Structures and Beyond

OXFORD STUDIES IN COMPARATIVE SYNTAX

Richard Kayne, *General Editor*

The Higher Functional Field: Evidence from North Italian Dialects
Cecilia Poletto

The Syntax of Verb-Initial Languages
Edited by Andrew Carnie and Eithne Guilfoyle

Parameters and Universals
Richard Kayne

Portuguese Syntax: New Comparative Studies
Dited by João Costa

XP-Adjunction in Universal Grammar: Scrambling and Bindiing in Hindi-Urdu
Ayesha Kidwai

Infinitive Constructions: A Syntactic Analysis of Romance Languages
Guido Mensching

Subject Inversion in Romance and the Theory of Universal Grammar
Edited by Aafke Hulk and Jean-Yves Pollock

Subjects, Expletives, and the EPP
Edited by Peter Svenonius

A Unified Theory of Verbal and Nominal Projections
Yoshiki Ogawa

Functional Structures in DP and IP: The Cartography of Syntactic Structures, Volume 1
Edited by Guglielmo Cinque

Syntactic Heads and Word Formation
Marit Julien

The Syntax of Italian Dialects
Christina Tortora

The Morphosyntax of Complement-Head Sequences: Clause Structure and Word Order Patterns in Kwa
Enoch Oladé Aboh

The Structure of CP and IP: The Cartography of Syntactic Structures, Volume 2
Edited by Luigi Rizzi

The Syntax of Anaphora
Ken Safir

Principles and Paremeters in a VSO Language: A Case Study in Welsh
Ian G. Roberts

Structures and Beyond: The Cartography of Syntactic Structures, Volume 3
Edited by Adriana Belletti

Structures and Beyond

The Cartography of Syntactic Structures, Volume 3

EDITED BY
ADRIANA BELLETTI

OXFORD
UNIVERSITY PRESS

2004

OXFORD
UNIVERSITY PRESS

Oxford New York
Auckland Bangkok Buenos Aires Cape Town Chennai
Dar es Salaam Delhi Hong Kong Istanbul Karachi Kolkata
Kuala Lumpur Madrid Melbourne Mexico City Mumbai Nairobi
São Paulo Shanghai Taipei Tokyo Toronto

Published by Oxford University Press, Inc.
198 Madison Avenue, New York, New York, 10016

www.oup.com

Library of Congress Cataloging-in-Publication Data
Structures and beyond / editd by Adriana Belletti.
p. cm — (Oxford studies in comparative syntax) (The cartography of syntactic structures ; v. 3)
Revised presentations given at a workshop held during the fall of 1999 and hosted by Certosa di Pontignano of the University of Siena.
Includes bibliographical references and index.
ISBN 0-19-517197-7; 0-19-517196-9 (pbk.)
1. Grammar, Comparative and general—Syntax—Congresses. I. Belletti, Adriana, II. Certosa di Pontignano (Pontignano, Italy) III. Series. IV. Series: The cartography of syntactic structures ; v. 3

P291.S695 2004
415—dc22 2003058029

9 8 7 6 5 4 3 2 1

Printed in the United States of America
on acid-free paper

CONTENTS

Structures and Beyond

ADRIANNA BELLETTI

Introduction

1. The event

In November 1999 the Certosa di Pontignano of the University of Siena hosted a comprehensive workshop primarily devoted to the research undertaken under the Cartographic Project (a research project funded by the Italian Ministry of the University and of Scientific and Technological Research); articles directly related to the project are collected in the Oxford University Press volume *The Structure of CP and IP,* edited by L. Rizzi. A previous workshop related to the project (Venice, January 1999) had given rise to the volume *Functional Structure in DP and IP,* edited by Guglielmo Cinque, and also published by Oxford (Cinque 2002). Immediately after the Pontignano event, specifically dedicated to cartographic issues and themes, another workshop took place that was primarily intended to provide a broader perspective touching upon various aspects of current theoretical and experimental research on language. Issues directly connecting the cartographic studies with the most recent developments of the Minimalist program, of the Antisymmetric approach, of the study on the semantic-syntax interface, and of the study of locality principles, as well as issues related to experimental neurolinguistics and psycholinguistics, were discussed by leading researchers and theoreticians. The workshop, which was held in connection with Noam Chomsky's visit to the University of Siena during the fall of 1999, thus became a comprehensive, state-of-the-art workshop. The present volume collects the revised version of the presentations given at this event.

Twenty years after the Principles and Parameters framework found its first systematization in the *Pisa Lectures* and almost a decade after the Minimalist Program

(MP) started taking shape, it seemed that the time was appropriate to produce an in-depth reflection on the state of the art. The very strict connection, both in timing and content, with the preceding workshop entirely devoted to the Cartographic Project suggested the title of the present volume: *Structures and Beyond*. Any reflection on language must include the structural dimension of the hierarchical organization of syntactic constituents; the cartographic enterprise addresses this dimension in a systematic and detailed way with the identification of complex representations specifying positions dedicated to different interpretations. This was the starting point for a general reflection intended to go beyond the purely structural dimension and to touch upon some central theoretical and empirical issues with the confrontation of partly different points of view.

Before briefly introducing the different contributions, I will devote the following section to a presentation of some particularly prominent theoretical issues that the different contributions have commonly addressed, in some cases identifying domains of tension among the different points of view. This should help to tease apart those aspects and aims that constitute the sense of a common enterprise and those in which technical decisions diverge. It appears that, although the authors have addressed different and unrelated topics in a way that is peculiar to their interests and competence, nevertheless a general picture results from the works collected here, giving the sense of a remarkable coherence of intents. There are several points of convergence in the identification of the central questions and aims (in an unordered list): accounting for the richness of (the interpretable component of) syntactic representations; aiming at the optimization of syntactic computations; clarifying the relation of the computational system with other cognitive systems at the interface; defining the nature and scope of formal syntactic/semantic computations; and searching for special evidence from other domains, most notably neurolinguistics (language pathology) and psycholinguistics (language acquisition), two privileged sources of evidence in addition to the most common reference to speakers' grammaticality and interpretive judgments. But let us address some of the general theoretical issues in closer detail.

2. On some theoretical issues in the state of the art

2.1. Minimalism, cartography, "interpretability" and the role of the interfaces

Despite a prima facie distance between the aims of the Minimalist program (Chomsky 1995 and subsequent work) and the cartographic approach, which is suggested by the apparent different conception of syntactic structures, crucial points of convergence make the distance much smaller and local and identify a deep convergence of research intents. The role of interface conditions has acquired prominence within the Minimalist program. A well-designed faculty of language (FL) is such if it can interact in an optimal way with the conditions imposed by other cognitive systems within the human mind. So, the identification of the role and nature of the conditions at the interface between the FL and other cognitive systems becomes one of the fundamental aims of the research program. This goes together with the effort of identifying how much of the properties involved in the various computational mechanisms introduced in the work undertaken within the guidelines of the Principles and Parameters (P&P) approach over the last twenty years or so is actually to be considered proper to the FL per se and how much is in fact a consequence of the operation of conditions at the interface between the FL and other cognitive systems. One of the technical mechanisms implemented by MP is the notion of "interpretable" feature/head: syntactic representations should end up containing only information that can be visible, hence interpretable, to the other cognitive systems, external to the FL proper, the SM (sensory motor) system and the C-I (conceptual intentional) system, in particular. One of the fundamental aims of the Cartographic Project is that of drawing maps as fine-grained as possible of the clause structure with the identification of different types of positions. Among the most significant and characteristic results of the project is precisely the identification of several distinct positions within the clause dedicated to different interpretations, both at the level of the clause proper (traditional IP) and at the (left) peripheral level (traditional CP). So, the numerous heads that are contained in the typical cartographic syntactic structure are all 'interpretable' in the sense relevant for the MP. The complex syntactic representations are assumed to provide information to the semantic/pragmatic systems in a simple and transparent manner. The identification of interface conditions are thus both a central aim of the MP and a direct contribution of the Cartographic Project. The following quote from Chomsky's (2002: 123) interview on Minimalism, held in the same period as the workshops, effectively synthesizes the commonality and the sharing of the research aims in these areas: "This kind of work [cartographic research] leads us to inquire more closely into the nature of interface relations. . . . And beyond that, it leads us to investigate the 'external' systems themselves, and the conditions they impose on a well designed language faculty. As is common, these questions have traditional antecedents, but it seems that they can now be addressed on much firmer grounds."

2.2. On the complexity of syntactic representations

The syntactic representations uncovered under the impulse of the cartographic studies are very complex and articulated objects. They constitute an extreme development of the original "split IP" hypothesis of Pollock (1989), the most direct ancestor of this style of approach. The complexity of these representations derives from the combination of several very simple, basic syntactic projections, essentially the replication of the X'-schema; the computations undertaken within these representations use elementary mechanisms (merge, move, and agreement). This is very close in spirit to the simplicity of minimalist representations and computations (as in bare phrase structures, as well as antisymmetric ones (Kayne 1994)), despite, once again, prima facie impressions to the contrary. The poverty of the typical minimalist representation can be considered a notational tool, a convenient abbreviation (see also Rizzi forthcoming). Let us refer to Chomsky's words on this point, going back to the interview on Minimalism once again: "To a first approximation the clause seems to be of the general form [. . . C . . . [. . . T . . . [. . . V . . .]]]. . . . But the cartographic studies have made it very clear that this is only a first approximation: the positions indicated by . . . have a rich structure" (Chomsky 2002: 123). Some of the most studied areas of "richness" are the left periphery of the clause, with force indicators and dedicated positions for focus, topic, and further discourse-related positions (Rizzi 1997 and forthcoming; this volume and references cited therein); the IP internal system of inflectional heads brought to light by Cinque's (1999) hierarchy of adverbs and functional heads; low zones of the clause surrounding the VP area, sometimes called the VP-periphery (Belletti 2004 and reference cited therein). The proliferation of positions can be further enriched by taking certain prepositions as "probe" heads, as in Kayne's proposal (see his contribution to this volume); they become part of the functional structure of the clause, attracting elements to their specifiers (and then moving further up and incorporating into one of the functional heads of Cinque's hierarchy, which determines the right word order "*à* DP," e.g., in French causatives; Kayne, this volume, p. 192). "Richness" of syntactic structures is then not at all at odds with minimalist assumptions; furthermore, there seems to be a convergence toward the enrichment of the functional architecture of the clause between the cartographic studies and recent analyses involving "remnant movement" (Kayne 2000). Of course, it remains to be understood in detail how much of the style of the derivations undertaken within minimalist assumptions can be literally preserved and extended to the complex representations, such as those assumed under cartographic analyses. The chapters in this volume provide material for an in-depth reflection on this important technical point.

2.3. Specifiers and heads

Traditional X'-theory set an important distinction between the specifier of a maximal projection and the complement of a head. Much work in P&P has capitalized on this distinction, giving a special status to the Spec-head relation identified as the core configuration of agreement phenomena and relations. Early work in the MP (Chomsky 1993) also gave a central role to this relation, which was assumed to implement checking operations. The Spec-head relation is also a fundamental relation, in much cartographic work, where the nature of specifiers is determined by the nature of the head, through the agreement relation. Agreement may involve features of the inflectional system, such as mood, aspect, tense, and voice in Cinque's hierarchy, and features related to aspects of the scope- and discourse-related semantics, such as interrogative wh-features, Focus, and Topic of, for example, Rizzi (1997 and this volume). These latter relations extend to the interpretable (in minimalist terms) set of functional heads expressing the clause structure the same kind of agreement relation assumed in the checking of φ-features, as in the analysis of the subject-verb agreement relation in full (tensed) clauses (e.g., in Chomsky 1995) and in the tradition established by Kayne's (1989) analysis of past participle agreement phenomena in Romance. Recent versions of the MP, including Chomsky's chapter in this volume, propose the elimination of the privileged status of the Spec-head agreement relation in favor of the reduction to the unique existence of the head-head type of relation—A conclusion close to the one also reached by Starke (in this volume), who underscores the unnecessary complexity and redundancy introduced in syntactic representations and computations by the notion specifier.

According to Chomsky's system, agreement is established between a "probe" head and an active "goal" head contained in its complement. Can the results obtained through a vast use of the relation Spec-head be reproduced in a system that does not recognize any special status to it? And how can one deal with cases in which an element is directly merged in a Spec position, not moved there from a lower position? This is an important technical research area, given the new proposals on this topic in minimalism. Its centrality becomes particularly clear in the context of many discussions in the present volume, in particular Cinque's contribution, based on Cinque (1999), where the central role of the Spec-head relation is crucially assumed, and Rizzi's chapter, where the relation comes into play also in the determination of the fine-grained principle of locality proposed there.

2.4. Other issues in brief

2.4.1. The status of Movement

Is Movement a last-resort operation? Is it an "imperfection," to use Chomsky's minimalist terminology? The metaphor of movement has always been utilized in theoretical works to account for the displacement property pervasively manifested by natural languages: a constituent is pronounced in a position different from the one where it is interpreted, at least thematically interpreted. In the first works in the minimalist vein, the assumption was that movement is an unexpected property, one that would be missing from a "perfectly designed system"—whence much discussion on the motivations and justifications of movement. In cartographic studies, movement is always justified: it occurs in order to assign a certain interpretative property to an element by moving it to a position dedicated to that interpretation (as in the case of focus or topic movement or wh-movement). In Kayne's antisymmetric approach, movement operations are widespread and are directly responsible for the different orders displayed by different languages in various contexts, including the fundamental head-complement order. Within the antisymmetric approach, the justification of the various movements hypothesized is not always made explicit, as in the case of the massive use of derivations involving movements of remnant constituents. Kayne's chapter in this volume has examples of these kinds of movement operations. According to Chomsky's chapter, movement and the related displacement property of natural languages should not be considered an imperfection (p. 104) as movement is now interpreted as the "internal" version of the fundamental operation of Merge. Thus, several questions remain open in this connection: if movement is not an imperfection, should we expect it to be even more pervasive in natural languages? Should movement still be interpreted as a "last resort," or should the need of justification for it, still present under recent minimalist proposals and under cartographic research, be interpreted differently, possibly related to the interpretability of the landing sites? If all of this holds, are antisymmetric derivations, with their wide use of movement operations, closer to being optimal, as movement is by and large "costless" in natural languages, or should they still look for clearer and explicit justifications? The proposals developed in the chapters here directly or indirectly bear on this issue and should contribute to clarify at least some of its various implications.

2.4.2. *Toward a "uniform" locality principle*

Rizzi (in this volume) speculates that the proposed locality principle could be the manifestation, at the syntactic level, of a possibly more general principle of locality also applying at the phonological level. Chierchia, in his chapter, suggests that a somewhat similar principle may condition the phenomena discussed there, at the interface between semantics and pragmatics (see 3.2 below). Much work is needed in particular for the determination of what the notion "intervener," relevant for the principle, should necessarily imply to really be operative. This is a potentially central point, as it would seem that a general cognitive principle of locality could be uncovered, conditioning formal linguistic computations at different levels, as well as at the interface with other cognitive systems. The question still awaits detailed investigations in the interface areas, but it is suggestive that potential empirical evidence bearing on it has started being identified, as it is the case in Rizzi's and Chierchia's contributions.

3. The contributions

The chapters in this volume can be divided into three groups: those more directly connected to Minimalist questions and Antisymmetric analyses (Chomsky, Kayne, Starke); those more directly connected with Cartographic issues and questions on the relations at the interface between syntax and semantics/pragmatics (Cinque, Rizzi, Chierchia); those related with domains "external" to the computational system of the faculty of language *stricto sensu* but "internal" to the mind, dealing with data and issues from language pathology and language acquisition (Caramazza & Shapiro, Mehler & Nespor). I will now briefly introduce some aspects of the different contributions, in particular those that appear to be the most innovative in the various proposals, with special attention to some common general issues that they take into account.

3.1. Chomsky, Starke, Kayne

Many of the ideas in Chomsky's chapter are very innovative. We have already referred to the elimination of the operation Move of previous work in favor of the operation Internal Merge and also the attempt to eliminate the privileged status of the Spec-head relation, reducing it to one of the manifestations of the Head-complement relation, through the operation Agree in combination with the checking of uninterpretable features (such as Case and EPP). As discussed in section 2.3, this is certainly a major change in current syntactic theorizing, where Spec-head agreement relations have been taken to play a crucial role in implementing several instances of syntactic displacements (both IP internally and externally, toward the CP-area). The challenge is to reinterpret the results so far obtained through the assumption that the relation between a head and its specifier is somehow privileged; and this both in the realm of agreement phenomena involving uninterpretable φ-features (see the overview in Belletti 2000), as well as in the "criterial" type of agreement relations, involving interpretable features (cf. Rizzi's work on the wh-criterion and related contributions, some also contained in Rizzi forthcoming).

Several other innovative aspects of the system are proposed in *Beyond Explanatory Adequacy*; they are all characterized by the effort of reducing language-specific mechanisms to a minimum, both in the sense of providing optimally simple computations and in the sense of precisely identifying what properties and mechanisms should be considered specific to the FL proper, among the other cognitive systems.

There is an interesting convergence between the proposal of eliminating the privileged status of the Spec-head relation put forth by Chomsky and a similar conclusion argued for by Starke in his chapter. Although completely internal to the view that syntactic structure is rich and complex in the sense developed since Pollock's (1989) seminal article and, more recently, in Cinque's (1999) detailed syntactic hierarchy of functional heads, Starke's contribution tries to show that the Spec-head relation is an unnecessary complication, which should be eliminated in any optimal computation. He gives various indications of either the redundancy or the potentially misleading effect of the assumption that syntactic structures contain Specifiers, and he proposes their elimination in favor of the reduction to one single syntactic relation directly resulting from the Merge operation: the head-complement relation. This contribution provides material for the necessary rethinking that the radical proposal requires, both on the empirical and on the conceptual side.

Kayne's chapter makes a central use of the notion probe, also a minimalist notion taken to be responsible for triggering movement, an instance of internal Merge. The probe Kayne concentrates on is the preposition *à*, found in causative constructions in French, as well as in double object constructions of the French type (DO IO) or of the English type (DO1 DO2). The main aim is to first correlate the presence of *à* in front of the subordinate (typically transitive) subject of the infinitival clausal complement of the causative verb to the very presence in the matrix clause of the causative verb itself, a selectional property that is not neatly captured by previous approaches. In developing his analysis, Kayne also makes use of typical antisymmetric derivations that lead to the final word order found in French and Romance causatives, on the one side, and English and Germanic causatives and double object constructions on the other. The assumed derivation is also meant to extend to other prepositions, for example, the preposition *de* in French. By utilizing minimalist and antisymmetric ingredients, Kayne arrives at a very unconventional conception of constituent structure to the effect that not all P + DP sequences are considered to be constituents: datives typically are not. Thus, this chapter invites a fresh reconsideration of standardly assumed structural analyses of prepositional constructions.

3.2. Cinque, Rizzi, Chierchia

Perfectly internal to the spirit of the cartographic approach, Cinque's chapter provides a new analysis of the phenomenon known as Restructuring (from Rizzi 1978 and related work started in the mid-1970s). In his important monograph, *Adverbs and Functional Heads*, Cinque (1999) has provided a systematic classification of adverb positions across languages. According to Cinque's hypothesis, the clausal map of any language conforms to a universal hierarchy of functional heads. The hierarchy is made visible in one of two possible ways in different types of languages: either through the manifestation of different heads, typically in the form of an affix, or through the manifestation of the constituent filling the specifier of the various head projections, typically in the form of an adverb. In his chapter, Cinque argues that verbs that enter the Restructuring phenomenon in Romance are indeed the realization of some of the functional heads assumed in the universal hierarchy; these verbs are then "functional verbs." Cinque gives the reader a fresh perspective on old and classical questions related to Restructuring, which have accompanied this research area over the last twenty-five years or so. According to Cinque's proposal, the clause structure containing Restructuring verbs is always monoclausal. Hence, there is no real Restructuring *process* to account for; rather, restructuring verbs appear to follow the order of the universal hierarchy in a coherent and systematic way. Apart from various details of the empirical analysis, which the reader will appreciate directly, Cinque provides an extremely elegant and instructive example of the contribution of the cartographic approach in accounting for complex patterns in a most transparent way. Transparency comes from the fact that the clause structure contains the necessary information for the interpretation of the functional verbs through the presence of different head positions dedicated for different interpretations. As restructuring verbs are one possible realization of the various head positions of the universal hierarchy, the functional nature of restructuring verbs and the nature of the positions they fill in the universal hierarchy make a crucial part of the interpretation completely transparent.

As noted in section 2.2, the apparent tension that seems to arise between the aims of the Cartographic Project, which postulates very rich structures, and the Minimalist program, which tends to simplify them, can in fact be taken to be only apparent if, as it is the case with Cinque's hierarchy, richness of structure corresponds to the presence of syntactically justified functional positions, which are all interpretable in the sense relevant for the MP.

A similar consideration can be made with respect to the conclusions drawn in Rizzi's chapter. The main theoretical issue here is locality. Syntactic computations are local, in the sense that Rizzi's work over the nineties has defined in terms of the Relativized Minimality (RM) principle. Actually, different kinds of linguistic computations, not just strictly syntactic ones, appear to be local in a way that is systematically reminiscent of RM. One significant point of Rizzi's chapter is precisely the discussion of this more general application of the RM principle to other linguistic computations, such as those dealing with phonological processes. The very general RM principle, first proposed in Rizzi (1990), appears to be in need of further refinements since the notion of "intervener" is not able, in its original formulation, to account for a number of subtle contrasts arising in the domain of A'-syntax. The refinement of the RM principle is the primary aim of Rizzi's contribution. The result is the formulation of a typology of positions that is assumed to characterize the left periphery of the clause. Thus, the article is also a development of Rizzi's (1997) original work dealing with the drawing of a detailed map of the left periphery of the clause. Once again, much as in the case of Cinque's chapter for the IP internal area, a typology of interpretable positions is identified here within the CP area. The main empirical domain is adverb syntax and in particular the syntax of adverb preposing phenomena, which turn out to interact in nontrivial ways with the locality principle and which can be made sense of through the assumed typology of dedicated positions. Various related issues are dealt with, most notably the discussion of the difference between simple preposing phenomena, on the one side, and the topic interpretation, on the other, also involving preposing into left peripheral positions. The developed approach is potentially full of consequences for the general issue concerning the relation of the computational system with other interacting cognitive systems at the interface, in particular in connection to the pragmatics of discourse exchanges.

The relation between the syntactic/semantic computational system with pragmatics is the central concern of Chierchia's chapter, dealing with the semantics of Scalar Implicatures (SI) and their "suspension" or "recalibration," in Chierchia's terms, within contexts of D(ownward) E(ntailing). The DE contexts are also those where Negative Polaritity Items (NPI), such as *any*, are licensed (Ladusaw 1979). The chapter puts forth an innovative proposal: SI do not belong to a different interpretive domain applying when the syntactic computation is completed, but rather they are computed "locally," bottom up, as soon as the syntactic tree is built up. We may say that they are computed in a cyclic, "phase"-related manner (Chomsky 2001). The SI-"suspension"/"recalibration" occurs when the computation moves on to the next higher phase and the domain is thus enlarged as in standard cyclic derivations. All of this sounds very familiar to the syntactician, who is used to dealing with the cyclicity of syntactic derivations. The proposal that is put forth, supported by a rich and subtle semantic argumentation, looks far-reaching in that a bridge is built between the functioning of two sides of linguistic phenomena that are traditionally kept separate: formal syntactic/semantic derivation and pragmatics (with the computation of SI and NPI taken as a case in point). Aspects of pragmatic entailing, which speakers are aware of as much as they are aware of formal grammaticality judgments, on the one side, and the building of syntactic structure, on the other, appear to be computed in parallel, within the very same formal domains: the phases. Furthermore, Chierchia shows that both licensing of NPIs (as discussed in Linebarger 1981) and SI appear to be subject, in their computation (although in different ways), to a locality condition that closely resembles the RM-locality principle of Rizzi (1990 and subsequent work). Once again, it is tempting to claim that the very same principle applies to different domains. Chierchia's discussion tries to make the notion "intervener" in the particular computation of both SI and NPIs as precise as possible in a way that also captures the relation between the two phenomena, SI and NPI. This aim appears to be very close in spirit to the one discussed above (and in 2.4.2), presented in Rizzi's chapter, although it refers to a completely different and seemingly unrelated empirical domain. The pragmatic principle that Chierchia comes up with consists of a revision of a Gricean approach, according to which, in discourse exchanges, speakers tend to use strategies that "strengthen" the informational content of their statements: both SI and NPI provide a way to reach this result in the complex and intricate fashion that Chierchia's chapter and previous work on the topic bring to light (notably Kadmon & Landman 1993; Krifka 1995; discussed by Chierchia).

3.3. Caramazza and Shapiro; Mehler and Nespor

How specific to the language module organ of the brain are the linguistic categories that linguists currently use in their attempt to characterize the human language capacity? This is an interesting question per se, but certainly it acquires further centrality within the recent developments in the MP. As discussed above (section 2), one fundamental aim of MP is that of determining if the language faculty of human beings can be considered a system optimally designed to interact with other cognitive systems internal to the mind/brain, such as the conceptual-intentional system and the sensorimotor system (C-I and SM; see the discussion above). Given this enterprise, any kind of evidence that can contribute to the understanding of what property is to be considered specific to language is a highly relevant contribution. I believe that this is the case of Caramazza and Shapiro's contribution to this volume. They offer a clear presentation and discussion of data from language pathology (aphasia) indicating that linguistic categories such as nouns and verbs and also, at the phonological level, consonants and vowels are very likely to be primitives of the cognitive module specifically dedicated to language. The evidence they discuss comes from various experiments on different tasks (repetition of nouns vs. verbs, with homonyms and with invented words; recordings of natural productions; picture naming; etc.), which show a number of modality-specific deficits manifested in the behavior of several brain-damaged patients. The modality-specific nature of the deficits is particularly relevant in that it makes it very unlikely to assume that difficulties that patients find in some task, for example, with respect to nouns and not with respect to verbs, but do not find in other tasks could be due to some unique language-independent (semantic?) feature(s). The argument is even stronger in the pure formal domain of phonology with selective impairment of consonants and vowels in different patients with respect to different tasks. These kinds of pathologies indicate that the deficits may affect both the way in which categorical information is stored in the brain and the way it gets into the computational system of morphosyntax, where nouns and verbs are computed differently. Interesting questions are raised by this kind of evidence for current versions of morphological theory, such as Halle and Marantz's (1993) "Distributed Morphology"and Chomsky (this volume), where roots are "category neutral" and are introduced in the syntactic tree, where they are computed either as nouns or as verbs.

Language acquisition has been identified as the central empirical question in the work in generative grammar ever since its origins. It has become even more so within the Principles and Parameters approach, where the very notion of parameter setting represents a plausible model of the way in which language acquisition may proceed in infancy. Parameter setting simultaneously accounts for language variation and for the ability that children manifest in acquiring any language they are exposed to in their first years of life. The chapter by Mehler and Nespor addresses the central issue of language acquisition from the peculiar perspective of how very basic parameter values can be bootstrapped from the noisy environment where the young infant is inserted from birth. The proposal that is put forth is based on a number of experiments undertaken by Mehler and his collaborators over the last decade or so (e.g., Mehler et al. 1988, 1996). It consists in suggesting that linguistically relevant notions defining language types, such as "syllable timed" versus "stress timed" versus "mora timed" languages, could be primed by the general, not just language-specific, property that is usually referred to as "rhythm." The chapter provides a careful overview of recent results in this domain and speculates on a possible way in which the language organ might interact with the interfaces (here, the SM interface) from the onset of the language acquisition process.

The contributions collected in this volume give a rich sample of some currently addressed issues in theoretical linguistics. They are representative of the state of the debate on these issues and of their centrality, both for the cartographic perspective and for linguistic theory in general, thus providing a stimulating picture of the state of the art of the field at the beginning of the new century. I am profoundly grateful to all the contributors for making the Pontignano workshop such an inspiring event. I also thank them for preparing a written version of their contribution to that event, thus making the compilation of this volume possible. I am confident that it will help us go beyond our current understanding of the functioning and of the properties of the fascinating and intriguing component of our human nature: language.

References

Belletti, A. (2000). "Agreement Projections." In M. Baltin & C. Collins, eds., *The Handbook of Contemporary Syntactic Theory*, Oxford: Blackwell, 483–510.

Belletti, A. (2004). "Aspects of the Low IP Area." In L. Rizzi, ed., *The Structure of CP and IP, The Cartography of Syntactic Structures,* vol. 2. New York: Oxford University Press.

Chomsky, N. (1993). "A Minimalist Program for Linguistic Theory." In K. Hale & S. J. Keyser, eds., *The View from Building 20.* Cambridge, MA: MIT Press.

Chomsky, N. (1995). *The Minimalist Program*. Cambridge, Mass.: MIT Press.

Chomsky, N. (2001). "Derivation by Phase." In M. Kenstowicz, ed., *Ken Hale: A Life in Language*. Cambridge, Mass.: MIT Press.

Chomsky, N. (2002). *On Nature and Language*. Cambridge: Cambridge University Press.

Cinque, G. (1999). *Adverbs and Functional Heads*. New York: Oxford University Press.

Cinque, G. (2002). *Functional Structure in DP and IP. The Cartography of Syntactic Structures,* vol. 1. New York: Oxford University Press.

Halle, M., & A. Marantz. (1993). "Distributed Morphology." In K. Hale & S. J. Keyser, eds., *The View from Building 20.* Cambridge, MA: MIT Press.

Kadmon, N., & F. Landman. (1993). "*Any*." *Linguistic and Philosophy* 15.

Kayne, R. (1989). "Facets of Romance Past Participle Agreement." In P. Benincà, ed., *Dialect Variation on the Theory of Grammar*. Dordrecht: Foris.

Kayne, R. (1994). *The Antisymmetry of Syntax*. Cambridge, Mass.: MIT Press.

Kayne, R. (2000). *Parameters and Universals*. New York: Oxford University Press.

Krifka, M. (1995). "The Semantics and Pragmatics of Polarity Items." *Linguistic Analysis* 25.

Ladusaw, W. (1979). Polarity Sensitivity as Inherent Scope Relation. Ph.D. diss., University of Texas, Austin; distributed by IULC.

Linebarger, M. (1981). The Grammar of Negative Polarity, Ph.D. diss., Massachusetts Institute of Technology, Cambridge Mass.

Mehler, J., E. Dupoux, T. Nazzi, & G. Dehaene-Lambertz. (1996). "Coping with Linguistic Diversity: The Infant's Viewpoint." In J. L. Morgan and K. Demuth, eds., *Signal to Syntax: Bootstrapping from Speech to Grammar in Early Acquisition*. Mahwah, N.J.: Lawrence Erlbaum.

Mehler, J., P. W. Jusczyk, G. Lambertz, N. Halsted, J. Bertoncini, & C. Amiel-Tison. (1988). "A Precursor of Language Acquisition in Young Infants," *Cognition* 29.

Pollock, J. Y. (1989). "Verb Movement, Universal Grammar and the Structure of IP." *Linguistic Inquiry* 20.

Rizzi, L. (1978). "A Restructuring Rule in Italian Syntax." In S. J. Keyser, ed., *Current Transformational Studies in the European Languages.* Cambridge, Mass.: MIT Press.

Rizzi, L. (1990). *Relativized Minimality.* Cambridge, Mass.: MIT Press.

Rizzi, L. (1997). "The Fine Structure of the Left Periphery." In L. Haegeman, ed., *Elements of Grammar.* Dordrecht: Kluwer.

Rizzi, L. (forthcoming). *The Structure of CP and IP. The Cartography of Syntactic Structures,* vol. 2. New York: Oxford University Press.

1

ALFONSO CARAMAZZA AND KEVIN SHAPIRO

Language Categories in the Brain: Evidence from Aphasia

1. Introduction

1.1. Two plans for a brain

A central question in the study of cognition concerns the way conceptual information is represented and organized in the mind/brain. If we presuppose, as most experimental scientists do, that cognitive processes are computational processes, it becomes self-evident that the presumably enormous amount of information over which these processes operate must be structured in some way in order to be accessible and useful.

Given these two minimal criteria (accessibility and usefulness), along with the straightforward assumption of computational efficiency, we can reject as doubtful a host of potential models of organization—for example, Borges's Chinese encyclopedia, the Boston telephone directory, and the Internet. The task of the cognitive scientist is then to sort through the remaining options and divine which has been preferred in the course of neural evolution. In practice, of course, this undertaking is informed as much by intuition about how the brain is likely to operate as by empirical observation.

Intuitive approaches to the problem of categorical representation have tended to cluster around two poles. Associationist accounts (including connectionism), the intellectual descendants of eighteenth-century (capital E) Empiricism, see the brain as a powerful statistical engine that stores and retrieves information in terms of elementary continuous variables, like perceptual features. Theoretical constructs at the categorical level—like "animal," "noun," "consonant," and so forth—are taken to reflect correlated clusters of these features; they are not thought to correspond to discrete internal representations.

Cognitivist accounts, on the other hand, hold in common the view that the brain actually does make use of discrete, categorial representations in processing information. As a class, though, they do not necessarily share any assumptions about how these categories come into being. That is, cognitive accounts may differ over whether and to what degree given categories are either given innately or "bootstrapped" from qualitatively different types of information.

As with nearly any scientific controversy so broad in scope, it is unlikely that there is a single solution to the problem of conceptual representation that falls neatly into either the associationist or the cognitivist paradigm. On the other hand, several kinds of empirical evidence can help us to decide which of the two models is most appropriate in accounting for a given set of observations.

Beginning with the work of authors like Piaget (1923) and Vygotsky (1962), a vast literature has accumulated over the past six decades on the subject of concept acquisition by infants and children, yielding many important clues to the ways in which concepts and categories are formed. By the same token, the careful investigation of cognitive deficits in brain-damaged individuals can help us understand this problem empirically by exposing the functional and neuroanatomical lines along which cognitive mechanisms break down. And the study of nonhuman animals has provided important insights about mechanisms of concept formation that may be shared across evolutionary lineages.

1.2. Face recognition: A paradigm case

Not surprisingly, many of the most productive areas of inquiry in the study of conceptual representation have been defined by converging evidence from neuropsychology and developmental and comparative neuroscience. Face recognition is a case in point. Both newborn human infants, in looking-time experiments (Goren et al. 1975; Johnson & Morton 1991), and monkeys, in recordings from single neurons in the ventral occipitotempal pathway (Gross et al. 1972; Perrett et al. 1982), seem to react differently to upright faces than to other types of stimuli, including inverted faces and faces with displaced features. At the same time, neurological patients classified as prosopagnosic seem to present with selective difficulties in recognizing previously familiar faces, though their knowledge of other objects and of words is generally intact (Bodamer 1947).

There is good reason to believe that the differences observed between the processing of faces and of other kinds of visual stimuli cannot be explained simply by assuming that faces are in some general way more difficult to recognize than other objects. If this were true, we might predict, for example, that any brain damage severe enough to affect object recognition would disproportionately hinder face recognition. As it turns out, this prediction is plainly false. CK, a patient described by Moscovitch et al. (1997), presents with a drastic impairment in recognizing objects and words but is completely normal at recognizing faces.

The contrast between CK's visual recognition performance and the patterns presented by prosopagnosic patients strongly implies the existence of separate neural mechanisms that are dedicated to different kinds of visual recognition tasks and which can be spared or impaired selectively by neurological trauma. Indeed, a series of electrophysiological and functional neuroimaging studies of normal subjects has highlighted neural regions in the ventral pathway that are implicated in face recognition tasks but not in object recognition (for review see Kanwisher et al. in press).

Despite all this, it remains controversial whether the neural regions in question, and the cognitive operations associated with them, are devoted specifically to processing faces (a cognitivist view) or whether they subserve a more general kind of computation that happens to be heavily engaged in face recognition, but not in recognizing most other objects (an associationist view)—for instance, the ability to make fine-grained visual discriminations between different exemplars of a highly familiar class (Diamond & Carey 1986; Gauthier et al. 1997).

1.3. Category-specific semantic impairments

Neuropsychology is rich in reports of other cognitive fractionations that can arise as a result of brain damage, many of them just as specific and just as difficult to interpret as prosopagnosia. Another well-known example is the phenomenon of so-called semantic category-specific deficits (e.g., Warrington & Shallice 1984; Caramazza 1998). Patients with disorders of this type are selectively impaired at processing words that represent one category of objects (like living things) but are able to name and comprehend the names of other objects (like artifacts) without difficulty. Here again the argument from difficulty is rendered unlikely merely by the existence of double dissociations across categories between patients using the same test materials (Hillis & Caramazza 1991), but the precise nature of the deficit(s) involved is far from clear (see Figure 1.1).

The earliest and perhaps most widely defended account, which has been dubbed the sensory/functional theory (Caramazza & Shelton 1998), assumes that conceptual representations of animals rely more heavily on sensory or perceptual features than do representations of inanimate objects (variants of this theory have been advanced by Warrington & McCarthy 1983, 1987; Warrington & Shallice 1984; Allport 1985; Shallice 1988; Silveri & Gainotti 1988; Farah & McClelland 1991; Hart & Gordon 1992; Gainotti & Silveri 1996). Therefore brain damage selectively affecting the representation of or access to perceptual semantic features may generally result in an observed deficit in naming animals. Conversely, damage to functional or encyclopedic features may result in an observed deficit in naming artifacts.

The sensory/functional theory fits well within the rubric of associationism, explaining an apparent categorical effect as a byproduct of correlations between categories defined by the experimenter and various kinds of information thought to be associated with conceptual representations. However, as Caramazza and Shelton (1998) have pointed out, the basis for these supposed correlations is empirically suspect. Not only is it not obvious or true that unimpaired individuals associate sensory information more with living things and functional information more with nonliving items (Garrard et al. in press; McRae & Cree in press), but several recent studies have described patients with category-specific deficits for living things who are equally impaired with these items' visual and functional attributes and equally unimpaired

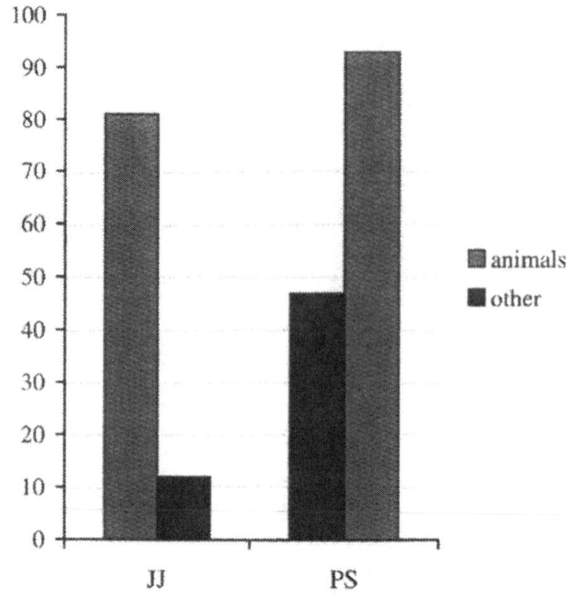

FIGURE 1.1. Picture-naming performance of two patients (JJ and PS) with semantic category specific deficits (Hillis & Caramazza 1991). The bars indicate correctly named animate and inanimate items. A double dissociation across patients using the same test materials indicates that semantic category effects cannot be explained trivially as resulting from the greater difficulty of one category.

with both attribute types for nonliving things (Laiacona et al. 1993, 1997; Caramazza & Shelton 1998). Other reports have shown that at least some patients with difficulties in processing visual attributes of objects do *not* also show evidence of impaired knowledge of living things (Coltheart et al. 1998; Lambon Ralph et al. 1998).

In light of these and other criticisms of the sensory/functional theory (Caramazza & Shelton 1998; Shapiro & Caramazza 2001), Caramazza and Shelton have offered an alternative cognitivist account of category-specific semantic impairments, the "domain-specific knowledge hypothesis," which suggests that knowledge of certain categories may be anatomically and functionally "modular," provided that there is an evolutionary rationale for this special status.

It is not hard to imagine the advantages that might be afforded by dedicated neural mechanisms for processing information about, for example, animals, foods, and conspecifics, and Caramazza and Shelton (1998) point to a good deal of converging evidence for such mechanisms from the literature on concept acquisition. All the same, the most serious objection to the domain-specific knowledge hypothesis is that it does not clearly articulate a framework for the segregated processing of different categories, or indeed for deciding *which* categories might be specially represented (but see Santos & Caramazza in press).

Yet even if we had such an explanatory scheme, we would still be faced with the problem of what is meant here by a "category." Does the term refer only to the spatial segregation of neural populations that subserve different kinds of concepts into distinct anatomical domains, or might there be an additional, more abstract level of representation that defines category membership? In other words, are animals, for example, spared or impaired as a group because they live together in the same part of the brain (perhaps for ease of recognition) or because they are linked to a higher order property (say, +ANIMATE) that is invoked in tasks that probe knowledge about animals? (Why, indeed, would this kind of property be useful?) In the absence of a principled approach to such questions, we may not make much headway in disentangling associationist and cognitivist explanations through the study of semantic deficits.

2. Language categories in the brain

2.1. On what do linguistic rules operate?

The theoretical motivation for postulating categorical (as opposed to featural) representations becomes clearer when we move away from categories that ostensibly reflect knowledge about the external world and consider categories that are relevant only in the specialized domain of language, like "noun" and "consonant." Grammarians and linguists from Panini to Chomsky have described language use (at the levels of phonology, morphology, and syntax) as a function of rules operating over discrete categories, based largely on intuitions about the way linguistic elements are processed in various contexts: consonants behave differently from vowels in syllable formation, nouns behave differently from verbs in sentence generation and morphological production, nouns and verbs both behave differently from prepositions and articles, and so forth.

On the other hand, some researchers have advanced alternative notions of linguistic categories, according to which hypothetical constructs like "noun" and "consonant" are to be understood merely as convenient labels for elements representing values along a featural continuum—for example, lexical items with a high ratio of concrete or sensory features (e.g., Bird et al. 2000) and phonemes that are relatively low on the scale of sonority (e.g., Goldsmith 1990), respectively. From these points of view, intuition-based categories are suspect because they fail to represent adequately the diversity of information associated with linguistic objects.

It is our view that the evidence from aphasia largely corroborates the existence of intuition-based categories, inasmuch as patients like the ones we will describe here exhibit deficits that appear to be categorical in nature and are not easily explained as reflecting damage to one region or another of a featural continuum. This is not to say that none of the myriad patterns of performance presented by aphasic patients can be interpreted in terms of feature gradients or correlations between perceptual properties of linguistic items and their structural roles. Rather, our point is that to understand the various forms of aphasic deficits, and by extension the language-processing system whose disruption leads to these observed deficits, we are compelled to conclude that labels such as "noun," "syllable," "vowel," and so forth reflect real internal representations and are not merely epiphenomena of lower level feature correlations.

2.2. Agrammatism: What it doesn't tell us

Several reports have demonstrated that brain damage can selectively disrupt access to words of one morphosyntactic class, leaving access to words of other classes relatively intact. An example is the well-documented pattern of production known clinically as "agrammatism." Patients with agrammatic or Broca's aphasia are in general more severely impaired at producing closed-class function words, like determiners, prepositions, and auxiliaries, than open-class content words, including nouns, verbs, and adjectives (Goodglass 1968; Berndt & Caramazza 1980).

The basis for this dissociation is not as obvious as it may seem. Intuition tells us that function words and content words play very different roles in sentence production (e.g., Garrett 1980)—but it is also the case that function words, as a class, differ substantially from content words in phonology, being generally shorter and prosodically less salient (Grosjean & Gee 1987; Shattuck-Hufnagel 1987). Kean (1978) has suggested that it is the phonological status of function words that is the root cause of their selective loss in agrammatism; specifically, she posits that agrammatic aphasics may simply omit morphological elements, like function words and certain affixes, that cannot be realized independently as phonological words.

We will not take a stand here on the plausibility of this claim, except to say that it cannot be dismissed out of hand. Rather, we would submit that function words and content words diverge too sharply along too many dimensions (syntactic, phonological, and possibly semantic) to allow us to pinpoint unambiguously the locus of their dissociation, at least given the evidence currently available.

2.3. Noun-verb dissociations as test cases for associationism

It is interesting that some agrammatic patients also present with a dissociation between classes in the larger category of content words, faring relatively worse with verbs than with nouns in speech production. This pattern was first in a seminal article by Luria and Tsvetkova (1967) and has since been confirmed in careful investigations of the performance of agrammatic and anomic patients (Miceli et al. 1984, 1988).

Using a task in which patients were asked to name pictures of either single objects or actions, Miceli et al. (1984) found that agrammatics produce fewer correct responses and many cross-category (noun) responses (25%) to actions; anomics produce fewer correct responses and many omission errors to objects (26%). A number of more recent reports have likewise documented selective impairments in producing either verbs (McCarthy & Warrington 1985; Williams & Canter 1987; Kohn et al. 1989; Caramazza & Hillis 1991; Hillis & Caramazza 1995; Berndt et al. 1997a, 1997b; Silveri & di Betta 1997; Breedin et al. 1998; Rapp & Caramazza 1998) or nouns (Zingeser & Berndt 1988, 1990; Bates et al. 1991; De Renzi & di Pellegrino 1995; Rapp & Caramazza 1997; Silveri & di Betta 1997; Robinson et al. 1999; Shapiro et al. 2000) in various tasks.

What do these observed dissociations between nouns and verbs tell us about the representation and organization of grammatical classes of words in the brain? To begin with, the existence of a double dissociation of noun-verb deficits across patients makes it unlikely that one class of words is simply harder to produce than another, just as we argued earlier for semantic category-specific deficits. The possibility of a "difficulty effect" becomes even more remote in light of double dissociations observed even in some individual patients across comprehension and production tasks (Hillis & Caramazza 1995)—but this is, again, where any consensus ends. Like function and content words, nouns and verbs differ along several potential dimensions of representation. At the same time, the two major classes of content words are (by most accounts) formally similar enough that we can make empirically testable predictions about the kinds of dissociations that might emerge between them, depending on where the system is thought to be disrupted.

Along these lines, Bates and colleagues (1991) have distinguished three basic classes of explanations that have been offered for noun-verb dissociations in aphasia: "grammatical" explanations, which hinge on the different roles nouns and verbs play in constructing sentences; "lexical" explanations, which trace dissociations between nouns and verbs to differences in morphosyntactic form class; and "semantic-conceptual" explanations, which reduce differences between the two categories to effects of concreteness, imageability, or some other dimension related to lexical meaning.[1]

Most grammatical explanations hold that agrammatics' difficulties in producing verbs may be related to the role played by verbs in determining the thematic and argument structures of sentences ("who did what to whom"). For instance, the "mapping deficit hypothesis" (Saffran et al. 1980) postulates that agrammatic aphasics have lost the ability to map thematic roles (agent, patient, etc.) from verbs to their nominal arguments. Since this mapping process is critical in producing sentences, a breakdown in thematic role assignment may account for agrammatics' syntactic difficulties, as well as their problems processing lexical items that take obligatory grammatical arguments—not only main verbs, but also, for example, prepositions.

Parsimonious as this account may be, it clearly does not (and is not intended to) extend to patients with selective noun deficits, or even patients who show an "anomic" pattern with respect to verb retrieval but have no problems with sentence construction. Such patterns can be accommodated by lexical explanations, which hold that dissociations arise because of damage to a component of the lexicon that is concerned specifically with the processing of one form class. In this view, subtle distinctions between individual patients' patterns of performance depend on the way in which access to this component is impaired, regardless of other damage elsewhere in the system.

Semantic-conceptual accounts can also handle a wide range of selective deficits in noun or verb retrieval but without referring to a special component of the lexicon that encodes grammatical class. Rather, these explanations hold that grammatical class distinctions are incidentally correlated with semantic properties of words; it is damage to these semantic properties, then, that gives rise to apparent noun- and verb-specific deficits. Thus McCarthy and Warrington (1985) originally proposed that difficulty in producing verbs relative to nouns is the result of damage to the semantic category of actions, whereas difficulty in producing nouns results from damage to the category of objects. This is certainly a reasonable interpretation of any differences that might arise in picture naming—the more so since (at least in English) the grammatical class of action words can be ambiguous (Kohn et al. 1989). (Consider *singing*, which is a verb in the sentence *the man is singing* but a noun in *the man's awful singing disturbed me*.)

For noun-verb dissociations in production and comprehension tasks that do not rely on differences in naming picturable words, such as reading and sentence generation, more nuanced accounts are necessary. These generally do not refer to the categories of objects and actions per se but concentrate on semantic dimensions whose extremes are associated with "prototypical" nouns and verbs. For example, conceptual representations of object names, and of nouns generally, are expected to be more concrete and imageable on average than those of verbs. In this respect, semantic-conceptual explanations can be characterized as associationist, in contrast to lexical explanations, which are cognitivist insofar as they posit damage to functionally segregated categories. (McCarthy and Warrington's 1985 proposal, in a certain reading, can also be considered cognitivist.)

Crucially, such associationist explanations predict that apparent grammatical class effects should vanish when some critical semantic variable is controlled. The nature of the variable depends on the theory under consideration. Marshall and colleagues (1996a, 1996b) explain difficulties in producing nouns as a consequence of a deficit in processing highly concrete words, whereas difficulties with verbs reflect problems with abstract or relational properties. Hence they predict that abstract nouns should be just as impaired as verbs in production, which is just what they observe for their patient RG. In a similar vein, Breedin et al. (1998) propose that difficulties in producing verbs reflect these words' more abstract semantic content. Verb-impaired patients should therefore be relatively spared with verbs whose meanings are well elaborated in their perceptual dimensions (e.g., *shout* or *whisper* as opposed to *talk*)—the assumption being that sensory features relating to manner will provide cues to production or comprehension even when relational information is unavailable.

Finally, Bird et al. (2000) offer a two-pronged semantic hypothesis to account for noun-verb dissociations. They claim that representations of nouns tend to include a high proportion of sensory features compared to nonsensory features, which is not the case for verbs; therefore, difficulties with nouns principally reflect damage to sensory information. Difficulties with verbs, on the other hand, arise as a consequence of diffuse damage to the semantic system. Because verbs, by hypothesis, have fewer semantic features on average than do nouns, a distributed semantic impairment will tend to affect them disproportionately.

It is possible that each of the three types of explanation just outlined (grammatical, lexical, semantic-conceptual) is applicable to at least some cases of putative grammatical class deficits. In other words, the verb impairment observed in some aphasic patients may in fact be due to difficulties in computing argument structure given a verb's complement of permissible thematic roles, whereas some (even many) other patients who appear to present with grammatical class impairments may in fact have semantic deficits masquerading as deficits with nouns or verbs. However, given that semantic accounts have often been marshalled to argue against the existence of categories per se, the issue at stake is whether or not there are cases for which a semantic account is simply improbable.

Several types of evidence can be brought to bear on this problem. For instance, indications that the semantic system is intact in patients with putative grammatical class deficits would tend to cast doubt on the assumption that the root cause of the deficits in these patients is semantic. Such evidence is provided by patients with modality-specific difficulties in producing nouns and verbs—that is, patients who are selectively impaired in producing words of one grammatical class either in speaking or in writing (Caramazza & Hillis 1991; Hillis & Caramazza 1995; Rapp & Caramazza 2002).

Moreover, there is evidence that the semantic dimensions that supposedly underlie the distinction between nouns and verbs cannot explain the dissociations observed in some patients. One carefully designed study by Berndt et al. (2002) has shown that selective difficulties producing verbs in picture naming persist for some patients even when imageability is matched for target nouns and verbs in a sentence-completion task. On the other hand, at least one patient with a marked deficit for low imageability words in reading and sentence completion showed no discernible difficulty in producing verbs. Reports of other patients suggest that the concreteness-abstractness dimension also does not play a role in some grammatical class deficits (Caramazza & Hillis 1991; Shapiro et al. 2000).

Finally, in some cases where there is independent evidence for a deficit involving grammatical processing, it may be most parsimonious to assume that an observed deficit in processing nouns or verbs also results in an impairment in the representation of grammatical class, rather than at the semantic level (Shapiro et al. 2000; Tsapkini et al. 2002; Shapiro & Caramazza submitted).

Let us now look closely at some of this evidence.

2.4. Modality-specific dissociations

Caramazza and Hillis (1991) were the first to describe dissociations in lexical production specific both to one grammatical class of words *and* to one modality of output. The two patients they reported showed complementary deficits in verb production following left-hemisphere cerebrovascular accidents (CVAs). HW, a 62-year-old right-handed woman with parietal and occipital lesions, correctly produced 56% of object names but only 22% of action names in spoken naming tasks, though she was able to access both action and object names in writing virtually flawlessly. By contrast, SJD, a right-handed woman who was 48 at the time of testing and had suffered damage to frontotemporal regions, was able to write correctly only 70% of action names, whereas she was not impaired in naming actions orally (97% correct) or in producing nouns in either modality (99% in both speaking and writing). Both patients presented with fluent but paraphasic speech, normal in prosody and phrase length, and naming performance for both was affected by the frequency of the stimuli but not by concretness values.

It is interesting that the same patterns of performance obtained when the patients were tested with homonyms, that is, words that can be used in English as either nouns or verbs (e.g., *to watch/a watch*). HW was able to read correctly 88% of noun homonyms but only 46% of verb homonyms in a sentence context, whereas she was largely unimpaired in writing the same nouns and verbs to fill blanks in the same sentences presented in written form. SJD, on the other hand, produced both noun and verb homonyms perfectly in the spoken modality but could write only 56% of the verbs correctly, as opposed to 98% of the nouns.

A third patient PW, whose performance profile is similar to SJD's, was reported by Rapp and Caramazza (1998; see figures 1.2 and 1.3). PW is a 51-year-old right-handed man, with damage to anterior parietal and posterior frontal areas resulting from a left CVA. His speech is grammatically correct but with hesitations due to word-finding difficulty; there are no signs of phonemic or articulatory disturbance. Like SJD, PW was able to produce both nouns and verbs normally in the spoken modality in oral picture naming and scene description tasks. However, when asked to perform the same tasks in writing, PW's performance deteriorated markedly with verbs,

P. W.
The boy The fence
The boy is climbing the fence
The wife is The
The female is fixing the dress
The boy is move The wooD box.
The boy is moving the wooden box

FIGURE 1.2. Sample of patient PW's responses in a written and spoken picture description task (Rapp & Caramazza 1998). PW is unable to produce the written forms of verbs that he produces correctly in speech.

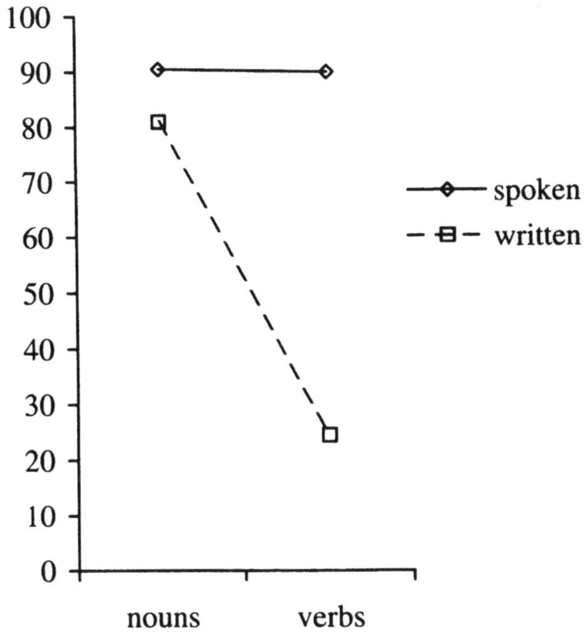

FIGURE 1.3. Summary of the proportions of correct responses produced by PW in spoken and written naming tasks (Rapp & Caramazza 1998).

whereas nouns were unaffected. In many cases he was able to provide written descriptions of pictures in which only the main verb was missing or ill formed (e.g., "The wife is ______ the dress"; "The boy is move the wood box").

Because the naming performance of these patients is normal in one modality of output, it is hard to see how the grammatical class deficits they show in the other modality can be attributed to a strictly semantic deficit. Attempts to explain such patterns of performance in semantic terms (Gainotti et al. 1995; Bird et al. 2000) simply fail to account for all the data (Shapiro & Caramazza 2001). Moreover, because the same effect was obtained with homonyms as with unambiguous nouns and verbs, it cannot plausibly be argued that the grammatical class effect is due to a phonological or orthographic processing deficit.

At the same time, it might be noted that all three of the patients just described showed deficits in processing verbs. This coincidence invites speculation about whether verbs might have a special status in lexical production. We have already argued that it is unlikely that they are generally harder to produce than nouns since some patients have trouble producing nouns but have no trouble with verbs; yet it is possible that some dimension of verb representation makes verbs more difficult to produce in the context of a very mild phonological or orthographic output deficit. (Such a deficit would, indeed, have to be so mild that it would have no observable impact on noun production.) This possibility can be rejected if we find a patient who shows a double dissociation of nouns and verbs across modalities.

Patient EBA (Hillis & Caramazza 1995) is just such a case. EBA at the time of testing (in 1993) was a 57-year-old right-handed woman who had suffered an ischemic stroke in 1985 involving the left frontal and basal ganglia, resulting in anomic aphasia and severe writing difficulties. An additional stroke five years later involving a "watershed" area in the left frontal-temporal-parietal region rendered her unable to read and increased her difficulty in retrieving words. As a consequence of these two strokes EBA presented with a profound impairment in naming and reading despite fluent, grammatical, and well-articulated speech, as in this sample: "Oh Lordy, she's making a mess. She let the thing go, and it's getting on the floor. They're stealing something. He's falling; he's gonna hurt himself. She's cleaning these things. She's looking at him falling, and she's gonna get some of the stuff he's giving her."

It is evident from these few utterances that EBA has severe difficulties in producing nouns in the oral modality, and she relies heavily on pronouns (*she, he, they*) and very frequent, generic nouns (*thing, stuff*). On the other hand, she seems to have few problems in producing appropriate and semantically meaningful verbs (*stealing, falling, gonna hurt, cleaning*). In a picture-naming task she accurately named 72% of action pictures but only 12% of object pictures. Moreover, in a naming to definition task using noun-verb homonyms, EBA was significantly more impaired in naming the homonyms defined as nouns (19%) than in naming the same words defined as verbs (75%). When asked to generate nouns in ten categories (e.g., things you use outdoors) and verbs in ten categories (e.g., things you do outdoors), EBA produced an average of 5.5 responses per category for verbs and 0.5 responses per category for nouns.

In marked contrast to her naming performance, EBA was able to comprehend visually presented nouns much more readily than verbs in the same modality. She was able to match written verbs to pictures only 43% of the time, as opposed to 98% of the time for nouns. (EBA performed perfectly in an auditory version of the same task.) Likewise, in a visual lexical decision task, she was much more accurate in accepting nouns as real words (92%) than in accepting verbs, with which she performed essentially at chance (58%). EBA correctly rejected 96% of nonwords (see figure 1.4).

To summarize, EBA showed normal auditory comprehension of nouns and verbs but impaired visual comprehension of verbs only and impaired spoken production of nouns only. It is highly unlikely that such a pattern of performance could result from a root deficit at the semantic level.

Another example of a patient with a double dissociation of grammatical class deficits across modalities is KSR (Rapp & Caramazza 2002). KSR has more difficulty in producing nouns than verbs in speech but is relatively more impaired with verbs in writing. He was able to produce correctly 92% of verbs but only 76% of nouns in oral naming tasks; this pattern was mirrored neatly in written naming (96% of nouns, 57% of verbs). Again, the interaction between grammatical class and modality in this case cannot be attributed to differences in the relative difficulty of nouns and verbs, for the very plain reason that the *same* items were used in speaking and writing tasks. Moreover, since KSR (unlike EBA) shows a double dissociation between grammatical categories in *production* tasks, we cannot appeal to the possibility that comprehension and production place different demands on the lexical access system as an explanation for this patient's pattern of performance (see figure 1.5).

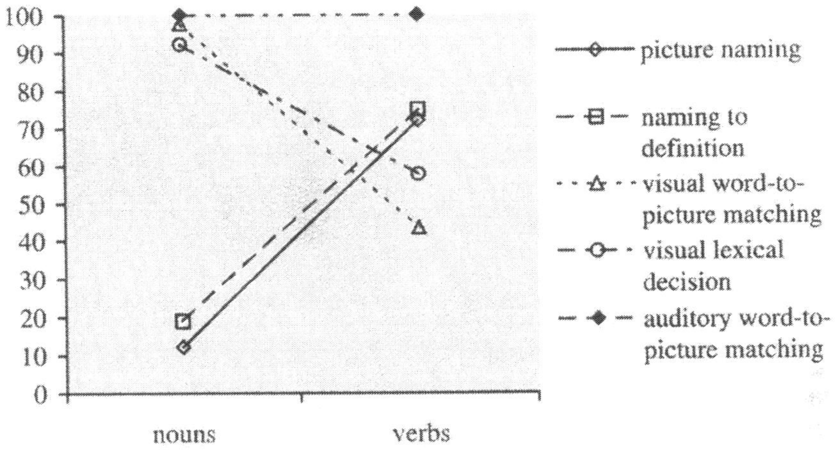

FIGURE 1.4. Rates of correct performance of patient EBA on a variety of production and comprehension tasks involving nouns and verbs (Hillis & Caramazza 1995). EBA was better with nouns than verbs in comprehending written stimuli—the reverse of the pattern observed in oral production.

2.5. Further evidence for deficits restricted by grammatical category

We have argued that the modality-specific nature of the grammatical category specific deficits observed in HW, SJD, PW, EBA, KSR, and potentially other patients precludes locating the source of all such deficits at either the semantic level or at the level of peripheral phonological or orthographic processes.

However, it might still be the case that grammatical class effects arise as a consequence of the way the semantic system is organized in relation to lexical representations. For instance, suppose that there are spatially segregated semantic systems that subserve the representation of concrete and abstract features and that these systems send activation to modality-specific lexical systems. A given phonological or orthographic lexical item (lexeme) would then receive different amounts of activation from each of the two semantic subsystems depending on whether the lexeme represents a more concrete word (a noun) or a more abstract one (a verb). Brain damage resulting in a functional disconnection of one of the semantic subsystems from one of the lexical subsystems might then give rise to the kind of modality-specific grammatical class effects observed in the patients we have described.

Although we cannot reject this account directly, there is other evidence in at least three patients for a grammatically based deficit restricted to one category (nouns or verbs). In each case, the crucial evidence relates to the patient's ability to process morphological affixes specific to words in the impaired grammatical category.

JR (Shapiro et al. 2000) is a 55-year-old former professor of philosophy who became anomic in the aftermath of a left CVA affecting the left frontal-temporal-parietal region. His speech is fluent but is marked by word-finding difficulties that often result in circumlocutions. In a picture-naming task, JR correctly produced 83%

Speaking:	The girl is holding the [baɪg]	The man is putting gas in the car.
Writing:	The girl is actions a wagon.	The woman is hold gas the car.

FIGURE 1.5. Sample of patient KSR's written and oral descriptions of two pictorial stimuli (Rapp & Caramazza 2002).

of action names but only 50% of object names. The same pattern of spared verb production in the face of impaired noun production is evident in a wide range of tasks including delayed repetition, homonym naming, and sentence generation (see figure 1.6). In the latter task, not only did JR use only 25% of unambiguous target nouns as nouns in well-formed utterances (as against 73% of verbs), he also displayed a marked preference for incorporating ambiguous words into utterances as verbs (78%) compared to nouns (6%).

It seems unlikely that semantic variables such as concreteness could account for JR's pattern of production. Indeed, there was a small but significant *positive* effect of concreteness on JR's naming performance, suggesting that he was better, or at least not worse (as might be expected on the basis of many semantic-conceptual accounts), at producing concrete words than abstract words. Moreover, the deficit for nouns in JR's production was not evident in comprehension. In a task that required him to identify which one of three words was least similar in meaning to the other two, JR responded correctly to 80% of noun triplets and 50% of verb triplets. When the task compared abstract and concrete nouns, JR was slightly but not significantly better with concrete nouns (62%) than with abstract nouns (46%). These findings argue against a semantic interpretation of JR's grammatical class effect in production.

Evidence that JR's deficit involves the grammatical category "noun" comes from a morphological processing task, in which he was asked to complete sentences of the type "This is a *judge*; these are . . ." (for nouns) or "This person *judges*; these people . . ." (for verbs). When the task involved noun-verb homonyms (e.g., *he judges/the judges*), JR was worse at producing the plurals of nouns (76%) than producing the phonologically identical third-person singular verb forms (94%). The same pattern resulted when the task involved pseudowords (e.g., *it wugs/the wugs*): JR was able to produce the correct plural forms of only 38% of pseudonouns but correctly produced third-person singular forms 87% of the time when the same pseudowords were presented as verbs. The results of this task, together with JR's difficulty in pro-

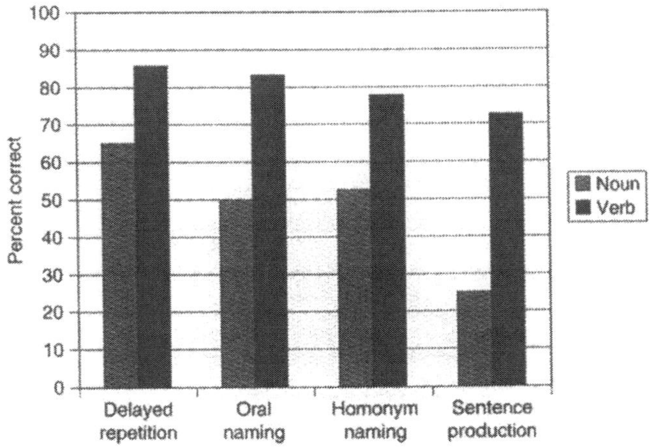

FIGURE 1.6. Summary of JR's correct performance with nouns and verbs in four production tasks (Shapiro et al. 2000).

ducing nouns in a wide range of other tasks, suggest that he is unable to access specific grammatical properties (such as morphological affixes) associated with the category of nouns.

In summary, JR presented with a disproportionate difficulty in producing nouns compared to verbs. This effect was not evident in comprehension and cannot be reduced to a deficit at the semantic level according to any account that has been proposed thus far. Moreover, JR's difficulty in producing nouns is associated with a specific difficulty with nominal morphology, which also extends to the morphological processing of pseudonouns. Since pseudowords cannot be said to have any stored semantic representation, it is extremely difficult to see how this effect could be accommodated by a semantic-conceptual account.

Is JR an isolated case? There is evidence to indicate that he is not. A second patient, RC (Shapiro & Caramazza 2003), shows analogous deficit with the category of verbs. A former transportation company manager, RC was 65 at the time of testing; after suffering a left CVA involving primarily left frontoparietal areas, he presented with articulatory problems and severely agrammatic speech. For instance, he defined the word *pan* as follows: "Lots of things. Cooking. Eggs. Bacon."

RC also showed a deficit for verbs relative to nouns across a variety of production tasks, including picture naming (nouns: 92%; verbs: 59%) and single-word repetition (nouns: 77%; verbs: 67%). Moreover, his performance on morphology tasks mirrored JR's. He produced correctly inflected verb forms on only 29% of trials, as opposed to 73% with nouns. A similar pattern obtained with pseudoverbs (28%) and pseudonouns (50%). As was the case with JR, this selective difficulty was not evident in RC's comprehension; he responded correctly to 69% of noun triplets and to 88% of verb triplets. Taken together, the patterns of performance displayed by RC and JR constitute strong evidence that grammatical knowledge about nouns and verbs may be impaired selectively following brain damage (see figures 1.7 and 1.8).

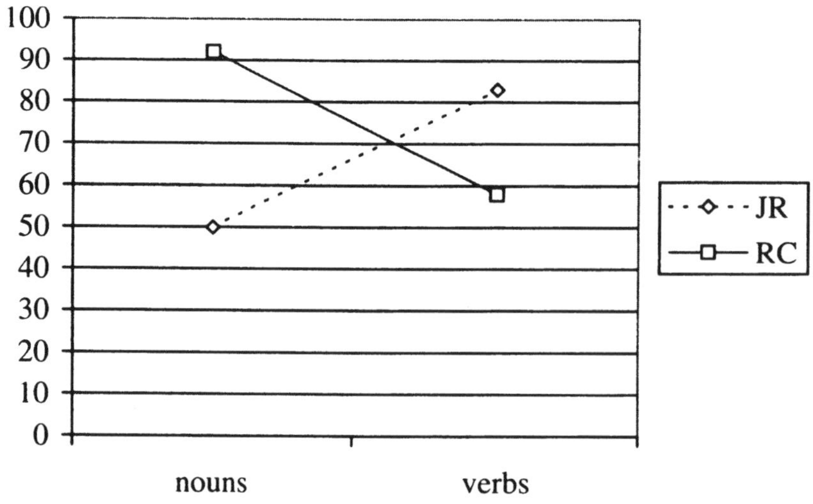

FIGURE 1.7. Comparative performance of JR (Shapiro et al. 2000) and RC (Shapiro & Caramazza 2003) on a picture-naming task with actions and objects.

It is true that the tasks we have described as crucial to establishing the presence of a grammatical deficit in JR and RC exploit a useful quirk of English morphology—namely, the fact that the third-person singular inflection for verbs is phonologically the same as the regular plural inflection for nouns. Although this provides an elegant way of controlling for phonological differences, it also nearly exhausts the inventory of comparable morphological manipulations in English, a fact that might raise questions about the generality of the effects that have been observed. However, similar dissociations in grammatical knowledge can arise in patients who speak other languages, including those with much richer inflectional systems than English.

Tsapkini et al. (2002) have described a Greek-speaking aphasic patient who presents with a deficit in verb morphology that may parallel the kinds of deficits observed in JR and RC. SK, a 58-year-old man, whose CT scan shows sizable hypodense areas in the left temporal lobe, was diagnosed with motor aphasia and displayed a very pronounced speech apraxia; Tsapkini and colleagues describe his spontaneous speech as "very limited and effortful with marked articulatory difficulties," though apparently he made more phonological errors on verb stems than on nouns with similarly complex phonetic structures.

When SK was asked to produce verbs in the past perfective form, he was unable to respond correctly 72% of the time. By contrast, he made only 9% of errors in producing the plural forms of neuter nouns, though Tsapkini and colleagues (2002) claim that the two manipulations being compared (forming plural neuter nouns and past perfective verbs) are essentially equivalent in morphophonological complexity. Sentence-to-picture-matching tasks indicated that SK had little difficulty in comprehending past perfective verbs (or plural nouns), and his repetition and reading were largely intact. The striking specificity of this patient's difficulty with verb morphology indicates, as the authors argue, that "grammatical class is an organizing principle in the lexicon."

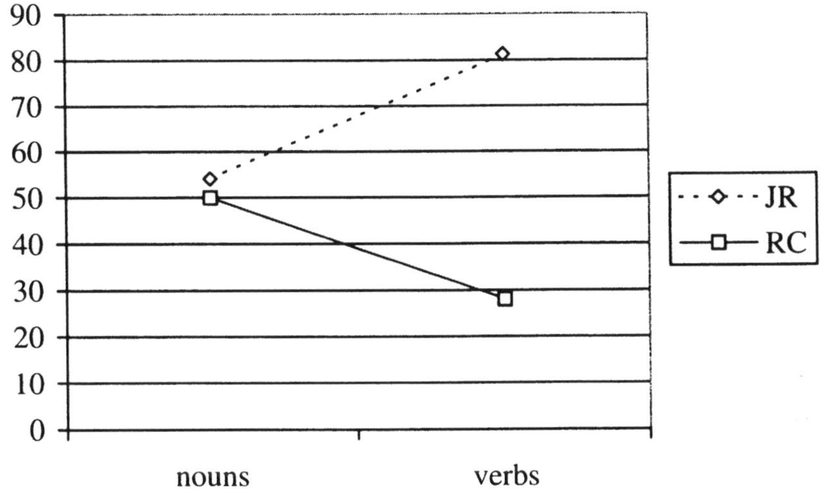

FIGURE 1.8. Comparative performance of JR (Shapiro et al. 2000) and RC (Shapiro & Caramazza submitted) on a task involving the production of morphologically inflected forms of pseudowords.

3. How is category information represented?

3.1. Category membership and the problem of determinism

The data and arguments outlined above support the view that at least some grammatical category dissociations are not amenable to semantic-conceptual explanations and are better explained as resulting from damage to processing components associated with the formal classes of nouns and verbs. By extension, these patients' patterns of performance tend to support the notion that grammatical categories are cognitive entities with, in some sense, irreducible internal representations.

However, these data do not speak to an important aspect of the distinction between associationist and cognitivist views of language processing, namely, whether or not grammatical categories are deterministic. Many generative theories of language view categories as discrete and deterministic in the sense that the members of a category form a finite (but expandable) set that is commonly accessible to certain rules and operations associated with that category—morphological affixation rules, for example.

Yet this need not be the case, even if it is true that computational processes relating to grammatical categories are autonomous and susceptible to selective impairment, as we have argued. We might imagine that a word's status as a noun or a verb is assigned online by syntactic operations involved in computing sentence structure and not stored as an aspect of that word's representation in the lexicon. To be sure, we would need to posit additional mechanisms to decide when it is appropriate to use a lexical item as a member of a given category, what morphological operations it must undergo (*the growth of fungus* but not **the flowth of water*), what phrasal structure it specifies (*to lord over someone* but not **to lord someone*), and what it signifies in a particular grammatical context (*to cat, an own*). But the problem is not theoretically insurmountable, and it can be approached in nondeterministic theories by means of such notions as prototypes (Rosch & Mervis 1975; Lakoff 1982), gradience (Bolinger 1961; Quirk et al. 1985), or fuzzy categories (Coates, 1983).

3.2. Phonological categories are discrete

Though the data from aphasia do not allow us to take a clear stand on this issue with respect to the grammatical categories of nouns and verbs, another potential categorical distinction in the brain—the distinction between consonants and vowels—can help us to decide whether at least some language categories are likely to be discrete and deterministic.

Caramazza et al. (2000) recently described two patients—AS and IFA—with selective deficits in the production of consonants and vowels, respectively. AS is a right-handed 41-year-old Italian woman who suffered an ischemic CVA and was left with a small lesion in the right parietal lobe, along with damage to larger areas of the left parietal and temporal lobes. She exhibits no visual, auditory, somatosensory, motor, or articulatory deficits, and her spontaneous speech is fluent but paraphasic. IFA is a right-handed 52-year-old Italian woman whose vascular stroke resulted in damage to the left supramarginal, angular, and superior temporal gyri. Like AS, she presents with fluent but paraphasic speech and no visual, auditory, somatosensory, motor, or articulatory deficits. For both patients verbal span was limited to three forward and three backward.

A striking feature of these patients' speech production performance is that they display contrasting patterns of error rates for vowels relative to consonants—a double dissociation. This general observation emerges from an analysis of substitution errors, in which the patients substituted one phonological segment for another (e.g., *salire* > *savite*, *solire*, *salene*). Within a corpus of words with which AS made substitution errors, she incorrectly produced 27% of vowel segments but only 9% of consonant segments. IFA, on the other hand, made errors on 28% of consonant segments but only 5% of vowel segments (see figures 1.9 and 1.10).

The substitution errors made by these patients were only slightly more likely to represent phonologically close segments (e.g., /t/~/d/) than phonologically distant ones (/t/~/f/). These results show contrasting selective impairments in the two patients but do not necessarily allow us to conclude whether or not consonants and vowels are represented categorically at some level of processing. It could be argued that the performance of these patients was largely a factor of sonority, that is, the degree of openness of the vocal apparatus during speech. Damage to the mechanism responsible for processing more sonorous (AS) or less sonorous (IFA) sounds would result in the observed double dissociation.

That view, however, predicts that the distribution of errors within the consonant class should be a function of sonority value: AS, who makes many errors on vowels, should also make more errors on the more sonorous consonants (e.g., /l/, /r/, /s/) than on the less sonorous consonants (e.g., /t/, /g/). IFA should show the opposite pattern. Yet when the error rates of these patients are analyzed as a function of the sonority

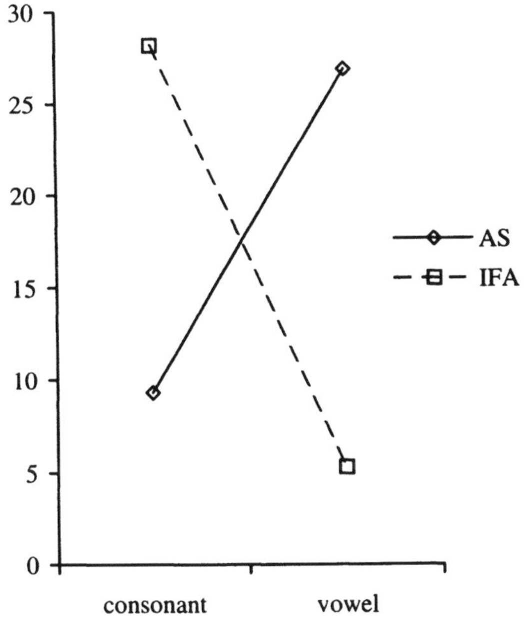

FIGURE 1.9. Error rates by segment type for patients AS and IFA (Caramazza et al. 2000).

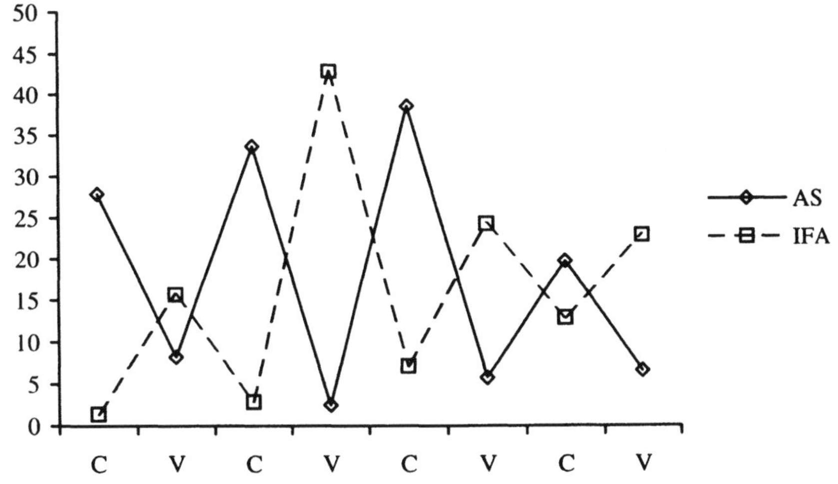

FIGURE 1.10. Percentage of substitution errors made by patients AS and IFA as a function of segment position in eight-phoneme Italian words with regular (CV) syllable structure (Caramazza et al. 2000). It is evident from the figure that AS made errors primarily on vowel segments, whereas IFA's errors were mostly restricted to consonant segments.

value of the target consonants, no correlation is observed for either AS (r = 0.16, n.s.) or IFA (r = 0.01, n.s.). Both patients are roughly equally likely to make errors with less sonorous consonants as with more sonorous consonants.

These patterns of dissociation constitute two simple but important observations. First, the double dissociation of error types between the two patients demonstrates that consonants and vowels can be damaged independently of each other. Second, the distribution of errors for consonants is not a function of their sonority value (or their dependence on other features that distinguish among both consonants and vowels).

The first observation rules out an explanation of these deficits based on the argument that consonants are more difficult to produce than vowels; the second implies that consonants and vowels are categorically distinct entities since performance is not a function of more basic phonetic parameters that distinguish members of the two categories. This does not imply, however, that sonority does not play a crucial role in speech production; the ordering of phonemes within syllables is undoubtedly a function of sonority, explaining why, for example, in English *plooze* is a licit nonword but *lpooze* is not. At the same time, a categorical distinction between consonants and vowels may also be critical in determining prosody and in computing online the syllabic structure of spoken utterances.[2]

4. Taking stock

What can we conclude from the evidence we have reviewed about apparently categorically based dissociations between nouns and verbs and between consonants and vowels? If nothing else, it seems that certain patterns of aphasic disturbance can be explained most readily if we assume that some of the processes carried out by the brain operate with discrete, categorical entities such as noun, verb, consonant, and vowel.

The evidence we have reviewed in favor of a cognitivist position on some aspects of language processing does not admittedly constitute a knock-down argument against associationist accounts, but it does place powerful constraints on theorizing about language processing, no matter what theoretical framework one adopts. Moreover, this type of data raises an important challenge for neuroscience generally: what is the nature of the neural mechanisms responsible for implementing discrete versus continuous representations? At the moment we may not have an answer to this question better than the explanation offered by JR for his problems in producing nouns: "I don't have in my brain a place where I'm familiar with that so that's why I can't do it. I don't know what to do . . . there's a hole there."

Notes

1. To these we might add "phonological" explanations, which suggest that there are subtle differences between phonological representations of nouns and verbs—in the case of English, for example, there may be differences in average length and vowel quality (Kelly 1992). Phonology generally has not been entertained as a possible locus of grammatical category effects (but see Black & Chiat 2000), and it is hard to imagine an argument from phonology

that can account for clearly described dissociations between noun and verb homophones (Caramazza & Hillis 1991; Shapiro et al. 2000).

2. Converging evidence for a categorical distinction between consonants and vowels is provided by patterns of spelling errors in certain types of dysgraphic patients, who may present with selective deficits in writing either vowels (Cubelli 1991) or consonants (Miceli et al. in preparation). One of the patients reported by Cubelli omitted all vowels, leaving blank spaces between consonants (e.g., writing *tavolino*, "small table," as T V L N), whereas the other produced errors almost exclusively on vowel segments. Such patterns accord with models of graphemic representation, which assume that the consonant/vowel status of a grapheme is discretely represented (Caramazza & Miceli 1990).

References

Allport, D. (1985). "Distributed Memory, Modular Subsystems and Dysphasia." In S. Newman & R. Epstein, eds., *Current Perspectives in Dysphasia*. Edinburgh: Churchill Livingstone.

Bates, E., S. Chen, O. Tzeng, P. Li, & M. Opie. (1991). "The Noun-Verb Problem in Chinese. *Brain and Language*, 41, 203–233.

Berndt, R., & A. Caramazza. (1980). "A Redefinition of Broca's Aphasia: Implications for a Neuropsychological Model of Language." *Applied Psycholinguistics* 1, 225–278.

Berndt, R., A. Haendiges, M. Burton, & C. Mitchum. (2002). "Grammatical Class and Imageability in Aphasic Word Production: Their Effects Are Independent." *Journal of Neurolinguistics* 13, 353–372.

Berndt, R., C. Mitchum, A. Haendiges, & J. Sandson, (1997a). "Verb Retrieval in Aphasia. 1. Characterizing Single Word Impairments." *Brain and Language*, 56, 68–106.

Berndt, R., A. Haendiges, C. Mitchum, & J. Sandson. (1997b). "Verb Retrieval in Aphasia. 2. Relationship to Sentence Processing." *Brain and Language*, 56, 107–137.

Bird, H., D. Howard, & S. Franklin. (2000). "Why Is a Verb Like an Inanimate Object? Grammatical Category and Semantic Category Deficits." *Brain and Language* 72, 246–309.

Black, M., & S. Chiat. (2000). "Noun-Verb Dissociations: A Multi-faceted Phenomenon." Paper presented at the XVII Annual BPS Cognitive Psychology Section Conference, Essex, England.

Bodamer, J. (1947). Die Prosopagnosie. *Archiv für Psychiatrie und Nervenkrankheiten* 179, 6–53.

Bolinger, D. (1961). *Generality, Gradience, and the All-or-none*. The Hague: Mouton.

Breedin, S., E. Saffran, & M. Schwartz (1998). "Semantic Factors in Verb Retrieval: An Effect of Complexity." *Brain and Language* 63, 1–31.

Caramazza, A. (1998). "The Interpretation of Category-specific Deficits: What Do They Reveal About the Organization of Conceptual Knowledge in the Brain?" *Neurocase* 4, 265–272.

Caramazza, A., D. Chialant, R. Capasso, & G. Miceli. (2000). "Separable Processing of Consonants and Vowels." *Nature*, 403, 428–430.

Caramazza, A., & A. Hillis. (1991). "Lexical Organization of Nouns and Verbs in the Brain." *Nature*, 349, 788–790.

Caramazza, A., & G. Miceli. (1990). "The Structure of Graphemic Representations." *Cognition* 37, 243–297.

Caramazza, A., & J. Shelton. (1998). "Domain-specific Knowledge Systems in the Brain: The Animate-Inanimate Distinction." *Journal of Cognitive Neuroscience* 10, 1–34.

Coates, J. (1983). *The Semantics of the Modal Auxiliaries*. London: Croom Helm.

Coltheart, M., L. Ingris, L. Cupples, P. Michie, A. Bates, & B. Budd, (1998). "A Semantic Subsystem Specific to the Storage of Information About the Visual Attributes of Animate and Inanimate Objects." *Neurocase* 4, 353–370.

Cubelli, R. (1991). "A Selective Deficit for Writing Vowels in Acquired Dysgraphia." *Nature* 353, 258–260.

De Renzi, E., & G. di Pellegrino. (1995). "Sparing of Verbs and Preserved but Ineffectual Reading in a Patient with Impaired Word Production." *Cortex* 31, 619–636.

Diamond, R., & S. Carey. (1986). "Why Faces Are and Are Not Special: An Effect of Expertise." *Journal of Experimental Psychology: General* 115, 107–117.

Farah, M., & J. McClelland. (1991). "A Computational Model of Semantic Memory Impairment: Modality Specificity and Emergent Category Specificity." *Journal of Experimental Psychology: General,* 120, 339–357.

Gainotti, G., & M. Silveri. (1996). "Cognitive and Anatomical Locus of Lesion in a Patient with a Category-specific Semantic Impairment for Living Beings." *Cognitive Neuropsychology* 13, 357–389.

Gainotti, G., M. Silveri, A. Daniele, & L. Giustolisi. (1995). "Neuroanatomical Correlates of Category-specific Semantic Disorders: A Critical Survey." *Memory* 3, 247–264.

Garrard, P., M. Lambon Ralph, J. Hodges, & K. Patterson. (in press). "Prototypicality, Distinctiveness and Intercorrelation: Analyses of the Semantic Attributes of Living and Nonliving concepts." *Cognitive Neuropsychology.*

Garrett, M. (1980). "Levels of Processing in Sentence Production." In B. Butterworth, ed., *Language Production,* vol. 1. London: Academic Press.

Gauthier, I., A. Anderson, M. Tarr, P. Skudlarski, & J. Gore, (1997). "Levels of Categorization in Visual Recognition Studied Using Functional Magnetic Resonance Imaging." *Current Biology* 7, 645–651.

Goldsmith, J. (1990). *Autosegmental and Metrical Phonology.* Oxford: Blackwell.

Goodglass, H. (1968). "Studies on the Grammar of Aphasics." In S. Rosenberg & K. Joplin, eds., *Developments in Applied Psycholinguistics Research.* New York: Macmillan.

Goren, C., M. Sarty, & P. Wu. (1975). "Visual Following and Pattern Discrimination of Facelike Stimuli by Newborn Infants." *Pediatrics* 55, 544–549.

Grosjean, F., & J. Gee. (1987). "Prosodic Structure and Spoken Word Recognition." *Cognition* 25, 135–155.

Gross, C., G. Roche-Miranda, & D. Bender. (1972). "Visual Properties of Neurons in the Inferotemporal Cortex of the Macaque." *Journal of Neurophysiology* 35, 96–111.

Hart, J., & B. Gordon. (1992). "Neural Subsystems for Object Knowledge." *Nature* 359, 60–64.

Hillis, A., & A. Caramazza. (1991). "Category-specific Naming and Comprehension Impairment: A Double Dissociation." *Brain* 114, 2081–2094.

Hillis, A., & A. Caramazza. (1995). "Representation of Grammatical Categories of Words in the Brain." *Journal of Cognitive Neuroscience* 7, 396–407.

Johnson, M., & J. Morton. (1991). *Biology and Cognitive Development: The Case of Face Recognition.* Oxford: Blackwell.

Kanwisher, N., P. Downing, R. Epstein, & Z. Kourtzi. (in press). "Functional Neuroimaging of Human Visual Recognition." In R. Cabeza & A. Kingstone, eds., Handbook of Functional Neuroimaging of Cognition. Cambridge, Mass.: MIT Press.

Kean, M. (1978). "The Linguistic Interpretation of Aphasic Syndromes: Agrammatism in Broca's Aphasia, an Example. *Cognition* 5, 9–46.

Kelly, M. (1992). "Using Sound to Solve Syntactic Problems: The Role of Phonology in Grammatical Category Assignments." *Psychological Review* 99, 349–364.

Kohn, S., Lorch, M., & Pearson, D. (1989). Verb finding in aphasia. *Cortex,* 25, 57–69.

Laiacona, M., R. Barbarotto, & E. Capitani. (1993). "Perceptual and Associative Knowledge in Category Specific Impairment of Semantic Memory: A Study of Two Cases." *Cortex* 29, 727–740.

Laiacona, M., E. Capitani, & R. Barbarotto. (1997). "Semantic Category Dissociations: A Longitudinal Study of Two Cases." *Cortex* 33, 441–461.

Lakoff, G. (1982). *Categories and Cognitive Models, Series A, Paper 96*. Trier, Ger.: Linguistic Agency, University of Trier.

Lambon Ralph, M., D. Howard, G. Nightingale, & A. Ellis. (1998). "Are Living and Nonliving Category-specific Deficits Causally Linked to Impaired Perceptual or Associative Knowledge? Evidence from a Category-specific Double Dissociation." *Neurocase*, 4, 311–338.

Luria, A. R., & L. S. Tsvetkova. (1967). "Towards the Mechanisms of 'Dynamic Aphasia'." *Acta Neurologica et Psychiatrica Belgica* 67, 1045–1057.

Marshall, J., T. Pring, S. Chiat, & J. Robson. (1996a). "Calling a Salad a Federation: An Investigation of Semantic Jargon. Part 1—Nouns." *Journal of Neurolinguistics*, 9, 237–250.

Marshall, J., S. Chiat, J. Robson, & T. Pring. (1996b). Calling a Salad a Federation: An Investigation of Semantic Jargon. Part 2—Verbs. *Journal of Neurolinguistics* 9, 251–260.

McCarthy, R., & E. Warrington. (1985). "Category Specificity in an Agrammatic Patient: The Relative Impairment of Verb Retrieval and Comprehension." *Neuropsychologia* 23, 709–727.

McRae, K., & G. Cree. (in press). "Factors Underlying Category-specific Semantic Deficits." In E. Forde & G. Humphreys, eds., Category Specificity in Brain and Mind. East Sussex, Eng.: Psychology Press.

Miceli, G., B. Benvegnú, R. Capasso, & A. Caramazza. (in preparation). "A Selective Deficit in Producing Consonants in Spelling."

Miceli, G., M. Silveri, U. Nocentini, & A. Caramazza. (1988). "Patterns of Dissociation in Comprehension and Production of Nouns and Verbs. *Aphasiology* 2, 351–358.

Miceli, G., M. Silveri, G. Villa, & A. Caramazza. (1984). "On the Basis for the Agrammatic's Difficulty in Producing Main Verbs. *Cortex* 20, 207–220.

Moscovich, M., G. Winocur, & M. Behrmann. (1997). "What Is Special About Face Recognition? Nineteen Experiments on a Person with Visual Object Agnosia and Dyslexia but Normal Face Recognition." *Journal of Cognitive Neuroscience* 9, 555–604.

Perrett, D., E. Rolls, & W. Caan. (1982). "Visual Neurones Responsive to Faces in the Monkey Temporal Cortex. *Experimental Brain Research* 47, 329–342.

Piaget, J. (1923). *La langage et la pensée chez l'enfant*. Paris: Delachaux & Niestle.

Quirk, R., S. Greenbaum, G. Leech, & J. Svartvik. (1985). A Comprehensive Grammar of the English Language. London: Longman.

Rapp, B., & A. Caramazza. (1997). "The Modality-specific Organization of Grammatical Categories: Evidence from Impaired Spoken and Written Sentence Production." *Brain and Language* 56, 248–286.

Rapp, B., & A. Caramazza. (1998). "A Case of Selective Difficulty in Writing Verbs." *Neurocase* 4, 127–140.

Rapp, B., & A. Caramazza. (2002). "Selective Difficulties with Spoken Nouns and Written Verbs: A Single Case Study." *Journal of Neurolinguistics* 15, 373–402.

Robinson, G., M. Rossor, & L. Cipolotti. (1999). "Selective Sparing of Verb Naming in a Case of Severe Alzheimer's Disease. *Cortex* 35, 443–450.

Rosch, E., & C. Mervis. (1975). "Family Resemblances: Studies in the Internal Structure of Categories." *Cognitive Science* 7, 573–605.

Saffran, E., M. Schwartz, & O. Marin. (1980). "The Word Order Problem in Agrammatism: II. Production. *Brain and Language* 10, 263–280.

Santos, L., & A. Caramazza. (in press). "The Domain-specific Hypothesis: A Developmental and Comparative Perspective on Category-specific Deficits." In E. Forde & G. Humphreys, eds., *Category-specificity in Brain and Mind*. East Sussex, Eng.: Psychology Press.

Shallice, T. (1988). "Specialisation Within the Semantic System." *Cognitive Neuropsychology* 5, 133–142.

Shapiro, K., & A. Caramazza. (2003). "Grammatical Processing of Nouns and Verbs in the Left Frontal Cortex?" *Neuropsychologia* 41, 1189–1198.

Shapiro, K., & A. Caramazza. (2001). "Sometimes a Noun Is Just a Noun: Comments on Bird, Howard, and Franklin" (2000). *Brain and Language* 76, 202–212.

Shapiro, K., J. Shelton, & A. Caramazza. (2000). "Grammatical Class in Lexical Production and Morphological Processing: Evidence from a Case of Fluent Aphasia." *Cognitive Neuropsychology* 17, 665–682.

Shattuck-Hufnagel, S. (1987). "The Role of Word-onset Consonants in Speech Production Planning: New Evidence from Speech Error Patterns." In E. Keller & M. Gopnik, eds., *Motor and Sensory Processes of Language: Neuropsychology and Neurolinguistics*. Hillsdale, N.J.: Lawrence Erlbaum.

Silveri, M., & A. di Betta. (1997). "Noun-Verb Dissociations in Brain-damaged Patients: Further Evidence. *Neurocase* 3, 477–488.

Silveri, M., & G. Gainotti. (1988). "Interaction Between Vision and Language in Category-specific Impairment." *Cognitive Neuropsychology* 5, 677–709.

Tsapkini, K., G. Jarema, & E. Kehayia. (2002). "A Morphological Processing Deficit in Verbs but not in Nouns: A Case Study in a Highly Inflected Language." *Journal of Neurolinguistics* 15, 265–288.

Vygotsky, L. (1962). *Thought and Language*. Cambridge, Mass.: MIT Press.

Warrington, E., & R. McCarthy. (1983). "Category Specific Access Dysphasia." *Brain* 106, 859–878.

Warrington, E., & R. McCarthy. (1987). "Categories of Knowledge: Further Fractionations of an Attempted Integration." *Brain* 110, 1273–1296.

Warrington, E., & T. Shallice. (1984). "Category Specific Semantic Impairments." *Brain* 107, 829–854.

Williams, S., & C. Canter. (1987). "Action-naming Performance in Four Syndromes of Aphasia." *Brain and Language* 32, 124–136.

Zingeser, L., & R. Berndt. (1988). "Grammatical Class and Context Effects in a Case of Pure Anomia: Implications for Models of Language Production." *Cognitive Neuropsychology* 5, 473–516.

Zingeser, L., & R. Berndt. (1990). "Retrieval of Nouns and Verbs in Agrammatism and Aphasia." *Brain and Language* 39, 14–32.

2

GENNARO CHIERCHIA

Scalar Implicatures, Polarity Phenomena, and the Syntax/Pragmatics Interface

1. Introduction

Negative polarity phenomena, as exemplified in the behavior of English *any*, and scalar implicatures, as exemplified by, say, the interpretations of *some* (i.e., "at least one and possibly all" vs. "at least one but not all"), have often been felt to be closely related.[1] However, the exact nature of such a relationship remains as of now not fully understood, insofar as I can tell. And in fact, some important empirical generalizations pertaining to it, if not altogether missed, have perhaps not been properly appreciated. In this chapter, I address the issue of what are the relevant factual connections between scalar implicature and negative polarity and what we can learn from this about the grammatical mechanisms at the basis of these phenomena. One of the features that makes the analysis of negative polarity items (NPIs) and scalar implicatures (SIs) particularly interesting is that they raise a number of key questions concerning how syntax, semantics, and pragmatics interact with each other. We will mostly focus on the interface of pragmatics with syntax and semantics. More specifically, here is a widespread view of the latter. Grammar (which includes syntax and semantics) is a computational system that delivers, say, pairs of phonetic representations and interpreted logical forms. The output of the computational system is passed onto the conceptual/pragmatic system that employs it for concrete communication. The computational system of grammar and the conceptual/pragmatic system are separate units and work in a modular way: each unit is blind to the inner workings of the other. Things like agreement or c-command belong to grammar; things like relevance or conversational maxims belong to the conceptual/pragmatic system. This view is very plausible and has been quite successful in explaining things. Yet, I would like to make a case that, in certain important respects, it is actually wrong.

Let me try to give, in broad outline, the structure of the main claims to be developed. An influential account of scalar implicatures stems from Grice (1989) and the work more or less directly inspired by it (e.g., Horn 1972, 1989; Atlas & Levinson 1981). I will take the (neo)Gricean view as our starting point. I will then try to establish a factual generalization relating scalar implicatures to polarity phenomena. The generalization, in rough terms, is the following: ordinary scalar implicatures are systematically suspended in the very contexts that license elements like *any*. This seems to entail that the two phenomena in question must be based on a device governed by uniform principles. At the same time, scalar implicature computation and NPI licensing are influenced by structural (i.e., locality) considerations in very different ways—so much so that it is hard not to draw the conclusion that they are driven by very different mechanisms after all. This is, then, the problem: SIs and NPIs are so similar in certain respects and so different in others. Why? How come? After discussing the limits within which current approaches manage to provide an account of this puzzle, I will make a specific proposal on how SIs are computed and on how NPIs are licensed. I will try to make a case that the interaction of these two proposals actually takes us some way to a better understanding of the relevant phenomena. As we will see, my proposal has interesting (though not uncontroversial) consequences for the overall architecture of grammar at the above mentioned interfaces. In particular, I will argue that pragmatic computations and grammar-driven ones are "interspersed." Implicatures are not computed *after* truth conditions of (root) sentences have been figured out; they are computed phrase by phrase in tandem with truth conditions (or whatever compositional semantics computes).

The structure of the chapter is the following. In section 2 I discuss the main empirical properties of SIs. Then in section 3, I will put forth a theory of SIs that hopefully sheds some light on such properties. I will argue that, contrary to the dominant view, SIs are introduced locally and projected upward in a way that mirrors the standard semantic recursion. In section 4 I turn to NPIs. In this area, recent proposals have been developed, which make us understand *why* NPIs are licensed in negative context (Kadmond & Landman 1993; Krifka 1995; Lahiri 1998). All such proposals are based on the idea that the semantics of NPIs involves a comparison among relevant alternatives (much as SI implicature computation involves a comparison with scalar alternatives). I will propose a modification of such views in order to overcome some difficulties they run into. The two proposals (on SIs and NPIs) will have an unexpected kind of interaction having to do with the so-called intervention effect that has been observed in connection with NPIs.

In the rest of this introduction, in order to set our baseline, I summarize (a version of) the neo-Gricean stand on implicatures. The phenomenon is well known. The truth conditional content of a sentence like (1a) is taken to be (1b). Yet, such a sentence typically implicates (1c) conversationally and similarly for the sentences in (2):

(1) a. John is singing or screaming
b. $\text{singing(j)} \vee (\text{screaming(j)}$
c. $\neg\ (\text{singing(j)} \wedge (\text{screaming(j)})$

(2) a. Some student did well
b. $\exists x[\text{student}(x) \wedge (\text{did well}(x)]$ (Some and possibly all students did well)
c. $\neg \forall x\ [\text{student}(x) \rightarrow (\text{did well}(x)]$ (Not every student did well)

Implicatures of this sort arise whenever expressions that may be viewed as partaking in an informational scale are involved. For example, the (positive) quantifiers can be thought of as being ordered along a scale of informativeness as follows:

(3) The (positive) quantifier scale: some < many < most < every

The reason why this is so is that, for example, a sentence like (4a) asymmetrically entails (and hence is informationally stronger than) a sentence like (4b):[2]

(4) a. Every man smokes
b. Some man smokes

More generally, whenever a determiner D occurs to the right of a determiner D^+ in the scale in (3), a sentence of the form D N V will entail a sentence of the form D^+ N V. Similarly, *and* and *or* can be thought of as part of an informational scale, as *p and q* (asymetrically) entails *p or q*, and hence the former is inherently more informative than the latter. The centrality of the notion of scale for implicatures has been especially motivated in Horn's (1972, 1989) work; what can constitute a natural scale is somewhat controversial and need not concern us here.[3] Typical scales, besides < or, and> and the positive quantifiers in (3), are the following:

(5) Examples of Horn scales:
a. Negative quantifiers: not all < few < none
b. Predicates: *cute < beautiful < stupendous*
discrete < good < excellent
. . .
c. Numerals: 1 < . . . n < . . . .
d. The modals: possibly < necessarily
may < must
where $\alpha < \beta$ ("α is informationally weaker than β") $=_{df}$ β (asymmetrically) entails α.[4]

SIs derive from the systematic exploitation of Grice's (1989) conversational maxims (especially relevance and quantity). The way in which they come about may be schematically illustrated by an example (inspired most directly by Landman 1998). Consider

(6) a. Who is in that room?
b. John or Bill
c. John and Bill

Suppose a hearer gets (6b) as an answer to question (6a); s/he will then typically come to conclude that the answer in (6b) implies that (6c) does not hold (i.e., that John and Bill are not both in the room) in the following (idealized) way:

(7) i. The speaker said (6b) and not (6c), which would have been also relevant
ii. (6c) entails (6b) [*or* and *and* are part of a scale]
iii. If the speaker had the info that (6c), she/he would have said so [quantity]
iv. The speaker has no evidence that (6c) holds
v. The speaker is well informed
Therefore,
vi. It is unlikely/not the case that (6c) holds

Whether one goes for the stronger or the weaker version of the conclusion in (8vi) will depend on various pragmatic factors. It is important to notice that in the view just sketched, SIs are computed "globally," that is, after grammar has done its job. One first computes the (plain) meaning of the sentences; then, taking into account the relevant alternatives, one strengthens that meaning by adding the implicature.

It might be useful to have a more explicit model of how SIs are computed. An interesting proposal in this sense may be found in Krifka (1995). Following recent discussions of the semantics of focus, Krifka argues that a sentence S is generally considered against the background of a relevant set of alternatives, that is, other statements that might have been made in place of S. When scalar items are involved, the relevant set of alternatives is constituted by propositions built up by using the other items on the scale. Consider, for example, a sentence like (8a). Its truth conditional content is given in (8b).

(8) a. John earns $200 an hour
b. earn (j, $200) (in the "at least" sense)

The relevant set of alternatives are the following:

(9) Relevant alternatives:
{ . . . earn (j, $100), ___, earn(j, $300), earn (j, $400) . . }
entailment : ←

The members of the relevant alternatives in (9) are presented in their natural order, going from the weakest to the strongest. That is, every item in (9) entails the items to its left. For example, if it is the case that John earns $400 an hour, it must also be the case that he earns $300 an hour, and so on. The arrow beneath (9) indicates the direction of entailment. The slash indicates where the assertion would fit (for simplicity I am assuming only multiples of $100 to be relevant). According to Krifka, the recursive part of the semantics is set up in such a way as to compute, next to the truth-conditional content of a sentence $||S||$, also its relevant set of alternatives $||S||^{ALT}$ (along lines similar to those proposed by Rooth 1985 for focus). Thus, we keep track simultaneously of truth conditions and alternative sets, which is tantamount to saying that what we call "meaning" is in fact a multidimensional phenomenon. At some point, we choose to assert our sentence. That is, we add it to a context c, which will include a shared body of information (the conversational background). It is at this point that SIs are factored in because to choose a proposition from a given set of alternatives will, reasonably, carry along the weaker ones (i.e., the entailed alternatives) and exclude the stronger ones (i.e., the entailing alternatives)—by something like the Gricean reasoning sketched above in (7). Krifka formalizes this by defining a notion of scalar context incrementation whereby adding (8a) to a context c amounts to adding to c the following:

(10) [earn (j, \$200) $\wedge \neg$ earn (j, \$n)] (\$200 < n)

Thus, there are two parts to this process: the recursive computation of meaning (truth-conditional content plus alternative set) and context incrementation (where SIs are added in). The second part necessarily follows the first in time. I refer to Krifka's (1995) article for details.

I have sketched a neo-Gricean model of how implicatures are computed that to the best of my knowledge pretty much represents the level of our current understanding of the phenomenon. (The existing variants of it, to the extent they are or can be made equally explicit, share the basic architecture of Krifka's 1995 proposal). To be sure, I have offered no arguments in favor of the neo-Gricean view. And, in fact, to do so would take us too far afield. However, I believe that there are a number of things that that approach explains reasonably well.

(11) What the (neo-)Gricean approach explains:
   a. Defeasability of scalar implicature
   b. Sistematicity and cross-linguistic stability of the phenomenon
   c. Lack of lexical ambiguity of scalar items
   d. Metalinguistic/echoic uses of negation (and other operators)

Let us briefly review how a neo-Gricean account of the properties of SIs listed in (11) would go. Scalar implicatures are defeasable for a number of reasons. Perhaps the most straightforward one is that something in the context may make the stronger alternatives irrelevant, thereby undermining the canonical reasons for assuming that they do not hold. [Imagine, e.g., uttering (8a) in a situation in which our explicit concern is to find out who earns *at least* \$200 an hour]. Moreover, the neo-Gricean reasoning applies in an equal manner to every item that may be construed as belonging to a scale of the type illustrated in (6); hence, whenever we find a set of items in any language that naturally forms a Horn scale, we will expect them to display similar behavior. And the reason that one does not find distinct lexical entries for the alternative interpretations of scalar items is also clear: the two interpretations of, for example, *some* can be derived by means of a fully general mechanism. Finally, the neo-Gricean view meshes well with the independent observation that negation (and, possibly, other connectives) may be used in a "echoic" or "metalinguistic" way (again see Horn 1989). I think it is desirable to hold on to these results. However, some further empirical generalizations relevant to SIs will lead us to change rather radically certain aspects of the picture I have just sketched. To these I now turn.

2. Empirical properties of scalar implicatures

In this section I will first present data that cast some doubts on the traditional, strictly modular view of how SIs come about. Such data will suggest that implicatures are (or, at the very least, can be) introduced locally (i.e., in the scope domain of the scalar term) and then projected to (i. e., inherited by) larger embedding structures. The main empirical generalizations that characterize implicature projection will be discussed.

2.1. Are there embedded implicatures?

As mentioned in the introduction, the dominant view maintains that implicatures are computed globally, that is, after the semantics of the whole root sentence has been computed. In this section I will present some preliminary evidence that goes against this idea. If this proves to be true, we then need a way of thinking about implicature computation differently from the standard neo-Gricean one.

Let us begin by pointing out that, according to the standard view, embedded implicatures should not exist. Consider, for example, a sentence like (12):

(12) John believes that some students are waiting for him.

If implicatures are factored in at the embedded level, this sentence should implicate this one:

(13) John believes that not every student is waiting for him.

If, on the other hand, implicatures are computed at the root level, sentence (12)'s relevant alternative would be (14a). And the implicature should be its negation, (14b).

(14) a. John believes that every student is waiting for him.
b. It is not the case that John believes that every student is waiting for him.

Sentence (14b) is much weaker than (13). The former merely says that it is *compatible* with John's beliefs that not every student is waiting. But this doesn't mean he excludes such a possibility, as (13) does. So, if (12) implicates (14a) [as opposed to (13)], the implicature normally associated with *some* is weakened to the point of being virtually suspended.

What are our intuitions like about these facts? Perhaps intuitions in this domain are not sharp enough to settle the issue. Let me add, then, some further relevant observations. Suppose John comes to us and utters sentence (15a). General conversational dynamics authorizes us to claim on the basis of John's utterance that (15b) holds:

(15) a. John: "Some students are waiting for me."
b. John believes that some students are waiting for him.

Uncontroversially, the "not all" implicature will normally be present in interpreting (15a), which will be taken to convey "Some, though not all sutdents are waiting for him." But if implicatures are computed globally, such implicature is absent from (15b). This seems odd, for after all we were just reporting what (15a) gives us grounds for. The same holds for numerals:

(16) a. John: "My colleague makes $100 an hour."
b. John believes that his colleague makes $100 an hour.

If the standard neo-Gricean view of numerals is correct, the phrase "$100 an hour" in (16a), via the scalar implicature, comes to have an "exactly" interpretation. But in sentence (16b), the same numerical phrase loses such an interpretation. In fact, if implicatures are global, there is no way for unmodified numerals in embedded clauses to get an "exactly" interpretation. To put it in slightly different terms, a sentence like (15b) or (16b) certainly can be understood as if it had an embedded implicature. For example, (16b) certainly can be understood as imputing to John the belief that his colleague makes exactly $100 an hour. If this attribution doesn't come about via a local implicature, then how does it come about?

A related set of problems comes from factive verbs, that is, verbs that are taken to presuppose the truth of their complement. As we know, presuppositions can normally be accommodated. Take a sentence such as "My bike is outside." If you didn't already know that I have a bike, you can accommodate such information without any problem. By the same token, suppose someone tells us,

(17) John knows that some students are waiting for him.

If we didn't know the relevant facts (namely, that some students are waiting for John), we would typically accommodate them. I think that, in fact, we will typically accommodate also the implicature generally associated with the embedded clause. That is, we interpret (17) as

(18) Some though not all students are waiting for John and he is aware of it.

This interpretation (and the way in which we accommodate) does not come for free at all if implicatures are computed globally, whereas it does if they are computed locally. In the local approach to implicatures, (17) is interpreted as

(19) John knows that some though not all students are waiting for him.

So we have right there the fact to be accommodated. The global mechanism, instead, would only authorize one to conclude, on the basis of (17),

(20) It is not the case that John knows that every student is waiting for him.

We obviously need some extra assumption to get from here to (18), and such assumptions are not so straightforward to state. The usual assumptions that the speaker (the speaker, not John, i.e., the knower) is well informed, cooperative, and so on do not straightforwardly enable us to arrive at (18). This does not mean, of course, that it cannot be done. But I'll let the globalists tell us exactly how.

Further evidence against global computation of implicatures comes from the interaction with sentential connectives. Consider the following sentences:

(21) a. (Right now) Mary is either working at her paper or seeing some of her students.
b. Mary is either working at her paper or seeing some (though not all) of her students.

Putting for the moment aside the implicature associated with *or*, sentence (21a) is typically understood as in (21b). That is, the implicature "not all" associated with *some* is clearly present. The question is how it comes about in the view that implicatures are computed globally. The relevant alternative would be as in (22a). Notice that (22a) is stronger than (21a). Hence, such alternatives should be understood as being implicitly negated, as in (22b):

(22) a. Mary is either working at her paper or seeing all of her students.
b. It is not the case that [Mary is either working at her paper or seeing all of her students].
c. Mary is not working at her paper.

So the expected relevant implicature should be (22b). But such an implicature entails (22c), that is, the negation of the first disjunct. This cannot be. It is not obvious how to fix this problem (without loosing the implicature). To put it differently, negation, in the globalist view, seems to wind up in the wrong place: it is expected to take scope over the whole disjunction, whereas we would want it to negate just the second disjunct of the alternative. This seems to constitute a problem.[5]

Difficulties of a similar sort arise for the standard view also from the interaction of implicature triggers and quantifiers.

Consider the following sentences:

(23) a. How did students satisfy the course requirement?
b. Some made a presentation or wrote a paper. Some took the final test.

The globalist predicts that (b) implies that no students whatsoever both wrote a paper and presented it. Again, this is so because negation always winds up having the widest scope in the globalist view. In this case, such a prediction appears to be exceedingly strong. Intuitions become even shaper if we put the scalar term in the restriction of *some*. So, for example, in the globalist's view, (24a) ought to implicate (24b).

(24) Who will get a good grade in that class?
a. Some students who read some J. D. Salinger stories will get a good grade.
b. No student who read all J. D. Salinger stories will get a good grade.

Again, this seems quite unwarranted by our intuitions. The problem with existential terms parallels the one with disjunction. In both cases, the globalist predicts implicatures that are exceedingly strong (to be expected, given that existential quantification can be defined as a generalized disjunction (or join) operator).[6]

A further argument is based on nonmonotone quantifiers. Consider the following sentence:

(25) Exactly two students wrote a term paper or made a class presentation.

Sentence (25) can certainly be construed exclusively (as much as it can be construed inclusively). That is, we can intend it to mean that the number of students who did one or the other (but not both) equals two. Or we can intend it to mean that the number of students who did one or the other or both equals two. The question is, how is this possible? In particular, how did this sentence get its exclusive interpretation? In the globalist's view, the relevant alternative would be

(26) Exactly two students wrote a term paper and made a class presentation.

But clearly, (26) does not entail (25). That is, because of the nonmonotonicity of the quantifier, the relevant alternatives are not ordered on a scale of informational strength. And the implicature cannot be computed. The engine that generates implicatures has nothing to work on. For the localist, per contra, this would be no problem. The implicature would be generated locally, before the subject comes in.

What emerges from these considerations is that if we look at it more closely, the idea that implicatures are computed globally (after the root sentence has been assigned its basic meaning by grammar) seems to face empirical difficulties. Hence, it seems wrong to take such an idea as the null hypothesis, in spite of its many prima facie desirable features. In all of the cases we have discussed above, one can try various moves, if one feels that the globalist view ought to be preserved. But we need theories of implicature more articulated than those currently available in order to assess the actual viability of the globalist view, rather than simply taking it for granted.

On the other hand, the facts under discussion also constitute preliminary evidence that justifies exploring an altogether different approach. Its guiding idea is that implicatures are introduced locally as soon as possible in the same order in which their trigger (the scalar terms) are introduced in the syntactic tree. Consider, for example, a sentence like (21a) above, repeated here as (27a). Its logical form would be roughly as (27b). The implicatures associated with the scalar terms would be introduced roughly at the points shown (imagining a bottom-up semantic computation):

(27) a. Mary is either working at her paper or seeing some of her students.

b.

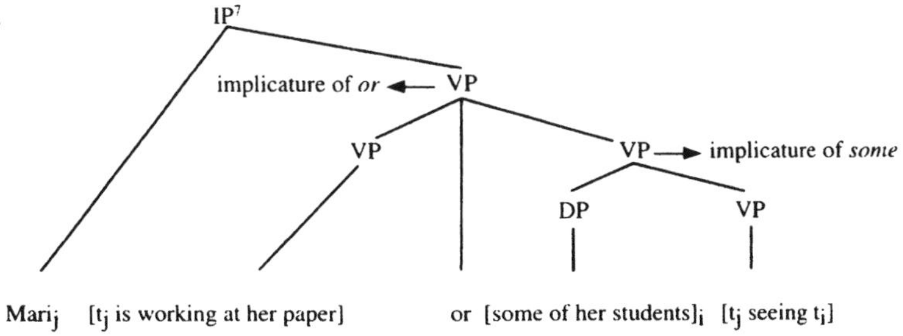

Once introduced, implicatures are projected upward and filtered out or adjusted, as the case may be, much like that which occurs with presuppositions.[8] As a matter of fact, the history of the problem of presuppositions offers a good analogy. In that case, too, it was thought early on that presuppositions constituted a purely pragmatic phenomenon, not amenable to a grammar-driven compositional treatment (see, e.g., Kempson 1975). But eventually it turned out that such a compositional, grammar-driven treatment is, in fact, the one that allows us a better understanding of the phenomenon. In what follows, we shall thus sketch a projection algorithm for scalar implicatures. To do so, we first need to have an idea of which contexts affect implicature projection. It is in this connection that the relation with NPIs becomes central. Let us see how.

2.2. *Any* licensing and contexts of scalar implicature suspension

If implicatures are introduced in the embedded position, which contexts affect them? It is useful to go back to one of the first attempts at developing a formal theory of implicatures, namely, Gazdar's (1979), who observes that SIs appear to be suspended under negation. It's worth going through the facts, as this will serve the purpose of illustrating the empirical methodology I will adopt. Take a sentence like (28a). If the implicature normally associated with *some* was added locally, together with its meaning, the result ought to be (28b). Hence, (28a) should be consistent with the continuation in (28c).

(28) Negation
  a. It's false that Sue harassed some students.
  b. It's false that Sue harassed some though not all the students.
  c. #Sue harassed all the students.

However, such a continuation is generally not possible, banning heavy metalinguistic uses of negation (I use the "#" sign to indicate the peculiar character of (28c) as a continuation of (28a)). Hence, we conclude that the implicature normally associated with *some* is absent under negation. The same happens with other scalar items. Consider, for example, disjunction under negation:

(29) a. Sue didn't meet Hugo or Theo.
  b. It is not the case that Sue met Hugo or Theo but not both.
  c. #She met both.

Here, too, the infelicity (apart from metalinguistic uses) of (29c) as a continuation for (29a) is, I take it, evidence that the implicature of exclusiveness is missing in (29a).[9] Now, in commenting on Gazdar's proposal, Horn (1989, 233–234) suggests that SIs are suspended not just under negation but more generally in downward-entailing (DE) contexts. Horn mentions only negation-like DE contexts (like *doubt*) and doesn't actually support his comment further. He gives away the culprit without presenting the evidence, so to say. For our present purposes it is important to see whether such a claim is actually empirically supported. In doing so, it is useful to depart slightly from Horn's suggestion and check whether SIs are affected by the contexts that license *any* (rather than in DE contexts). The DE-ness is a theoretical characterization of the relevant contexts, *any* licensing an empirical one. Since the seminal work of Ladusaw (1979), DE-ness has been identified as a key property in the licensing of NPIs. A function f is DE iff it licenses inferences from a set to its subsets [i.e., if f(A) entails f(B), whenever $B \subseteq A$]. Thus, for example, negation is DE because a sentence like (30a) entails (30b):

(30) a. John doesn't smoke.
 b. John doesn't smoke Muratti.

However, it is controversial whether DE-ness suffices in characterizing NPIs. In trying to establish the basic empirical generalizations, it is thus useful to keep *any* licensing and DE-ness separate (even though I do believe that DE-ness is, at present, our best bet). In my discussion, I will be using mostly the implicature associated with *or*. But I believe that things work in parallel ways for all scalar items.

Let us start with negative determiners like *no*. I will adopt here the classical relational analysis of determiners whereby a sentence like (31a) is analyzed as a relation between, roughly, the denotation of the noun and the verb as shown in (31b):

(31) a. No man smokes
 b. NO (MAN, SMOKES) = MAN $\cap$ smokes = $\emptyset$

Any is acceptable with *no* both within the VP and in the NP part.

(32) a. No italian eats any raw fish.
 b. No Italian who eats any fish will eat it raw.
 c. No more than *n*, at most *n*, few . . .

Following standard practice, I will refer to the NP part as the restriction of the determiner *no* and to the VP-part as the scope [as this generalizes to the cases in which a Determiner Phrase (DP) is assigned scope—say, via Quantifier Raising (QR)]. Other DE determiners such as those listed in (32c) behave exactly like *no* with respect to *any* licensing. Now, the observation that interests us in the present connection is that all such determiners, just like negation, also systematically suspend SIs. Relevant data are given in (33):

(33) Scope and restriction of DE quantifiers:
 a. No student with an incomplete or a failing grade is in good standing.
 b. #While/in fact a student with both is
 c. No student who missed class will take the exam or contact the advisor.
 d. #They will do both.

It may be useful to contrast the sentences in (33) with other non-DE determiners:

(34) a. There was some student who had an incomplete or a failing grade
b. Some student who missed class wanted to take the exam or contact the advisor

Here there is no expectation that the students mentioned in (34a) may have both an incomplete and a failing grade or that the student mentioned in (34b) wants to both take the exam and contact the advisor. That is, within the restriction and scope of *some*, the exclusiveness implicature of *or* is (or typically can be) assumed.

Another interesting contrast concerns the restriction versus the scope of the determiner *every*. As is well known, *any* is licensed in the restriction (which is DE) but not in the scope (which is not DE) of *every*. And, in fact, SIs behave accordingly.

(35) Restriction of *every*
a. Every student who wrote a squib or made a classroom presentation got extra credit.
b. #But not every student who did both got extra credit.
c. Every student wrote a squib or made a classroom presentation.

Sentence (35c) suggests that students didn't do both, although in sentence (35a) the implicature appears to be suspended, as witnessed by the oddity of (35b). In assessing their intuitions on cases such as this, readers should keep some caveats in mind. In particular, the defeasability of implicatures and the effect of shared contextual knowledge have to be taken into due consideration. Consider, for example, sentence (35c). If implicatures are introduced locally, such a sentence ought to be understood as "Every student wrote either a paper or made a presentation but not both." I think that this is what in fact happens in neutral contexts (i.e., contexts in which little is known about the relevant facts). Suppose, however, that we are considering a class where it is known beforehand that besides students that have done only one of the two chores there are also students that did both of them. We would still describe such a situation by means of (35c). The reason for this is fairly clear. We immediately see that the implicature is incompatible with the context, so we throw it out. Yet using *or* remains the best way to describe the relevant state of affairs. The same goes, mutatis mutandis, for implicature removal. Sentences like (35a) appear to favor an inclusive interpretation. But an exclusiveness condition may be *independently* present in the conversational background. For example, we may be talking about a school where you are actually penalized if you satisfy a course requirement in two ways. Or, to give another example, consider a sentence like:

(36) It was a two course meal. But everyone who skipped the first or the second course enjoyed it more, for he wasn't too full to appreciate it.

With a sentence like this, we don't mean to include among the most satisfied customers people who skipped both courses. We are told that the first and the second course cover, essentially, the whole meal. So under an inclusive construal, (36) winds up saying that also those who skipped the whole meal enjoyed it. But this is a contradiction. [Notice, incidentally, that the existence of cases like (36) seem to constitute further evidence against globalism. We seem to be in the presence here of an embedded scalar implicature.]

So what is being exactly claimed about SIs? The claim is that there are situations in which (standard) implicatures are by default present and situations in which they are by default absent, and such situations are determined by structural factors. By default interpretation, I simply mean the one that most people would give in circumstances in which the context is unbiased one way or the other. So the way in which you want to test your intuitions in assessing the above (and the following) claims is by resorting to situations that are as much as possible "neutral." Sometimes this may be hard to do, but by and large I think it is possible. At any rate, this is certainly an area of study where psycholinguistic experimentation can usefully supplement intuitions.

Let us move on to other relevant linguistic contexts and let us consider antecedents versus consequents of conditionals. *Any* is licensed in the former but not in the latter, and again SIs pattern accordingly.

(37) Antecedents of conditionals
  a. If Paul or Bill come, Mary will be upset.
  b. #But if Paul and Bill both come, Mary won't be.
  c. If Paul comes, Mary or Sue will be upset.

In (37c) the unmarked expectation is that Mary and Sue typically won't both be upset. There is a clear contrast with (37a), where the expectation is that if Paul and Bill both come, Mary will be upset all the more.

The next class of cases concerns clause-embedding verbs that have a negative coloring of some sort.

(38) Negative embedding predicates
  a. Dubitatives: doubt, deny
    i. John doubts that Paul or Bill are in that room.
    ii. # He doesn't doubt that Paul and Bill both are.
  b. Negative factives: regret, be sorry
    iii. John regrets that Paul or Bill are in that room.
    iv. #He doesn't regret that Paul and Bill both are.
  c. Negative propositional attitudes: fear, complain
    v. John fears that Paul or Bill might not come.
    vi. #John doesn't fear that Paul and Bill might both come.
  d. Predicates of minimum requirement: be enough, suffice
    vii. It's enough to know Italian or French (to be admitted to the program).
    viii. #It's not enough to know both Italian and French.

This list is by no means exhaustive. It is interesting to note that the verbs in (38) do not pattern wholly uniformly with respect to *any* licensing. The verbs in (38a) do license *any*. Those in (38b) typically do not. But they can be argued to have something close enough to the relevant property. For example, suppose I smoke and, in fact, I smoke only Muratti or Malboro. If I regret smoking, it must, then, be the case that I also regret smoking Muratti. Finally, there is a lot of debate in the literature on the distinction between negative polarity *any* versus free choice *any* (for insightful discussion and references, see, e.g., Dayal 1998). Now, the verbs in (38c and d) do not license negative polarity *any*, but they are very happy with the free choice one:

(39) It is sufficient to know any Romance language

Thus, here, too, there is an intriguing connection between the licensing of *any* and the suspension of SIs.

The next case is that of generic statements (on this plus the two that follow, cf. Higginbotham 1991). Generics express habits or regularities that involve generalizations across cases, in contrast with episodic sentences that describe a single event. Compare in this light the two sentences in (40):

(40) a. Tomorrow, a linguist or a philosopher will come to see me.
b. A linguist or a philosopher doesn't easily give in.

Sentence (40a) is episodic, sentence (40b) generic. Sentence (40a) appears to have the familiar exclusiveness implicature. In contrast, (40b) clearly has a reading according to which if you are a linguist or a philosopher, you don't give in. In this reading, *both* linguists and philosophers are claimed to be stubborn. Clearly, the exclusiveness of *or* is suspended.

In assessing (40b), it should be noticed that such a sentence is ambiguous. It also has a reading that can be brought out by the continuation in (41a), which is equivalent to (41b):

(41) a. I know you claimed that a linguist or a philosopher never gives in. But I don't remember which.
b. I know you claimed either that a philosopher never gives in or that a linguist never gives in, but I don't remember which.

In the construal brought out in (41a and b), *or* has wide scope with respect to the generic operator. In such a case, exclusiveness will typically be present, although in the reading we were considering before, the opposite is arguably the case: the generic operator has scope over disjunction. It is in this reading that *or* cannot, typically, be construed exclusively. I am assuming here, in line with much current work, that the generic operator is essentially a (modalized) universal quantifier whose restriction is partly supplied by the context and partly constructed out of the material structurally present in the sentence. What I mean, then, by "narrow scope" construal of disjunction is that the disjunction winds up in the restriction of the generic quantifier. In rough terms the Logical Form (and the corresponding interpretation) of (40b) can be spelled out as follows (where Gn is the generic quantifier—see, e.g., Chierchia 1995 and Krifka et al. 1995, for discussion):

(42) a. Gn x [x is a philosopher or x is a linguist][x doesn't give in easily]
b. For every x (in every "normal" circumstance), if x is a linguist or a philosopher, x does not give in easily.

If this is so, then the behavior of generics can be reduced to that of the universal quantifier (and of conditionals): in the restriction, exclusiveness is suspended.

Something related to this occurs in *before* clauses and *without* clauses, which are also known to be *any*-licensing contexts.

(43) Before/After
a. John arrived before Paul or Bill.
a'. John arrived before anybody else.
b. John arrived after Paul or Bill.
b'. *John arrived after anybody else.

(44) *Without* versus *with*
a. John will come without pen or notepads.
a'. John arrived without anything.
b. John will come with pens or notepads.
b'. *John came with anything.

I give in parallel, for comparison, sentences with scalar items and with *any*. Consider the paradigm in (44). Sentence (44b) tends to suggest that John will not come with both pens and notepads. On the other hand, sentence (44a) clearly has a reading suggesting that John will come without both (again, one must avoid getting interference with "wide scope" construals of *or*). The same, mutatis mutandis, seems to be going on in (43).

Here are further *any*-licensing contexts that also appear to inhibit SIs.

(45) Comparatives
a. Theo is taller than anybody else.
b. Theo is taller than Bill or John.

(46) Prefer (i.e., verbs of comparison)
a. I prefer Theo to any other linguist.
b. I prefer Theo to John or Bill.

These structures too appear to naturally admit a reading that may be paraphrased as follows:

(47) a. If x is Bill or John, then Theo is taller than x.
b. If x is Bill or John, then I prefer Theo to x.

(To be sure, (45b) and (46b) also admit the "but I don't remember which" reading, where exclusiveness pops out again).

An important set of constructions that are known to license NPIs are questions. And it seems clear that scalar items in questions typically get an inclusive interpretation. For example:

(48) Questions
Did John or Paul arrive?
a. #No; they both did.
b. Yes, they both did.

If the question was interpreted as "Did John or Paul but not both arrive?" the answer in (48a) would sound more natural than it does. The fact that, if they both arrived, the natural answer is yes suggests that *or* is being interpreted inclusively.

Consider next the case of modalities of permission:

(49) Modality of permission.
a. It is permitted/legal to smoke or drink.
(Expectation: it is permitted/legal to do both)
b. You may smoke or drink.

If we see posted something like (49a), we don't expect to be fined if we do both. Something similar happens with (49b). However, this also readily admits of a reading in which *or* is construed as having wide scope with respect to the modal ("You may smoke or you may drink"), in which case we get a (strong) exclusiveness implicature. Intonation matters. It favors the "inclusive" reading if "smoke or drink" form an intonational phrase of their own. Speakers seem to be a little less clear about imperatives, which nonetheless ought to be mentioned in this context because they, like the modals, are known to be licensors of (free choice) *any*.

(50) Imperatives (?)
Get me Paul or Bill.

The question is, If I get you both do I fulfill the order? It seems to me that there is a sense in which the answer is yes.

The final case I'd like to mention is the irrealis mood, which has also been identified as relevant to NPI licensing (see, e.g., the discussion in Giannakidou 1997) in interaction with suitable embedding predicates. To check the relevant facts, we have to go to a language that is a bit richer in its morphology than English. Italian will do. Consider the examples in (51):

(51) a. ??Ci sara' qualcuno che ha mai sentito nominare Pavarotti.[10]
There will be somebody who ever heard of Pavarotti.
b. Ci sara' qualcuno che abbia mai sentito nominare Pavarotti!
(I hope) there will be somebody who has-SUBJ heard of Pavarotti.

In (51a) we have a presentational construction, "there will be," with an embedded indicative future. The embedded clause contains the NPI *mai* 'ever,' and the result is marginal. If one switches to subjunctive, as in (51b), the presentational sentence acquires an optative meaning (I hope/wish that there will be . . .) and the sentence becomes grammatical. Thus the presentational future *plus* the subjunctive can license NPIs. Now, if we embed a scalar item in the construction in (51b), the interpretation one gets is the inclusive one:

(52) Irrealis constructions
  a. Lì ci sarà qualcuno che sa inglese o francese.
     In-that-place there will be somebody who knows English or French.
  b. Ci sara' qualcuno che sappia inglese o francese!
     (I hope) there will be somebody who knows English or French.
  c. #I don't hope that there will be somebody who knows both English and French.

Sentence (52a), with the indicative embedded under the future, is a (plain) prediction and it has a prominent exclusive construal (if in the relevant place we find only people who speak both languages, it is unclear whether the prediction we made was accurate). With the subjunctive embedded under the future, the favorite construal of *or* becomes inclusive, as witnessed by the oddity of the continuation in (52c).

In conclusion, a rather solid generalization seems to emerge from these considerations:

(53) Generalization on SIs
  (Ordinary) scalar implicatures are suspended in the contexts that license *any* (as a Neg Pol or Free-Choice Item).

So, we have, on the one hand, a class of specialized items (identified by a specific morphological makeup) whose distribution appears to be sensitive to contexts with a common semantic coloring (an extensively studied fact, which happens with remarkable cross-linguistic stability). We now also see that a certain well-established pragmatic phenomenon, the calculation of scalar implicatures, is also systematically sensitive to those very contexts (or to some closely related ones). Perhaps the extent to which generalization (53) holds hasn't been fully appreciated in the literature on these topics. One would like to understand exactly why this is case. In addressing this question, I am going to stick to Downward Entailingness as the property that comes closest to providing a characterization of the relevant contexts (while being aware of its problems).

2.3. Implicatures of negative contexts

Taking stock, we have gathered preliminary evidence in favor of the following two ideas: (a) implicatures are (or, at least, can be) added locally and (b) once an implicature has been added, upon being embedded within a DE element, it typically gets removed. Now a more careful consideration of the facts shows, I think, that what actually goes on in DE contexts is not simple cancellation of implicatures. What actually happens is that implicatures are in a way "recalibrated." Consider, for example, sentences like the following:

(54) a. In this class, no one read three papers (from the reading list).
b. In this class, no one read many papers (from the reading list).

Now intuitions tell us fairly firmly that these sentences have, respectively, the following implicature:

(55) a. No one read three papers ⇒ Someone read two papers.
b. No one read many papers ⇒ Someone read some papers.

Notice, for instance, the oddity of continuations that deny such implicatures, unless the typical means through which implicature cancellation is signaled are overtly present (i.e., interjections like *in fact* or *actually*):

(56) No students read many papers. *(In fact/actually) no student read any paper.

What is going on? As a first approximation, it looks as if in these cases (besides removing embedded implicatures), we add new ones created by the interaction of the embedding negative element and the embedded scalar terms. In the case of, for example, (54b), it is intuitively clear that the relevant alternative set will look as follows:

(57) { no student read some paper, no student read many papers, no student read every paper }

→

(Let's put aside the fact that for many speakers *some* is infelicitous under negation, as the issues this raises are related but orthogonal to our present concerns.) The direction of entailment is shown by the arrow. By the familiar reasoning, uttering (54b) will implicate the negation of the stronger alternatives. This corresponds to (58a), which is equivalent to (58b):

(58) a. ¬ no student read some paper.
b. Some student read some paper.

Clearly, this result would be (presumably) predicted if implicatures are computed globally. But we have seen that the globalist approach runs into problems (independent of those under consideration). So rather than computing them globally, we want to try to compute them at each step of the derivation (or, say, at each scope site or perhaps at each "phase"—cf. Chomsky 1999—or something of the sort). If we get it right, that should give us the good results of the globalist approach while avoiding its problems.

Let us see that facts of this sort are indeed quite general. An interesting case is that of the restriction of *every*. Since it creates (in its first argument) a DE context, it should not only remove implicatures when present but also induce new ones. And it does. A sentence like (59a) implicates (59b):

(59) a. Everyone who read two papers passed the exam.
b. Not everyone who read one paper passed the exam.

Fully parallel to these are cases concerning the antecedent of conditionals:

(60) a. If Bill has done two assignments, he will pass the exam.
b. It is not (necessarily) the case that if Bill has done one assignment, he will pass the exam.

By the same token, the sentences in (61a)–(63a) appear to convey the implicatures in (61b)–(63b), respectively:

(61) a. I doubt that most students will show up.
b. I think that some student will show up.

(62) a. It won't happen that every student will complain.
b. Some student will complain.

(63) a. Not every friend of mine has a car.
b. Some friend of mine has a car.

In (61)–(63), negation or a negative verb have scope over a quantifier like *most* or *every* and we get a positive implicature that typically involves *some*. Also *and*, embedded under negation, gives rise to an implicature:

(64) a. John doesn't eat and smoke.
b. John either eats or smokes.

(65) a. It never is the case that John drinks and drives.
b. John typically either drinks or drives.

The reasoning that justifies implicatures of this sort is, yet again, the same.

The role of scales in DE contexts (especially in connection with numerals) deserves perhaps some further discussion. According to the line we are taking, we expect that, for example, (66a) implicates (66b) and (67a) implicates (67b):

(66) a. John isn't 21 years old.
b. John is of an age pretty close to 20.

(67) a. John doesn't make $80,000 a year.
b. John makes something close to $80,000 a year.

In general, the predicted implicature of a sentence containing a numeral under negation is that the corresponding positive sentence containing the immediately lower numeral holds. Before commenting on whether this is indeed so, let me show briefly how these implicatures come about. Consider the alternative set for, say, (91). It will be something like

(68) $\{ \ldots \neg \mathbf{20Y(j)}, \neg 21Y(j), \neg 22Y(j) \ldots \}$
$\rightarrow$

The informational strength (i.e., entailment) goes the way indicated by the arrow. The strongest alternative to the assertion is the one in boldface. Hence, this is the one that, according to our Gricean procedure, gets negated. Is this expectation supported by our intuitions? The facts are not so clear. A sentence like (66a) seems to carry the expected implicature in most contexts; a sentence like (66a), less clearly so. This is part of a more general issue. Although there is systematicity in how implicatures get associated with negative sentences, such implicatures appear to be generally somewhat weaker and flimsier than their positive counterparts. For example, a sentence like (62a), repeated here rarely has the implicature "most students will complain," which is the one we would expect, given the mechanism we are assuming:

(62) a. It won't happen that every student will complain.
b. Some student will complain.

I believe that the reasons for this phenomenon have to be sought in two factors. The first is the "granularity" of the scale, that is, the intervals between the scale members that are taken to be contextually relevant. Clearly, not all the alternatives in a scale are always relevant. For example, in talking of age, we do not typically consider months (except for babies), and sometimes we talk in terms of decades. When we talk about money, we also tend to select a particular range of values (tenths of dollars in talking about restaurant prices, thousands in talking about yearly salaries, etc.), rounding off intermediate ones.[11] This interacts with the second factor, namely, the polarity under which the scalar term is embedded. If it's positive, the relevant alternative will be higher on the scale. Hence, no matter what granularity is chosen, one will get an "exactly" effect (relative to that granularity). But if the scale is embedded negatively, the relevant alternatives (i.e., those that can potentially yield stronger statements) have to be sought at the low end. This is schematized as follows:

(69)

		. . .	
		three	← next strongest element in positive embedding
target (i.e., uttered element)	→	two	
		one	← next strongest element in negative embedding

Now, it may happen that in a context, the only relevant element is the lowest on the scale. If that happens, one gets a very weak implicature, which may be tantamount to cancelling it. To give a concrete example, in talking about whether one can buy alcohol, the year immediately before the legal age will normally be relevant. In talking about money, it depends. But notice that if, in the latter case, we were to pick some small amount at the low end the scale, the implicature would be effectively cancelled, for having very little money is like having no money. That's why our intuitions are shakier in cases like (66) and (67). We will come back to this in section 3.3, after having put forth the specifics of our proposal.

In this section, I have first argued against adding implicatures all at once at the end, after the semantic computation. Then, on the assumption that implicatures get introduced locally, I have discussed the interaction of negative contexts with scalar term. Such contexts not only remove implicatures that may have been added in before. They also induce new ones by activating new alternatives. It may be useful to introduce an appropriate terminology to talk about this. Let us call the ordinary implicatures associated with a scalar term just in virtue of its position on a scale the *direct* implicatures (e.g., the direct implicature of "John read many linguistics books" would be that he didn't read all the linguistics books). We will instead call *indirect implicatures* those introduced by a scalar term in interaction with a higher negative element (such as "I doubt that John read many linguistics books" $\Rightarrow$ "I believe he read some," discussed in this section).

3. Scalar implicatures revisited

If we take the evidence we've gathered at face value, we are led to conclude that some of the Grice-inspired pragmatics is probably part of the computational system of grammar. We figure out SIs in tandem with "core" meaning, as facets of a parallel recursion. Or, an equivalent way of thinking about it is that intermediate phrases (maximal projections that are also scope sites or, possibly, just any maximal projections[12]), rather than root clauses, are shipped to the pragmatic module and that higher semantic components have access to the results of that. In what follows, I am going to formulate a hypothesis on the mechanism at the basis of such a process.

3.1. The proposal

I will assume that Logical Forms of the type familiar from the generative tradition are interpreted compositionally (bottom up) in the usual way, say, by translating them into a suitable logical language.[13] If α is any English expression, $\|\alpha\|$ will be its (plain) value, computed in the way familiar from your favorite semantic textbook. (I will sometimes abbreviate $\|\alpha\|$ as α'). Next to its plain value, each expression also has a "scalar" or "strengthened" value $\|\alpha\|^{\mathbf{s}}$, also recursively assigned. (I will sometimes abbreviate $\|\alpha\|^{\mathbf{s}}$ as $\alpha^{\mathbf{s}}$) Such a scalar value is computed (as in Krifka's 1995 proposal) by exploiting its alternatives, through a rather simple variant of the standard recursion. But rather than introducing implicatures at the end of the computation (or at some other arbitrarily stipulated site), I introduce them as soon as possible after a scalar term enters the computation. The strengthened value is thus provided by grammar. It is defeasible in the sense that whenever its addition to a given context results in inconsistency, one falls back on the plain value. In this section, I'll try to guide the reader through the characterization of strengthened meaning as informally as possible (without being exceedingly imprecise); all of the complete formal definitions necessary to the task are to be found in the appendix to this chapter.

The first step in defining strengthened values is identifying the relevant alternatives that enter into it. In the same spirit as Krifka's (1995) proposal, I assume that for any expression α, its alternatives $\|\alpha\|^{ALT}$ are a set of expressions of the same type as α (which I will abbreviate as α^{ALT}). Defining α^{ALT} is easy if α contains just one scalar term but might become quite complex if α contains more than one scalar term.

Now, since the plan is to deal with each implicature as soon as possible, I will define α^{ALT} in such a way that it yields the alternatives induced solely by the last scalar element in the tree (i.e., the highest or topmost one). The rationale for this is that scalar terms below the topmost (if present) will have been already taken care of (by the time we process the topmost). This is a locality constraint driven by the guiding idea of our attempt (namely, that implicatures are processed locally in the order in which their triggers appear). Let me illustrate how the intended definition works with a simple example. In the example below, I provide a sentence with two scalar terms, its simplified LF, and its alternative sets (throughout, I use logical formulas as stand-ins for the corresponding propositions):

(70) Some student smokes or drinks.

(71) a. LF: [some $student_i$ [t_i smokes or t_i drinks]]
b. [t_i smokes or t_i drinks]^{ALT} = { [smoke'(x_i) ∨ drink'(x_i)], [smoke'(x_i) ∧ drink'(x_i)]}
c. [some $student_i$ [t_i smokes or t_i drinks]]^{ALT} = {some'(student')(smoke' ∨ drink'), many'(student')(smoke' ∨ (drink'), every'(student')(smoke' ∨ drink')}

In (71b) we have the scalar alternatives of the embedded constituent; in (71c), those of the root. In the latter, the lower scalar term is ignored. Further examples (and a formal definition of $\| \|^{ALT}$) can be found in the appendix.[14]

Now, out of a given set of alternatives, we want to be able to pick the one that is immediately stronger than our target. For instance, if we have {some'(student')(smoke' ∨ drink'), many'(student')(smoke' ∨ drink'), every'(student')(smoke' ∨ drink')} as the alternatives for "some students smoke or drink," we will want to pick out "many students smoke or drink" (which is what will be denied when the implicature is factored in). Let us introduce some notation for this. Given a set of alternatives A and a member of such set β, $S_\beta(A)$ will be the weakest member of A that asymmetrically entails β (and if A does not contain anything that asymmetrically entails β, we let $S_\beta(A)$ be the contradiction, ⊥). Let me illustrate:

(72) a. $S_{\text{some students smoke or drink}}$ (some student smoke or drink ^{ALT}) = many students smoke or drink'.
b. $S_{\text{every students smoke or drink'}}$ (every student smokes or drinks^{ALT}) = ⊥

When the target is understood and no confusion arises, I will omit the subscript and write simply, for instance, S(some students smoke or drink ^{ALT}).

Let us see now how strong values are defined. The format is that of a recursive definition that parallels the standard one. The starting point is trivial. The strong meaning of a lexical item is simply identical to its plain one; and functional application (the core rule of any type of driven translation) is defined in the familiar way:

(73) a. For α lexical, $\|\alpha\|^{s} = \|\alpha\|$.
b. Functional application (first version): , $\|[\ \beta\gamma\ ]\|^{s} = \|\ \beta\ \|^{s}(\|\ \gamma\ \|^{s})$.

The effect of this is that ordinary meanings wind up qualifying as strong meanings, albeit as totally uninteresting ones. For example,

(74) a. John saw some students.
b. LF: [some student$_i$ [John saw t$_i$]]
c. $\|$[some student$_i$ [John saw t$_i$]]$\|^s$ = some'(student')(λx saw'(j,x)).

The next step is the "canonical" introduction of implicatures, which hopefully will make things more interesting. Let's assume that this is done at any scope site, through the following rule:

(75) If ϕ is a scope site (of type t), then $\|\phi\|^s = \|\phi\|^s \wedge \neg S(\phi^{ALT})$.[15]

This is simply a (slightly modified version of) Krifka's (1995) rule. Here is a simple computation that illustrates how it works:

(76) a. $\|$[some student$_i$ [John saw t$_i$]]$\|^s$ = $\|$[some student$_i$ [John saw t$_i$]]$\|^s$ ∧ ¬ S([some student$_i$ [John saw t$_i$]]$^{(ALT)}$), by (75)
b. $\|$[some student$_i$ [John saw t$_i$]]$\|^s$ = some'(student')(λx saw'(j,x)) ∧ ¬ S([some student$_i$ [John saw t$_i$]]$^{(ALT)}$), from (a) in virtue of (73b)
c. $\|$[some student$_i$ (John saw t$_i$]]$\|^s$ = some'(student')(λx saw'(j,x)) ∧ ¬ every'(student')(λx saw'(j,x)), by definition of ALT and S[16]

Setting things up in this way entails regarding interpretation as, in essence, a relation rather than as a function (i.e., for any expression α, $\|\alpha\|^s$ will be the *set* of its strong meanings, some of which will be innocuously trivial; see the appendix for details). The interaction between the canonical rules (73) with Krifka's rule lets us happily pile up implicatures in embedded contexts. Thus, in particular, a sentence like (77a) will wind up with the strong meanings listed in (77b):

(77) a. Someone smokes or drinks.
b. i. someone'(λx smoke'(x) ∨ drink'(x))
ii. someone'(λx smoke'(x) ∨ drink'(x) ∧ ¬ smoke'(x) ∧ (drink'(x))])
iii. someone'(λx smoke'(x) ∨ drink'(x) ∧ ¬ smoke'(x) ∧ (drink'(x))])
∧ ¬ everyone'(λx smoke'(x) ∨ drink'(x))

Of these, the strongest one is (iii); if nothing in the context blocks it, this is the one we'll tend to use. But we also have suitably weaker ones (all the way to the plain one), which will come in handy if the strongest meaning turns out to be inappropriate (e.g., inconsistent with contextually available information).

So far so good. We have a basis for our recursion and a way to introduce canonical implicatures locally. Now we have to make sure implicatures are filtered out or recalibrated, as the case may be, in accordance with our observations. The burden of this falls on functional application. Clearly, we cannot adopt it as is, for that would be tantamount to *always* keeping in the implicatures that have been introduced, whereas we have seen that they are removed in DE contexts. So DE functions must be treated differently from the others. When we hit a DE function, we must remove the implicature from the argument. In other words, the computation of strong values must be subject to an overall constraint (or, if you wish, presupposition): the strong value cannot become weaker than the plain value. This constraint (let us call it "the Strength Condition") is checked at each step of the derivation and involves a local comparison of potentially strong values with the corresponding plain value. Let me illustrate with a simple example. Imagine embedding (76c) under *believe*, as in "I believe that John saw some students." Focus on the interpretation of the VP and assume, just for the sake of explicitness, the classical possible worlds analysis of *believe*. Now, (78a) is the plain interpretation of the VP, whereas (78b) is the strong one:

(78) a. $\|\text{believe}\|(\|\text{that [some student}_i \text{ [John saw } t_i \text{]]}\|) =$
believe'(^some'(student')(λx saw'(j,x)))
b. $\|\text{believe}\|^{s}(\|\text{that (some student}_i \text{ (John saw } t_i \text{]]}\|^{s}) =$
believe'(some'(student')(λx saw'(j,x)) ∧ ¬ every'(students)(λx saw'(j,x)))

Since (78b) is indeed stronger than (78a), the strength condition is satisfied and it is possible to keep (78b) as the strong value of the VP. For comparison, let us imagine embedding, instead, the same sentence under *doubt*. Analyzing *doubt* as *not believe* (again, just for the sake of explicitness), we now get the following as candidate values for the plain and strong interpretations, respectively:

(79) a. $\|\text{doubt}\|(\|\text{that [some student}_i \text{ [John saw } t_i \text{]]}\|) =$
¬ believe'(^some'(student')(λx saw'(j,x))).
b. $\|\text{doubt}\|^{s}(\|\text{that [some student}_i \text{ [John saw } t_i \text{]]}\|^{s}) =$
= ¬ believe'(some'(student')(λx saw'(j,x)) ∧ ¬ every'(student)(λx saw'(j,x)))

Given the DE character of *doubt*, logical relations are inverted: (79a) is stronger than (i.e., it entails) (79b). So, if we took (79b) as the final strong value, the Strength Condition would be violated. In this case, we simply remove the implicature from the argument (i.e., we make the strong value of the argument identical to its weak value). Here is the modified general schema for application that formalizes the process we have informally described:

(80) Strong application (second version):
Suppose $\alpha = [\beta\ \gamma]$, where β is of type <a,b> type and γ of type a. Then

$$\|[\beta\ \gamma]\|^{S} = \begin{cases} \|\beta\|^{S}(\|\gamma\|^{S}), \text{ if } \|\beta\| \text{ is not DE} \\ \\ \|\beta\|^{S}(\|\gamma\|), \text{ otherwise} \end{cases}$$

We have now the beginning of a global picture of how strong values may be computed. Essentially, there are two modifications of the canonical interpretive rules.

First, we introduce implicatures at any scope site (including embedded ones). Second, we impose a general condition on application that filters out implicatures whenever they lead to a weakening of information content (by local comparison with plain meanings). The recursion through which we compute strong values is an arguably straightforward modification of the standard one. Having two interpretive procedures does not lead to loss of generality since one is a predictable variant of the other (somewhat in the same spirit of the way type shifting is used in much work since Partee 1987).

One last step: we have seen that DE operators are responsible for novel implicatures *in interaction with* the alternatives of their arguments (the indirect ones). We need to modify (80) in order to get this effect. Here is one way of doing so. When the Strength Condition fails, we do not merely remove implicatures; we also check the alternatives associated with the argument in the new context, making sure that new possible quantity implicatures are added. Again, let me resort to an example to illustrate what I have in mind. Consider a sentence like (81a) and its meaning in (81b) (ignoring irrelevant factors, e.g., genericity):

(81) a. John drinks and drives.
b. [drink'(j) ∧ drive'(j)]

Sentence (81a) won't have any implicature by itself. This follows from the fact that *and* is the strong element of its scale. But now embed (81a) under *doubt*, as in "I doubt that John drinks and drives," and again focus on the interpretation of the VP. What we want to do is reconsider the scale associated with the argument in the new context, and if there is now an element stronger than our target, we want to add the corresponding scalar assertion. The alternative set corresponding to (81a) is (82a). Combining this with *doubt* we get (82b):

(82) a. { [drink'(j) ∧ drive'(j)], [drink'(j) ∨ drive'(j)] }
→
b. doubt + { [drink'(j) ∧ drive'(j)], [drink'(j) ∨ drive'(j)] } =
= { doubt'(^[drink'(j) ∧ drive'(j)]), doubt'(^[drink'(j) ∨ drive'(j)]) }
←

Now, as indicated by the arrows below the alternative sets, *doubt* inverts the strength of the relevant alternatives. So when we combine *doubt* with its complement, we must add the relevant scalar term, thereby obtaining (83a), which is equivalent to (83b):

(83) a. doubt'(^[drink'(j) ∧ drive'(j)]) ∧ ¬ doubt'(^[drink'(j) ∨ drive'(j)])
b. doubt'(^[drink'(j) ∧ drive'(j)]) ∧ believe'(^[drink'(j) ∨ drive'(j)])

This is what we want. We must make it part of our definition of Strong Application, so that whenever a function combines with an argument, novel possible interactions between the two (with respect to scales already introduced) are duly taken into account. This takes us to the following definition:

(84) Strong Application (final version):
Suppose $\alpha = [\beta\ \gamma]$, where β is of type <a,b> type and γ of type a. Then

$$\|[\beta\,\gamma]\|^S = \begin{cases} \|\beta\|^S(\|\gamma\|^S), \text{ if } \|\beta\| \text{ is not DE} \\ \\ \|\beta\|^S(\|\gamma\|) \wedge \neg S(\|\beta\|(\gamma^{ALT})), \text{ otherwise} \end{cases}$$

So, in our final proposal on Strong Application, we simply enrich our previous definition with a novel scalar statement (i.e., $\|\beta\|(\gamma^{ALT})$), which corresponds to (83b) in our example).

Let us summarize so far. Grammar provides us with two related interpretive procedures that assigns two types of values to each expression: the plain value and its strengthened alternates. Plain values are defined in the usual way. The strengthened ones are defined in terms of the plain ones and the set of (local) relevant alternative values. The recursion through which strong values are defined is a simple modification of the standard one. Through this recursion, implicatures come in two ways, in correspondence with the two types of implicatures we have identified in the previous section. Direct implicatures come in at the first scope site of a scalar term, through Krifka's (1995) rule. Indirect implicatures come in through the interaction of a DE operator with an embedded scalar term, through Strong Application. The proper introduction of indirect implicatures is monitored at each step, as part of making sure that the strengthened value remains indeed stronger. The crucial thing is that, in this view, the level at which implicatures are added in (or removed) must not and cannot be freely set, but it simply is the most local relevant environment. Contrary to the dominant view (but consistently with our observations), implicatures, like core meaning, are computed compositionally bottom-up, off LF structures.[17]

One would expect that speakers will use the values grammar provides them with cooperatively. This means that they will tend to use the strongest interpretation (*consistent with the context*) for which they have evidence. So the default interpretation in a concrete communicative situation will be the one provided by strengthened values.[18] The idea that sentences have multiple values is what this proposal has in common with the semantics of focus. But unlike the focus value of a sentence, its scalar value is not accessible to operators. It is used for local comparison with the plain value.

Let us now turn to a more thorough discussion of some empirical consequences of the present approach.

3.2. Discussion

Insofar as I can see, the observations made in section 2 now follow and the relevant readings can be appropriately derived. Implicatures, introduced locally, appear to be projected by the theory according to intuition, through propositional connectives, quantifiers, modal operators, and embedding verbs. The reader can look up in the appendix some of the basic derivations, to get a better feel for how the proposal works. In the present section I will illustrate, informally, some more complicated cases.

3.2.1. Some complex DE contexts

Consider the following sentence:

(85) No one (here) lives to be 80.

Such a sentence implies that someone, however, lives to be 79 (or some other lesser age, according to the context). This implicature is indirect, as it arises from the interaction between the DE contexts and the scalar term in its argument. This is correctly predicted by our approach. Now insert another implicature trigger in the restriction of *no* in (85), as in the following example:

(86) No one who smokes and drinks lives to be 80.

We expect a novel indirect implicature to compound with the first one, so that (86) implies

(87) a. Someone who smokes and drinks lives to be 79 (or some other age fairly close to 80).
b. Someone who smokes or drinks lives to be 80.

Again, this seems to be in accordance with our intuitions. [See the appendix for a complete derivation of (87)].

Now change *no* to *few* in (86). Here are the results.

(87) Few people that smoke and drink live to be 80.
Expected implicatures:
a. Some people that smoke and drink live to be 80.
b. It is not the case that few people that smoke and drink live to be 79.
(≈ some people who smoke and drink live to be 79)
c. It is not the case that few people who smoke or drink live to be 80.
(≈ some people who smoke or drink live to be 80).

With respect to *no*, the sentence with *few* adds a new direct implicature, namely (88a). This is due to the fact that *few* is part of a (negative) scale with *no*; since *no* is stronger, it gets negated (by Krifka's 1995 rule). Moreover, *few* also essentially retains the same indirect implicatures as *no* because it is DE. Notice that such implicatures are, strictly speaking, of the form "not few," as in (88b and c). But this must be taken as the expression of the abstract content of the implicature and should not be confused with the actual content of the corresponding natural language expression. In particular, in no way should *not few* here be taken to suggest *many* (and that's why the paraphrasis in parenthesis with *some* is a better rendering of the implicature). Suppose, for example, we change the ambiguous *few* in (88) to *at most two* (i.e., one or two). The implicature then is that more than two (i.e., possibly three) people who smoke and drink live to the relevant lesser age. This seems right.

3.2.2. Default override

As we observed, the default is usually the strong meaning. However, implicatures can be cancelled. Under the present view, cancellation amounts to a simple kind of backtracking. Let me illustrate with a few examples. (In what follows, c + S stands for the incrementation of context c by S.)

(89) a. John or Theo are there. Maybe/in fact, they both are.
b. (c + there'(sue') $\vee^{s}$ there' (theo'))
c. (c + there'(sue') $\vee^{s}$ there' (theo')) + there' (sue') $\wedge$ (there'(theo')

Here is what one expects. One first processes the first sentence in (89a) and adds it to the context, as in (89b). At the point where the first sentence is processed, the hearer will hypothesize that the strong interpretation of (89a) is being intended (as that is the default). Then, the second sentence is processed and added to the context, as in (89c). But this results in a contradiction because the exclusive interpretation of *or* is incompatible with the second sentence. At that point, the hearer throws away the strong interpretation of the first sentence and switches to the plain one (in accordance with Stalnaker's 1978 felicity conditions). Items like *in fact* or *maybe* are markers to signal that some backtracking must take place.

We also noticed in section 2.2 that sometimes implicatures are not cancelled when one would expect them to be. The example we discussed there was

(90) It was a two course meal. But everyone who skipped the first or the second course enjoyed it more.

The point is that *or* in this sentence is not construed inclusively, because otherwise a contradiction would ensue (at least in "normal" contexts). Now in cases such as (90), my theory predicts that the strong interpretation and the plain interpretation are one and the same. So, how does such a sentence come to have the reading it seems to have ("Everyone who skipped the first or the second course but not both enjoyed the meal more")? How come we see what looks like an implicature in a context where we wouldn't expect one? A simple way of thinking about this is in terms of accommodation. We know that quantificational domains are subject quite generally to such phenomena. The interpretation of (90) requires a domain of people who don't skip both courses. This yields the same effect that we would obtain by not removing the locally added implicature.

Cases of a similar sort are also pointed out in Levinson (2000), who discusses, for example,

(91) If John has two cars, the third one parked outside must be somebody else's.

Notice how this sentence becomes a blatant non-sequitur if we introduce an overt "at least" in the antecedent:

(92) If John has at least two cars, the third one parked outside must be somebody else's.

Clearly, here too we want to accommodate in the antecedent of (92) an "and no more" proviso. I.e., we want to restrict our consideration to sets of worlds from which people with more than two cars are excluded. The effect of this accommodation is the same as the computation of an implicature. But if we are right, the mechanism through which this happens is very different from how implicatures come about normally. In (92) the implicature is not added locally. It is accommodated at some point to avoid a near contradiction.

A first consequence of this view is that we would expect phenomena like those exemplified in (90) and (91) to be hard to obtain in contexts where accommodation is hard. In particular, we know that accommodation with antecedents of conditional or quantificational domains is relatively common. But, for instance, it is quite hard in the scope of negation or of a negative quantifier (as in the famous "no one ate with the king because there is no king"), and indeed in such contexts it is much harder to have the appearance of implicature preservation.

(93) No one skipped the first or second course.

It is hard or impossible to construe (93) as equivalent to "no one skipped the first or second course but not both." To the extent that this happens, immediately the sentence gets a very strong metalinguistic flavor.

A second consequence is that if something prevents us from reintroducing a removed implicature, we should be in trouble (i.e., the sentence should sound awkward). Something like (94) might be a case in point:

(94) ?? No one who earns $40,000 a year can afford this house

I believe that this sentence out of the blue is strange (we need to add an understood "or less"). The reason is the following. First you remove the "exactly" implicature in the DE context of *no*. At that point we would get a sentence such as "No one who earns $40,000 a year or more can afford this house," which (given what *afford* means) is a contradiction (or a near contradiction). At that point, we try to introduce the implicature. But the result is not much better (why should it be that no one who earns exactly $40 a year should not be able to afford this house). So in the end we are left with a pragmatically odd sentence.

I should conclude this discussion by pointing out that the case of nonmonotone quantifiers like (95) now also follows.

(95) a. Exactly two students smoke or drink.
b. exactly two (student') (smoke' $\vee^{s}$ drink')
c. exactly two (student') (smoke' $\vee$ drink')

The scalar interpretation of (95a) is (95b), and the plain one is, of course, (95c), despite the fact that the strong and the weak interpretation are, in this case, informationally independent of each other (i.e., neither entails the other). The reason we expect the implicature to be kept in this case is the following. Implicatures are removed only when the plain meaning becomes stronger than the (candidate) strengthened one. In the case at hand, this doesn't happen, and the Strength Condition is thus satisfied. Of the interpretations made available in this case, none is stronger than the other. Hence, neither constitutes the default. That is, the hearer will need contextual clues to figure out which one is being intended by the speaker. Only in these cases do we get the effects we would get if *or* was ambiguous.

On the whole, the theory predicts that sentences have certain default interpretations. Defaults (when incompatible with the context) can be overridden in two ways. First, if a scalar implicature is absent in a positive context, backtracking takes place. We first try to increment the context with the strong meaning, and when that fails we revert to the plain one. Second, if a (direct) scalar implicature seems to be maintained in a negative context, accommodation takes place. That is, the implicature is not added at the first pass but accommodated at some point. Besides the purely linguistic evidence we have considered, these expectations might be (dis)confirmed through psycholinguistic experimentation.

3.3. Axioms on scales

We have noticed that indirect implicatures are somehow felt to be weaker than direct ones. We have suggested that this may be due, at least in part, to an interaction between scales and the context. Now that we have a precise device for implicature computation, it may be worth being more explicit about such an interaction. The question may be put in the following terms. Knowledge of scales is part of our knowledge of the lexicon. But when a scale has more than two elements (and possibly, as with numerals, a potential infinity of elements), the context may select some subset of such elements. That is, not every element of a scale needs to be salient (and hence in consideration) in any given context. Now, the choice of which elements of a scale may be disregarded cannot be totally free; otherwise, we would always be able to void the effects of scales. Consider, for example, the following sentence:

(96) I have many matches left.

Sentence (96) needs to be considered relatively to some total amount, say, a contextually salient matchbox. In this context, it implies that I don't have all of the matches originally left in the box or possibly that I don't have most of the matches left. These two options arise from the following scales:

(97) a. <many, most>
b. <many, every>

Those in (78) are the minimal scales that give the desired effect. "Smaller" amounts (e.g., the scale <some, many, every>) may also be salient. But in this case, the salience of such smaller amounts would remain without effect. Crucially, what we want to rule out is adopting the scale

(98) <some, many>

In the scale in (98), *many* is the strongest element. Under such a choice, the implicature would simply disappear, for sentence (96) would come out as the strongest of the relevant alternatives. And, by the usual scalar reasoning, no implicature would come about. But then we would no longer have any secure way of predicting any implicature. So, evidently, a choice such as (98) must be excluded. Accordingly, we might adopt the following simple axioms:

(99) In any given context where we utter a sentence S, containing a scalar term α,
  a. A subset of the lexical scale associated with α may be selected.
  b. The chosen scale must contain at least two elements.
  c. If possible, α must not be the strongest element of the chosen scale.

The proviso in (99c) is due to the fact that if α is itself the strongest element of the scale, we have no choice. For example, if we utter "I have all of the matches," *all* is necessarily the strongest member of its lexical scale, and thus the only kind of scale we can choose in the context has to be of the form <x, all>, with *all* as the strongest member.

Now the axioms in (99) have an interesting consequence once indirect implicature enters the picture. Imagine, in particular, embedding sentence (96) under negation:

(100) I don't have many matches left.

As we have noticed, our intuitions concerning the implicature of sentences like (100) are somewhat shaky. In particular, such a sentence may or may not imply that I have some matches left. Now we can be more precise about why. If "smaller" amounts are taken as relevant (i.e., if we choose the scale <some, many, every>), the implicature that I have some matches left, will be triggered. But if "small" amounts are irrelevant (because, say, having few matches is functionally equivalent, for the purpose at hand, to having none), then we might well select the scale <many, every>, as that is allowed by the axioms in (99). This is so because such axioms only constrain the scales associated with the lexical entry *many* (without having to consider how such a lexical entry winds up embedded). So, we can select in the case at hand <many, every>. In such a case the potential implicature of (100) will be absent, and the sentence will be fully compatible with having no matches. This is, I take it, the reason that sentence (100) sometimes can be used to convey that I have *no* matches (or, e.g., "I don't have much time" may wind up saying that I have *no* time): it is the combined action of the removal of the positive implicature plus small amounts not reaching the threshold of relevance.

This effect is also possible with numerals but is expected to be less easy to obtain. The reasons we may have for embedding a precise numeral under negation can be quite diverse and complex. What enables us to truncate a scale at the low end, as in the previous example, is that small amounts may be functionally equivalent to nothing. But when we use a numeral, precise amounts (even if small) are likely to be relevant. However, sometimes effects similar to those observed with *many* are also clearly visible with numerals. Suppose that, for example, classes are usually made up of twenty students. Take the following sentence uttered against such a background:

(101) Today, I won't address twenty lethargic students.

Clearly, B's utterance does not suggest "but I intend to address a smaller audience of students." In fact, it even suggests that I will simply not teach.

I think that this explains in principled terms the different intuitions we have on direct versus indirect implicatures and the "now you see it, now you don't" effect we observe with the latter (but not with the former). Intermediate quantifiers and numerals under negation typically give rise to a positive implicature. This is the default expectation. However, they may loose it because of scale truncation. This loss of the indirect (positive) implicature is perhaps harder with numerals (with respect to vague quantifiers). In general, it depends on which scale one selects; this in turn depends on the common ground and the particular aspects of the conversational dynamics.

3.4. Interim conclusions

Summing up, our theory of SIs is based on the idea of adding them in as soon as possible, as part of the computational system of grammar rather than as part of the interaction of such system with other extragrammatical modules. This addition is governed by one simple constraint: implicatures must lead to strengthening. The strength condition is checked at each step, and it leads to removal of implicatures as soon as their addition would wind up weakening what is said. The implementation of this idea, through the definition of the notion of strengthened values, is quite simple (maybe too much so to withstand closer scrutiny), and it leads to a number of detailed predictions, some of which have been discussed here.[19]

4. NPIs: Domain comparison versus scales

In this section, I will discuss how this approach to SIs and the theory of NPIs may be related. First, I will present some general issues that seem to arise in this area. Second, I will sketch a theory of NPIs that builds on recent semantic proposals. Finally, I will explore the consequences that such a theory has, once embedded in the general approach to scalar implicatures outlined in section 3.

4.1. Semantics of NPIs: The status of the debate

How is the sensitivity to the same type of contexts of such diverse phenomena to be explained? In the case of SIs, the line of explanation is fairly clear. The SIs are added in because they lead to strengthening (i.e., they constitute a gain in information). But strengthening is a context-dependent notion. More specifically, something that leads to a gain of information in a positive context turns into a loss once it gets embedded within a negative operator (as the latter reverses the monotonicity of its arguments).

Thus canonical SIs associated with certain terms (e.g., the strengthening of *some* to *some and not all*) are in general absent from DE contexts.

How about NPIs? Here is where recent semantic proposals have important new insights to offer. I am thinking, in particular, of such work as Kadmon and Landman (1993), Krifka (1995), and Lahiri (1998). Although quite different in many respects, these proposals have a common thread, which I'll briefly expose through a (much simplified) review of Kadmon and Landman's approach (K&L, henceforth).

Generally, quantifiers are associated with a certain quantificational domain, which the context supplies. For example, if I say, "Everyone was late," I typically don't mean everyone in the world but everyone in a salient domain of individuals. Following Westertahl (1988), let us assume that quantifiers are indexed to a domain (which is left for the context to specify). Accordingly, we will write "every_D(one')(was late')" for (the meaning of) *everyone (in D) was late* or "$\exists_D$ x [donkey (y)]" for *there is a donkey (in D)*.[20] Now, K&L propose that *any* is an existential quantifier that "widens" the domain of quantification that would otherwise be assumed. For example, if in using *potatoes* we have a certain domain in mind, which, say, excludes frozen ones, in saying, *I don't have any potato* we may enlarge that domain to include also frozen potatoes. But now the question immediately becomes, Why is domain extension limited to *negative* contexts? Consider a sentence with an existential quantifier in a positive context, say (102a):

(102) a There is a student who doesn't know me.
b. *There is any student who doesn't know me.

In uttering (102a), we will typically have some domain in mind, for if we meant some student or other in the world, then (102a) would hardly be news. In positive contexts, the more specifically constrained the quantificational domain of an existential will be, the more informative a sentence we get. To put it differently, domain widening in a positive context leads to a loss of information. That is why we don't do it in such contexts. The formal underpinning of this lies in the following elementary logical fact:

(103) Let g be an increasing function from sets into sets [i.e., for any set D, g(D) $\supseteq$ (D.]
Then
$\exists_D$ x [ϕ] entails $\exists_{g(D)}$ x [ϕ], where D is a quantificational domain.

So, in particular, the reason that (102b) is bad is the following: given a choice, we go for the most informative, relevant piece of information. Sentences (102a) and (102b) are semantically identical except for domain widening. Hence, we must go for (102a).

Under negation, things, of course, change. Since negation reverses entailments, we get the opposite of (103):

(104) $\neg \exists_{g(D)}$ x [ϕ] entails $\neg \exists_D$ x [ϕ]

This means that under negation, an *any* statement becomes stronger, and hence more informative, than its plain existential counterpart. That is, (105a) is stronger than (105b):

(105) a. There isn't any student that doesn't know me.
b. There isn't a student that doesn't know me.

What using *any* contributes is the information that there are no students of the relevant type in a domain larger than that one would otherwise assume. This looks like a sensible conversational move.

The explanatory potential of this approach is the following. It was discovered that NPI licensing takes place in contexts that have a certain abstract semantic property in common (idealizing a bit, DE-ness). This was an important breakthrough, but it remained an essentially descriptive statement; we didn't know why exactly such elements were so picky in their distribution. Now we have a fairly natural hypothesis on the meaning of the relevant lexical items (according to which, NPIs are simple modifications of the meaning of standard indefinites) that, given elementary considerations on how we communicate, makes us see why they should appear only in DE contexts. Of course many problems remain open, much needs to be worked out further, and so on. But what emerges is a line of argumentation one would wish to maintain (and Krifka 1995 or Lahiri 1998, e.g., constitute alternative accounts that do so).

On the basis of proposals on NPIs of this sort, we immediately also see the connection with SIs. In both cases, we are driven by a search for maximal information. And what is maximal in a positive context becomes minimal once embedded under negation-like operators—whence the sensitivity to the same structural semantic properties. So far we seem to have a success story, one that is largely independent of the localist view of implicatures I have been advocating.

However, there are things that don't quite work out so well, and this will force us to revise the picture we have so far. Let us consider some of the problems.

First, domain widening doesn't *have* to take place when we use *any*. Imagine a situation in which one is willing to utter (106a); in such a situation one might equally well utter (106b):

(106) a. Everybody in that class did poorly on the exam.
b. There isn't anybody in that class who did well.

The domains we implicitly refer to with (106a) versus (106b) seem to be just the same. In fact it is quite hard to imagine in exactly what way the intended domain might be expanded by using (106b). One might be led to conclude that whereas NPIs are good devices to widen a quantificational domain, domain widening can't be their only semantic function, for it doesn't always take place when we use them.

A second issue is the following. How are we to understand the condition that domain widening must lead to strengthening? The intuition is that domain widening and pragmatic strengthening are part and parcel of the lexical meaning of *any*. Yet it is not obvious how to exactly encode such an information in a lexical entry (in a way that is compatible with what is usually assumed on lexical meanings). To put it in different terms, it is not clear how we arrive at a compositional implementation of K&L's idea (see Lahiri 1998 for an elaboration on this criticism).

The two problems we just discussed are specific to K&L's proposal and do not apply to other proposals in the same spirit, such as Lahiri's (1998) or Krifka's (1995).

The next points, however, apply to them as well. They have to do with locality. Let me illustrate with examples. With K&L's proposal in mind, consider the sentence in (107a):

(107) a. It is not true that there aren't any potatoes.
b. Value on standard domain $\neg\neg\, \exists_D x$ [potatoes(x)]
c. Value on widened domain $\neg\neg\, \exists_{g(D)} x$ [potatoes(x)]

Here the two negations cancel each other out; the informational content of (107a) is the same as that of "there are potatoes." Hence, widening in (107a) cannot lead to strengthening, and we wouldn't expect *any* to be grammatical. But it is. The problem can be put in the following terms. The semantics of *any* is domain widening. This semantics naturally goes together with a pragmatic condition that domain widening must lead to strengthening. If this is truly a pragmatic condition and if the semantics/pragmatics interface is modular, pragmatic strengthening should be checked globally, after the computational system has done its job. But then we wouldn't expect the result in (107a). The grammaticality of (107a) shows that the condition that licenses *any* is, instead, checked locally; that is, what counts is the *first* DE operator that c-commands the NPI (which might be quite far from the NPI). This kind of locality (a "roofing" effect) is unexpected. Of course, one can always build locality into the theory, which is what, in essence, K&L or Krifka (1995) in different ways do.[21] But the point is that the logic of the theory is compatible with a variety of different ways of settling the locality issue. This can hardly be viewed as an asset of this family of approaches.

The presence of locality conditions on NPI licensing resonates well with my claim that implicatures are introduced (or removed) locally. Still one would like to understand better the exact relationships between the two kinds of locality. For example, how do implicatures behave with respect to roofing? If they worked like NPIs, we should expect that the first DE operator removes (or recalibrates) the implicature and whatever happens next has no further impact. But in fact, things do not seem to work this way. Consider, for example, the following sentences:

(108) a. It is warm outside.
b. I doubt that it isn't warm outside.
c. It's not boiling hot outside.

Sentence (108a) implicates (108c). Does (108b) have the same implicature? Whereas the double negation is hard to process, it seems that in one way of understanding (108b) it is just equivalent to (108a). In that interpretation, (108b) does implicate (108c). In other ways of understanding (108b), metalinguistic uses slide readily in. Such uses may remove the implicature. But that is no news, as metalinguistic uses can be construed as an objection to any aspect whatsoever of an utterance. So there is no roofing on implicature projection; we have rather a flip-flop effect: first implicatures are introduced, then they are removed or recalibrated at the first DE operator, then they are restored again at the next DE operator, and so on. This effect, which is predicted by my approach, sets implicatures aside from NPIs. This constitutes a serious problem for approaches that try to reduce NPIs and SIs to identical phenomena.[22]

The second problem is related to the first but adds, possibly, an extra twist. Since the work of Linebarger (1981), it has been known that NPI licensing is subject to an "intervention" or "minimality" effect. The problem is illustrated by paradigms of the following sort:

(109) a. I doubt that Sue has potatoes.
b. I doubt that Sue has any potatoes.
c. I doubt that every housemate of Sue has potatoes.
d. ??I doubt that every housemate of Sue has any potatoes.

In (109a), we have a plain indefinite. In (109b), we have the same sentence with an NPI replacing the plain indefinite (which, in the hypothesis we are entertaining, induces domain widening). In (109c), a universal quantifier intervenes between negation and the (plain) indefinite, and the result is perfectly grammatical. In (109d) we do the same with the NPI, and the sentence becomes noticeably degraded. *Every*, in that position, seems to interfere in the relationtionship between the NPI and the licensing context. This is surprising. Effects of this sort are quite familiar from syntax. Often enough we see syntactic relations that are affected by interveners. Often enough a relation between X and Y is disturbed by an intervening Z, which might in its own right establish the relevant relation with Y, as schematically illustrated in (110a) (taken from Rizzi 2001):

(110) a. . . . X . . . Z . . . Y . . .
b. I wonder who could solve the problem in this way.
c. *How do you wonder who could solve the problem t ?

For example, wh-island effects [such as the contrast between (110b) and (110c)] can be explained in this way. The relation between *how* and its trace in (110c) is disturbed by the intervention of another wh-element. The effect in (109d) appears to be of a similar nature. But if the relation in question is semantic in nature (i.e., check whether domain widening induced by A leads to strengthening under C), there is no obvious reason why we should expect effects of this sort. This is particularly so in view of the fact that though *every* is a potential NPI licensor, *any* in (109c) occurs on its wrong side, so to speak, that is, on the side in which *every* is upward entailing and could not license an NPI anyhow.

A point worth underscoring in this connection is that SIs aren't subject to anything like intervention, as seen in the following example:

(111) a. Every girl invited every boy three times. (exactly)
b. Every boy whom **every** girl has invited three times please stand up. (at least)

Sentence (111a) clearly has a highly prominent "exactly" reading. Sentence (111b) does not. The upper *every* removes the embedded implicature, and in doing so it is not disturbed by the intervention of the embedded *every*. Example (111) forms a minimal pair with (109c and d). So there are no intervention effects between scalar terms and what determines the presence or absence of the scalar implicature. Nor would we expect it in the theory I have outlined. Implicature calculation is a purely semantic process that involves the comparison of two potential values. For example, the upper *every* in (111b) compares the two available values of its argument and chooses the strongest, period.

Summing up, NPIs, unlike SIs, display both roofing and minimality effects (terms that I am using here and throughout in a purely descriptive manner). Now, it is conceivable, even a priori desirable, that phenomena of this sort, so similar to others that arise elsewhere in grammar, are to be accounted for in terms of a uniform theory of locality (but cf. section 4.3). Be that as it may, we see that the optimistic picture we had at the beginning of this section must be substantially qualified. We hoped we had a unified way to understand NPIs and SIs in terms of relative informational strength. An NPI broadens the quantificational domain of a plain indefinite; but this is informative (and hence felicitous) only in negative contexts. A SIs strengthens an assertion (taking into account the relevant scale); but this is informative (and hence felicitous) only in positive contexts. This makes us see why NPIs and SIs are sensitive to the same contexts. But we also see that the locality conditions in the phenomena at hand are very different from each other, and it is hard to understand why. In particular, if the key to NPIs is a pragmatic condition and if such conditions kick in the conceptual/intentional system *after* the computational system of grammar has done its job, locality effects are unexpected to begin with. If, instead, pragmatics work as in our proposal, the locality effects would be different from what they in fact are. This is the dilemma.

4.2. Theory outline

The main insight of recent semantic proposals on NPIs is that they make explicit the intuition that such items involve a comparison of some sort. In K&L, NPIs involve a comparison of two domains; in Krifka's (1995) proposal, a comparison among a whole scale of domains; in Lahiri's (1998) approach, a comparison of likelihood (analogous to that involved in the analysis of focal particles like *even*). I will stick to this general view and propose a variant of K&L's approach, which blends with aspects of the other two. The result, coupled with my approach to SIs, should lead to a better understanding of the relevant phenomena.

Here is the basic idea. NPIs are parasitic upon indefinites. They differ from the meaning of basic indefinites (say, the meaning of *some*) in that they invite us to consider possible domain expansions—not necessarily a specific one: any reasonable domain expansion will do. Let me elaborate on this idea to make it clearer. The meaning of NPIs comes, as it were, in two parts. First, as in the version of K&L's idea discussed in the previous section, they introduce into the domain variable associated with indefinites a variable ranging over increasing functions:

(112) $\text{any}' = \lambda P \lambda Q\ \text{some}_{g(D)}'(P)(Q)$ (where, for any D, $g(D) \supseteq (D)$)

Second, this domain-extending function must be *universally* closed at some point in the derivation. Crucially, such an operation of quantificational closure is subject to a condition (or, if you wish, carries a presupposition). Its result must lead to something stronger than the corresponding meaning with a plain indefinite. I will make this idea more precise shortly. Meanwhile, let me enunciate the principle:

(113) Strengthening/blocking
Domain expansions must be universally closed. Such closure must lead to strengthening with respect to the meaning of the plain indefinite.

What quantificational closure over domain-expanding functions achieves is twofold. First, we are freed from having to assume that NPIs require a *specific* way of extending the domain. Second, we can compositionally implement pragmatic strengthening as a condition on quantificational closure. Let me illustrate. Suppose we have an NPI in a positive sentence such as *any man walked in*. Its base meaning, according to our hypothesis, would be as in (114a). If we apply closure to it, we get (114b):

(114) a. $\text{some}_{g(D)}$'(man')(walked in')
b. $\forall g \in \Delta[\text{some}_{g(D)}$'(man')(walked in')]
c. some_{D}'(man')(walked in')

I am assuming that no form of quantification is ever possible without a domain restriction, and universal closure is no exception. So Δ in (114b) ranges over the domain expansions the speaker may be willing to entertain. Formula (115c) represents, instead, the sentence meaning corresponding to *any man walked in*, with the plain indefinite replacing the NPI (i.e., the competitor). Now, (114c) asymmetrically entails (114b).[23] Hence, the condition on strengthening, which closure must satisfy, is not met. Consequently, the sentence is ungrammatical.

Suppose now we embed our example sentence under some DE operator as in *it is false that any man walked in*. The base meaning is (115a). The presence of negation gives us another possible site for quantificational closure, that is, above negation. The result is given in (115b).

(115) a. $\neg\ \text{some}_{g(D)}$'(man')(walked in')
b. $\forall g \in \Delta$ [$\neg\ \text{some}_{g(D)}$'(man')(walked in')]
c. $\neg\ \text{some}_{D}$'(man')(walked in')

Formula (115b) says, "For any (reasonable) way of expanding the domain of quantification it is not the case that some man in the extended domain walked in." Clearly, (115b) asymmetrically entails (115c). Hence, the competitor of the NPI-sentence is weaker and the condition on closure is met. Moreover, the sentence is grammatical. Obviously the basic insight is just K&L's. However, I borrow from Lahiri (1998) the idea that NPIs must be assigned scope (in our version, the site of quantificational closure). And, like him, I make this operation contingent upon strengthening. There are two differences with respect to Lahiri's proposal, one of form, the other of substance. First, Lahiri requires that the sentence with the NPI be "less likely" than its alternatives (as he is analyzing the Hindi "even one" construction). My condition is just equivalent to his since being stronger entails being less likely. Second, Lahiri identifies NPI scope assignment with association with focus. This, for Hindi, is plausible since NPIs in Hindi are literally formed with the use of the focus particle *even*. But if we wanted to generalize Lahiri's proposal to other languages (which Lahiri is careful not to do), we face a problem. For although NPIs are compatible with focusing, they do not *require* any special focus assignment (in the form of, say, a special stress contour). The relevant alternatives are not evocated via focus. It's just a lexical property of *any* that it contrasts with ordinary indefinites.[24]

I mentioned also that with my proposed modification, domain expansion is no longer an absolute requirement. More specifically, it may just happen that the base domain (i.e., what I have been indicating as D) is already, so to speak, the largest reasonable domain. In this case the only "extension" of D to be considered will be D itself (which is allowed since g is not required to be properly increasing). This, as we saw, is in keeping with our intuitions. To put it differently, an NPI, in the present modified view, does not necessarily signal an actual, specific domain expansion; it signals, rather, willingness to expand the domain (an effective way of couching its role, which I owe to A. von Stechow). Notice that even in the limiting case in which there is no suitable expansion around, the proposed semantics still serves a useful purpose, namely, that of signaling that the indefinite must wind up within the scope of a DE operator (and hence it reduces potential ambiguities). But such an effect is not stipulated as the primary role of NPIs. It is rather a byproduct of how their semantics works out (and, more specifically, of the requirement that the use of NPIs leads to formal strengthening).

One further remark: I think that the proper way of thinking of (113) is in terms of something like "blocking", as is familiar from much work in morphology. The presupposition to which NPIs are subject puts them in an "elsewhere" relation with indefinites, on the assumption that the former are parasitic upon the latter. Intuitively, NPIs are a more marked version of indefinites (not dissimilar from, say, the relation between pronouns and their clitic counterparts). This brings about a sort of blocking effect, whereby the use of NPIs is blocked by the indefinites whenever the former don't give rise to a communicational advantage over the latter. Distributed morphology may provide a good framework for fleshing this out. For the time being, I am not in condition of being less vague.

Let me now try to be more explicit on how strengthening is formally implemented. I will first describe its semantics and then its syntax. (Readers not interested in formal details may safely skip this paragraph). Imagine introducing in our logical form a variable binding operator $\mathbf{O}_\Delta$ with the following semantics:

(116) Strengthening (/blocking)
$\|\mathbf{O}_\Delta, g\phi\| = \forall g \in \Delta \|\phi\|$, if $\forall g \in \Delta \|\phi\|$ entails $\|\phi'\|$; otherwise $\|\mathbf{O}_\Delta, g\phi\|$ is undefined, where ϕ' is identical to ϕ, with all occurrences of g removed.

Such an operator is what we would use to close off a domain-expanding function. The semantics given in (116) is still a first approximation, which might be improved on in many ways,[25] but it is sufficiently precise to give the reader something to work with. Let me use a simple example. Consider a sentence such as *I din't eat any potato*. Before closure, its logical form will be (117a); after closure, it will be (117b):

(117) a. not ($any_{g(D)}$ $potato_i$ [I ate t_i]] $\Rightarrow \neg\ some_{g(D)}$'(potato')($\lambda$x I ate x))
b. $\mathbf{O}_{\Delta,g}$ not ($any_{g(D)}$ $potato_i$ [I ate t_i]] $\Rightarrow \forall g \in \Delta\ \neg\ some_{g(D)}$'(potato')($\lambda$x I ate x))

According to (116), the closure of a sentence ϕ [i.e., in this case, (117a)] must be stronger than ϕ', which is identical to ϕ with all occurrences of g removed. That is, (117b) must be stronger than

(118) $\neg\ some_D$'(potato')(λx I ate x))

Since (117b) is in fact stronger than (118), the result of closing (117a) is well defined. Essentially, **O** is a presuppositional universal quantifier restricted to domain-extending functions. The presupposition is that the result must entail the meaning of the corresponding sentence with *some*.

Usually quantificational closure is taken to be subject to mapping conditions (Diesing 1992). We may exploit this general line of approach to closure to enforce the requirement that domain-extending functions (present in the lexical entry of NPIs) must be eventually closed. Here is one way of executing it. First, observe that in the case of scalar terms, the individuation of the relevant alternatives is done through lexically specified scales (a list of words in paradigmatic opposition with each other). Because of this, scalar terms need no special morphology to flag that their use may lead to strengthening. Quantificational domains, on the other hand, are not coded in lexicalized scales but in covert domain variables. So if one wants to signal domain expansion, one *must* resort to some morphological device specialized to this task. And morphological features enter into agreement relations. It is thus to be expected that the morphology of NPIs must agree with the morphology of some suitable head, just as, say, wh-words must enter into such a relation with, for example, interrogative complementizers. The second issue is what counts as a suitabile head. Given the semantics of NPIs, it must be a DE-head (any other choice would lead the interpretive component to crash). So we may assume that DE-heads carry a feature that, when active, must be checked by an NPI. This feature marks in syntax possible scope sites for closure, the relevant mapping hypothesis being now obvious:

(119) The domain of a +DE-head maps onto the scope of **O**.

To recapitulate, suppose an NPI is selected in an enumeration. There will have to be a head with the appropriate semantic quality and an active feature that will constitute the domain of quantificational closure. Any other option will lead the derivation to crash either in the syntax or in the semantics.[26]

As an immediate consequence of this way of implementing quantificational closure (through a feature that may be associated with negative heads), we get an account of why NPI licensing is subject to a roofing constraint. If you have an NPI and a string of DE-heads C-commanding it, clearly only the closest relevant head may agree with the NPI (however, you will want to cash this in formally):

```
(120) [ . . . NEG. . . . [ . . . NEG. . . . [ . . . NPI . . . ] . . . ] . . . ]
                          |_______________|
           |__________X___________________|
```

This, given my mapping hypothesis, forces the closest DE-head to act as the scope site for universal closure (and hence as the level at which the condition on strengthening must be checked). What happens above that level (i.e., how many negative operators there may be) remains without consequence.[27]

To sum up, my hypothesis is that NPIs are parasitic on weak quantifiers and close off quantificationally the domain (or situation) variable implicit in the former. In positive contexts, this constitutes a loss of information with respect to plain existentials; in negative contexts, it leads, instead, to strengthening. Hence, pragmatic and/or morphological considerations prevent NPIs from occurring in positive contexts (not embedded under a DE-head). The NPIs involve a comparison of domains (as proposed by K&L) but not a lexicalized scale (like scalar terms).

4.3. Intervention

The approach to NPIs outlined above captures their sensitivity to DE-contexts, a property NPIs share with SIs. However, the two phenomena also differ in some important respects. One difference between the two phenomena is the flip-flop versus roofing effects. This difference, too, now makes sense. The SIs are in turn inserted and removed across DE-operators, in a pistonlike fashion because the scalar requirements are checked at every step of the derivation (as is necessary to keep the strengthened meaning stronger)—whence the flip-flop effect. The NPIs, per contra, are not part of scales. They involve a generalization over quantificational domains that must lead to a stronger statement than plain indefinites. In virtue of their parasitic nature, they are subject to a constraint that relates their contribution to that of their host. Roofing follows from this. In particular, I suggest (in the spirit of much previous work) that this constraint takes the form of a morphological requirement. If their special morphology (necessary to signal potential domain widening) enters into an agreement relation with a negative head (the only kind of heads they could agree with, in virtue of their semantics), then roofing follows from the properties of agreement (e.g., the probe must seek out the closest goal). But even if such a morphological requirement were not there, if strengthening or blocking is just freely checked, the empirical effects of roofing would also be expected: in the presence of c-commanding negative heads, we would always have a site at which strengthening can be satisfied (namely, the closest one), and nothing that happens thereafter would affect that.

So we have a proposal that does arguably improve some on the previous semantic ones that directly inspired it, namely K&L's, Krifka's, and Lahiri's. With respect to K&L, besides the general issues just mentioned, we no longer have to posit a specific domain extension (which, in fact, does not seem to always take place). Krifka (1995) tries to directly reduce NPIs to scalar implicatures (albeit of an abstract kind, involving a hierarchy of domains), which makes it difficult to account for the differences between the two phenomena. Lahiri (1998) links NPI licensing closely to focus, which may be fine for Hindi, but it's problematic for NPIs in general. Be that as it may, there is an outstanding problem for all the theories we have considered (including my own), and that is the intervention effect.

Let us briefly review the facts. Here is a representative sample:

(121) a. I doubt that Theo drank the leftover wine or any coffee.
a'. *I doubt that Theo drank the leftover wine and any coffee.
b. Mary doesn't wear any hearing at every party (Linebarger 1981).
O.K.: not [any hearing$_y$ [every party$_x$ [Mary wears t_y at t_x]]]
*not [every party$_x$ [any hearing$_y$ [Mary wears t_y at t_x]]]
c. I didn't meet a person who read any of my poetry.
c'. *I din't meet ten/the people that read any of my poetry.
d. I won't marry a woman who has little money because I get any advantage out of it.
d'. *I won't marry a woman who has any money because I get any advantage out of it.

The general puzzle at hand is that in all of the ungrammatical cases, the semantic condition required for NPI licensing is met. Consider, for example, the following pair of sentences:

(122) a. It is not the case that everyone has some potatoes.
a'. $\neg\ \forall x\ \text{some}_D'(\text{potatoes})(\lambda y\ \text{has}(x,y))$
b. *It is not the case that everyone has any potatoes.
b'. $\forall g \in \Delta \neg\ \forall x\ \text{some}_{g(D)}'(\text{potatoes})(\lambda y\ \text{has}(x,y))$

The semantic value of the (agrammatical) *any* sentence (122b) is indeed stronger than the one of the corresponding *some* sentence (122a), as is shown by their respective meanings. Hence, we would expect no blocking effect (i.e., insofar as semantics goes, the sentence should be grammatical). It seems reasonable to conclude that semantics cannot be the cause of intervention. Of course, one can always tack an extralocality condition on any theory.[28] But this does not make us understand why effects of this sort arise in this way and with these specific items.

We seem to have an argument to go with a syntactic account. Intervention effects are known from much work on locality in syntax, where they are extensively discussed. We have hypothesized that NPIs enter into an agreement relation with negative heads. It is then to be expected that such a relation will be disturbed by the intervention of a class of operators. I have argued that this is what in fact happens for roofing. I also noted that the roofing effects might in fact be derived in some other fashion. So, although roofing lends some plausibility to the overall idea of a syntactic relationship between the licensor and the NPI, it does not constitute an exceedingly strong argument in favor of it. Now, however, we have arguably more of the same. In (121), we see that a relationship between a potential licensor and an NPI is quite clearly disturbed by a class of operators, and this time no other account is readily forthcoming. On the syntactic tack we have taken all we need to do is assume that the relevant operators carry some feature that disturbs the agreement relation between the NPI and its licensor. Roofing, viewed as a syntactic phenomenon, sets the stage. Intervention phenomena provide us with seemingly independent evidence that syntax (e.g., agreement) is indeed the right way to look at NPI licensing. And we can live happily ever after.

But some outstanding puzzles do remain. I'll mention three. The first concerns the class of interveners. They are strong determiners (*every*, *most*, and the definite article); also numerals seem to intervene (cf. 121c), even if with them our intuitions are a bit shakier. Nonnumeral indefinites (the indefinite article, *some*, and bare plurals) do not intervene. In the realm of sentential operators, *and* intervenes but *or* does not. (cf. 121a vs. 121a'). So, strong quantifiers, numerals, and *and* must carry the disturbing feature. The problem here is that it is not clear in what sense the interveners form a natural class that would justify them in carrying the same feature. One might try saying that the culprit is universal quantification (as, e.g., Lahiri 1998 suggests). A reason for thinking that this is the right idea is that conjunction is a meet operator, just like universals, whereas disjunction corresponds to existential quantification. The numerals, however, do not fit smoothly with this idea. One would have to claim that, at least in one reading, they, too, involve universal quantification. But this is not so plausible (especially if the "exactly" reading of numerals is an implicature and hence not part of their core meaning). At any rate, even if this hypothesis was right, why exactly would universals intervene?

Be that as it may, we seem to face a problem here. In accounting for roofing in syntactic terms, we didn't face any such problem. In that case, we simply have to say that the NPI agrees with the closest DE head. But in extending this idea to intervention, we are forced to say that a number of other operators that are clearly not DE (like the numerals or *and*) carry a feature that disturbs licensing of NPIs. Because it is not clear that such a feature has any independent status, we run the risk of making up a diacritic that simply means +intervener.

There is also a second reason to doubt that universal quantification is the culprit. Consider the case of *if* clauses. They do not intervene (cf. 123a), yet their (default) interpretation is generally taken to involve a universal operator (over worlds or situations), as illustrated in (123b):

(123) a. I doubt that if John gets drunk, anyone will be surprised.
b. $\neg \forall w$ [if John gets drunk in w][anyone will notice in w]

Formula (123b) is a rough representation of the meaning of (123a), in reflection of the idea that in general *if* clauses are restrictors of an operator, whose default interpretation is that of a universal quantifier. So the semantics of (123a) is isomorphic to that of, say, (121b) or (122b), with the same (or the same type of) operator involved. Yet in (123) we see no sign of intervention. This constitutes a second puzzle: if universals intervene, why don't *if* clauses, which involve a universal operator, intervene?

Finally, consider the case of *because* clauses, which are closely related to *if* clauses. According to some—see, for example, Dowty (1979)—*because* clauses are defined in terms of *if* clauses. Yet the former behave very differently from the latter with respect to the problem at hand. Whereas *if* clauses do not intervene, *because* clauses do. Consider the contrast in (121d and d'). In both sentences, negation has scope over the *because* clause. This is necessary in order to get the NPI contained in the *because* clause properly licensed. The relevant logical forms are roughly the following:

(124) a. ¬ BECAUSE (I get any advantage out of it, I will marry a woman that has any money).
b. ¬ BECAUSE (I get any advantage out of it, I will marry a woman that has little money).

Notice that (124a) parallels (123b). Yet whereas (123a) is grammatical, (124a) is not. Why? Moreover, as (124b) shows, licensing across the *because* operator per se is permissible. So it is not the *because* operator as such that intervenes but the *because clause* as a whole. Or, in different terms, if we regard *because* as a two-place operator, the intervention effect takes place only with respect to its second argument, not with respect to the first. Why would this be so?

What these considerations jointly show is that the paradigm in (121) cannot be so readily understood by hypothesizing that certain heads carry a feature that disturbs a syntactic relationship between the NPI and its licensor. With enough assumptions, we can surely get a feature base approach to work. But quite a few quirks remain, and I don't see a profound explanation coming out of it as readily as one might have hoped. Maybe intervention is doomed to remain a mystery.

Wait. We forgot about implicatures. What could implicatures possibly have to say about intervention? Against any prima facie plausibility, I would like to suggest that they are actually the real culprits. Let me try to make my case by first looking back at examples like (122). In trying to decide whether the semantic condition that licenses *any* was met, we considered and compared just *plain* meanings of (122a) and (122b) (and concluded on this basis that the semantic condition on strengthening was duly met). But sentences have implicatures; that is, they have strong meanings that, in our approach, are assigned by the computational system (or by a computational system parallel to and accessible from that of core grammar). In particular, a sentence like (122a) is expected to have an implicature of the following sort:

(125) a. Strong meaning of *it is not the case that everyone has some potatoes*:
$\neg \forall x\ \text{some}_D{}'(\text{potatoes})(\lambda y\ \text{has}(x,y)) \wedge \exists x\ \text{some}_D{}'(\text{potatoes})(\lambda y\ \text{has}(x,y))$
b. It is not the case the case that everyone has some potatoes, but someone does.

The strong meaning of the relevant sentence in plain English is given in (125b). Compare with this the meaning of the ungrammatical sentence with *any*, repeated here:

(126) Meaning of of *it is not the case that everyone has any potatoes*:
$\forall g \in \Delta \neg \forall x\ \text{some}_{g(D)}{}'(\text{potatoes})(\lambda y\ \text{has}(x,y))$

Clearly, (126) does not entail (125a), even though it entails its first conjunct. So if we assume that strengthening must be met with respect to strong meanings, we see that in the case at hand it cannot be. *Any* here is not properly licensed after all.

The idea is that NPIs compete not with the plain meanings of the corresponding sentences with indefinites but with their strengthened meanings. This is not implausible. If their role is to lead to a stronger statement than that which one otherwise would get, they should, in fact, compete with the strongest possible assertion that could be made with the relevant alternative. Accordingly, strengthening and blocking should be reformulated as follows:

(127) a. Universal closure of a sentence with *any* is defined only if the result is stronger than the *strong* meaning of the corresponding sentence with some.
b. $\|\mathbf{O}_{\Delta}, g\phi\| = \forall g \in \Delta \|\phi\|$, if $\forall g \in \Delta \|\phi\|$ entails $\|\phi'\|^{s}$; otherwise $\|\mathbf{O}_{\Delta}, g\phi\|$ is undefined, where ϕ' is identical to ϕ, with all occurrences of g removed.

Here (127b) is the formal counterpart of (127a). This constitutes a trivial modification of our original proposal. But as a consequence of it, strong meanings become the blockers of *any*. This simple move has the effect of ruling out all the bad cases in (121). To illustrate it further, consider the case of *and*:

(128) a. *I doubt that John ate the cake and drank any coffee.
b. $\forall g \in \Delta \neg$ (ate (j, the cake) $\wedge$ some$_{g(D)}$'(coffe)(drank(j, y))

The competitor and its strong meaning (in plain English) are given in what follows:

(129) a. I doubt that John ate the cake and drank some coffee.
b. I doubt that John ate the cake and drank some coffee, but I believe that he did one of the two.

Again, whereas (128) would entail the first conjunct of (129b), which corresponds to its plain meaning, it fails to entail the conjunct as a whole. Hence *any* is blocked.

Don't we run the risk of ruling out too much by switching to (127)? Not really. There will be plenty of cases in which strong meanings and plain ones are predicted to coincide. In such cases, our present formulation of blocking will make the same predictions as our previous one. This is trivial and will occur whenever no scalar term is involved. Thus, for example, in *I doubt that John has any money*, beating the strengthened meaning tantamounts to beating the plain one (and this will indeed happen, thanks to the presence of negation). It is more interesting, that this is expected to happen also in the presence of scalar terms, under certain circumstances. Consider, for example, the counterpart of (129a), with *or* replacing *and.*

(130) a. I doubt that John ate the cake or drank any coffee.
b. I doubt that John ate any cake or drank some coffee.

Here *or* is the weakest member of its scale. This means that in positive contexts it will trigger an implicature (the familiar exclusive construal). But in a negative context, last becomes first: *or* becomes the *strongest* member of the scale, and the strongest members of a scale can trigger no implicature. In fact, (130a) has none. So the strong meaning of (130a) is just its plain meaning, and potential domain widening follows its due course. That is, when we apply universal closure to (130a) we obtain something that is stronger (and more informative) than its competitor (viz. 130b). And so *any* in (130a) is properly licensed. The same goes, mutatis mutandis, for simple existentials like *some* or *a*; just like *or*, they are the weakest members of their respective scales; under negation they become the strongest, and no implicature gets in the way of NPI licensing.

Putting *because* clauses aside for the moment and looking at quantifiers and operators, we now see why interveners and noninterveners divide up the way they do. Interveners are strong members of a scale; noninterveners are the weakest ones. Whether my proposal is right or wrong, this generalization seems to be on the right track—presumably, not by accident. The intervention effect must be related to the scalar nature of the elements involved. Our conjecture is that under negation strong members of a scale give rise to an implicature that blocks NPIs. This in a sense is turning Linebarger's (1981) theory on its head. Linebarger used implicatures to license certain occurrences of *any* that her immediate scope constraint was not able to accommodate. I am proposing that the so-called intervention effect is a byproduct of a positive scalar implicature that (some) negative sentences carry along. Such an implicature prevents NPIs from satisfying the strengthening condition to which they are subject. They fail, in the relevant contexts, to yield something stronger than the alternative with the plain indefinite.

The behavior of numerals now also falls into place. Under negation, they, too, have (a possibly rather weak but nonetheless present) positive scalar implicature. In section 4, I discussed the case of (131a), which implicates (131b):

(131) a. John isn't twenty.
b. John is close to twenty.

Also something like (132a) normally implicates something like (132b):

(132) a. I doubt I met eleven people that read some of my poetry.
b. I believe I met at least someone who read some of my poetry.

Now take the sentence parallel to (132a), in which *any* replaces *some*, namely, the deviant (121c') discussed above and repeated here:

(121) c'. *I din't meet eleven people that read any of my poetry.

This sentence fails to entail the conjunction of (132a) and (132b), which corresponds to the strong meaning of the relevant competitor, and *any* is blocked.

As we saw, sometimes intermediate values of a scale in a negative context lose their implicature. The reason is due to the fact that the scale gets "truncated." That is, the mentioned amount is selected as the smallest relevant value of the scale. In this case, under negation, such an element will become the strongest and no implicature will come about. Hence, the intervention effect should disappear. Contrast, for example, (121c') with

(133) I never had eleven kids who won any championship. (said by a soccer coach)

As eleven is the minimal number of players on a soccer team, this number can naturally be selected as the smallest element of the contextually relevant scale. Under negation, it becomes the strongest and no implicature comes about. As soon as this happens, intervention indeed gets weaker. In other words, the scales that are naturally associated with (132a) and (133), respectively, are

(134) a. < x, 11, 12>, where x is some nonnull number minor that 11
b. <11, 22, 33 . . . >, where we group numerals by multiples of 11 (i.e., by teams)

So, under negation, (132a) has a positive implicature, whereas (133) does not. With numerals, this kind of "now you see it, now you don't" effect, though clearly present, is not so easy to construct because in the typical contexts in which mentioning a specific numeral is appropriate, a relatively fine-grained scale with several intermediate ladders will typically be salient. This explains why, in general, numerals will tend to display intervention [i.e., cases like (133) are harder to come across than cases like (121c')]. But with the quantifiers, especially with vague ones like *many*, where no specific amount is mentioned, the suspension of negative implicature under negation is much easier to come across, as we saw. This explains why often enough intermediate quantifiers like *many* don't show intervention:

(135) I typically don't have many students with any background in linguistics.

The reason, I think, is because in this case we are leaving open the possibility that in fact we may well have no student with any background. That is, the positive implicature is absent. The mechanism that allows this to happen is always the same, as in the case of numerals. We can select a truncated scale <many, every> in which, under negation, *many* becomes the strongest member. With such a scale, the positive implicature that *many* under negation would otherwise trigger, disappears. If we choose a context in which the implicature is present, we also get intervention back with *many*. This can be accomplished by focusing *many* or by making the relevant background assumptions sufficiently explicit:

(136) Typically in that course you do get some students that are interested. ?? But don't expect that many students will show any interest.

Sentence (136) clearly has a positive implicature parallel to (132b). Because of such an implicature, *any* winds up being positively embedded. Thus the *any* sentence fails to lead to strengthening, as it should in order to be properly licensed; and sentence (136) is degraded. This kind of behavior of numerals and intermediate quantifiers with respect to intervention seems to be very hard to explain in a feature-based approach.

This raises, however, a general issue for our proposal. Let me try to lay it out as clearly as I can. Implicatures are, in general, cancellable. Shouldn't we expect, therefore, that when they are removed, intervention effects should disappear or be weakened with *any* kind of intervener? Shouldn't we, in other words, expect that if we remove the relevant implicature, *every* should behave like *many*? For that matter, how can we possibly rely on implicatures, generally held to be an extragrammatical phenomenon, to account for the degraded grammatical status of certain sentences?

The point is that, for independent reasons, the claim that implicatures are extragrammatical is probably wrong. Or rather, whether we like to think of them as extragrammatical or not, scalar implicatures are computed in parallel to the syntactic computation, and (at appropriate stages) the results of the two computational processes are accessible to each other. Look in particular at the present setup. For any expression α, we have a well-defined characterization of its plain meaning $\|\alpha\|$ and of its strong one $\|\alpha\|^S$. This enables us to directly state a condition in NPI-licensing in terms of strong meanings. Strengthening must be checked with respect to *strong* meanings. The fact that implicatures can be cancelled (i.e., that in certain contexts we want to use plain meanings) does not and cannot affect this fact. If sentences with *any* fail to be stronger than the strong version of the corresponding sentences with *some*, the condition on *any* licensing cannot be met. And that's the end of it.

To clarify further, suppose, for example, I try to say, "I doubt that every student has any background." Grammar gives me two meanings, the plain one || I doubt that every student has any background|| and the strong one ||I doubt that every student has any background||^S. It does not matter which one I choose. Whichever one I choose, I am required to check whether it entails the relevant competitor, which is ||I doubt that every student has some background||^S. Since that fails, the sentence in question is ruled out. The disappearance of intervention with numerals or a quantifier like *many* is an all together different matter. In that case, by simply choosing a suitable scale (which we independently know that we must be able to do), we can get a strong meaning ||I doubt that many students have any background||^S, which is equivalent to its plain meaning; with respect to such an interpretation, strengthening is met and *any* is grammatical. Independently motivated axioms on scales prevent me from doing the same with *every* (and other operators).

Let us now turn to other types of sentential operators—*if* and *because* clauses. A puzzling aspect of intervention noted above was the fact that *if* clauses, although involving a universal quantifier over worlds, show no intervention effect. The answer to that, from the present point of view, is straightforward. It is not the inherent feature of an operator that causes intervention. It is, rather, its position on a scale (if any). *If* clauses are not part of a lexicalized scale. Hence, under negation they don't have a positive implicature of the sort that could get in the way of NPI-licensing. This leads us to the issue of *because* clauses. They do show intervention effects. However, just like *if* clauses, *because* clauses do not seem to belong to a scale. Hence, it is not obvious what my approach might have to say about them. Although this might well turn out to be a problem, there are a few preliminary considerations that are worth pointing out. The obvious observation is that *because* clauses are strongly factive. This, per se, is not enough to conclude much. We know that NPIs may be licensed by certain factives, like *be surprised*,[29] and thus factivity by itself can hardly be the cause of ungrammaticality in intervention cases. However, I think that the specific form in which factivity gets realized in *because* clauses is indeed responsible for their peculiar behavior vis-à-vis intervention. Let me try to illustrate this idea. Consider a sentence like (137a) on the LF schematically indicated in (137b):

(137) a. John didn't complain because Mary was in a bad mood.
b. not [John complained BECAUSE Mary was in a bad mood]

The problem is the following. If, assuming an LF-isomorphic to (137b), we embed an NPI in the main clause, we get intervention (whereas if we embed it in the subordinate clause, we do not). Now suppose that the factive nature of *because* clauses is due to the circumstance that they actually involve a double assertion. Suppose, in other terms, that a sentence such as "John complained because Mary was in a bad mood" is literally interpreted as "John complained and that was caused by Mary's being in a bad mood." Accordingly, the logical form of a plain (nonnegated) *because* clause like (138a) is as shown in (138b):

(138) a. John complained because Mary was in a bad mood
b. [John complained]$_i$ and CAUSE (Mary was in a bad mood, x_i)

So, *because* clauses are covert conjunctive statements where the first conjunct is the main clause (which is actually asserted) and the second conjunct is formed by the CAUSE operator; the second argument of the latter [x_i in (138b)] is a covert pronominal element bound by the main clause. This reflects the intuition that "p because q" does two things: asserts p and adds to it a specification of what causes it. Now consider what would happen if we embed a structure like (138b) under negation, as in (139):

(139) not [[John complained]$_i$ and CAUSE (Mary was in a bad mood, x_i)]

Formula (139) is of the form $\neg$ (p $\wedge$ q); such formulas, as we saw above, generally implicate (p $\vee$ q). That is, the strong meaning of (139) would be

(140) $\neg$ [[John complained]$_i$ $\wedge$ CAUSE (Mary was in a bad mood, x_i)]
$\wedge$ [[John complained]$_i$ $\vee$ CAUSE (Mary was in a bad mood, x_i)]

Given the factivity of CAUSE (i.e., the fact that *CAUSE (p, q)* entails $p \wedge q$), formula (140) is provably equivalent to

(141) [John complained]$_i$ $\wedge$ $\neg$ CAUSE (Mary was in a bad mood, x_i)

In other words, the strong meaning of (139) would be (141). This would explain why wide scope negation of a *because* clause is generally construed as negating just the cause, not what gets caused. A further consequence of this approach is that whenever negation is construed as having wide scope, an NPI in the main clause can never be licensed. Consider, for example, (121d'), whose logical form (under the current hypothesis) is given in what follows:

(142) [I will marry any woman]$_i$ ∧ ¬ CAUSE (I get any advantage out of it, x_i)

I leave it to the reader to verify that this sentence so construed fails to be stronger than its competitor (in which a plain existential replaces *any*). On the other hand, if *any* is embedded just in the subordinate clause [i.e., as in (143)] strengthening will be met and *any* is, therefore, properly licensed:

(143) a. I won't marry a woman because I get any advantage out of it.
b. [I will marry a woman]$_i$ ∧ ¬ CAUSE (I get any advantage out of it, x_i) competitor:
c. I won't marry a woman because I get some advantage our of it.

Again, I must leave it to the reader to verify that this is indeed so.

The key to this proposal is that *because* clauses are hidden conjunctive statements, which, like overt conjunctions, carry a positive implicature under negation. In other words, they are sort of covertly scalar terms (in the sense that they involve conjunction). If this proves tenable, we would have a general explanation of the behavior of *because* clauses under negation, including the failure of NPIs to be licensed whenever negation is assigned wide scope over *because*. The viability of such a hypothesis needs, of course, a much closer scrutiny than that which we are able to do here. The purpose of the present exercise is to give some preliminary plausibility to the idea that positive implicatures are also likely to play a role in this case, once the factivity of *because* clauses is better understood.[30]

A further interesting problem needs some attention.[31] It has to do with negative scalar quantifiers like *few*. As is well known, such quantifiers license NPIs:

(144) Typically, few students know any linguistics.

However, sentences of this form also have a robust positive scalar implicature, so the strong meaning of (144) can be paraphrased as in (145a):

(145) a. Few students know any linguistics but some do.
b. Few students know some linguistics but some do.

The problem is that if (145a) is the strong meaning of (144), *any* is not expected to be licensed under the present view. If we compute the meaning of (144), we see that it fails to entail its competitor, (145b). Taking (145a) as an informal representative of the (strong) meaning of (144), we see that the first conjunct of (145a) entails the first conjunct of (145b), as *any* there is negatively embedded. But the second conjunct of (145a) would fail to entail the second conjunct of (145b) (as *any* there is positively embedded); as a consequence, (145a) as a whole fails to be stronger than (145b) as a whole. Hence, *any* should be blocked, contrary to fact.

I think that in spite of what prima facie appears, this behavior of *few* does actually make sense from the perspective we are adopting. I will first give what I think is the empirical generalization behind the fact under discussion. Then I will illustrate how it follows. Take another look at the basic intervention cases, for example, at the pattern in (121). Our claim is that there are certain positive implicatures that get in the way and provoke intervention. Notice that in all the cases of intervention documented in the literature, we are invariably dealing with what we have called *indirect* scalar implicatures. The schema is always the same, namely,

(146)

```
          ____________
          | implicature |
  . . . NEG . . . SCALAR TERM . . . NPI . . .
     |_________________________________|
          licensing
```

The generalization, therefore, is that licensing is degraded whenever, through the interaction of the upper negation and an intervening scalar term, an implicature comes about. It is in exactly this configuration that scalar terms that are not the weakest in their scales become interveners. In contrast, the implicature with *few* is a direct one. It arises from *few* by itself, not from its interaction with a higher polarity-reversing function. I believe that direct implicatures can never cause intervention. If we were to give a schematic representation to the case of *few*, we might go for the following:

(147)

```
      . . . FEW . . . NPI
        ⇑       |______|
  implicature  licensing
```

Perhaps, the most appropriate way to think of this is in terms of processing. Direct implicatures can arise only after a scalar term has been introduced. For direct implicatures to be added, we first have to compute the regular meaning and then the implicature. In my system, this is done via Krifka's (1995) rule. But independently of implementation, the crucial thing here is that we must compute the plain meaning *before* computing the strong one. This, in turn, gives us a chance to check *any* licensing *before* the scalar implicature has been factored in. That is, we can check the condition on *any* licensing before Krifka's rule applies; and at that stage, strengthening will be satisfied and *any* licensed. Moreover, nothing that happens thereafter (namely, the introduction of the implicature) will affect this fact. In contrast, the way in which indirect implicatures are computed is very different. In computing strong meanings, we must use a special form of functional application, one that is sensitive to the character of functions. If a function is not DE, we use the regular function application. If the function is DE, we have to recalibrate. Indirect implicatures arise through this process of recalibration, which is part and parcel of functional application. So there is no way around indirect implicatures; they are not added after the plain meaning (of the whole expression) has been computed. Consider (126) again and imagine having to check the condition on *any*. If we check it right after the scalar term, we are still in a positive context (and the semantic computation will crash). If we check it after negation, we are in a negative context all right, but the implicature will be there (as it arises when we apply negation to the rest) and strengthening will fail. So the fact that not all positive implicatures get in the way of NPI licensing is, in fact, predicted. Only indirect implicatures can play such a role.[32]

The difference between direct and indirect implicatures, on which I am relying to account for the behavior of quantifiers like *few*, does not seem to be an artifact of the present way of looking at things. Some preliminary evidence suggests that direct and indirect implicatures are in fact processed differently. It has been observed in the psychological literature that unjustified violation of implicatures encounters strong resistance in adults. For instance, Gualmini et al. (2001) show that in a truth-value judgment task, a sentence like (148) is rejected by adults in a situation in which the relevant implicature is violated.

(148) Every pirate stole a jewel or a necklace.

In a situation in which in fact every pirate steals a jewel and a necklace, we have, in our current terms, a direct implicature violation, which adults reject. In contrast with this, Gualmini et al. run the same type of task with the following sentence:

(149) No pirate stole a jewel and a necklace.

Such a sentence has an *indirect* scalar implicature, namely, that some pirate stole a jewel or a necklace. If adults are asked to evaluate the sentence in a situation in which such an implicature is violated (i.e., in a situation in which pirates stole various things, but no pirate stole a necklace and no pirate stole a jewel), the acceptance rate is significantly higher than with (148). This happens in spite of the fact that adults do get the implicature associated with (149).[33] Thus, whereas direct and indirect implicatures are both computed online, adults seem to be more ready to tolerate violations of indirect implicatures, which means that these two types of implicatures must be distinguished by our processing system. This, in turn, may lend some independent plausibility to my idea that direct and indirect implicatures also play a different role vis-à-vis the intervention effect.

Taking stock, we see that specific aspects of my implementation are clearly amenable to further developments and improvements. But the basic idea should be clear: NPIs compete with strong meanings of indefinites. The presence of certain positive implicatures in negative sentences sometimes prevents NPIs from fulfilling their raison d'être in contexts in which we would otherwise expect them to do so. The main advantage I see to this idea is that we no longer have to hypothesize that, say, conjunction has a feature that interferes with NPI licensing, but disjunction does not; that *every* does, but *some* does not; and so on. We now see why certain elements (the interveners) form a natural class. And this leads to a rather principled (if surprising) account of the facts. If the present approach is on the right track, intervention in NPI-licensing is epiphenomenon. It has no formal status. It arises from the interplay of the general licensing condition on *any* (it must lead to strengthening with respect to *some*) and the way strong meanings (i.e., implicatures) are computed.[34]

5. Concluding remarks

I started with an observation that had been made several times in the literature: scalar implicatures and items like *any* are sensitive to the polarity of the context in which occur. We have first explored to what extent and in what form this observation holds. The main outcome (that surely needs further refinements) is that the contexts in which *any* is licensed (in both its NPI and free-choice variant) appear to be to a remarkable degree the same as those in which scalar implicatures are recalibrated (i.e., direct implicatures are removed and indirect ones come about). This fact, by itself, raises many interesting issues. The mechanisms at the basis of both phenomena must be somehow sensitive to similar factors. To find out whether this is indeed so, one has to go through a careful examination of how SIs are computed and NPIs licensed. Let us review the main (provisional) conclusions we've reached on these matters.

The dominant view on SIs is that they are computed at the level of root sentences, after grammar stricto sensu has finished its job. We have seen, however, that this position leads to difficulties. The interaction of SI-computation with several connectives and quantifiers (like disjunction, existentials, and nonmonotone quantifiers) turns out to be problematic. We have therefore explored a different view, according to which SIs are introduced locally and projected upward. The basic idea is that SIs are factored in by a recursive computation parallel to the standard one that builds up and interprets Logical Forms. Just as we have a well-defined notion of "standard" or "plain" meaning for any expression α, we also have a notion of "strengthened" or "scalar" meanings for any α. The latter is, in fact, a simple variant of the former, computed in a similar way. Essentially, whenever we hit a scalar term (computing bottom up) we introduce the corresponding implicature. This is then maintained until we find a monotonicity-reversing function. Upon encountering such a function, we remove the implicatures introduced thus far and perform a local recalibration (introducing the indirect implicatures). It is as if phrases (rather than root sentences) are passed through a pragmatic component, that is, a component sensitive to the quantity of information of relevant alternatives and other such factors. As a consequence of this shift, the problems with the recalcitrant connectives and quantifiers fall into place, some fairly complex cases of implicature come out right, and the resulting system remains computationally tractable. The next question (for further research) is whether other phenomena generally held to fall within pragmatics may be treated in a similar way or whether this is a characteristic of scalar implicatures and scalar reasoning.

On the NPI front, what seems to be going on is somewhat different. Essentially, NPIs are a marked form of indefinites. Their specificity is perhaps the presence of some kind of domain expansion (or willingness to consider alternative domains), which gives them a modal flavor. Being marked alter ego's of more basic forms, NPIs cannot be freely used. We need some justification to use them in place of their less marked alternatives. The idea here is that the use of NPIs (and, thus, modification of quantificational domains) must turn out to be more informative than the use of basic forms. This looks like a reasonable condition or presupposition of NPI use: generalizing over domain expansions is admissible only when it yields something stronger than that which one gets without such a generalization. And, given that NPIs are potential domain wideners of indefinites, strengthening can happen only in negative (DE) contexts—whence their peculiar distribution.

This leads immediately to the question, How exactly does the generalization over domain expansions (i.e., the universal closure) come about? How is it enforced? Several plausible answers can be explored. We have considered two. Such a closure may be viewed as an inherent semantic requirement to which NPIs are subject, a sort of "somewhere" condition of semantic well-formedness. Or perhaps closure is associated with a feature of elements that agrees with NPIs (where such elements, or rather their projection, map onto the scope of the relevant closure operation). In either case, we get the beginning of an interesting account of similarities and differences between NPIs and SIs. What they have in common is (local) comparison of degree of informativeness with a set of competitors: for SIs, their comparison among items on a scale, for NPIs, comparison with indefinites. Such comparison in informativeness is responsible for the sensitivity to polarity reversals. Where SIs and NPIs differ is in the dimensions of the respective comparisons. For SIs, such comparison is built into a recursive bottom-up interpretive process, where the relevant condition is checked at each step all the way up (whence the flip-flop of implicatures). For SIs, it is morphologically (i.e., lexically) driven. Hence, once the relevant condition is checked, that's it (no flip-flop). And if such a condition is part of a form of agreement (at a distance), some kind of locality effect is to be expected. We get, thus, a seemingly well-balanced overall picture of the two phenomena under discussion. Moreover, as we saw, this approach to NPIs might also solve some more specific problems of the immediate predecessors that inspire it.

The final main point of this investigation concerns a further difference between NPIs and SIs, namely, the fact that whereas the former display intervention effects, the latter do not. It is conceivable that intervention is just a facet of locality; this is particularly plausible since, as we saw, locality considerations play a very different role in SI-computation than in NPI licensing. However, a direct syntactic approach to intervention does not readily account for why interveners and noninterveners divide up the way they do. An interesting empirical generalization, in this connection, is that if we look at quantifiers and sentential operators, the interveners are all strong scalar terms; the noninterveners are, instead, weak ones. This suggests that intervention, in the case at hand, may have to do with the way in which implicatures come about. Our conjecture is that NPIs compete with the scalar meaning of indefinites. That is, NPIs are licensed only if they turn out to be stronger than the scalar value of the corresponding sentences with plain indefinites. What happens in intervention contexts is that an indirect implicature comes about (in presence of strong scalar terms), and this prevents NPIs from meeting the strengthening condition. On the other hand, if the interveners are weak scalar elements, no indirect implicature comes about and the NPI turns out to be stronger than its competitor.

In the standard view of the syntax/pragmatics interface, this kind of phenomena is just the type of things that shouldn't exist. And the explanation I have provided should in principle be impossible. If the computational system of grammar sets up interpreted logical forms for root sentences and then passes them onto the conceptual/intentional system for pragmatic processing, it clearly can have no access during its computation to the results of the latter. It is one of the tenets (or, as the case may be, dogmas) of such a view that syntactic (and semantic) computations cannot have direct access to pragmatics. In my proposed modification, this is, instead, quite conceivable. The condition in NPI-licensing is a clear illustration. A grammatical (morphosemantic) well-formedness condition in NPIs has to check on something that is usually held to belong to pragmatics. The resulting system is still, I would say, modular. The syntactic and semantic computation and the pragmatic one are autonomous. But now we don't wait until the end to do our pragmatics; we compute recursively. Consequently, at any stage or phase of the recursion, each one of the two systems can in principle have access to the results of the immediately previous phases of the other (nota bene: the results, not the inner workings).

My proposal on the intervention effect may well turn out to be wrong. Insofar as I can see, this would not, by itself, immediately undermine the proposals on SI-computation and NPI-licensing. They have been motivated on independent grounds (internal to the respective phenomena). It is true, however, that if my proposal on intervention is not wholly off the mark, it would constitute a particularly robust confirmation of the basic idea we have explored here: namely, that some aspects of pragmatic processing fall under the purview of grammar or, equivalently, that some aspects of the pragmatic system are more grammar-like than we thought so far.

Besides these general questions that concern central aspects of how grammar is organized, there are a host of side issues that call for further research. In investigating SIs, I've often appealed to intuitions about "default" values or about accommodation. Isn't this pushing the current linguistic methodology (of relying on intuitions) a bit far? Aren't some of the key judgments a bit too subtle? Well, perhaps this is an area (or another area) in which psycholinguistic experimentation and linguistic theorizing may fruitfully interact. Experiments may be designed to actually test the presence or absence of the relevant SIs in the target contexts. I've already mentioned Gualmini's et al. (2001) work in this connection. Noveck et al. (2001) try to explore the consequences on reasoning of the generalization on the distribution of SIs explored here. In particular, they set up a reasoning task in which pairs of premises, such as those in (150) and (151) are given out and subjects are asked whether a certain conclusion is warranted:

(150) a. If P or Q, then R; P and Q — Does R follow?
b. If P then P or Q; P — Does P and Q follow?

The inference in (150a) is overwhelmingly accepted [in contrast with what happens with (150b)], in spite of the fact that the second premise is given in conjunctive form. This confirms that the default interpretation of disjunction in the antecedent of a conditional is inclusive. What is interesting here is that we are dealing with abstract syllogistic frames with letter variables, where the only "real" words are *or* and *if*. . . *then*. Hence the relevant effect cannot be imputed to anything like scripts and lexical or world knowledge of any kind. It must be due to the meaning of the only "real" items that occur in the experimental material.

There are also interesting issues having to do with acquisition. Consider the pair in (151) and contrast it with the pair in (152):

(151) a. *Every student read anything.
b. Every student who read anything on language will know these facts.

(152) a. Every student wrote a paper or made a classroom presentation.
b. Every student who wrote a paper or read a classroom presentation will get an A.

It is not easy to figure out how a child can learn the contrast in (151). But it is even harder to imagine how she could learn the difference in meaning between (152a) and (152b). After all, in (151) we are dealing with the distribution of an overt morpheme. And it is conceivable (though not very plausible) that a sophisticated detector of statistical correlations might eventually zero in onto such a distributional quirk. But in cases like (152), all the action concerns meaning. Morphology or distributional patterns play no role. What goes on in (152) is simply that we interpret *or* in one way in (152a) and in another way in (152b). How is the child going to figure that out? It seems to me that the generalization under discussion yields a particularly strong version of the poverty of stimulus argument. It is thus interesting to find out when exactly the child starts acting in an adultlike manner with respect to implicature. Noveck (2001) finds out that children learn certain SIs relatively late because, for a fairly long time, they accept SI violations much more readily than the adult controls. He attributes this to a lack of (or slower maturation of) pragmatic knowledge. Reinhart (1999) has made some interesting suggestions relevant to Noveck's findings, inspired by the well-known difficulties children encounter with nonreflexive pronouns (i.e., principle B of the binding theory). Couching Reinhart's suggestions in the terminology adopted here, I can say that the non-adultlike behavior of children vis-à-vis implicatures may be due to the fact that implicature computation involves a comparison with a set of competitors. This task presumably requires more working memory than the plain meaning, and the relevant resources are not available to children. Thus, according to Reinhart, the problem is not so much in the lack of knowledge of pragmatic principles (say, quantity) or in the capacity of using them in reasoning. It is a task-specific limitation of working memory. Perhaps the present approach may help bring this issue into sharper focus. I have distinguished between the definition of "strong" meaning—namely, α^{s}, which involves taking into account relevant alternatives—and the final choice on how to increment the context, given a choice between two options. These two processes are clearly distinguished, and to the extent that they use similar principles (like quantity), they use them in very different ways. Perhaps the reasons for children's behavior is to be sought in these differences. Noveck's results are partly confirmed by the work of Gualmini et al. (2001), who, however, also find groups of children that perform in an adultlike manner quite early on. It is interesting that through a pragmatic felicity task (which involves inviting children to judge which of two target sentences better describes a given scene), Gualmini et al. also find out that the children who do not perform in an adultlike manner appear to be attuned to the fact that certain sentences are pragmatically more appropriate than others. Although they accept sentences with implicature violation, they also show a preference for the competitors. This seems consistent with Reinhart's hypothesis, interpreted in the light of the present approach. Children have pragmatic principles and apply them competently; but the working-memory resources necessary to compute α^{s} may take time to mature. Obviously, more work needs to be done in this area.

Besides these interface questions, there are many open problems internal to the phenomena we have investigated that I simply have to leave open at this point. In particular, there are several cases of intervention I either discussed in a very preliminary fashion (like *because* clauses) or could not discuss at all (e.g., the contrast of bridge and nonbridge verbs). I also said nothing on different types of NPIs (like minimizers, so called N-words in Romance, or Zwart's 1996 typology). Nor did I address the issue of the relation between Free-Choice items and NPIs. The viability of the present approach and of the overall perspective on which it is based ultimately rests also on how these matters will eventually be addressed.

Appendix: Formal definitions and examples

(1) For any expression α, $\|\alpha\|^{ALT}$, the set of potentially relevant alternatives to α, is defined as follows:
a. For α lexical,

$$\|\alpha\|^{ALT} = \begin{cases} \{\alpha_1, \ldots, \alpha_n, \ldots\}, \text{ if } \alpha \text{ is part of a scale } < \alpha_1, \ldots, \alpha_n, \ldots >, \\ \{\alpha\} \text{ otherwise} \end{cases}$$

To go on with the definition, it is useful to define a generalized operation of application that allows us to apply a set of functions to a set of arguments of the appropriate type. Let us call such an operation Ap. Here is its definition:

b. If B is a set of functions and A a set of arguments of a type appropriate to the functions in B, then

$$Ap(B,A) = \{\beta(\alpha); \beta \in B\ \alpha \in A\}$$

Whenever no confusion arises, I will simply write B(A) for Ap(B,A).

I now complete the definition of the set of relevant alternatives of an expression. I only consider the case corresponding to functional application (generalization to rules of binding is straightforward).

c. For $\alpha = [\beta\ \gamma]$, where β is of a functional type and γ of a suitable argumental type,

$$\|\alpha\|^{ALT} = \begin{cases} Ap(\{\|\beta\|\}, \|\gamma\|^{ALT}), & \text{if } \|\beta\|^{ALT} \text{ is a singleton} \\ Ap(\|\beta\|^{ALT}, \{\|\gamma\|\}), & \text{otherwise} \end{cases}$$

d. Examples:
$\|$John smokes $\|^{ALT}$ = {smoke' (j)}
$\|$John smokes or Mary smokes $\|^{ALT}$ =$\|$John smokes and Mary smokes $\|^{ALT}$ =
= { smoke(j) ∨ smoke'(m), smoke'(j) ∧ smoke'(m)}
$\|$it is not the case that John smokes or Mary smokes $\|^{ALT}$ =
= $\|$it is not the case that John smokes and Mary smokes $\|^{ALT}$ =
= { ¬ (smoke(j) ∨ smoke'(m)), ¬ (smoke'(j) ∧ smoke'(m))}
From now on, we write α^{ALT} for $\|\alpha\|^{ALT}$.

The next step is defining a function that selects the member from an alternative set that is immediately stronger than our designated target. If β is the target [i.e., what gets uttered) and α^{ALT} the relevant alternative set, the member of α^{ALT} immediately stronger than β [in symbols $S_\beta(\alpha^{ALT})$] is defined as follows:

(2)

$$S_\beta(\alpha^{ALT}) = \begin{cases} \alpha', \text{ where } \alpha' \text{ is the weakest member of } \alpha^{ALT} \text{ such that } \alpha' \text{ entails } \beta \text{ and not vice versa, if there is such an } \alpha'. \\ \bot \text{ (the contradiction), otherwise} \end{cases}$$

When β is understood (e.g., as being identical to α), I'll omit marking it explicitly and simply write $S(\alpha^{ALT})$.

We now define for any α, the set $\|\alpha\|^{S}$ of its admissible strong meanings. It will be the *smallest* set of semantic values of the appropriate type that satisfies the following conditions:

(3) a. For α lexical, $\|\alpha\|^{S} = \{ \|\alpha\| \}$ (B: base of the recursion)

b. Suppose $\|\alpha\|$ is of type t. Then
$\|\alpha\|^{S} \supseteq \xi \wedge \neg S(\alpha^{ALT})$: $\xi \in (\|\alpha\|^{S} \}$ (KR: Krifka's rule)

c. Suppose $\alpha = [\beta\ \gamma]$, where $\|\beta\|^{S}$ is of type <a,b> and $\|\gamma\|^{S}$ of type a. Then (SA: Strong apply)

$$\|[\beta\ \gamma]\|^{S} \supseteq \begin{cases} Ap(\|\beta\|^{S}, \|\gamma\|^{S}), \text{ if } \|\beta\| \text{ is not DE} \\ \{ \|\beta\|^{S}(\|\gamma\|) \wedge \neg S_{\|\beta\|(\|\gamma\|)}(\|\beta\|(\gamma^{ALT})) \}, \text{ otherwise} \end{cases}$$

I assume that Boolean operators $\subset$, $\wedge$, $\neg$ are generalized to all types that "end in t" in the usual manner. Strictly speaking, $\|\alpha\|^{S}$ is a relation, not a function (see examples):

(4) John smokes or Mary smokes.

a. $\|$John smokes$\|^{S} \supseteq (\|$smoke$\|^{S}(\|$John$\|^{S})$ [by SA]= {smoke'(j)} [by B]

b. $\|$Mary smokes$\|^{S} \supseteq \|$smoke$\|^{S}(\|$Mary$\|^{S})$ = {smoke'(m)}

c. $\|$John smokes or Mary smokes$\|^{S} \supseteq$ {smoke'(j) $\vee$ (smoke'(m)} [by SA]

d. $\|$John smokes or Mary smokes$\|^{S} \supseteq \|$Mary smokes or John smokes$\|^{S} \supseteq \{ \xi \wedge \neg S_{[smoke'(m) \vee smoke'(j)}$ ([smoke'(m) $\vee$ smoke'(j)] (^{AL}) : $\xi \in \|$John smokes or Mary smokes$\|^{S}$ } [by KR]

e. $\|$John smokes or Mary smokes$\|^{S} \supseteq \|$Mary smokes or John smokes$\|^{S} \supseteq$ { ([smoke'(m) $\vee$ smoke'(j)] $\wedge \neg S_{[smoke'(m) \vee smoke'(j)}$ ([smoke'(m) $\vee$ smoke'(j)]^{ALT} } [from (c) and d) and tautologous transformations]

f. $\|$Mary smokes or John smokes$\|^{S} \supseteq$ { [smoke'(m) $\vee$ smoke'(j)] $\wedge \neg S_{[smoke'(m) \vee smoke'(j)}$ ({ [smoke'(m) $\vee$ smoke'(j)], [smoke'(m) $\wedge$ smoke'(j)]})} [def. of ALT]

g. $\|$Mary smokes or John smokes$\|^{S} \supseteq$\{ [smoke'(m) $\vee$ smoke'(j)] $\wedge \neg$ [smoke'(m) $\wedge$ smoke'(j)]}, [def. of S]

We abbreviate (g) as follows:

h. $\|$Mary smokes or John smokes$\|^{S} \supseteq$\{ [smoke'(m) $\vee^{S}$ smoke'(j)]}

i. $\|$Mary smokes or John smokes$\|^{S}$ = {[smoke'(m) $\vee$ smoke'(j)], [smoke'(m) $\vee^{S}$smoke'(j)]} [from (c) and (g), by the smallest set condition].

(5) The following derivation contains a slight abuse in the use of lambas. It could be easily avoided at the cost of being more precise or pedantic on the semantics of abstraction.

Someone$_i$ [e$_i$ smokes or e$_i$ drinks].

a. $\|$ e$_i$ smokes or e$_i$ smokes$\|^S$ = {[smoke'(e$_i$) $\vee$ smoke'(e$_i$)], [smoke'(e$_i$) $\vee^S$ smoke'(e$_i$)]}

b. $\|$ someone$_i$ [e$_i$ smokes or e$_i$ smokes]$\|^S$ $\supseteq$ ($\|$ someone$_i$ $\|^S$(λe$_i$ $\|$[e$_i$ smokes or e$_i$ smokes]$\|^S$) [SA + slight abuse of notation] $\supseteq$ {(someone$_I$ λe$_i$ [smoke'(e$_i$) $\vee$ smoke'(e$_i$)], (someone$_I$ λe$_i$ [smoke'(e$_i$) $\vee^S$ smoke'(e$_i$)]}

c. $\|$ someone$_i$ [e$_i$ smokes or e$_i$ smokes]$\|^S$ $\supseteq$ {(someone$_i$ λe$_i$ [smoke'(e$_i$) $\vee$ smoke'(e$_i$)] $\wedge\neg$ S (someone$_i$ λe$_i$ [smoke'(e$_i$) $\vee$ smoke'(e$_i$)]]^{ALT}), (someone$_I$ λe$_i$ [smoke'(e$_i$) $\vee^S$ smoke'(e$_i$)] $\wedge\neg$ S (someone$_i$ λe$_i$ [smoke'(e$_i$) $\vee$ smoke'(e$_i$)]]^{ALT})} [KR]

d. $\|$ someone$_i$ [e$_i$ smokes or e$_i$ smokes]$\|^S$ $\supseteq$ {(someone$_i$ λe$_i$ [smoke'(e$_i$) $\vee$ smoke'(e$_i$)] $\wedge\neg$ everyone$_I$ λe$_i$ [smoke'(e$_i$) $\vee$ smoke'(e$_i$)], someone$_I$ λe$_i$ [smoke'(e$_i$) $\vee^S$ smoke'(e$_i$)] $\wedge\neg$ everyone$_i$ λe$_i$ [smoke'(e$_i$) $\vee$ smoke'(e$_i$)]} [def. of ALT]

e. $\|$ someone$_i$ [e$_i$ smokes or e$_i$ smokes]$\|^S$ = { someone$_i$ λe$_i$ [smoke'(e$_i$) $\vee$ smoke'(e$_i$)], someone$_i$ λe$_i$ [smoke'(e$_i$) $\vee$ smoke'(e$_i$)] $\wedge\neg$ everyone$_i$ λe$_i$ [smoke'(e$_i$) $\vee$ smoke'(e$_i$)], someone$_I$ λe$_i$[smoke'(e$_i$) $\vee^S$ smoke'(e$_i$)] $\wedge\neg$ everyone$_i$ λe$_i$ [smoke'(e$_i$) $\vee$ smoke'(e$_i$)]} [from (d) and (b) by the smallest set condition]

(6) It is not the case that John smokes or Mary smokes.

a. $\|$it is not the case that John smokes or Mary smokes$\|^S$ $\supseteq$ { $\|$not$\|^S$ ($\|$ John smokes or Mary smokes$\|$) $\wedge$ $\neg$ S($\|$not $\|$($\|$ John smokes or Mary smokes$\|^{ALT}$)) } [by SA]

b. $\|$it is not the case that John smokes or Mary smokes$\|^S$ $\supseteq$ { $\neg$ $\|$ John smokes or Mary smokes$\|$ $\wedge$ $\neg$ S($\|$not $\|$($\|$ John smokes or Mary smokes$\|^{ALT}$)) } [B]

c. $\neg$ [smoke'(j) smoke'(m)] $\wedge$ $\neg$ S($\|$not $\|$($\|$ John smokes or Mary smokes$\|^{ALT}$))}

d. {$\neg$ [smoke'(j) $\vee$ smoke'(m)] $\wedge$ $\neg$ S($\|$not$\|$({ smoke'(j) $\vee$ smoke'(m), smoke'(j) $\wedge$ smoke'(m)}))} [def. of $\|$ $\|^{ALT}$]

d. $\|$not $\|$({ smoke'(j) $\vee$ smoke'(m), smoke'(j) $\wedge$ smoke'(m)}) = { $\neg$ [smoke'(j) $\vee$ smoke'(m)], $\neg$ [smoke'(j) $\wedge$ smoke'(m)]} [def. of Ap]

e. Since no member of the set in (e) is stronger than $\neg$[smoke'(j) $\vee$ smoke'(m)], it follows that

$$\text{S}(\|\text{not }\|(\{\text{ smoke'(j)} \vee \text{smoke'(m), smoke'(j)} \wedge \text{smoke'(m)}\})) = \bot$$

Hence,

f. {$\neg$ [smoke'(j) $\vee$ smoke'(m)] $\wedge$ $\neg$ $\bot$} [from (c) by substitution of identicals]

g. {$\neg$ [smoke'(j) $\vee$ smoke'(m)]} [from (f) by tautologous transformations]

(7) a. I doubt that it is not the case that John or Mary smokes.
To simplify things a bit, let us represent (a) as not [not [John smokes or Mary smokes]].

b. $\|$ not [not [John smokes or Mary smokes]($\|^S$ $\supseteq$ { $\neg$ ($\|$ (not (John smokes or Mary smokes]] $\|$)$\wedge\neg$ S ($\neg$ $\neg$[smoke'(j) $\vee$ smoke'(m)(^{ALT})} [by SA]

c. {$\neg$ $\neg$[smoke'(j) $\vee$ smoke'(m)] $\wedge$ $\neg$ S ({$\neg$ $\neg$[smoke'(j) $\vee$ smoke'(m)], $\neg$ $\neg$[smoke'(j) $\wedge$ smoke'(m)] })} [by def. of $\|$ $\|^{ALT}$]

d. $\{[smoke'(j) \vee smoke'(m)] \wedge \neg S(\{[smoke'(j) \vee smoke'(m)], [smoke'(j) \wedge smoke'(m)]\})\}$ [tautologous transformations]

e. $\{[smoke'(j) \vee smoke'(m)] \wedge \neg [smoke'(j) \wedge smoke'(m)]\}$ [by def. of S]

(8) Nobody that smokes and drinks gets to be 60.
LF: [[No [body that t smokes and drinks]] [t gets to be sixty]]

a. Let us write 60(x) for "x gets to be (at least) sixty."

b. $\|[t \text{ gets to be sixty}]\|^s \supseteq \{60(x) \wedge \neg 61(x)\}$ [by KR]

c. $\|$ No body that smokes and drinks $\| = NO(\lambda x[person'(x) \wedge [smoke'(x) \wedge drink'(x)]])$

d. $\|$ No body that smokes and drinks $\|^s \supseteq \{NO(\lambda x[person'(x) \wedge [smoke'(x) \wedge drink'(x)]]) \wedge \neg S(NO(\lambda x[person'(x) \wedge [smoke'(x) \wedge drink'(x)]^{ALT}))\}$ [by SA]

e. $\|$ No body that smokes and drinks $\|^s \supseteq \{NO(\lambda x[person'(x) \wedge [smoke'(x) \wedge drink'(x)]]) \wedge \neg S(\{NO(\lambda x[person'(x) \wedge [smoke'(x) \wedge drink'(x)]), NO(\lambda x[person'(x) \wedge [smoke'(x) \vee drink'(x)])\})\}$ [by def. of ALT and Ap]

f. $\|$ Nobody that smokes and drinks $\|^s \supseteq \{NO(\lambda x[person'(x) \wedge [smoke'(x) \wedge drink'(x)]]) \wedge \neg NO(\lambda x[person'(x) \wedge [smoke'(x) \vee drink'(x)])\})\}$ [by def. S]

g. $\|$ Nobody that smokes and drinks $\|^s \supseteq \{\lambda P[NO(\lambda x[person'(x) \wedge [smoke'(x) \wedge drink'(x)]])(P) \wedge SOME((\lambda x[person'(x) \wedge [smoke'(x) \vee drink'(x)])(P)]\}$ [tautologous transformations]

h. $\|$ [[No [body that t smokes and drinks]([t gets to be sixty]] $\|^s \supseteq \{\lambda P[NO(\lambda x[person'(x) \wedge [smoke'(x) \wedge drink'(x)]])(P) \wedge SOME((\lambda x[person'(x) \wedge [smoke'(x) \vee drink'(x)])(P)] (\lambda x[60(x)]) \wedge \neg S(NO(\lambda x[person(x) \wedge [smoke(x) \wedge drink(x)]) ((\lambda x[60(x)]^{ALT}))\}$ [by SA]

i. $\|$ ([No [body that t smokes and drinks]] [t gets to be sixty]] $\|^s \supseteq \{NO(\lambda x[person'(x) \wedge [smoke'(x) \wedge drink'(x)]])((\lambda x[60(x)]) \wedge SOME((\lambda x[person'(x) \wedge [smoke'(x) \vee drink'(x)]])((\lambda lx[60(x)]) \wedge \neg S(\{NO(\lambda x[person'(x) \wedge [smoke'(x) \wedge drink'(x)]) ((\lambda x[59 (x)]), NO(\lambda x[person'(x) \wedge [smoke'(x) \wedge drink'(x)]) ((\lambda x[60(x)]), (NO(\lambda x[person(x) \wedge [smoke'(x) \wedge drink'(x)]) ((\lambda x[61(x)])\})\}$ [def. of ALT and GenAp

j. $\|$ [[No [body that t smokes and drinks]] [t gets to be sixty]] $\|^s \supseteq \{NO(\lambda x[person'(x) \wedge [smoke'(x) \wedge drink'(x)]])((\lambda x[60(x)]) \wedge SOME((\lambda x[person'(x) \wedge [smoke'(x) \vee drink'(x)])((\lambda x[60(x)]) \wedge \neg NO(\lambda x[person'(x) \wedge [smoke'(x) \wedge drink'(x)]) ((\lambda x[59 (x)])\}$ [def. of S]

k. $\|$ [[No [body that t smokes and drinks]] [t gets to be sixty]] $\|^s = NO(\lambda x[person'(x) \wedge [smoke'(x) \wedge drink'(x)]])((\lambda x[60(x)]) \wedge SOME((\lambda x[person'(x) \wedge [smoke'(x) \vee drink'(x)])((\lambda x[60(x)])] \wedge SOME(\lambda x[person'(x) \wedge [smoke'(x) \wedge drink'(x)]) ((\lambda x[59 (x)])$ [tautologous transformations; smallest set condition]

Notes

The first version of this work was presented in the fall of 1999 at the Center for Cognitive Science in Lyon and at the Pontignano workshop (which concluded Chomsky's visit to Italy). Subsequent versions were presented at NELS, University of California at Irvine, UCLA, University of Tuebingen (Fall 2000); at the DGfS meeting in Leipzig and at Massachusetts Institute of Technology (Spring 2001). All those audiences contributed significantly to give shape to the original ideas. I also would like to thank I. Caponigro, C. Cecchetto, S. Crain, J. Gajewski, A. Gualmini, T. Guasti, E. Guerzoni, L. Meroni, F. Panzeri, O. Percus, and U. Sauerland.

1. See, for example, Fauconnier (1975), Horn (1989: 230ff.), Krifka (1995), Landman (1998), Israel (1998), among many others.

2. The relevant entailment holds whenever the set of men is nonempty. Or, equivalently, we will be assuming a presuppositional view of determiners like *every*, according to which *every N* is taken to be uninterpretable as there are no Ns in the domain of quantification. See, for example, de Jong and Verkuyl (1985).

3. On scales, besides the works cited in the text, see, for example, Gazdar (1979) and Hirschberg (1985). Heim (class lectures, Fall 1999) individuates in monotonicity a necessary condition for being part of a scale. For arguments that monotonicity is not also a sufficient condition, see Landman (1998).

4. Two caveats are in order. First, the notion of entailment is to be understood as generalized in the usual way to all types (that "end in t"—see Partee and Rooth 1983). Second, entailment must be understood as being relativized to contextually shared knowledge in the sense of Stalnaker (1978). See Heim (1984) and von Fintel (1999) for relevant elaborations of Stalnaker's view.

5. U. Sauerland (personal communication) suggests that one way around this problem might be analyzing disjunction $p \vee q$ by using such epistemic possibility operators as $[\Diamond p \wedge \Diamond q]$. The consequences of this move need careful consideration. For example, it is not clear that a scalar treatment of the exclusiveness implicature associated with disjunction can be maintained under such a view (without ad hoc assumptions).

6. The localist may be accused of predicting too strong truth implicatures with universal quantifiers. (a) is predicted to implicate (b):

(a) Everyone wrote a paper or made a presentation.
(b) Everyone either wrote a paper or made a classroom presentation and not both.

The localist would predict the implicature to be

(c) It is not the case that everyone did both.

I think that the (possible) presence of the strong implicature (b) is plausible. Suppose we make a bet on (the truth of) (a). I bet that everyone wrote a paper or made a classroom presentation. Then we find out that half of the people did both (while the other half, one of the two). What would happen? I think there would be discussion on who won the bet. If the embedded strong implicature was simply not there, there should be no ground whatsoever for arguing in such a case.

7. I am assuming that (i) subjects originate within the VP, (ii) *or* can coordinate VPs, and (iii) QR can apply at the VP level. Accordingly, the subject *Mary* in (27b) is extracted across the board out of the coordinated VP. These assumptions are made just for explicitness sake. None is crucial to the conceptual point at hand.

8. One of the few authors who takes an explicit position in favor of such a view is Landman (1998). His arguments are developed in the context of a treatment of numerals within an event-based semantics. The present chapter is an attempt at pursuing his proposal for all implicatures (while remaining neutral with respect to event semantics).

9. An alternative methodology would involve considering the implicature separately from the meaning. Thus, for example (28a), repeated here, would implicate (b):

(a) It's false that Sue harassed some students.
(b) It's false that Sue harassed some though not all the students.

But the results would not change. If (a) implicates (b), then (28c) ought to be a possible continuation.

10. For some speakers (more tolerant in the use of the indicative future for optatives)

the contrast is not as sharp; however, in most dialects the subjuntive contrasts with the indicative future in forcing the optative interpretation.

11. Something similar also happens with the quantifiers. Even in positive contexts, we do not often consider all of the possible values of a given scale. For example, a sentence like (a) below clearly has (c) as an implicature; whether it also implicates (b) is much less clear. It will depend on what is specifically at issue in the context:

a. Some students will do well.
b. Not many students will do well.
c. Not every student will do well.

This means that out of a certain scale (say <some, many, most, every>) we select the contextually most relevant segment. In the case of quantifiers, in the absence of information to the contrary, the safest bet is often <some, every>.

12. I owe this way of putting it to a suggestion of H. Truckenbrodt.

13. The system I have in mind is the version of Dynamic Intensional Logic developed in Chierchia (1995). The dynamic aspect has its importance because implicatures interact with presuppositions. The basic idea of dynamic semantics is that sentences are interpreted as functions from contexts into new contexts. Such functions are undefined for contexts that do not satisfy the presuppositions of the sentence. Thus (modulo accommodation) it is impossible to update a context c through a sentence S if c does not satisfy S's presuppositions. The reader not familiar with dynamic semantics won't need anything beyond this general idea to follow the proposal.

14. The formal definition employs a generalized notion of functional application Ap(A,B), which lets us apply sets of functions to sets of arguments.

15. Thanks to Jon Gajewski and Irene Heim for pointing out a bug in a previous formulation of this rule.

16. An assumption I will be making is that every Boolean operator is generalized to functional types (that "end in t"—cf. Partee and Rooth 1983 for discussion) through a "pointwise" definition. For example, if P and Q are predicates (in Montague's notation, of type $\langle e,t \rangle$), then

(b) $P \wedge Q = \lambda x\ [P(x) \wedge Q(x)]$

and so on.

17. My interpretive procedure has a seemingly odd consequence. Consider the following sentences:

(a) John smokes or drinks.
(b) It is not true that John doesn't smoke or drink.

Sentence (b) involves a double negation and it is truth conditionally equivalent to sentence (a). Furthermore, they have the same implicature (that John doesn't do both). However, the set of strong meaning of sentence (a) technically includes also its plain one, whereas this is not so for sentence (b):

(c) Strong meanings of sentence (a): $\{\text{smoke}(j) \vee \text{drink}(j),\ \text{smoke}(j) \vee \text{drink}(j) \wedge \neg\ \text{smoke}(j) \wedge \text{drink}(j)\}$.
(d) Strong meanings of sentence (b): $\{\ \text{smoke}(j) \vee \text{drink}(j) \wedge \neg\ \text{smoke}(j) \wedge \text{drink}(j)\}$.

The strong meanings of sentence (a) are built up directly via Krifka's rule, whereas the strong meanings of sentence (b) come in indirectly via functional application. This looks like a quirk, without any empirical effect. But it turns out to have interesting (if controversial) consequences in connection with the intervention effect of NPIs. We will come back to this point in section 4.3.

18. This can be seen as part of the general conditions for felicitous use of a sentence S in a context c, in the spirit of Stalnaker (1978). Schematically,

Felicity conditions on context updates.
A sentence S is felicitous in a context c relative to its value V(S) iff:
i. S's presuppositions relative to V(S) are met in c

$$(c + V(S) \text{ is defined})$$

ii. V(S) is the most informative interpretation that doesn't lead to contradiction

$$(c + V(S) \neq \emptyset$$
$$c + V(S) \subset c$$
$$c + V(S) \subseteq c + V'(S), \text{ for all } V' \neq V)$$

19. In slightly different terms, we may view the proposal as follows. The plain semantic value of a sentence ϕ tells us how a context c may be modified by it (i.e., it yields a recursive characterization of a context incrementation function $c + \phi$). The strengthened semantic value yields a notion of strengthened context incrementation ($c +^{s} \phi$) by taking into account the role of relevant alternatives. Speakers will tend to use cooperatively these two manners of adding information to the context that grammar makes available.

20. Much of the same effect can be obtained by indexing formulas to situation variables (see Percus 2000 for a recent discussion). All that I say about quantificational domains can be recouched in terms of situations.

21. Lahiri (1998) doesn't explicitly discuss the issue of locality. But Sauerland (1999) has presented a minimality-based account of intervention that builds on Lahiri's proposal.

22. See, for example, the discussion in Haspelmath (1997: 106ff. and references quoted there); cf. also Israel (1998).

23. This holds, of course, if Δ is nonempty (i.e., nontrivial).

24. I believe that the approach just sketched in terms of universal closure of the domain (or situation) variable might also be extended in an interesting way to Free-Choice *any*, in the spirit of Dayal's (1998) proposal. But exploration of this must be left to some other occasion.

25. The operator O can be given a generalized quantifier version. And the *some* alternatives can be specified in model theoretic terms through a recursive definition (akin, once again, the how Rooth (1985) defines focal alternatives or to how I define scalar alternatives).

26. Some kind of feature checking also seems to be necessary to mark the varying strength of NPIs. As Zwarts (1996) shows, NPIs may require negative heads of varying strength (DE, antiadditive, or antimorphic). My semantics of NPIs has the potential to explain why NPIs requires DE-ness. But any more stringent requirement must come from something else. Also relevant is the question of how local the relation between the NPI and the trigger is allowed to be. Here, too, there is some cross-linguistic variation that may be related to different properties of the relevant morphological features.

27. Roofing might also be derived from the semantics alone. Suppose, for example, you have two negative heads stacked up.

(a) . . . NEG1 . . . NEG2 . . . NPI . . .

If we close at the level of NEG1, the derivation crashes, for strengthening cannot be met because the two negations cancel each other out. Closing at the level of NEG2 is permissible. This predicts that if we have a sequence of negative heads, we could have closure (i.e., check that strengthening is met) at any odd-numbered negative site insofar as semantics goes:

(b) . . . NEG 1 . . . NEG2 . . . NEG3 . . . NPI . . .

So, for the moment, I don't have a strong argument against a purely semantic account of roofing. But it strikes me as implausible that things work this way.

28. For example, Krifka (1995) builds into his theory conditions on where the "assertion" operators that check the semantic condition on NPI licensing may be inserted.

29. For a discussion of how this may occur consistent with the general line we are exploring here, see von Fintel (1999).

30. Space prevents me from getting into intervention effects with the definite article and with nonbridge verbs. I think, however, that that also comes for free, roughly along the lines suggested in Krifka (1995).

31. I owe this point to Dominique Sportiche.

32. Recall that in my approach, a sentence such as *Few students know any linguistics* has two strong values, one with the implicature, the other without it (whereas sentences with indirect implicatures have only one strong value). This is where treating $\| \|^{s}$ as a relation, rather than as a function, comes in handy since it provides a straightforward mechanics to capture the idea discussed in the text.

33. In Gualmini et al. (2001), adults where asked which sentence, between (136) and "no pirate stole a jewel or a necklace," would better describe the situation at hand. The reply was overwhelmingly in favor of the latter, thus showing that adults were attuned to the pragmatic infelicity of (149) in this situation.

34. It seems to me that the spirit of the present proposal on intervention is close to that of Szabolcsi and Zwarts's (1992) on weak islands. But obviously we cannot jump to conclusions concerning all sorts of intervention-type effects.

References

Atlas, J., & S. Levinson. (1981). "It-Clefts, Informativeness, and Logical Form: Radical Pragmatics." In P. Cole, ed., *Radical Pragmatics*. New York: Academic Press.

Chierchia, G. (1995). "Individual Level Predicates as Inherent Generics." In G. Carlson and J. Pelletier, eds., *The Generic Book*. Chicago: University of Chicago Press.

Chomsky, N. (1999). *Derivation by Phase*. MITWPL 18.

Dayal, V. (1998). "Any as Inherent Modal." *Linguistics and Philosophy*, 21: 433–476.

Diesing, M. (1992). *Indefinites*. Cambridge, Mass.: MIT Press.

Dowty, D. (1979). *Word Meaning in Montague Grammar*. Dordrecht: Reidel.

Fauconnier, G. (1975). "Pragmatic Scales and Logical Structure." *Linguistic Inquiry* 6.

Fintel, K. von. (1999). "NPI-Licensing, Strawson-Entailment, and Context Dependency." *Journal of Semantics* 16, 97–148.

Gazdar, G. (1979). *Pragmatics: Implicature, Presupposition, and Logical Form*. New York: Academic Press.

Giannakidou, A. (1997). The Landscape of Polarity Items. Ph.D. diss., University of Groeningen, Germany.

Grice, P. (1989). *Studies in the Way of Words*. Cambridge, Mass.: Harvard University Press.

Gualmini, A., S. Crain, L. Meroni, G. Chierchia, M. T. Guasti. (2001). The Semantics-Pragmatics Interface in Child Language. Paper presented at Salt XI, New York University, New York.

Haspelmath, M. (1997). *Indefinite Pronouns*. Oxford: Oxford University Press.

Heim, I. (1984). "A Note on Polarity Sensitivity and Downward Entailingness." NELS 14.

Higginbotham, J. (1991). "Either/Or." *Proceedings of NELS* 21.

Hirschberg, J. (1985). A Theory of Scalar Implicature. Ph.D. diss., University of Pennsylvania, Philadelphia.

Horn, L. (1972). On the Semantic Properties of Logical Operators in English. Ph.D. diss., UCLA; distributed by IULC.

Horn, L. (1989). *A Natural History of Negation*. Chicago: University of Chicago Press.

Israel, M. (1998). *The Rhetoric of Grammar: Scalar Reasoning and Polarity Sensitivity*. Ph.D. diss., University of California, San Diego.

Jong, F. de, and H. Verkuyl. (1985). "Generalized Quantifiers: The Properness of their Strength." In J. van Benthem & A. ter Meulen, eds., *Generalized Quantifiers in Natural Language*. Dordrecht: Foris.

Kadmon, N., & F. Landman. (1993). "*Any*." *Linguistics and Philosophy* 15, 353–422.

Kempson, R. (1975). *Presuppositions and the Delimitation of Semantics*. Cambridge: Cambridge University Press.

Krifka, M. (1995). "The Semantics and Pragmatics of Polarity Items." *Linguistic Analysis* 25, 209–257.

Krifka, M., et al. (1995). "Genericity: An Introduction." In G. Carlson & J. Pelletier, eds., *The Generic Book.* Chicago: University of Chicago Press.

Ladusaw, W. (1979). Polarity Sensitivity as Inherent Scope Relation. Ph.D. diss., University of Texas, Austin; distributed by IULC.

Lahiri, U. (1998). "Focus and Negative Polarity in Hindi." *Natural Language Semantics* 6, 57–125.

Landman, F. (1998). "Plurals and Maximalization." In S. Rothstein, ed., *Events and Grammar*. Dordrecht: Kluwer.

Levinson, S. (2000). *Presumptive Meanings*. Cambridge, Mass.: MIT Press.

Linebarger, M. (1981). The Grammar of Negative Polarity. Ph.D. diss., Massachusetts Institute of Technology, Cambridge.

Noveck, I. (2001). "When Children Are More Logical Than Adults: Investigations of Scalar Implicature." *Cognition* 78/2, 165–188.

Noveck, I., G. Chierchia, F. Chevaux, R. Guelmiuger, E. Sylvestre. (2001). "Linguistic-Pragmatic Factors in Interpreting Disjunctions," ms., Centre for Cognitive Science, Lyon.

Partee, B. H. (1987). "Noun Phrase Interpretation and Type-shifting Principles." In J. Groenendijk, M. Stokhov, F. Veltman. eds., *Studies in Discourse Representation Theory and the Theory of Generalized Quantifiers*. Dordrecht: Foris.

Partee, B. H., & M. Rooth. (1983). "Generalized Conjunction and Type Ambiguity." In R. Bauerle, C. Schwarze, & A. von Stechow, eds., *Meaning, Use and Interpretation of Language*. Berlin: de Gruyter.

Percus, O. (2000). "Constraints on Some Other Variables in Syntax." *Natural Language Semantics* 8, 175–229.

Reinhart, T. (1999). "The Processing Cost of Reference-Set Computation: Guess Patterns in Acquisition." OTS Working Papers, Utrecht.

Rizzi, L. (2001). "Relativized Minimality Effects." In M. Baltin & C. Collins, ed., *Handbook of Syntactic Theory*. Oxford: Blackwell.

Rooth, M. (1985). *Association with Focus*. Ph.D. diss., University of Massachusetts, Amherst.

Sauerland, U. (1999). Paper presented at the meeting at the Centre for Cognitive Science, Lyon.

Stalnaker, R. (1978). "Assertion." In P. Cole, ed., *Syntax and Semantics 9: Pragmatics*. New York: Academic Press.

Szabolcsi, A., & F. Zwarts. (1992). "Weak Islands and an Algebraic Semantics for Scope Taking." *Natural Language Semantics* 1, 235–284.

Westertahl, D. (1988). "Quantifiers in Formal and natural Languages." In D. Gabbay & F. Guenthner, eds., *Handbook of Philosophical Logic*, vol. 4. Dordrecht: Kluwer.

Zwarts, F. (1996). "Three Types of Polarity." In F. Hamm & E. Hinrichs, eds., *Plural Quantification*. Dordrecht: Kluwer.

3

NOAM CHOMSKY

Beyond Explanatory Adequacy

I will assume here an approach to the study of language that takes the object of inquiry to be an internal property of persons, a subcomponent of (mostly) the brain that is dedicated specifically to language:[1] the human "Faculty of Language" (FL), to adapt a traditional term to a new context. This "biolinguistic approach" was controversial when it took shape almost half a century ago, and remains so, but without warrant, in my opinion.[2] A stronger thesis is that the biolinguistic approach has a kind of privileged status, in that every constructive approach to human language and its use presupposes it, or something similar, at least tacitly. That, too, seems to me tenable, but I will not pursue the issue here.

FL appears to be a species property, close to uniform across a broad range. It has a genetically determined initial state S_0, which determines the possible states it can assume. Suppose we also adopt—if it is too strong, only for convenience—a strong uniformity thesis for language acquisition that holds that each attainable state of FL is a further specification of S_0 with parameters valued;[3] at S_0, all parameters are set with unmarked values. Then each attained state (including S_0) is a possible (I-)language L. We can then formulate without complication the familiar idealization: S_0 (= LAD) maps primary linguistic data (PLD) to L. We then seek to discover theories that meet the conditions of descriptive and explanatory adequacy—that are true, respectively, of L (particular grammars) and of S_0 (universal grammar, UG).

It was clear from the outset that within the biolinguistic framework, this formulation is oversimplified in crucial respects. The initial conditions for (the abstract model of) language acquisition include more than S_0. The properties of the attained language L result from the interaction of three factors:[4]

(1) 1. Individual experience (PLD), which selects among the options allowed by S_0
2. S_0 itself, a product of evolution
3. General properties of organic systems

in this case computational systems incorporating, it is reasonable to expect, principles of efficient computation. The picture is familiar in the general study of organic systems. Work of D'Arcy Thompson and Alan Turing on form and morphogenesis is a classic illustration of 3. but recognition of its importance goes back to the origins of evolutionary biology, and the basic point is a virtual truism: natural selection can only function within a "channel" of options afforded by natural law, including properties of complex systems. One current example that may be suggestive in the present context is work by Christopher Cherniak, who has been exploring the idea that minimization of "wire length," as in microchip design, should produce the "best of all possible brains," and has sought to explain in these terms the neuroanatomy of nematodes and some properties of nervous systems generally, such as the fact that the brain is as far forward as possible on the body axis.[5]

One can plausibly trace interest in factor 3. back to the Galilean intuition that "nature is perfect," from the tides to the flight of birds, and that it is the task of the scientist to discover in just what sense this is true. However obscure it may be, that intuition about what Haeckel called nature's "Sinn für das Schone" has been a guiding theme of modern science ever since, perhaps its defining characteristic.[6]

In principle, then, we can seek a level of explanation deeper than explanatory adequacy, asking not only *what* the properties of language are but also *why* they are that way.

For familiar and substantial reasons, research concentrated on the problems of descriptive and explanatory adequacy, restricted to factors 1. and 2. The choice of terminology reflects the feeling that factors of category 3. were beyond the range of feasible inquiry, though they are always prominent even in pursuit of the narrower concerns, as part of the motivation for "best theory" considerations. That these limits might be transcended was suggested by the crystallization of the Principles and Parameters program in discussions at the Scuola Normale Superiore in Pisa in 1979 and subsequently. This approach offered a way to overcome the tension between descriptive and explanatory adequacy for the first time and at once suggested that questions of category 3. might be directly addressed in a serious way. Various efforts were made through the 1980s, which a few years later attained some substantive results (e.g., in recasting problems of "reconstruction" in terms of reduction of the theory of movement to its bare essentials) and seemed to show considerable promise, coming to be called "the minimalist program," by now with a rich and varied literature. Whether further optimism is warranted is hardly a topic for useful debate; as always in the case of research intuitions, time will tell.

Assuming that these questions can now be seriously placed on the research agenda, we can proceed further to disaggregate S_0 into elements that have a principled explanation, as well as others that remain unexplained at this level of analysis and must be attributed to something independent: perhaps path-dependent evolutionary processes or properties of the brain that remain unknown. These would have to be studied along similar lines, sorting out the effect of general principles (physical, chemical, mathematical), interface conditions, and a residue to be accounted for in other terms. The principled elements of S_0 are the conditions imposed on FL by the systems with which it interacts. If language is to be usable at all, its design must satisfy an "interface condition" IC: the information in the expressions generated by L must be accessible to other systems, including the sensorimotor (SM) and conceptual-intentional (C-I) systems that enter into thought and action. We can therefore restate the deeper *why* question. Insofar as properties of L can be accounted for in terms of IC and general properties of computational efficiency and the like, they have a principled explanation: we will have validated the Galilean intuition of perfection of nature in this domain.

The minimalist program is the attempt to explore these questions. Its task is to examine every device (principle, idea, etc.) that is employed in characterizing languages to determine to what extent it can be eliminated in favor of a principled account in terms of general conditions of computational efficiency and the interface condition that the organ must satisfy for it to function at all. Put differently, the goal is to determine just what aspects of the structure and use of language are specific to the language faculty, hence lacking principled explanation at this level.[7]

Summarizing, the initial conditions on language acquisition fall into the categories (i), (ii), and (iii):

(2) i. Unexplained elements of S_0.
ii. IC (the principled part of S_0)
iii. General properties

Principled explanation, going beyond explanatory adequacy, keeps to (ii) and (iii). An extremely strong minimalist thesis SMT—too much to expect—would be (3):

(3) (2i) is empty.

Evidently, there are no a priori instructions about how to proceed on this path. The questions are empirical at every point, including the kinds of computational efficiency that FL selects; such elements of category (iii) are external to S_0, just as there is no gene that determines how particular proteins fold, but unexplained (category i) elements of S_0 may choose among these options. I will begin by adopting fairly standard assumptions (which are by no means innocent), proceeding along more controversial lines that seem to me reasonable and promising,[8] assuming the best case to hold unless the contrary is demonstrated, and putting to the side many attractive alternatives that are currently being pursued.

The language L generates a set of derivations. The last line of each derivation D is a pair <PHON, SEM>, where PHON is accessed by SM and SEM by C-I. D *converges* if PHON and SEM each satisfy IC; otherwise it *crashes* at one or the other interface. IC must be strong enough to allow sufficient diversity of "legible" expressions at the SEM interface. Exactly how this requirement should be formulated is not obvious. At least infinite legibility is presumably required, but that condition is not strong enough: it could be satisfied, for example, by indefinite reiteration of an element with no features that are uninterpretable at the interfaces, for example, "No,

No. . . ." A very strong condition would be that each derivation is "failure proof": there must be a way to extend it to a convergent derivation.[9] Though this condition may be too strong (see below), something like it has motivated much recent work, which has sought to eliminate comparison of derivations, backtracking and look-ahead, and "nonlocal" operations generally.

S_0 determines the set {F} of properties ("features") available for languages. Each L makes a one-time[10] selection of a subset [F] of {F} and a one-time assembly of elements of [F] as its lexicon LEX, which we can take to be a classical "list of exceptions," putting aside further issues.[11] More controversially, for each derivation D, L makes a one-time selection of elements of LEX that will be accessed in D: a *lexical array* LA (a *numeration* if elements of LEX are accessed more than once). Each of these decisions involves a tradeoff: memory requirements are restricted (massively, in the case of LA), but new concepts are introduced. Whether the decisions are correct is, as always, a (rather subtle) question of fact about language design. I will assume they are, but nothing here hinges directly on this.

Assume further that L has three components: *narrow syntax* (NS) maps LA to a derivation D-NS; the *phonological component* Φ maps D-NS to PHON; the *semantic component* Σ maps D-NS to SEM. Σ is assumed to be uniform for all L; NS is as well, if parameters can be restricted to LEX (as I will assume). Φ, in contrast, is highly variable among Ls. Optimally, mappings will satisfy the *inclusiveness condition*, introducing no new elements but only rearranging those of the domain. Assume this strong condition to be true of NS. It is surely not true of Φ nor (on usual assumptions) of Σ.[12]

Assume that all three components are cyclic, a very natural optimality requirement and fairly conventional. In the worst case, the three cycles are independent;[13] the best case is that there is a single cycle only. Assume that to be true. Then Φ and Σ apply to units constructed by NS, and the three components of the derivation of <PHON, SEM> proceed cyclically in parallel. L contains operations that transfer each unit to Φ and to Σ. In the best case, these apply at the same stage of the cycle. Assume so. Then there is an operation TRANSFER, applying to the narrow-syntactic derivation D-NS:

(4) TRANSFER hands D-NS over to Φ and to Σ.

We focus here primarily on the mapping to Φ, returning to its integration later: call it *Spell-Out* (S-O).[14]

In this conception there is no LF: rather, the computation maps LA to <PHON, SEM> piece by piece, cyclically. There are, therefore, no LF properties and no interpretation of LF, strictly speaking, though Σ and Φ interpret units that are part of something like LF in a noncyclic conception.

Call the relevant units "phases."[15] It remains to determine what the phases are, and exactly how the operations work. I will assume, following *DbP*, that the phases are CP and *v*P, but crucially not TP, returning later to some reasons for this.[16] When a phase is transferred to Φ, it is converted to PHON. Φ proceeds in parallel with the NS derivation. Φ is greatly simplified if it can "forget about" what has been transferred to it at earlier phases; otherwise, the advantages of cyclic computation are lost.

Although the assumption may be somewhat too strong, let us assume it to be basically true, so that global properties of phonology (e.g., intonation contour) are superimposed on the outcome of the cyclic operation of Φ.

Applied to a phase PH, S-O must be able to spell out PH in full, or root clauses would never be spelled out.[17] But we know that S-O cannot be *required* to spell out PH in full, or displacement would never be possible. Consider a typical phase (5), with H as its head:

(5) PH = [α [H β]]

Call α-H the *edge* of PH. It is a fact that elements of the edge may (or sometimes must) raise. A natural condition, which permits spell-out of root phrases and allows for meaningful cyclic computation, is that β must be spelled out at PH, but not the edge: that allows for head-raising, raising of Predicate-internal subject to Spec-T, and an "escape hatch" for successive-cyclic movement through the edge. Call this condition the Phase Impenetrability Condition (PIC). However PIC is formulated exactly, it should have as a consequence that, at the phase ZP containing phase HP,

(6) The domain of H is not accessible to operations, but only the edge of HP.[18]

If ZP = [C [T *v*P]], then T can access Quirky NOM object within *v*P (modifying its feature structure and also that of T),[19] but C can access only the edge of *v*P, so that movement from the domain of *v* must pass through the escape hatch at the edge of *v*. PIC sharply restricts search and memory for Φ, and thus plausibly falls within the range of principled explanation (2ii and iii). It could be that PIC extends to NS as well, restricting search in computation to the next lower phase.

Let us focus on NS, taken to be the "generative engine" of L. Given LA, NS constructs a derivation D. LA is a set of elements of LEX. In the best case, these are "atoms" for D, undergoing no internal tampering in NS. Let us assume so, understanding this to mean that there is no feature movement and hence no "modified lexical items" (MLIs) with features attached to them.[20] That improvement is of some importance: feature movement is a complex operation, requiring some notion of "feature occurrence" that is not very clear; MLIs also introduce many complications, best avoided if possible. Informally, we can refer to these atoms as the "heads of constructions."

NS has one operation that comes "free," in that it is required in some form for any recursive system: the operation Merge, which takes two elements α, β, already constructed, and creates a new one consisting of the two—in the simplest case, {α, β}.[21] The operation yields the relation ε of membership, and assuming iterability, the relations dominate (contain) and term-of. The derived relation c-command (= sister of contain) functions at SEM (e.g., for binding theory), but perhaps not within NS. Any operation other than Merge requires empirical motivation and is a prima facie departure from SMT [= (3)].

Informally, the new unit {α, β} is regarded as a "projection" of some head of α or β. In phrase structure grammars, including X-bar theories, the projection is identified by a new element (N, N-bar, NP, etc.), violating the inclusiveness condition.

We therefore assume that {α, β} is identified either by α or by β (its *label*); a label, then, is always a head. In the worst case, the label is determined by an explicit rule for each choice of α, β. A preferable result is that the label is predictable by a general rule. A still more attractive outcome is that L requires no labels at all.[22]

If computation keeps to these austere conditions, it cannot rely on a head-to-Spec relation R(H, Spec)—the relation called "m-command" in earlier work. There is no such relation. There is a relation R(Spec, H), namely, c-command, but no relation R(LB,H) where LB is the label of Spec since H is not in the minimal search space for LB (unless LB = Spec). If operations are "driven" by labels, as we expect, then there can be no general Spec-head relation at all, a strong and highly controversial conclusion to which we return later. Computation driven by the label LB will keep to its domain, the category that guarantees minimal search, in accord with SMT.

In standard terminology, the first element merged to a head is its complement, later ones its specifiers (Spec). In the best case, there should be no further restrictions on Merge; in particular, no stipulation on the number of Specs, as in X-bar theories. There are further reasons to be skeptical about such stipulations. Typically, they are redundant; the limitations on Merge follow from selectional and other conditions that are independent. If empirical arguments are offered in support of restrictions on Merge, one must be careful to ensure that they do not follow from these independent considerations. It is sometimes supposed that stipulated restrictions have a conceptual advantage in that they reduce the number of possible configurations, but that is a dubious argument. Suppose we have a head H and three elements K, L, M to be successively merged to it. Free Merge yields the syntactic object SO_1 = {M, {L, {H,K}}} (L, M Specs of H). Stipulation that Merge can apply only twice yields SO_2 = {M, {H', {L, {H, K}}}} (L the Spec of H, M the Spec of a new head H'). Stipulation that Merge can apply only once yields SO_3 = {M, {H", {L, {H', {H, K}}}}}, with two new heads H' and H". Each more restrictive stipulation reduces the types of possible configurations (under some interpretations), but there is no clear sense in which requiring SO_3 is preferable to SO_2 or either is preferable to SO_1; if anything, the opposite would appear to be the case. Empirical arguments might be offered to show that H' and H" really exist, but if so, no restriction of Multiple Merge is necessary.

I will assume that there are no stipulated restrictions on Merge and no projections or other violations of inclusiveness, keeping to "bare phrase structure."

Elementary considerations of efficient computation require that Merge of α to β[23] involves minimal search of β to determine where α is introduced, as well as least tampering with β: search therefore satisfies some locality condition (let us say, defined by least embedding, "closest" under c-command), and Merge satisfies an *extension condition*, with zero search. One possibility is that β is completely unchanged (the strong extension condition); another natural possibility is that α is as close as possible to the head that is the label of β, so that any Spec of β now becomes a higher Spec ("tucking in," in Norvin Richards's sense). Further questions arise under Merge with multiple Specs.[24] Assume some version of the extension condition to hold, in accord with SMT.

The SM system requires that PHON indicate (ultimately temporal) order. A fairly standard assumption today, though not in earlier work, is that SEM involves only hierarchy, not order.[25] This version of IC is reasonable: let us adopt it—noting, however, that it is by no means easy to satisfy and is often violated in practice, even when adopted as a general principle. Holmberg's (to my mind, very convincing) theory of Object Shift, for example, requires explicit reference to the left border of a category (see Holmberg 1999, *DbP*), and other current work within a framework close to the one adopted here also requires left-right distinctions. The same is true much more broadly, but on the most austere assumptions about IC such devices must be recast in different terms.

The C-I system requires that SEM express a variety of semantic properties. These include at least argument structure; call such properties "theta-theoretic," without commitment to one or another version of interpretability at the C-I interface. But beyond theta theory, C-I makes use of other kinds of semantic information, including scopal and discourse-related properties (new/old information, specificity, etc.). The NS derivation therefore has to provide the basis for assignment of order at the SM interface, and for multiplicity of semantic properties at the C-I interface—presumably, one aspect of the diversity required by IC at SEM. Let us consider how these requirements are met.

Begin with order, determined by ϕ. The worst case is that it is construction-specific. A better possibility is that it is fixed once and for all for L: the head-parameter, along with a principle that determines that specifier (Spec) precedes head—perhaps, as has sometimes been proposed, a reflection of a more general property that holds at other levels, too (specifically, syllable structure: C-VC rather than CV-C), and may reduce to more general cognitive principles.[26] An alternative, developed by Kayne (1994) and a great deal of subsequent work, is that order reflects hierarchy. That approach eliminates the head-parameter, but at the cost of introducing many others (options for movement required to yield the proper hierarchies) and also some technical complications.[27] Hence the proposal requires empirical rather than conceptual argument, and that is the approach that has properly been adopted in pursuing these ideas. If correct, it appears to be a departure from SMT, contrary to what has commonly been assumed (by me in particular).

Let us turn to the multiplicity of semantic properties required at the C-I interface. Of these, the most fundamental are theta-theoretic properties (also incorporated in some fashion in artificial symbolic systems). Let us then reduce the multiplicity to duality: argument structure and everything else. IC therefore imposes order at PHON and duality of semantic interpretation at SEM, with no interaction between Φ-PHON and Σ-SEM.[28]

NS is based on the free operation Merge. SMT entails that Merge of α, β is unconstrained, therefore either *external* or *internal*. Under external Merge, α and β are separate objects; under internal Merge, one is part of the other, and Merge yields the property of "displacement," which is ubiquitous in language and must be captured in some manner in any theory. It is hard to think of a simpler approach than allowing internal Merge (a grammatical transformation), an operation that is freely available. Accordingly, displacement is not an "imperfection" of language; its absence would be an imperfection.[29] The extension condition requires that displacement from within α be to the edge of α, yielding a new Spec.

Internal Merge leaves a "copy" in place. Hence reconstruction is not an operation: it applies obligatorily in the base position. In A-movement, one position is selected for binding and scopal purposes; there is no need for a countercyclic operation of quantifier-lowering QL.[30] This "copy theory of movement" is sometimes regarded as a controversial innovation. It is not: it is the null hypothesis.[31]

By definition, the operation TRANSFER [see (4)] applies at the phase level. At this level, internal Merge can apply either before or after TRANSFER, hence before or after Spell-Out S-O. The former case yields overt movement, the latter case covert movement, with the displaced element spelled out in situ.[32]

Covert and overt movements yield pairs $\langle\alpha, \beta\rangle$, α an edge element c-commanding β, where either α or β loses its phonological features under S-O: α under covert Move, β under overt Move. If we understand "copy" to cover both cases,

(7) K is a copy of L if K and L are identical except that K lacks the phonological features of L.[33]

Both external and internal Merge are constrained in how they apply. We would like to show that the constraints are principled, deriving from (2ii and iii) but not (i). It is unlikely that they have to do with PHON, which lacks relevant structure, so presumably they are imposed at the C-I interface, as conditions on SEM. There are two kinds of Merge (external and internal) and two kinds of semantic conditions at C-I (the duality noted earlier). We therefore expect them to correlate. That appears to be true. Argument structure is associated with external Merge (base structure), everything else with internal Merge (derived structure).

Although plausibly regarded as the optimal outcome, the correlation is, of course, not a logical necessity. There could be in principle internal Merge to theta-positions,[34] and other devices might be employed to indicate scope and discourse-related properties: say, extra features on heads. But such devices have no independent motivation and would also require new rules. In contrast, internal Merge is free, so on minimalist assumptions it is to be expected that FL will use this device, as appears to be the case. FL takes scopal and discourse-related properties to be "edge phenomena" (hence involving c-command).

Uncontroversially, theta-theoretic properties depend in part on configuration and the semantic properties SEM(H) of the head (label). In the best case, they depend on nothing else (the Hale-Keyser version of theta theory). Assuming so, there are no s-selectional features or thetagrids distinct from SEM(H), which is typically a rich and complex structure,[35] and theta-theoretic failures at the interface do not cause the derivation to crash; such structures yield "deviant" interpretations of a great many kinds. The only other possibility is merger of a semantically uninterpretable element in a configuration that lacks a theta theoretic interpretation, in which case it will have to be deleted before SEM. Reference to s-selection below is to be understood as informal reference to the effects of SEM(H) in particular configurations.

Elimination of s-selection and related notions is motivated by other considerations beyond their redundancy in pure-configurational theta theory. Suppose that the transitivity marker *v* has an s-selection feature F requiring an external argument EA. One immediate problem is that the requirement is formulated as a head-to-Spec relation, and we have seen good reason to believe that this cannot exist (nor the broader symmetric Spec-head relation, in the general case). But even extending relations to m-command leaves problems. Suppose we have derived (8):

(8) *v* [see [the picture]]

To satisfy F, EA must be merged before the derivation moves on, or F will remain unchecked (because of cyclicity of Merge) and the derivation will crash at SEM. But this condition is unnecessary, therefore unwanted: it amounts to stipulating a part of Burzio's generalization, which follows independently from Case-theoretic considerations.[36] These problems become more severe if there are no categories, only roots, so that *v* in (8) determines that the root *see* is verbal—on many grounds a reasonable assumption, which also yields the otherwise unexplained conclusion that V → *v* movement is obligatory. Then given, say, the root *arrive*, we do not know whether it is verbal (selecting an internal argument IA) or nominal (with no IA required) until the next stage of derivation, at which point it is too late to merge IA (by cyclicity). There are still further problems; for example, how do we know which s-selectional feature must be satisfied first?[37] For a variety of reasons, then, s-selection should be dispensable.

Elimination of s-selection has a number of consequences: it undermines at least the simplest ways of predicting labels (as in *MI*), requiring a restatement in terms of SEM(H). It also entails that derivations cannot be failure-proof ("crash-free"), thus undermining the strong version of IC mentioned earlier. But these cannot be reasons for insisting on s-selection features, plainly. We have to find other ways to determine labels, or show that they are dispensable. And IC must be weakened. Perhaps the condition should be that L yields an infinite variety of propositional configurations (CP or *v*P), and that each element of LEX enters into these.

Properties of the C-I interface, then, determine generally the application of external Merge. If we dispense with s-selectional features, failure to satisfy the selectional properties they were taken to express does not block convergence but yields deviance, an outcome that can be detected instantly in the cyclic NS derivation.

What about internal Merge? We expect its application to be motivated by the nontheta-theoretic C-I conditions: scopal and discourse-related (informational) properties in particular. That appears to be the case as well. Scope has the familiar "long-distance" property: scope of wh-, for example, can be well outside its phase. Given PIC, it follows that internal Merge (movement) must be successive-cyclic, passing through the edge of successive phases. The same is true of discourse-related properties. Note that these properties are not built into artificial symbolic systems, which need not satisfy IC and do not resort to internal Merge.

The extra edge position in α, required by internal Merge, is optional and has no theta role. Assuming options to be determined in LEX, the head H of α must have a feature that makes this position available: an EPP-feature in standard terminology, or from another point of view, the feature OCC that means "I must be an occurrence of some β."[38] Optimally, OCC should be available only when necessary, that is, when it contributes to an outcome at SEM that is not otherwise expressible—the basic Fox-Reinhart intuition about optionality.[39] Hence H has OCC only if that yields new scopal or discourse-related properties (or if required for other reasons; see *DbP*). No nonlocal or look-ahead conditions are introduced. If H has OCC, then the new interpretive options are established if OCC is checked by internal Move; it is only necessary that the cyclic derivation D can continue so that they are ultimately satisfied with convergence of D. Informally, we can think of OCC as having the "function" of providing new interpretations; in the analysis of any process or action (the operation of the kidney, organizing motor action, generating expressions, etc.) such functional accounts are eliminated in terms of mechanisms.[40]

Note that no Spec-head relation is involved. The new interpretive options result from checking of OCC by internal rather than external Merge, the former a reflex of a head-head relation in the *MI-DbP* framework assumed here; it is not the Spec-head relation but the way it is satisfied that is crucial. It therefore conforms to the empirical thesis (9):

(9) Apparent Spec-H relations are in reality head-head relations involving minimal search (local c-command).

The thesis conforms to SMT but faces serious empirical challenge.

IC requires that all features be interpretable. But it is clear that there are uninterpretable features that must somehow be eliminated before the NS derivation is transferred to Φ, a prima facie "imperfection" that appears to fall within the unexplained category (2i). One example is the OCC-feature, but insofar as it can be accounted for in the terms just outlined, it moves to the preferred category (2ii) and (2iii).

Case-agreement systems involve a richer array of uninterpretable features and are of particular interest for this reason in the minimalist context: structural Case for nouns and φ-features for categories that agree with nouns; assume these to include T for subject agreement and *v* for object agreement.[41] These must be eliminated in NS. Let's first consider some of their general properties, then ask why they exist.

Uninterpretable features are eliminated when they satisfy certain structural conditions: an uninterpretable feature of α must be in an appropriate relation to interpretable features of some β. Furthermore, β must be *complete*, with a full set of features. Nouns are always complete since their φ-features are always present (and interpretable); hence nouns check the φ-features of agreeing categories. Participles are not complete (lacking person) and do not check Case.[42] T may be complete or *defective*; if the latter, it does not check Case. Feature checking, then, resolves to pairs of heads <H, H'>, where at least one is complete and they are in an appropriate relation. For optimal computation, one member of the pair must be available with no search. It must, therefore, be the head H of the construction α under consideration, α = {H, XP}. Call H a *probe* P, which seeks a *goal* G within XP; P = H c-commands G, but that is a consequence of minimal search. If the P-G relation satisfies relevant conditions, then uninterpretable features of P, G delete.

We therefore conclude that in addition to Merge, there is a relation Agree holding between probe P and goal G, which deletes uninterpretable features if P and G are appropriately related. It remains to determine its properties.

These considerations lend further support to the conclusion that the Spec-head relation does not exist. But there is strong empirical evidence that it does exist. Much work relies on Spec-head relations to provide positions for surface phrase structure.[43] It is also well established that raising tends to yield richer visible morphological realization of inflection than long-distance agreement.[44] We therefore either conclude that the unexplained category (2i) is more comprehensive than we would like, or we have to reanalyze this evidence in other terms. In some cases, this may be fairly straightforward. For example, morphological richness of H in the Spec-H relation (as compared with long-distance agreement) is not actually a reflex of the Spec-H relation but of the way it is satisfied: by internal rather than external Merge. It therefore correlates with the new interpretive options provided by H when OCC (= EPP) is satisfied by internal Merge; in both cases, we are dealing with the same property of H, and the Spec-head relation plays no role, conforming again to thesis (9). A similar observation holds for successive-cyclic A'-movement that yields a special form of C at the intermediate and final positions, as in Irish. McCloskey (2000c) shows that the forms of C are determined not by the Spec-head relation but by the way it is satisfied: external or internal Merge, again conforming to (9).[45] The more general task is not trivial and remains an interesting research project.

If there is no Spec-head relation, then the EPP-feature OCC cannot be satisfied by Merge alone. It follows that internal Merge requires Agree. Therefore, Move = Agree + Pied-piping + Merge. Note the weakness of the hypothesis. It would be refuted only by a configuration H-XP in which any arbitrary term of XP could raise to Spec-H. But it seems that the raising of α from XP is always restricted to some category of constituents of XP, hence some feature F of α (or complex of features) that matches OCC. The (nontrivial) question then reduces to what F is.[46]

It also follows that external Merge does not suffice to check OCC. The only relevant case is expletive EXPL. EXPL externally merged in Spec-T must delete the OCC-feature of T and lose its own uninterpretable features (if T is complete). The interesting case is a *there*-type EXPL lacking a theta role. EXPL must have some feature [uF], or it could not be raised.[47] Suppose EXPL is a simple head, not formed by Merge. In a label-free system, EXPL is accessible without search as a probe and can match and agree with the goal T. If T is selected by C (hence complete), then [uF] is valued and disappears, and the derivation can converge. If T is defective, EXPL will await a higher complete probe (either C-T or *v*). Whatever probe values and deletes, [uF] must still seek a complete goal, to eliminate its own uninterpretable features: the normal case of *there* constructions with long-distance agreement. Suppose that EXPL has all φ-features, like French *il*. When merged in Spec-T, T complete, it can no longer raise: therefore, T must value and eliminate the φ-features of EXPL. But that can happen only if T finds a goal to value its own features—which, however, are overridden by the EXPL-T relation (possibly a reflection of the property of richness of morphological realization already mentioned). We conclude that such expletives must be simple heads and that there is an additional empirical argument in favor of Collins-style label-free phrase structure—noting that some problems remain unresolved, at least in any clean way.

If the head H of α has the feature OCC, then something must be Merged in Spec-H to check and eliminate it. If external Merge of EXPL is inapplicable, internal Merge must find an agreeing active goal G, which induces Pied-piping to yield K(G), then merged in Spec-H. Suppose G is unable to check and delete the features of H; for example, Quirky Dative G that raises to Spec-T but does not satisfy the requirement that the features of T can be checked only by Nominative. Then T can either have a default inflection, if the language allows that option, or it can find a lower active Nominative with which it can agree, deleting its uninterpretable features.[48]

Covert movement to the escape hatch Spec-*v*P is possible for a direct object only if it undergoes further A'-movement (in the informal sense: see note 30). Thus there is covert wh-movement but not covert Object-Shift OS (yielding the semantic edge properties but without overt movement). If OS is Case-driven and Move includes Agree, then we cannot have this sequence of operations: Agree (*v*, Object), TRANSFER, OS. That would require that Agree apply both before and after TRANSFER (specifically, S-O).[49] But wh-movement is plainly driven by a different feature, as successive-cyclic and adjunct movement make clear. Therefore, it can apply (covertly) in a unitary fashion after TRANSFER.

In the probe-goal system, or any approach based on Attract rather than Move, it follows from optimal computational considerations that Merge must be binary, minimizing search for the goal. The conclusion has been generally assumed but has resisted explanation and is not obvious; some considerations might yield a preference for n-ary categories.[50]

Returning to the relation Agree, we see that the problem is to show, if possible, that it is reducible to categories (2ii and iii), thus conforming to SMT.

The simplest version of Agree would be based on the free relation Match: identity of features. For Agree to delete the features of P or G, the paired element (G or P, respectively) must be complete. Furthermore, P and G must be *active*: once their features are checked and deleted, these elements can no longer enter into the Agree relation; the Case-checked subject of a finite clause, for example, cannot check uninterpretable features of the next higher phase head or raise to this position. To minimize search, the P, G relation must be local. In *DbP*, it is assumed that G must be the closest matching H, but there is good reason to believe that, like others, this property must be relativized to phases so that P can find any matching G in the phase PH that it heads, simultaneously deleting uninterpretable features. It follows that intervention effects will hold only if the intervening element is not rendered inactive by P itself.[51]

This modification is both natural and empirically motivated. It means that the operations driven by the head H of α—Merge (external and internal) and Agree—are, in effect, simultaneous. We have already implicitly made this assumption by taking the probe H in $\alpha = \{H, XP\}$ to be detectable with no search. Of course, α might have Specs, but these are added simultaneously with probe for G.

It is unexpected that *v* and T (rather than the two phase heads *v* and C) should be the probes for the Case-agreement system. The departure from expectation is an illusion, however. T functions in the Case-agreement system only if it is selected by C, in which case it is also complete.[52] Furthermore, in just this case T has the semantic properties of true Tense. These cannot be added by the φ-features, which are uninterpretable; they must therefore be added by C.[53] Hence T enters into feature-checking only in the C-T configuration, and the symmetry is restored: the two phase heads C and *v* are the operative elements. There is further evidence to support this conclusion. Successive-cyclic A'-movement often leaves a reflex, sometimes in C (where we would expect it), but commonly in the agreement system headed by T (where we would not).[54] That makes sense if C-T are really functioning as a unit in inducing agreement.

We would expect to find similar properties for *v*. A possible example is Indonesian. There is a transitivity marker and two options for wh-questions: in-situ or successive-cyclic movement. With wh-in situ, the marker remains; with the movement strategy, it disappears at each stage.[55]

An uninterpretable feature F must be distinguished somehow in LEX from interpretable features. The simplest way, introducing no new devices, is to enter F without value: for example, [uNumber]. That is particularly natural because the value is redundant, determined by Agree. Therefore, Match is nondistinctness rather than identity. Uninterpretable [uF] has several important properties: (1) it must be valued under Agree for the NS derivation D to converge; (2) once valued, it must be eliminated from D; (3) it must be transferred to Φ by TRANSFER before it is eliminated since it may have a phonetic reflex. Furthermore, (2) must be carried out quickly, without need for search to earlier stages of derivation. The optimal way to deal with all properties is to regard valuation of [uF] as, in effect, part of TRANSFER. This operation removes features that would cause D to crash at SEM, including phonological/morphological features of LEX and [uF] if it has just been valued. We therefore conclude that TRANSFER (hence S-O) must be cyclic, confirming the earlier conclusion based on computational efficiency. Note that TRANSFER has a "memory" of phase length, meaning again that operations at the phase level are in effect simultaneous. It follows that phases should be as small as possible, to minimize memory for S-O, and independently, to maximize the effect of cyclic derivation in simplifying Φ.

A major problem is why uninterpretable features and Agree exist at all. We have an answer for OCC at the phase level but not for OCC at T: the original Extended Projection Principle—perhaps universal, perhaps not; the jury is still out on that, I think.[56] More important are the features of the Case-agreement system. These features fall into three types:

(10) i. φ-features on the probe (T, *v*) (with T tensed and complete, i.e., really C-T)
ii. Structural Case on the goal (N or D)
iii. EPP-feature (OCC) on the probe

A suggestive fact is that internal Merge requires just these three kinds of information. The target is determined by the probe (i), which also determines what kind of category can be merged to it. The moved element is determined by the goal (ii) (which has to be active). The availability of a position for Merge is determined by (iii) (which may allow long-distance agreement if the feature is valued in some cheaper way, and it may allow a multiple subject if the language allows OCC to be satisfied in both of the possible ways, by external and internal Merge, as in Icelandic).

All of this falls into place if uninterpretable features are the mechanism for displacement, perhaps even an optimal mechanism. But displacement comes "free," and its application is determined by IC: the duality of semantic interpretation at SEM. If this line of reasoning is tenable, then uninterpretable features and the extra relation Agree move from the unexplained category (2i) to the category of principled explanation (ii and iii), and the discussion so far continues to conform pretty closely to the strong minimalist thesis (3).

Cyclicity of derivation requires that Merge to α always be at the edge of α, satisfying an extension condition, strong or weak ("tucking in"). Non-cyclic Merge to a term properly contained in α complicates all three parallel derivations: NS, Φ, Σ. There appears to be one significant counterexample to cyclic Merge: late insertion of adjuncts,[57] as in (11):

(11) $[_{wh}$ which $[_{\alpha}$ $[_{NP}$ picture $[_{\beta}$ of Bill]] $[_{ADJ}$ that John liked]]] did he buy t_{wh}

Despite complexities, the tendencies are fairly clear: linking of *Bill* to *he* induces a Condition (C) effect, but linking of *John* to *he* does not. The effect for (*he, Bill*) is expected by (obligatory) reconstruction but not its obviation for (*he, John*). That would follow, however, if adjuncts can be late-merged at the root, though not complements, consistent with the fact that the complement β is s-selected but the adjunct ADJ is not.

Is there a way to deal with these problems while preserving cyclicity in a single cycle in accord with SMT [= (3)]?

More fundamental questions arise at this point. There has never, to my knowledge, been a really satisfactory theory of adjunction, and to construct one is no slight task. That has been recognized since the earliest efforts to construct a reasonable version of phrase-structure grammar, what came to be called X-bar theory.[58] An adjunction construction is plainly not the projection of a head: for NP-adjuncts, for example, the constituent structure appears to be something like [NP XP]. The construction is crucially asymmetric: if α is adjoined to β, the construction behaves as if α isn't there apart from semantic interpretation, which is not that of standard X-bar-theoretic constructions; island properties differ as well. β retains all its properties, including its role in selection. There is no selectional relation between β and α, so determination of label evidently relies on the asymmetry to determine, say, that "the picture of John's" is an NP, not a PP, while "the picture of John" is an NP; and "destruction of the army" is one or the other, in one case interpreted as in "the achievement of the army." The adjunct α has no theta role in $\langle\alpha, \beta\rangle$, though the structure does—the same one as β.

Suppose we see how far we can go, starting from first principles, assuming SMT, and keeping to core problems—concentrating on what should be captured by some eventual formalization.

For structure building, we have so far assumed only the free symmetrical operation Merge, yielding syntactic objects that are sets, all binary: call them *simple*. The relations that come "free" (contain, c-command, etc.) are defined on simple structures. But it is an empirical fact that there is also an asymmetric operation of adjunction, which takes two objects β and α and forms the ordered pair $\langle\alpha, \beta\rangle$, α adjoined to β. Set Merge and pair Merge are descendants of substitution and adjunction in earlier theories. Given the basic properties of adjunction, we might intuitively think of α as attached to β on a separate plane, with β retaining all its properties on the "primary plane," the simple structure.

Two questions arise about adjunction: (1) Why does it exist? (2) How does it work?

The natural place to seek an answer to question (1) is at the SEM interface. Recall that the strong interface condition (however formulated precisely) requires sufficient diversity at SEM. Possibly richness of expressive power requires an operation of predicate composition: that is not provided by set Merge, which yields the duality of interpretation discussed earlier: argument structure and edge properties. But it is the essential semantic contribution of pair Merge. If the C-I-system imposes this condition, then the existence of a device to yield predicate composition would conform to SMT—a promissory note, given the limitations of understanding of C-I, but not unreasonable.

Let's turn to the second question: how does adjunction work? We have to determine how relations and operations apply to complex objects formed by asymmetric pair Merge in such a way as to capture the basic properties of the construction, keeping to SMT as far as possible.

Assume that like other operations, adjunction of α to β applies cyclically. β behaves throughout as if it were in a simple structure formed by set Merge. We can implement the observation by taking β to be in fact set-merged in the standard way; adjunction then applies to replace β by $<\alpha, \beta>$, where the information that β is set-merged is captured by the asymmetry (it is part of the interpretation of the pair). The semantic role of $<\alpha, \beta>$ is determined compositionally under Σ. In (11), for example, ADJ is pair-merged to NP in the base position, and [DET <ADJ, NP>] receives its theta role in the normal way, with composition of the predicates NP, ADJ. We take [DET $<\alpha, \beta>$] to be "in a configuration" at SEM, but that seems unproblematic: "in a configuration" is not one of the relations defined for simple structures, and the assumption here is as natural as any. Any role played by β in selection or other semantic interpretation is preserved because it is interpreted to be set-merged, in a simple structure.

What about Condition (C) at SEM? When X c-commands $<\alpha, \beta>$, does it also c-command α and β? β was introduced by set Merge, and before α was adjoined to it, X c-commanded β. But the central property of adjunction is that adjunction of α to β does not change the properties of β. For β to lose some property when α adjoins to it would be a complication, an "imperfection." The relation c-command(X, β) is therefore not lost when α is adjoined to β: accordingly, X still c-commands β in $<\alpha, \beta>$, as before adjunction. But extension of c-command to the adjoined element α would be a new operation, to be avoided unless empirically motivated. Happily, the empirical evidence disconfirms the complication. Cases of type (11) fall into place, insofar as they are clear.[59]

We know that at the stage where $<\alpha, \beta>$ is spelled out, it also becomes a simple structure at SEM. Thus if (11) is embedded in the context "he asked———," *Bill* is subject to Condition (C) and hence must be c-commanded by matrix *he*. Therefore, there is an operation SIMPL that converts $<\alpha, \beta>$ to $\{\alpha, \beta\}$; in effect, it is part of Σ. Since SIMPL applies at the stage of the derivation at which Spell-Out S-O applies, it is also in effect part of S-O. We conclude, then, that it is part of the operation TRANSFER [=(4)], which transfers the NS derivation (specifically, its last line) to both Φ and Σ.[60]

Suppose SIMPL is optional. Recall that overt movement, as in (11), requires the ordering of operations: Move TRANSFER. For overt movement, then, optionality of SIMPL will have no effect at the PHON level because S-O does not apply to the trace in any event.[61] But it might have an effect at SEM. Thus in such structures as (11), application of SIMPL to the trace (copy) yields reconstruction effects, obviated if SIMPL applies only where it must: at the phase where S-O applies. In the case of covert movement, with the ordering TRANSFER Move, S-O applies, and therefore SIMPL feeds Σ as well.

The account so far is consistent with the basic assumption throughout that ordering is required only at PHON. Within Φ, α of $<\alpha, \beta>$ is integrated into the primary plane, in the informal version.[62] Along with S-O in general, ordering is not part of NS. It can therefore apply no earlier than TRANSFER. If it applies later than TRANSFER, computation will be more complex since it will have to apply separately in the mappings Φ or Σ. We therefore assume that SIMPL applies at the point of transfer, so that SIMPL—an optional component of TRANSFER—is in effect part of both Φ and Σ. SIMPL converts $<\alpha, \beta>$ to $\{\alpha, \beta\}$, which is then ordered, using the information that this is pair Merge, not set Merge (unproblematic because SIMPL is in effect part of S-O). The instantaneous and uniform operation Σ retains the same information at SEM, so that even when simplified, $<\alpha, \beta>$ is interpreted as adjunction.

It follows that in the structure $<\alpha, \beta>$, α is integrated into the linearly ordered structure at the stage of derivation where β is spelled out. Perhaps α is adjacent to β, perhaps not; that depends on properties of adjuncts, which are not all the same in this regard. These are separate issues, which have to be addressed however adjunction is handled. The crucial point is that we will not find β spelled out in one place with α appearing somewhere else as a result of movement of β—either covert Move, carrying α along, or overt Move, leaving it behind. In short, principle (12) holds:

(12) In $<\alpha, \beta>$, α is spelled out where β is.

Suppose (12) is rejected: integration of the adjunct α can be dissociated from spell-out of β. That raises all sorts of conceptual problems, but even if these can be resolved, the proposal requires a new rule INSERT that applies to $<\alpha, \text{Copy}(\beta)>$, inserting α into the simplified structure.[63] These complications are unwanted and seem empirically incorrect.

Consider successive-cyclic movement, applying to an underlying expression of the form (13), with ADJ-P = "with great annoyance" or "every day of his life" (or both, to bring out the intended interpretation, with ADJ-P understood as qualifying "remember"; the extra phrase "he heard" is inserted to avoid *that*-trace issues):

(13) Bill remembered [that he heard [John had insulted him]] ADJ-P

Now replace *John* by *which person*, which raises to the root either overtly or covertly, yielding (14), where wh_2 = Copy(*which person*) if raising is overt, and wh_1 = Copy(*which person*) if it is covert (in the latter case, take *Bill* to be replaced by *who*, raising to Spec-C):

(14) wh_1 (1) [Bill [(2) remembered [(3) that he [(4) heard
[wh_2 (5) [had [(6) insulted him (7)]]]]]]] ADJ-P

Whether overtly or covertly, *which person* passes through positions (1)–(6).

Suppose REL = "who taught at Harvard" is adjoined to *which person*, necessarily in the base position (6). Suppose dissociation of Spell-Out is allowed (contrary to (12), the extra rule INSERT exists, and the conceptual problems are somehow overcome. Then REL should be able to appear at PHON at positions (1)–(6)—or (7), if INSERT places the adjunct to the right. But it can appear only at (1) (if wh_1 = *which person*, after overt movement) or at (5) (if wh_2 = *which person*, with covert movement; possibly (7)). That is, REL must be spelled out where *which person* is spelled out; any other choice yields severe deviance. Therefore, we can avoid the conceptual problems and the new rule INSERT: SIMPL is part of TRANSFER with no further complication, and Spell-Out accords with (12).

Let us turn to application of Move to <α, β>. Here a preliminary question arises: do we take Move to be a literal internal Merge (overt and covert movement), or do we adopt the approach outlined at the end of *DbP*, with no internal Merge but only marking of the OCC feature of the probe? If the latter, no special problems seem to arise, but let us continue to adopt internal Merge. Clearly <α, β> can be moved as a unit, as in (11), where SIMPL applies at the root. That means that the operation of Pied-piping, triggered by the active element of β [the wh-feature in (11)], can pick up the adjunct along with everything else in the category it identifies. Exactly how Pied-piping works remains somewhat unclear, with well-known problems still outstanding, but it must at least have this property. Is there also an option for Pied-piping to keep just to the simple part of the construction, hence moving β while leaving α in situ? That would violate (12), yielding the dissociation of S-O that we have just rejected on conceptual and empirical grounds, so we dismiss this option. Note that the same considerations apply to the countercyclic late-Merge approach to adjunction of α to β: it should be permitted only where β is spelled out, in accord with (12). Merge cannot apply to a copy: a trace or an empty category that has moved covertly.[64]

If this line of reasoning is correct, then the complications of countercyclic late Merge can be eliminated at least in the standard cases. Given the (presumed) interface condition that requires compositionality of predicates, the properties of these structures follow from minimal conditions on SIMPL: optional application at TRANSFER. Furthermore, (12) holds.

More generally, we have the basic outlines of a theory of adjunction that satisfies SMT.

The late-Merge operation for adjuncts has recently been exploited in work by Danny Fox and Jon Nissenbaum to deal with such constructions as (15), in which the adjunct is apparently extraposed in conflict with the general principle that only complements, not adjuncts, can be extracted from NP (we ignore NP-DP distinctions where irrelevant); and, in (ii), the Condition (C) effect is obviated for the pair (*he*, *John*), though it would be expected (by reconstruction) if ADJ is extraposed from NP:[65]

(15) i. We saw [$_{NP}$ a painting] yesterday [$_{ADJ}$ from the museum].
ii. I gave him [$_{NP}$ a painting] yesterday [$_{ADJ}$ from John's collection].

Fox and Nissenbaum argue that strange properties of these and many more complex constructions can be explained if *a painting* is covertly raised to the right (by QR), and ADJ is then merged postcyclically.

Though the results are impressive for a wide range of constructions, there are a number of problems. One is that late Merge is employed. Possibly the analysis can be reconstructed in terms of cyclic adjunction, but even if so, other problems remain. Dissociation of Spell-Out of adjunct and host is required in violation of (12), but that is problematic, as just discussed. It is also unclear why QR is to the right; a covert operation should have no ordering properties. One cannot—at least in any obvious way—appeal to the fact that authentic extraposition is to the right since a crucial (and well-motivated) part of the analysis is that there is no adjunct extraposition; nor can Heavy-NP-Shift (HNPS) be invoked because of the dissociation of Spell-Out of *a painting*, not true for HNPS. There is also a conceptual question: apart from serving as an empty bearer of adjunction, QR typically does not feed Φ. It should, then, not be part of NS, just as ordering is not.

An alternative approach is suggested by the fact that very similar expressions are generated independently, namely, those that introduce qualifications or afterthoughts, as in (16):[66]

(16) i. We saw [$_{NP}$ a painting] yesterday, (that is,) a painting (one) [$_{ADJ}$ from the museum].
ii. I gave him [$_{NP}$ a painting] yesterday, (more precisely,) a painting (one) [$_{ADJ}$ from John's collection].

Here "a painting" is destressed in the adjoined phrase and can undergo ellipsis in the normal way, yielding (15). The scopal and other properties of (15) follow without recourse to QR or countercyclic Merge. There is no need to violate the theoretically well-motivated and apparently empirically valid principle (12). It also follows that the adjunct is to the right. The adjunct-complement distinctions that Fox and Nissenbaum (1999) describe are also accommodated: if the "afterthought" is, say, "a [picture of his father]," then "a picture," not being a unit, cannot delete.

Fox (2001) applies similar ideas to the intricate problems of antecedent-contained deletion (ACD). Still keeping to the simplest case, we now consider (17):

(17) John [$_{vP}$ likes [$_{NP}$ every boy Mary does <likes t>]]

Here < . . . > is elided with VP as antecedent. But the parallelism requirement for ellipsis is violated. For such reasons, ACD-resolution is standardly assumed to involve QR, raising NP. But this solution is inconsistent with the simplest theory of movement (the "copy theory"), which reintroduces the problem. Furthermore, condition (C) effects would be induced if movement leaves a copy, but they are not.

Fox (2001) develops a very simple analysis along the lines of the analysis of (15) just reviewed and shows that it deals with a wide range of cases. The base-generated form for (17) is (18):

(18) John [$_{vP}$ likes [$_{NP}$ every boy]].

QR raises NP to the right, at which point the relative clause is late-merged. Parallelism is straightforward; there are no condition (C) or other reconstruction effects; scopal properties and complement-adjunct distinctions fall into place.

Though the results are again impressive, the same problems arise as for (15). It is natural to ask, then, whether the alternative approach just outlined can overcome them. Suppose that the underlying structure for (18) is (19)—which, again, is generated independently as one of a large class of cases:

(19) John likes every boy (that is, more accurately . . .) every boy Mary likes.

We derive essentially the same results without the problems associated with late-Merge, violation of (12), and QR. There might also be other advantages: ACD-resolution requires application of QR in constructions in which it is usually barred.[67] These problems might be obviated if the scope of ACD is determined in the manner suggested here, without QR. If something like this approach is tenable, then ACD essentially disappears as a phenomenon.

This discussion only scratches the surface.[68] A great many important questions remain, but it seems that cyclic Merge is at least compatible with the empirical evidence, perhaps supported by it, and, more generally, that the theory of adjunction conforms to SMT in crucial aspects—maybe entirely. If so, another large category of phenomena shifts from "unexplained" to "explained in a principled manner"—from (2i) to (2ii and iii).

Let's consider finally the place of Spell-Out S-O—that is, the choice of phases. We know that S-O cannot apply at each stage of cyclic Merge. Relevant information may not yet be available. Suppose, for example, that Merge has constructed {see, OB}, where the object OB equal *that* or *what*. At this stage we do not know whether OB or *see* is spelled out in situ or whether they move on overtly to be spelled out in a higher position. If they move on (either sometimes or always), then S-O plainly cannot apply at this stage. In a cyclic theory, we do not want to wait too long to determine whether they are spelled out in situ. Ideally, it should be at the next Merge. Suppose further that *see* is a root—a reasonable assumption, as noted earlier. Then the next Merge should also tell us what kind of element it is: the verb *see* or the noun *sight*. In the best case, then, the next Merge should yield (20), where α is the verbalizer v or the nominalizer n:

(20) {α, {see, OB}}

If $\alpha = n$, then OB receives inherent Case and can be spelled out at this stage. Suppose it is v. We now have the conventional v-vP analysis. V raises to v, but we do not yet know whether it is spelled out.[69] v can be of various types. Suppose v is transitive.

Then Agree holds between *v* and OB, and structural Case of OB can be assigned the value ACC, with φ-features of *v* valued by OB. Whether OB raises further at this stage depends on whether *v* has an OCC- (= EPP-) feature. Suppose it does. Then OB raises to SPEC-*v*, either above or below the externally Merged subject SU that is required for convergence; see note 36. If below, then there will be an ultimate theta-theory violation, detectable at once. Proper positioning might be automatic under various assumptions, for example, if the simultaneous satisfaction of properties of *v* involves an internal cyclic order, with raising of OB first, then "tucking in" of externally Merged SU. Recall that it cannot be required that every subsequent extension converges, only that there are convergent extensions.

S-O should apply as early as possible, for reasons already discussed. It cannot be before the *v* level, but it can be at this level, as long as only the sister of *v* is spelled out (in accord with PIC). Therefore *v*P is a phase. We understand PIC as before: the sister of the head is spelled out obligatorily; the fate of the edge—the head and its Specs—is not determined until *later*; see note 19.

Suppose T is merged with (20). If T is defective, SU may raise to Spec-T, but it remains active. If T is complete, the next Merge is C. Though SU may raise to Spec-T before C is merged, valuing and inactivating Case, this is really a reflex of the C-T-relation, as we have seen. For the other two elements of the edge of *v*, *v* itself and the extra Specs, we know their local destination by the C level but in general not before: A'-movement is to Spec-C, and the same appears to be true for V-topicalization (Holmberg 1999). Relevant considerations therefore converge to the conclusion that the next higher phase is CP (or *v*P if T is defective).

Spell-Out applies at the phase level (by definition), and as discussed, all operations within the phase are in effect simultaneous. Furthermore, their applicability is evaluated at the phase level, yielding apparent countercyclic effects within the phase; see *DbP*. The phenomenon is illustrated most simply by A'-movement to Spec-C, as in (21) [abstracting from effects of T-to-C, -*do*- support, and -*seem*-to-T raising, as well as *t* the trace (copy) of the wh-phrase, *t'* of *he*]:

(21) i. What C [he T [t [t' see t]]]
ii. To-whom C [he T [t seem [t' to be intelligent]]

Applying cyclically, T first raises *he* to Spec-T, skipping wh- in apparent violation of the Minimal Link Condition, MLC. After Merge of C, wh- is raised to Spec-C, voiding the violation of MLC at the phase level.[70] Again, it is "as if" all operations are applying simultaneously at the phase level, as we should now expect.

Phase-level evaluation has other consequences. One is that if XP is raised to Spec-*v*, it cannot remain there, or the external argument will not be accessible to the higher complete category with which it must agree (C-T or *v*), and the derivation will crash. We expect, then, that under successive-cyclic movement, wh-phrases cannot be stranded in Spec-*v*, though they could be strandable in Spec-C. Both conclusions are apparently correct: to my knowledge, no clear case of stranding in Spec-*v* is known, but stranding in Spec-C is a plausible analysis of the German *was* constructions. It also follows that if Object Shift is to Spec-*v*, it must then move on to a higher position; see *DbP* for discussion.[71]

We have good reason, then, to regard *v*P and CP (but not TP) as phases.[72]

Why should these be the phases, and the only ones? Ideally, phases should have a natural characterization in terms of IC: they should be semantically and phonologically coherent and independent. At SEM, *v*P and CP (but not TP) are propositional constructions: *v*P has full argument structure, and CP is the minimal construction that includes Tense and event structure[73] and (at the matrix, at least) force. At PHON, these categories are relatively isolable (in clefts, VP-movement, etc.). These properties do not, however, yield exactly the right distinctions: *v*P with *v* nontransitive is relatively isolated and is a domain for QR, though these cannot be phases for Spell-Out. Call these *weak phases*. Then the strong phases are those that have an an EPP-position as an escape hatch for movement and are, therefore, the smallest constructions that qualify for Spell-Out.[74]

So far, we have remained reasonably close to the strong minimalist thesis (3), that is, within the categories (2ii and iii). That seems rather surprising. One reason is that even much weaker versions of the thesis are surprising (and difficult to discover and poorly understood for organic systems except at the simplest levels). Another is that nothing remotely similar would have been anticipated only a few years ago. How far this kind of analysis can proceed, or along what paths, one can only conjecture. Insofar as it can, the conclusions are of some significance, not only for the study of language itself.

Notes

1. As a system, that is; its elements might be recruited from, or used for, other functions.

2. For some recent discussion, see Chomsky (2000b, 2001) and Jenkins (2000).

3. Or with the set of remaining choices narrowed in a "grammar competition model" of the kind investigated in Roeper (2000) and Yang (2000); see the latter on antecedents and alternatives.

4. See Chomsky (1965: 59). See also Chomsky et al. (1982: 23).

5. Cherniak (1995). For an illuminating review of the state of the art, see Stewart (1998); in briefer comments, Maynard Smith (1998). A more technical review appears in Maynard Smith et al. (1985). On Turing's contributions particularly, see Leiber (2001).

6. For recent commentary relevant to linguistics, see Uriagereka (1998), Jenkins (2000), Martin & Uriagereka (2000), and Freidin and Vergnaud (2001).

7. The approach is complementary to others, for example, studies of language acquired under sensory deficit or studies of other species that seek to identify properties that may be recruited for language but not specific to it. For suggestive recent results of these two categories, see Petitto et al. (2000) and Ramus et al. (2000).

8. See Chomsky 2000a (henceforth *MI*) and 2001(henceforth *DbP*), presupposed in what follows, though with significant modification.

9. See Frampton & Gutmann (2000).

10. For discussion and references to other works on these particular topics (by Chris Collins, Sam Epstein, John Frampton and Sam Gutmann, Howard Lasnik, and others), see *MI* and *DbP*.

11. Note that this convention entails that L changes when a new lexical item is introduced. Alternatively, LEX could be replaced by a generative system for constructing the possible lexical elements of L.

12. These asymmetries allow for investigation of the internal structure of NS and Φ in

ways that are not possible for Σ, which is invariant and does not satisfy economy conditions of type (2iii) in any obvious way. It is somewhat paradoxical, perhaps, that logically equivalent versions of Σ, decomposing it in different ways, have important consequences. A further asymmetry is that Φ introduces only elements that are in [F] (though typically not in LEX), whereas the new elements introduced by Σ never enter NS and are accordingly not in [F]; and if inclusiveness holds for NS, it introduces no features, even of [F].

13. A still worse case is the EST-model, with two cycles in NS, overt and covert.

14. For a very strong version of the thesis, see Epstein (1999). On cyclic Spell-Out see *MI* and *DbP*; and for related ideas, see Uriagereka (1999). S-O removes from NS all features that do not reach SEM. For expository simplicity, I refer to all these as "phonological."

15. For an intriguing generalization of the notion to incorporate binding theory properties, see Freidin and Vergnaud (2001). For another possible generalization, see note 51.

16. Possibly DP as well, but this raises many questions. I will put the topic aside here, keeping to the basic clausal architecture and the phases CP, *v*P.

17. This requirement could reduce to Spell-Out of sister of the head if we adopt some variant of Ross's phonologically empty performative analysis; Nissenbaum, personal communication.

18. *MI* (p. 21): *DbP* (p. 11). See also Nissenbaum (2000).

19. Here and below, assume Quirky Case to be inherent Case with a structural Case feature. Note that the NOM object neither raises nor undergoes any phonetic change in situ, the structural Case feature being invisible in this case. If properties of FL conspire to ensure that this is true generally of the domain of H in (6), the sister of H can be spelled out at HP (as in Nissenbaum's modification of PIC; see preceding note), with a universally invisible unvalued feature understood to be, in effect, a morphological convention rather than an actual feature, so that there is no crash at PHON. For expository convenience, let's assume that PIC can be formulated in terms of Spell-Out of domain (sister) of the head, ignoring these problems.

20. Contrary to *MI* and earlier work but not *DbP*.

21. On binary versus n-ary sets, see below.

22. On the last two possibilities, respectively, see *MI* and Collins (1999).

23. Note that the asymmetry is for expository convenience only; α and β are merged with no asymmetry.

24. On these topics, see, inter alia, Richards (1997), Boskovic (1998a and b), Pesetsky (2000), Nissenbaum (2000), and Brody (1995), on which much of this work relies, with reinterpretation. On tampering, see *MI*.

25. On arguments to the contrary, see Fukui (2001).

26. See Gil (1987) and Carstairs-McCarthy (1999).

27. See Collins (1999), *MI*, and Fukui (2001).

28. Another questionable assumption; see *MI* and sources cited.

29. Contrary to what I have assumed in earlier work. For over forty years, there have been efforts to motivate displacement. That seems to have been a mistake. Recourse to any device to account for the displacement phenomena also is mistaken, unless it is independently motivated (as is internal Merge). If this is correct, then the radically simplified form of transformational grammar that has become familiar ("Move-α" and its variants) is a kind of conceptual necessity, given the undeniable existence of the displacement phenomena.

30. Many questions arise about when and where reconstruction takes place. A particularly important contribution is Fox (2000). For some alternative conceptions, see Lasnik (1999a) and Lebeaux (1999). For A'-movement, see particularly Barss (1986). Note that A- and A'-movement have no status in the present framework; the terms are used only for convenience. It follows that no principles can be formulated in terms of the A-/A'-distinction, a strong and highly controversial conclusion.

31. On the confusion of logic and history in this case, see *MI*.

32. See Nissenbaum (2000). See also Pesetsky (2000). I will assume this to be correct, contrary to *MI* and *DbP*, which interpreted covert movement as long-distance agreement.

33. On "phonological" as used here, see note 14. Since we are assuming a "classical LEX," with phonological and semantic features of roots included, pure synonyms are distinguished in the lexical array (numeration), so no false chains will be introduced.

34. See, for example, Horstein (1999).

35. There is nothing to say, then, about the fact that they are not morphologically manifested, though argument position may be marked morphologically, a different matter.

36. If the internal argument receives Case, a higher element that requires agreement (T or *v*), which must appear in a well-formed construction for independent reasons, will not be able to have its features checked. We assume that once Case of α is checked, α is "frozen"; it cannot enter into further agreement relations. See below.

37. See Collins (1999), who also proposes that c-selection is a head-head property that avoids labels, with some interesting empirical consequences, but some problems as well. Note that nothing requires that EA be an actual argument: it could be a *there*-type expletive with φ-features (similar to French *il*). For a possible example from Greek, see Iatridou (2001).

38. Taking an occurrence of β to be its sister, as in the theory of chains without indexes; see *DbP* and sources cited.

39. Ibid.

40. Ibid. See also Lasnik (1999c) and Frampton & Gutmann (2000).

41. With provisos discussed in *DbP* and elsewhere. We keep here to Nominative-Accusative systems, but the same reasoning should apply to Ergative-Absolutive systems. Theta-related (inherent) Case is a separate matter.

42. But a participle PRT may have Case, shared with that of its object OB. See *DbP* for discussion within a phase-theoretic framework, with Case determined by the higher Case-assigner (NOM with T; ACC with *v*). If OB has only structural Case, the PRT-OB-relation in itself cannot determine the (uninterpretable) Case of either; but if OB has inherent Case, the relation suffices to determine case of PRT, as in the Icelandic counterpart of (i) (from Boeckx 2000):

(i) me(DAT) seems(Default) t [John(DAT) be believed(NOM, Pl) like horses(NOM, pl)

Here OB (= *horses*) has inherent Case, optionally Quirky (but not here).

43. One important recent discussion is McCloskey (2000a).

44. See Guasti and Rizzi (1999). For extensive evidence that Spec-head agreement not only exists but also plays a decisive role, see Chung (1998).

45. McCloskey also provides evidence that the resumptive pronoun strategy involves external Merge of pro in Spec-C, yielding an operator-variable structure that may form "mixed chains" with raising. Hence the attempt in *MI* to describe (not account for) the appearance of EXPL in Spec-T, but not Spec-*v* in phase-theoretic terms, cannot be correct. The problem of accounting for the distribution of EXPL in some principled way (noted some years ago by Julie Legate) remains open.

46. One might seek to appeal to universal conditions C: α is allowed to raise only if it satisfies C. Even if this is possible, to show that Merge alone checks OCC, it would be necessary to show that C does not invoke head-head relations (as in standard formulations of MLC). A technical question is how checking of the EPP-feature by internal Merge (Move) is effected by a head-head relation alone. Neither Agree nor (by assumption) Merge can check the feature, so it must be a property of Pied-piping, still in many ways a mysterious operation.

47. Perhaps, for example, structural Case, as proposed by Lasnik (1999b: chap. 4).

48. See *DbP* and sources cited for further detail. For much more extensive discussion of related issues, see Boeckx (2000).

49. Possibly this falls together with the Maximization principle [see *DbP*, (14), and (21)]. Recall that Agree must apply to the direct object before S-O because of phonetic reflexes and to remove the uninterpretable Case feature from NS, and that Case-driven movement covers Quirky Case as well. On problems concerning A'-movement, see note 51.

50. That was assumed in early efforts to motivate transformations in processing terms; see Miller and Chomsky (1963) for a review. On binary structures, see particularly Kayne (1981).

51. Frampton et al. (1999); Hiraiwa (2000). See the latter for extensive discussion of intervention effects and multiple Agree, with parametric variation. The former points out that this proposal can overcome a problem they note in the analysis of participial constructions in *DbP*, which works if the object remains in situ but fails if it raises, blocking Case checking of the participle; as they note, this could also be overcome along lines of the proposal at the end of *DbP*, which dispenses with literal movement. Multiple Agree eliminates unvalued features of traces, as desired. Although this is the right result for A-movement, it may not be for A'-movement; for example, the *wh*-feature of a trace is not valued until a higher phase. The asymmetry reflects another one: all A-movement properties are handled within a phase, but not A'-movement properties. That suggests that there might be a more abstract notion of phase, based on the concept of valuation of features rather than just the size of the category, as here and in earlier work.

52. There are unstated assumptions here, for example, that control structures are CPs.

53. Additional evidence is provided by languages like Greek, in which T with a complete set of φ-features, but not selected by C, lacks semantic tense and is defective with regard to Case and agreement; Iatridou 1993, and much subsequent work.

54. See Chung (1998) for review; also Collins (1993). Irish is the best-studied case of C-reflex. See McCloskey (2000c). Inflectional marking of C in some languages yields further support. For more on C-T-relations, assuming literal head movement, see Pesetsky and Torrego (2001).

55. Aguero (2001); data from Saddy (1991). A host of further questions arises in this connection, including differences of richness of inflection of T, *v*, and correlated differences of overt Case marking in Nominative-Accusative vs. Ergative-Absolutive languages.

56. For English it appears to hold invariably for T, as we can see in raising constructions (awkward because there are so few relevant raising verbs, but the point is clear), as in (i), *ti* the trace of *John*:

(i) John seems to Y [t_1 to appear to X [t_2 to like Mary]]

Suppose Y = *her*. At the relevant level (presumably SEM), Y c-commands *Mary*, inducing a Condition (C) effect. It therefore c-commands X, which can however be *her* linked to Y or *himself* linked to *John* (despite intervening Y); both facts imply that t_1 = *John*. Therefore, intermediate T, though defective, must satisfy EPP. For an argument that Irish does not have EPP, see McCloskey (2000a).

57. Proposed by Lebeaux (1988) to deal with problems noted by Robert Freidin, Henk van Riemsdijk, and Edwin Williams.

58. See, for example, the discussion of "house in the woods" versus "book in the woods" and other such matters in Chomsky (1970).

59. Judgments fade as the r-expression in the adjunct [*John* in (11)] is more deeply embedded. It is tempting to relate this to the fact that a deeper search is required at the root to spell out the pair <α, β>, along the lines to which we turn directly.

60. We are assuming that S-O applies at the point of transfer: that is, there are no pho-

nological operations that must apply before S-O (and ordering). If there are, the account becomes more complex but unchanged in essentials.

61. Apart from the possibility mentioned in note 64.

62. Note that α may have already been spelled out, in part at least, prior to adjunction. The question is how and where it is integrated into the simple configuration that is spelled out. Recall that lots of computation is proceeding in parallel.

63. Copy is asymmetrical: Copy(β) is β stripped of its phonological features—either the trace of β or covertly raised β. See (7). Since operations at the phase level are in effect simultaneous, the asymmetry of Copy is determined by TRANSFER, Move, and their ordering at the phase level.

64. Perhaps Merge cannot apply to any empty category ec, not really a generalization if a copy is just a syntactic object with no phonological features. Alternatively it could be that trace is destressed, entering into ellipsis under the usual paradigm but obligatorily in this case. Here questions arise about apparent phonetic effects of trace versus lexically determined ec's. Barring of adjunction to ec's seems correct for PRO and pro, but there might be other reasons. Note that phonological features do not affect NS-derivations, but their presence or absence may (see note 33). On this matter, see *DbP*. The conclusion would leave intact the results of Distributed Morphology while abandoning the condition of obligatory late insertion for roots, questionable on other grounds; see *DbP*.

65. See Fox and Nissenbaum (1999), Fox (2001), and Nissenbaum (2000) for extensive discussions and references to the earlier work of Peter Culicover and Michael Rochement and Tarald Taraldsen.

66. We know that these are to the right, independently (and for obvious reasons), because of the variety of such constructions; the simplest of them are relevant here, but the others clearly exist.

67. See von Fintel and Iatridou (2001) for a review and some new cases.

68. It also omits entirely the parasitic gap and other constructions that are the primary focus of Nissenbaum's work because of their intricacy; but I think that an analysis similar to that proposed below may be possible here as well.

69. I will omit further comment on head raising, including the possibility, which I think is real, that it is part of Φ; see *DbP*. Also ignored are other possibilities, for example, automatic raising of α to some position above V but below *v*, as in recent work of Masatoshi Koizumi, Howard Lasnik, and others.

70. Note that this provides still another reason to conclude that TP is not a phase.

71. For German, see McDaniel (1989). Suppose that Spec-*v* is the position of overt *wh* (and possibly focus). We might ask whether in such cases *v* has raised to T, so that the Spec position does not intervene between T and EA. Many questions remain concerning Heavy-NP-Shift, Object Shift, and overt and covert *wh*-movement, all assumed here to move to Spec-*v*, though they have different properties.

72. See note 16.

73. Recall that T has these properties only as a reflex of C-T.

74. On nontransitives, see Legate (1998). On the escape hatch in strong phases and parasitic gaps, see Nissenbaum (2000).

References

Aguero, C. (2001). The Scope of Wh-phrases. Ms, MIT

Barss, A. (1986). Chains and Anaphoric Dependence. Ph.D. diss., MIT, Cambridge.

Boeckx, C. (2000). "Quirky Agreement." *Studia Linguistica* 54(3).

Boeckx, C. (2001). Experiencer-Intervention Across Languages. Ms., University of Connecticut, Storrs. To appear in P. Pica and J. Rooryck, eds., *Syntax Yearbook* (Amsterdam: John Benjamins).

Boskovic, Z. (1998a). "Multiple *wh*-fronting and Economy of Derivation." In E. Curtis, J. Lyle, and G. Webster, eds., *Proceedings of the 16th West Coast Conference on Formal Linguistics*. Stanford, Cal.: CSLI Publications. (Distributed by Cambridge University Press), 49–63.

Boskovic, Z. (1998b). "*Wh*-phrases and *Wh*-movement in Slavic." Comparative Slavic Morphosyntax Workshop, Bloomington, Ind.

Brody, M. (1995). *Lexico-Logical Form: A Radically Minimalist Theory*. Cambridge, Mass.: MIT Press.

Carstairs-McCarthy (1999). *The Origins of Complex Language*. Oxford: Oxford University Press.

Cherniak, C. (1995). "Neural Component Placement" *Trends in Neuroscience* 18, 522–527.

Chomsky, N. (1965). *Aspects of the Theory of Syntax*. Cambridge, Mass.: MIT Press.

Chomsky, N. (1970). "Remarks on Nominalization." In R. Jacobs and P. Rosenbaum, eds., *Readings in English Transformational Grammar*. Waltham, Mass.: Ginn. Reprinted in Chomsky, *Studies on Semantics in Generative Grammar*. The Hague: Mouton, 1972.

Chomsky, N. (2000a). "Minimalist Inquiries" (*MI*). In Martin et al., eds. (2000)

Chomsky, N. (2000b). *New Horizons in the Study of Language and Mind*. Cambridge: Cambridge University Press.

Chomsky, N. (2001). "Derivation by Phase" (*DbP*). In Kenstowicz (2001).

Chomsky, N., R. Huybregts, & H. van Riemsdijk. (1982). *The Generative Enterprise*. Dordrecht: Foris.

Chung, S. (1998). *The Design of Agreement*. Chicago: University of Chicago Press.

Collins, C. (1993). Topics in Ewe Syntax. Ph.D. Diss. MIT, Cambridge.

Collins, C. (1999). Eliminating Labels. Ms., Cornell University, Ithaca, N.Y.

Epstein, S. (1999). "Un-Principled Syntax: The Derivation of Syntactic Relations. In Epstein and Hornstein (1999).

Epstein, S., & N. Hornstein, eds. (1999). *Working Minimalism*. Cambridge, Mass.: MIT Press.

Fintel, K. von, & S. Iatridou. (2001). On the Interaction of Modals, Quantifiers, and *If*-Clauses. Ms., MIT, Cambridge.

Fox, D. (2000). *Economy and Semantic Interpretation*. Cambridge, Mass.: MIT Press.

Fox, D. (2001). Antecedent Contained Delection and the Copy Theory of Movement. Ms., Harvard University, Cambridge, Mass.

Fox, D., & J. Nissenbaum. (1999). Extraposition and the Nature of Covert Movement. Ms., Harvard University, Cambridge, Mass.

Frampton, J., & S. Gutmann. (2000). Crash-Proof Syntax. Ms, Northeastern University, Boston.

Frampton, J., S. Gutmann, J. Legate, & C. Yang. (1999). Remarks on DBP, Agreement, and Intervention. Ms., Northeastern University, Boston, and MIT, Cambridge.

Freidin, R., & J.-R. Vergnaud. (2001). Exquisite Connections: Some Remarks on the Evolution of Linguistic Theory. Ms., Princeton University, Princeton, N.J., and the University of Southern California, Los Angeles.

Fukui, N. (2001). "Phrase Structure." In M. Baltin and C. Collins, eds., *The Handbook of Contemporary Syntactic Theory*. Malden, Mass., and Oxford: Blackwell.

Gil, D. (1987). "On the Scope of Grammatical Theory." In S. Mogdil and C. Mogdil, eds., *Noam Chomsky: Consensus and Controversy*. Philadelphia: Taylor & Francis.

Guasti, M. T., & L. Rizzi. (1999). Agreement and Tense as Distinct Syntactic Positions: Evidence from Acquisition. In G. Cinque, ed., *Functional Structure in DP and IP—The Cartography of Syntactic Structures*, vol. 1. Oxford University Press, N.Y.

Hiraiwa, K. (2000). Multiple Agree and the Defective Intervention Constraint in Japanese. Ms, MIT, Cambridge.

Holmberg, A. (1999). "Remarks on Holmberg's Generalization." *Studia Linguistica* 53(1), 1–39, April.

Hornstein, N. (1999). "Movement and Control." *Linguistic Inquiry* 30, 69–96.

Iatridou, S. (1993). "On Nominative Case Assignment and a Few Related Things." In C. Phillips, ed., *MIT Working Papers in Linguistics: Vol. 2, Papers on Case & Agreement*, 175–196.

Iatridou, S. (2001). Temporal Existentials? Ms., MIT, Cambridge.

Jenkins, L. (2000). *Biolinguistics*. Cambridge: Cambridge University Press.

Kayne, R. (1981). "Unambiguous paths." In R. May and J. Koster, eds., *Levels of Syntactic Representation*. Dordrecht: Foris.

Kayne, R. (1994). *The Antisymmetry of Syntax*. Cambridge, Mass.: MIT Press.

Kenstowicz, M., ed. (2001). *Ken Hale: A Life in Language*. Cambridge, Mass.: MIT Press.

Lasnik, H. (1999a). "Chains of Arguments." In S. Epstein & N. Hornstein, eds., *Working Minimalism*. Cambridge, Mass.: MIT Press.

Lasnik, H. (1999b). *Minimalist Analysis*. Malden, Mass., and Oxford: Blackwell.

Lasnik, H. (1999c). "On the Locality of Movement: Formalist Syntax Position Paper." In M. Darnell, E. Moravcsik, F. Newmeyer, M. Noonan, & K. Wheatley, eds., *Functionalism and Formalism in Linguistics*, vol. 1. Amsterdam: John Benjamins.

Lebeaux, D. (1988). Language Acquisition and the Form of Grammar. Ph.D. Diss., University of Massachusetts, Amherst. Revised and extended edition, Amsterdam: John Benjamins, 2000.

Lebeaux, D. (1999). Where Does the Binding Theory Apply? Ms., NEC Research Institute.

Legate, J. (1998). Verb Phrase Types and the Notion of a Phase. Ms., MIT, Cambridge.

Leiber, J. (2001). "Turing and the Fragility and Insubstantiality of Evolutionary Explanations: A Puzzle About the Unity of Alan Turing's Work with Some Larger Implications." *Philosophical Psychology* 14, 1.

Martin, R, D. Michaels, and J. Uriagereka, eds. (2000). *Step by Step: Essays in Minimalist Syntax in Honor of Howard Lasnik*. Cambridge, Mass.: MIT Press.

Martin, R., & J. Uriagereka (2000). "Introduction: Some Possible Foundations for the Minimalist Program." In Martin et al. 2000.

Maynard Smith, J. (1998). *Shaping Life: Genes, Embryos and Evolution*. London: Weidenfeld & Nicolson.

Maynard Smith, J., R. Burian, S. Kauffman, P. Alberch, J. Campbell, B. Goodwin, R. Lande, D. Raup, & L. Wolpert. (1985). "Developmental Constraints in Evolution." *Quarterly Review of Biology* 60(3), 265–287.

McCloskey, J. (2000a). "The Distribution of Subject Properties in Irish." Ms., University of California, Santa Cruz. To appear in S. Dubinsky and W. Davies, eds., *The Role of Grammatical Functions in Transformational Syntax*. Dordrecht: Kluwer.

McCloskey, J. (2000b). "Quantifier Float and Wh-movement in an Irish English. *Linguistic Inquiry* 31(1), 57–84.

McCloskey, J. (2000c). Resumption, Successive Cyclicity, and the Locality of Operations. Ms., University of California, Santa Cruz.

McDaniel, D. (1989). "Partial and Multiple *WH*-movement." *Natural Language and Linguistic Theory* 7, 565–604.

Miller, G., & N. Chomsky (1963). "Finitary Models of Language Users." In R. Luce, R. Bush, & E. Galanter, eds., *Handbook of Mathematical Psychology*, vol. 2, chap. 13. New York: Wiley, 419–492.

Nissenbaum, J. (2000). Investigations of Covert Phrase Movement. Ph.D. diss., MIT, Cambridge.

Pesetsky, D. (2000). *Phrasal Movement and its Kin*. Cambridge, Mass.: MIT Press.

Pesetsky, D., & E. Torrego (2001). In Kenstowicz (2001).

Petitto, L., R. Zatorre, K. Gauna, E. Nikelski, D. Dostie, & A. Evans (2000). "Speech-like Cerebral Activity in Profoundly Deaf People While Processing Signed Languages: Implications for the Neural Basis of Human Language." *Proceedings of the National Academy of Sciences USA* 97(25), 13961–13966, December 5.

Ramus, F., M. Hauser, C. Miller, D. Morris, & J. Mehler (2000). "Language Discrimination by Human Newborns and by Cotton-Top Tamarin Monkeys." *Science* 288, 349–351.

Richards, N. (1997). What Moves Where in Which Language. Ph.D. diss., MIT, Cambridge.

Roeper, T. (2000). "Universal Bilingualism." *Bilingualism: Language and Cognition* 2.

Saddy, J. (1991). Investigations Into Grammatical Knowledge. Ph.D. diss., MIT, Cambridge.

Stewart, I. (1998). *Life's Other Secret*. New York: Wiley.

Uriagereka, J. (1998). *Rhyme and Reason*. Cambridge, Mass.: MIT Press.

Uriagereka, J. (1999). "Multiple Spell-Out." In Epstein & Horstein (1999).

Yang, C. (2000). Knowledge and Learning in Natural Language. Ph.D. diss., MIT, Cambridge.

4

GUGLIELMO CINQUE

"Restructuring" and Functional Structure

1. Introduction

In what follows I would like to show how the articulated functional structure of the clause suggested in Cinque (1999) may shed new light on the "restructuring" phenomenon (Rizzi 1976a,b; 1978) and perhaps afford a deeper understanding of it.

In the past twenty-five years, numerous analyses have been proposed to explain why certain phenomena that are otherwise clause-bound [such as Clitic Placement—see (1)] appear to be able to span over two clauses when the matrix verb is either a *modal*, an *aspectual*, or a *motion* verb and the complement is nonfinite [see the "climbing" of the clitic in (2)]:[1]

(1) a. ***Lo** detesto [vedere **t** in quello stato] '(I) him detest seeing in that state'
b. ***Lo** ammetto [di conoscere **t** appena] '(I) him admit to barely know'
c. ***Lo** rinuncio [ad avere **t** per me] '(I) it give up having for me'

(2) a. **Lo** volevo [vedere **t** subito]'(I) him wanted to see immediately' (*modal*)
b. **Lo** finisco [di vedere **t** domani]'(I) it finish to see tomorrow' (*aspectual*)
c. **Lo** vengo [a prendere **t** domani]'(I) it come to fetch tomorrow' (*motion*)

Even if each of the proposed analyses captures one or another aspect of restructuring, it is fair to say that none of them manages to answer the two most basic questions that the phenomenon raises; namely, why it should exist at all, and why it should exist with those particular verb classes (modal, aspectual, and motion). The fact that one finds transparency phenomena comparable to Clitic Climbing language after language, and with the same set of verbs (or subsets thereof), suggests that the phenomenon is universal and should thus follow from some general property of UG.[2] Here I would like to propose an analysis that derives its universality and answers at the same time the two basic questions just mentioned. The analysis is a natural extension of proposals made in Cinque (1999), where, on the basis of the relative order of functional morphemes in head position and of the corresponding classes of AdvPs, I suggested that the functional portion of the clause, in all languages, is constituted by the same, richly articulated and rigidly ordered, hierarchy of functional projections, a subset of which is shown in (3):[3]

(3) $\text{MoodP}_{\text{speech act}}$ > $\text{MoodP}_{\text{evaluative}}$ > $\text{MoodP}_{\text{evidential}}$ > $\text{ModP}_{\text{epistemic}}$ > TP(Past) > TP(Future) > $\text{MoodP}_{\text{irrealis}}$ > $\text{ModP}_{\text{alethic}}$ > $\text{AspP}_{\text{habitual}}$ > $\text{AspP}_{\text{repetitive(I)}}$ > $\text{AspP}_{\text{frequentative(I)}}$ > $\text{ModP}_{\text{volitional}}$ $\text{AspP}_{\text{celerative(I)}}$ > TP(Anterior) > $\text{AspP}_{\text{terminative}}$ > $\text{AspP}_{\text{continuative}}$ > $\text{AspP}_{\text{retrospective}}$ $\text{AspP}_{\text{proximative}}$ > $\text{AspP}_{\text{durative}}$ > $\text{AspP}_{\text{generic/progressive}}$ > $\text{AspP}_{\text{prospective}}$ > $\text{ModP}_{\text{obligation}}$ $\text{ModP}_{\text{permission/ability}}$ > $\text{AspP}_{\text{Completive}}$ > VoiceP > $\text{AspP}_{\text{celerative(II)}}$ > $\text{AspP}_{\text{repetitive(II)}}$ > $\text{AspP}_{\text{frequentative(II)}}$

The verbs that enter the restructuring construction appear to correspond to distinct heads of (3), in the sense that each seems to lexicalize the content of one or another functional head. This is obvious for the various modal and aspectual verbs, but it is true for motion verbs as well.[4]

In previous work (Cinque 2001, 2002a, originally written and circulated in 1997, and Cinque 1998), I had suggested that this striking correspondence rendered the following hypothesis appealing: only those verbs that happen to match semantically the content of a certain functional head admit of two distinct possibilities. They are either regular verbs, heading a VP [in which case they take a fulfledged sentential complement (CP)—cf. (4a)], or functional verbs, directly inserted in the head position of the corresponding functional projection (cf. (4b):

(4) a. $[_{\text{CP}} \ldots [_{\text{FP}} \ldots [_{\text{FP}} \ldots [_{\text{VP}} \text{V}_{\text{restr}} [_{\text{CP}} \ldots [_{\text{FP}} \ldots [_{\text{FP}} \ldots [_{\text{VP}} \text{V}]]]]]]]]$
b. $[_{\text{CP}} \ldots [_{\text{FP}} \ldots [_{\text{FP}} \text{V}_{\text{restr}} [_{\text{FP}} \ldots [_{\text{VP}} \text{V}]]]]$

Following the received opinion, I had also assumed that the presence or absence of transparency effects reduced to two mutually exclusive options: the obligatory *presence* of transparency effects in the monoclausal structure (4b) and the obligatory *absence* of transparency effects in the biclausal structure (4a).

Here, after arguing that *when transparency effects obtain,* "restructuring" verbs are functional verbs in a monoclausal configuration (sections 2–5), I will explore the stronger and at first sight more difficult claim that they are *always* functional verbs in a monoclausal configuration (*even in the variant that shows no transparency effects*—section 6). This implies that restructuring verbs have no other option but to enter structure (4b) (ultimately, a consequence of their corresponding to the semantic content of a distinct functional head). This also requires interpreting the differences between the variant with and the variant without transparency effects in a different manner (section 7).[5]

2. The constituency issue

The analysis whereby, when transparency effects obtain, restructuring verbs are functional verbs (directly inserted under the corresponding functional heads) leads one to expect a constituent structure quite different from that of Rizzi (1976a, 1978). According to Rizzi's analysis, modal, aspectual and motion verbs can trigger a process of structural simplification (Restructuring), which turns an original biclausal configuration into a monoclausal one, forming a complex verb out of the complement and matrix verbs, as shown in (5):

(5) a. [$_{CP}$ io [verrò [$_{CP}$ a parlar**ti** di questi problemi]]] RESTRUCTURING →
(I will come to talk-to-you about these problems.)
b. [$_{CP}$ io [$_{V}$ **ti** verrò a parlare] di questi problemi]

As a result of this complex verb formation, the embedded verb is taken to no longer form a constituent with its own complements [cf. (5b)].

In the present analysis, instead, the expected constituent structure is (6), with the embedded verb still forming a constituent with its complements:

(6) [$_{CP}$ io [$_{AndativeP}$ **ti** verrò [$_{VP}$ a parlare [di questi problemi]]]]

This requires reassessing the arguments brought forth by Rizzi (1976a, 1978) in support of the constituency in (5b). He shows, for example, that when transparency effects obtain a number of operations apparently cease to apply to the sequence formed by the embedded verb and its complements, taking this to support the derived structure (5b). Let us consider these cases in turn.

2.1. Cleft Sentence Formation

As shown by the contrast between (7a and b), when the clitic has climbed to the matrix verb the embedded verb cannot be clefted together with its complement:

(7) a. E' proprio a parlar**ti** di questi problemi che verrà
'It's just to talk to-you about these problems that he'll come.'
b.*E' proprio a parlare di questi problemi che **ti** verrà

This would seem to follow from the constituency in (5b). Notice, however, that with other fronting rules (such as Focus Movement and Topicalization) no such restriction obtains:

(8) a. A PARLARE DEI SUOI PROBLEMI, **ti** verrà! Vedrai.[6]
'To speak about his problems (focus), he'll to-you come! You'll see'
b. PORTARE A CASA, **lo** voleva! 'Take home (focus), he it wanted'
c. Leggere a tutti, non **lo** potevo 'Read to everybody, I it couldn't'

As the latter constructions are no less valid constituency diagnostics than Cleft Sentence Formation, we must conclude that the embedded verb *does* form a constituent with its complement, just as (6) implies, and that the ungrammaticality of (7b) is due to some other reason (not dependent on constituency). Note that there are quite severe restrictions on what can be clefted [cf. (9) and (10)] that do not hold with Focus Movement or Topicalization of the same sequences [cf. (11) and (12)]. These same restrictions, then, might be at the basis of the ungrammaticality of (7b) versus (8) (see section 7 below for discussion of a possible reason).

(9) a. *Era bella che sembrava
It was beautiful that she seemed
b. *E' completamente che l'ha rovinato
It is completely that he ruined it
c. *E' tutti che li ha visti
It is all that he saw them

(10) a. *E' parlato di questo che (gli) avrà 'It's spoken about this that he (to-him) will have'[7]
b. *Era parlando di questo che (gli) stavo 'It's speaking about this that I (to-him) was'
c. *E' stato portato a casa che è 'It's been taken home that he has'

(11) a. BELLA, sembrava 'Beautiful (focus), she seemed'
b. COMPLETAMENTE, l'ha rovinato 'Completely (focus), he ruined it'
c. Tutti, non li ha visti 'All, he hasn't seen them'

(12) a. PARLATO DI QUESTO, (gli) avrà! 'Spoken about this (focus), he (to-him) will have'
b. PARLANDO DI QUESTO, (gli) stavo! 'Speaking about this (focus), (to-him) I was'
c. Portato a casa, non era stato, ancora 'Taken home, he hadn't been, yet'
d. ?Stato portato a casa, non era, ancora 'Been taken home, he hadn't, yet'

All in all, we have no reason to interpret (7b) as showing that the embedded verb and its complement do not form a constituent. If anything, (8) shows just the opposite.[8]

2.2. Right Node Raising

As Rizzi (1976a, 1978) also notes, the embedded verb and its complement can be Right Node Raised only in the absence of trasparency effects. See the contrast between (13a and b):

(13) a. Piero voleva—ma francamente adesso non so se vorrà ancora—parlar**ne** con Gianni
'P. wanted to—but frankly now I don't know if he still will—speak about it with G.'
b. *Piero **ne** voleva—ma francamente adesso non so se **ne** vorrà ancora—parlare con Gianni
'P. about it wanted to—but frankly now I don't know if he still will—speak about it with G.'

Once again this would seem to follow from the assumption that in the presence of Clitic Climbing the embedded verb and its complement do not form a constituent. But this conclusion is not necessary. Another possibility exists, which is compatible with the idea that the embedded verb continues to form a constituent with its complements.[9]

In the framework in which Rizzi (1976a, 1978) was working, Right Node Raising was considered a rightward movement rule (cf. Postal 1974: 125–128). More recently, Kayne (1994: 67f.), following Wexler and Culicover (1980: 298ff.), has proposed to reinterpret it as a deletion rule deleting under identity the lefthand copy of the "raised" phrase: *Piero voleva ~~parlarne con Gianni~~—ma francamente adesso non so se vorrà ancora—parlarne con Gianni*. The following contrasts between Italian and English indeed appear to support Kayne's reinterpretation of Right Node Raising. As noted in Napoli (1981: 846), Right Node Raising of the complement of an auxiliary is impossible in Italian. See (14):

(14) a. *Mario ha—ma dirà di non avere—capito la lezione 'M. has—but he will say he hasn't—understood the lesson'
b. *Gianni allora era—ma non so se ancora oggi sarebbe—apprezzato per il suo autoritarismo 'G. then was—but I don't know whether today still he would be—appreciated for his authoritarianism'

Right Node Raising of the complement of an auxiliary is instead possible in English:

(15) Tony should have—and Pete probably would have—called Grace (Postal 1974: 126)

Now, the two languages also differ with respect to the deletion of the complement of an auxiliary, as shown in (16):

(16) a. Have you called John? Yes. I have______.
b. Hai chiamato John? *Sì. Ho______

If Right Node Raising involves deletion, the first contrast reduces to the second. No such reduction is possible under the Movement analysis of Right Node Raising. In the more restrictive deletion analysis, which crucially relates (14) to (16b), the ungrammaticality of (13b) can, then, be attributed not to the fact that *parlare con Gianni* fails to be a constituent but to the impossibility of deleting an infinitival complement in the presence of transparency effects. See (17), noted in Radford (1977a: 113) (whatever the right analysis of this phenomenon is; see Depiante 1998 and section 7 below):

(17) a. Gianni voleva parlare di questo, ma Piero non (*ne) voleva______
G. wanted to talk about this, but P. not (about-it) wanted
b. *Certe cose si possono fare, ma queste non si possono______
Certain things one can do, but these not one can
c. Gianni poteva andare a casa, ma non ha/*è voluto______
G. could go home, but not has/is wanted

2.3. Heavy NP-Shift

Another rule considered in this context by Rizzi is Heavy (or Complex) NP-Shift, which at the time was taken to move a heavy or complex constituent rightward, deriving for example (18b) from (18a) by moving the constituent *ad esporti la mia idea* to the right of the PP *a Firenze*.

(18) a. Fra qualche giorno, verrò ad espor**ti** la mia idea a Firenze 'In a few days, I'll come to explain to-you my idea in Florence.'
b. Fra qualche giorno, verrò a Firenze ad espor**ti** la mia idea 'In a few days, I'll come to Florence to explain to-you my idea.'

Rizzi (1976a, 1978) notes that this movement is no longer possible if Clitic Climbing has applied [cf.(19)], taking this to suggest that *ad esporre la mia idea* in (19b) cannot be moved because after Restructuring it is no longer a constituent:

(19) a. Fra qualche giorno, **ti** verrò ad esporre la mia idea a Firenze
b. *Fra qualche giorno, **ti** verrò a Firenze ad esporre la mia idea

More recently, the existence of rightward movement rules has been called into question (Kayne 1994). Kayne reanalyzes Heavy NP-Shift as involving the leftward movement of what in the previous analysis was crossed over by the rightward moved phrase. Within such an analysis, there is a natural account for the ungrammaticality of (19b) that does not depend on the nonconstituenthood of *ad esporre la mia idea*. It is bad for the same reason that (20) is; namely, a locative PP has been moved (scrambled) to an illicit position in the lower functional field between a functional head and its complement:[10]

(20) *Lo ho a Firenze messo al corrente della nostra decisione
'I him have in Florence notified of our decision'

Thus it seems that there is no reason to abandon the idea that the embedded infinitival and its complements form a constituent when transparency effects obtain, and hence no particular reason to assume that the "restructuring" and the infinitival verb come to form a complex predicate (cf. Hinterhölzl 1999 for a similar conclusion concerning the "restructuring" construction of Germanic).[11]

2.4. Aux-to-COMP

I mention here a possible additional piece of evidence in favor of the structure $[_{FP}\ V_{restruct} \ldots [_{VP}\ V\ ZP]]$ and against the idea that the restructuring verb and the embedded infinitive come to form a constituent that leaves out the infinitive's complements. Consider the behavior of a restructuring verb and its embedded infinitive in the Aux-to-COMP construction studied in Rizzi (1981, 1982a). Even in the presence of Clitic Climbing, only the restructuring verb can raise to C, never both, which is unexpected if the two verbs form a complex V (unless *obligatory* excorporation of the matrix verb is posited):

(21) a. Non potendo**lo** [egli restituire a nessuno] 'Not being able it he to give back to anybody'
b.*Non potendo**lo** restituire [egli a nessuno] 'Not being able it to give back he to anybody'

(22) a. Ritenevamo non dover**ne** [egli parlare neanche con voi] 'We thought not to have he to talk not even with you'
b.*Ritenevamo non dover**ne** parlare [egli neanche con voi] 'We thought not to have to talk he not even with you'

3. Monoclausality versus biclausality

In this section I examine some potential evidence (in addition to that recently discussed in Wurmbrand 1998, 2001) for the monoclausal nature of the construction when transparency effects obtain (sections 3.1–3.2), and consider in section 3.3 some of the apparent evidence for its biclausality, concluding that it is unconvincing.

3.1. Prohibition against using the same adverb twice

Adverbs that in a simple clause can occur only once (like *già* 'already' and *sempre* 'always')[12] in contexts with *volere* appear to be able to occur twice if no transparency effects obtain (and there is a pause after the first adverb). They no longer can when transparency effects obtain:

(23) a. Maria vorrebbe **già** aver**lo** **già** lasciato
Mary would already want to have already left him.
b.*Maria **lo** vorrebbe **già** aver **già** lasciato (Clitic Climbing)

(24) a. Si vorrebbe **sempre** aver **sempre** esperienze come queste
One would always want to always have experiences like these.
b.*Esperienze come queste si vorrebbero **sempre** aver **sempre** (Long NP-Movement)

(25) a. Maria vorrà **già** esser **loro** **già** stata presentata
M. will already want to have to-them already been introduced.
b.*Maria vorrà **loro** **già** esser **già** stata presentata (*Loro* Climbing)

(26) a. Gianni **avrebbe** **sempre** voluto arrivare **sempre** tra i primi
G. would always have liked to always arrive among the first.
b.*Gianni **sarebbe** **sempre** voluto arrivare **sempre** tra i primi (Auxiliary Selection)

The contrast becomes understandable if the (a) variants contain two clauses and the (b) variants are strictly monoclausal.[13]

3.2. The relative order of "restructuring" verbs

If more "restructuring" verbs occur, their relative order appears to be quite rigid when transparency effects obtain [cf. (27)–(30)]. Although this is unexpected under biclausal analyses, it is to be expected in a monoclausal one in which "restructuring" verbs are 'functional' verbs directly inserted into the corresponding functional heads. This occurs because functional heads are themselves rigidly ordered.

So, for example, when the "restructuring" verb *solere* 'use' (cf. *Lo soleva dire anche mio padre* 'it my father too used to say'), related to the Habitual Aspect head, co-occurs with the "restructuring" verb *tendere* 'tend' (cf. *Lo tendo a credere anch'io* 'it I tend to believe myself'),[14] the only possible order for most speakers is *solere* > *tendere* (suggesting the order of heads $\mathbf{Asp_{habitual}} > \mathbf{Asp_{predispositional}}$):[15]

(27) a. ?Certe cose, le si suole tendere ad evitare 'Certain things, them one usually tends to avoid.'
b. *Certe cose, le si tende a soler evitare 'Certain things, them one tends to usually avoid.'

When *tendere* and *volere* 'want' co-occur, the order is rigidly *tendere* > *volere*, in turn suggesting the order $\mathbf{Asp_{predispositional}} > \mathbf{Mod_{volitional}}$:

(28) a. Lo tenderebbe a voler fare sempre lui 'He would tend to want to always do it he himself.'
b. *Lo vorrebbe tendere a fare sempre lui 'He would want to tend to always do it he himself.'

When *volere* and *smettere* 'stop' (related to what in other languages is a Terminative Aspect suffix or particle) co-occur, the order is *volere* > *smettere*, suggesting the order of heads: $\mathbf{Mod_{volitional}} > \mathbf{Asp_{terminative}}$.

(29) a. Non vi vuole smettere di importunare 'He you doesn't want to stop bothering'
b. *Non vi smette di voler importunare 'He you doesn't stop wanting to bother'

A final example here (see Cinque 2001 for a more systematic investigation of these orderings) is the relative order of *smettere* and *continuare* 'continue,' the latter corresponding to the Continuative Aspect head morphology found in many languages. When they co-occur the order is *smettere* > *continuare*, once again suggestive of the order of heads: $\mathbf{Asp_{terminative}} > \mathbf{Asp_{continuative}}$.[16]

(30) a. ?La smise di continuare a importunare '(He) her stopped continuing to bother'
b. *La continuò a smettere di importunare '(He) her continued to stop bothering'

Putting together the various relative orders, one arrives at the order of verbs in (31), corresponding to the order of functional heads shown in (32):[17]

(31) *solere > tendere > volere > smettere > continuare*

(32) $\mathbf{Asp_{habitual}} > \mathbf{Asp_{predispositional}} > \mathbf{Mod_{volitional}} > \mathbf{Asp_{terminative}} > \mathbf{Asp_{continuative}}$[18]

3.3. Apparent cases of transparency effects across CP

A strong case for the biclausal character of restructuring would seem to come from two instances of Clitic Climbing across what looks like a CP-boundary.

The first is already discussed in Rizzi (1978: 151f.), where such cases as (33) are noted:

(33) a. [. . .] non **ti** saprei che dire 'I you wouldn't know what to tell'
b. ?Mario, non **lo** saprei a chi affidare, [. . .] 'M., I him wouldn't know to whom to entrust'
c. ??[. . .] proprio, non **lo** saprei come risolvere 'Really, I it wouldn't know how to solve'

As Rizzi himself (n. 38) observes (cf. also Napoli 1981: 855; Moore 1994: n. 3; Rooryck 1994: 420ff.; etc.), the productivity of the construction is, however, severely limited. Among the predicates that take embedded interrogatives, only *sapere* (*come*) 'know (how)' allows it [compare (33) with (34)], and even it has various limitations [cf. (35)]:

(34) a.*Me lo chiedevo come fare 'I myself it wondered how to do'
b.*Gli si domanda che cosa dare 'He himself to-him asks what to give'
c.*Me lo ha detto a chi dare 'He to-me it told to whom to give'

(35) a.*Non ne saprei quando parlare
'Of-it I wouldn't know when to speak' (cf. Rizzi 1978: n. 38)
b.*[. . .] non lo saprei se consigliare o no
'I him wouldn't know whether to advise or not' (Rizzi 1978: n. 38)
c.*Non lo saprei perché fare 'I it wouldn't know why to do'

The generalization appears to be that Clitic Climbing is allowed across a wh-phrase with *sapere* either if *sapere* means "know how" (33c) or if the sentence allows for a rhetorical reading without the wh-phrase; with *sapere* meaning "be able" (33a) is equivalent to *Non ti saprei dire niente* 'I to-you wouldn't be able to say anything', and (33b) to *Non lo saprei affidare a nessuno* 'I him wouldn't be able to entrust to anybody').[19]

In either case, the verb embedding a wh-phrase is interpreted as a modal of mental ability (a notion often distinguished from physical ability in the languages of the world). This makes the verb a natural candidate for direct insertion under the root modal head of ability, like other restructuring verbs, an option not open to the verbs in (34) and (35), whose interpretation is not one of mental ability. The only auxiliary assumption that needs to be made is that the root modal head of *mental* ability can take a single wh-CP-layer above its ordinary functional XP-complement (without full recursion of the extended functional projection).[20]

In sum, the very selective nature of Clitic Climbing across a wh-CP in mental ability contexts and the interpretation of it just sketched render the argument based on (33) for the biclausal character of restructuring very dubious. If anything, the properties of (33) point, once again, to the functional nature of the verb, a modal (and to the monoclausal character of the construction).

More problematic would seem to be the apparent case of Clitic Climbing out of finite complements of restructuring verbs in certain varieties of Salentino, discussed in Calabrese (1993) and Terzi (1992: 151ff., 1994, 1996), and in the varieties of Serbo-Croatian, discussed in Progovac (1991, 1993) and Terzi (1996: 289ff.); see also Stjepanović (1998).

In the Salentino of Brindisi, for example, when the mood particle *ku* is missing, a clitic can climb out of the apparently finite complement and cliticize to the restructuring verb [cf. (36b), from Terzi 1992: 159]:[21]

(36) a. Voggyu (ku) lu kkattu
(I) want (I) it buy 'I want to buy it'
b. Lu voggyu (*ku) kkattu
(I) it want (I) buy

A similar situation (modulo the nondeletability of the mood particle *da*) is found in Serbo-Croatian (Progovac 1993: 119):

(37) a. Milan želi da **ga** vidi
M. want-3sg particle him see-3sg
b. ?Milan **ga** želi da vidi
M. him want-3sg particle see-3sg
'M. wishes to see him.'

Despite appearances, there is some reason to doubt that (36) and (37) involve the extraction of a clitic from a finite clausal complement.

First, in both Salentino and Serbo-Croatian, the apparently finite embedded verb of (36) and (37) displays severe restrictions on its form: it can only appear in the present tense, which is equal to the verb stem plus person and number agreement. In particular, no past (or periphrastic) tense forms are possible:[22]

(38) a. ***Lu** vulia kattavu (Salentino—Andrea Calabrese, personal communication)
It wanted-1sg bought-1sg 'I wished I bought it.'
b. *Ja bih **ga** voleo da sam posetio (Serbo-Croatian—Lijljana Progovac, personal communication)
I would him like PART be-1sg visited 'I would like to have visited him.'
(Cf. Ja bih voleo da sam **ga** posetio 'I would like to have visited him.')

This is unexpected in a biclausal analysis of such structures. But it makes sense in an analysis in which particle + stem agreement is treated as a surrogate form of infinitive (itself absent, or highly restricted, in these varieties). In fact, it is tempting to view agreement here as nothing other than a way to render the stem a well-formed morphological word. If so, the possibility arises again of viewing the sequence (particle +) stem-agreement as part of one and the same clause with the restructuring verb (in which case the observed unavailability of past tense on the embedded verb would follow from the fact that this is already marked on the restructuring verb or higher up).

The monoclausal nature of such structures (when they display Clitic Climbing) may be glimpsed from the following property of Serbo-Croatian. As (39a) shows, when no Clitic Climbing is present, the subject of the embedded verb can be expressed by an overt (focused) pronominal even when it is coreferential with the matrix subject. This possibility is, however, lost in the presence of Clitic Climbing (Ljiljana Progovac, personal communication). See (39b):

(39) a. Milan želi da ga ON vidi 'M. wishes HE HIMSELF to see him'
b. *Milan ga želi da ON vidi 'M. him wishes HE HIMSELF to see'

While unexpected under a biclausal analysis of "restructuring"/Clitic Climbing, the contrast follows from the monoclausal one proposed in the next section, where evidence is provided that even apparently 'control' verbs such as 'want' inherit, in "restructuring" contexts, their subject from the embedded lexical verb (as happens with auxiliaries). Under such a monoclausal analysis, (39b) is bad because either *Milan* or *ON*, but not both, can be generated in the subject position of the embedded verb *vidi* (Stjepanović 2001 also argues for the monoclausal character of both (37a and b)].[23]

4. The functional status of restructuring verbs in the presence of transparency effects

One consequence of the idea that (when transparency effects obtain) "restructuring" verbs are "functional" verbs directly inserted under the corresponding functional heads is that, like auxiliaries (cf. Pollock 1989), they should have no thematic roles to assign, and hence no arguments of their own.[24] Despite certain appearances, this will prove a welcome (and correct) consequence.

4.1. The unavailability of internal arguments

Kayne (1989b: 248) observes, "Virtually all the standard cases of clitic climbing are cases of subject control or raising. What is conspicuously absent is object control."[25] He takes his analysis of "restructuring" in terms of INFL raising from the embedded to the matrix clause (via COMP) to provide the required explanation. As INFL is coindexed with its Spec (containing the subject DP), the embedded INFL raising to the higher INFL will force coindexation of the lower with the higher subject. In object control structures, however, there would be "two AGR whose respective subjects are themselves not essentially coindexed."[26]

The analysis developed here instead takes the absence of object-control restructuring verbs to be a special case of a more general phenomenon, namely, the fact that no verb with an object complement (i.e., assigning a thematic role) can be used as a functional verb. This more stringent condition indeed appears to predict the nonexistence of cases that the I-to- (C-to-) I hypothesis does not exclude.

Consider the case of a raising verb that can optionally take a complement. *Sembrare* 'seem' in Italian is such a verb:

(40) a. Gianni non sembra apprezzarlo 'G. does not seem to appreciate it.'
b. Gianni non ci sembra apprezzarlo 'G. does not seem **to-us** to appreciate it.'

For many speakers, myself included, *sembrare* allows Clitic Climbing [cf. (41a)][27] but, crucially, not if it takes a (dative) complement [cf. (41b)]:[28]

(41) a. Gianni non lo sembra apprezzare abbastanza 'G. does not it seem to appreciate enough'
b. *Gianni non **ce** lo sembra apprezzare abbastanza 'G. doesn't **to-us** it seem to appreciate enough'

A comparable contrast concerning 'long' L-*tous* in French (also found only with "restructuring" verbs) is noted in Pollock (1978: 97f.) (I thank Richard Kayne for pointing this out to me):[29]

(42) a. ?Elle a tous semblé/paru les avoir lus
She seemed/ appeared to have read them all
b. *Pierre **m**'a tous semblé/paru les avoir lus
She seemed/ appeared **to-me** to have read them all

These contrasts, which are very sharp, seem to indicate that it is the presence of the dative complements of 'seem,' *ce* 'to us,' *me* 'to me,' which inhibits Clitic Climbing and 'long' L-*tous*, respectively. For such contrasts, the I-to- (C-to-) I account has nothing to say, as in neither case would there be contraindexing as a result of I raising.[30]

In conclusion, there are no object control "restructuring" verbs because, being functional (directly inserted under a functional head), such verbs can have no complements. Nor can there be any unaccusative subject control "restructuring" verb (with the subject originating in object position), natural candidates being motion verbs. As the ill-formedness of (43b) shows, this expectation is also confirmed. Whenever the subject of *venire* remains in the inverted subject (i.e., structural object) position, which in the present analysis excludes its restructuring usage, the downstairs clitic cannot climb to *venire*:[31]

(43) a. Ne sono venuti molti a porta**ti** un regalo?
Of-them are come many to bring to-you a present
'Did many come to bring you a present?'
b. ***Te** ne sono venuti molti a portare un regalo?
To-you of-them are come many to bring a present
'Did many come to bring you a present?'

Again, in the I-to- (C-to-) I analysis it is not clear why Clitic Climbing should be blocked in this case, as the matrix and the embedded subjects are coindexed.[32] The intervention of material between the "restructuring" and the embedded verb in (43b) should not matter. Various cases of intervening material, documented in the literature, do not block Clitic Climbing (see Napoli 1981: 865f.; Aissen & Perlmutter 1983: 395f.; & LaPolla 1988: 220), one being floating quantifiers: ***Ti*** *sono venuti* ***tutti*** *a portare un regalo* 'All have come to bring you a present.') It thus seems plausible to take the unavailability of Clitic Climbing in (43b) to depend on the fact that *venire* has an internal argument.[33]

4.2. Some apparent cases of object control "restructuring" verbs

If the general unavailability of object control "restructuring" verbs is derived from the fact that functional verbs cannot take internal arguments, something needs to be said about the few cases claimed in the literature to be object control "restructuring" verbs. Luján (1978: 123), and Suñer (1980: 318), for example, analyze cases like the following, containing Clitic Climbing, as cases of "restructuring":[34]

(44) a. **Me** permitió tocar**la**
b. **Me la** permitió tocar 'She allowed me to play it' (Luján 1978: 123).

(45) a. **Nos** ordenaron ver**la**
b. **Nos la** ordenaron ver 'They ordered us to see it' (Suñer 1980: 318).

Although sentences corresponding to (44b) and (45b) are impossible in Italian (**Me la permise di suonare; *Ce la ordinarono di vedere*) and Portuguese (cf. Martins 1995: 228), a comparable case of an apparently object control verb that allows Clitic Climbing in Italian is *insegnare* 'teach.'[35] See (46):

(46) a. **Gli** ho insegnato a far**lo** io
b. **Gliel'**ho insegnato a fare io
'I taught him (DAT) to do it.'

Kayne (1989b: 248), observing the general nonexistence of object control restructuring verbs, conjectures that the few existing cases [like (44)–(46) above] are actually hidden instances of the causative construction (which also has Clitic Climbing).[36]

Indeed there is evidence to support his intuition. These putative "restructuring" verbs appear to be subject to restrictions that typically hold for the combination of a causative verb and its infinitival complement and are not found with ordinary "restructuring" verbs. For example, as noted in Suñer (1980: 316), where the observation is attributed to Bordelois (1974) and Luján (1978) in Spanish, "causative verbs permit Clitic Promotion provided that the object of the infinitive is [-animate]." See the contrast between (47) and (48):

(47) a. Juan **le** dejó/hizo/vio/oyó armar**la** 'J. let/made/saw/heard him assemble it'
b. Juan **se la** dejó/hizo/vio/oyó armar 'J. let/made/saw/heard him assemble it'

(48) a. Juan **le** dejó/hizo/vio/oyó llamar**la** 'J. let/made/saw/heard him call her'
b.*Juan **se la** dejó/hizo/vio/oyó llamar 'J. let/made/saw/heard him call her'

Now, exactly the same restriction has been observed by Luján (1978: 180f.), Contreras (1979: 181, n. 11), Pizzini (1982), and Moore (1990: 321ff.) to hold with *permitir* 'allow' and the other hidden causatives. Compare (44) with (49), and (45) with (50):

(49) a. **Me** permitieron saludar**la** '(they) me permitted to greet her'
b.***Me la** permitieron saludar '(they) me her permitted to greet'

(50) a. **Nos** ordenaron saludar**la** '(they) us ordered to greet her'
b.***Nos la** ordenaron saludar '(they) us her ordered to greet'

Crucially, no such restriction holds for the ordinary (subject control and raising) cases of "restructuring". Similarly, in Italian, a restriction found with overt causatives is also found with *insegnare* 'teach.' The subject of a transitive verb embedded under causative *fare* (syntactically a dative) cannot cliticize to the causative if it is a reflexive or a reciprocal pronoun coreferent with the causative subject:

(51) a. Gianni e Mario fecero imparare la procedura a Carlo/l'uno all'altro
G. and M. had C. each other learn the procedure
b. Gianni e Mario gli/*si fecero imparare la procedura
G. and M. had him/each other learn the procedure

Analogously, the dative of (the hidden causative) *insegnare* (52), as opposed to the dative of an ordinary verb (53), cannot cliticize to the verb if it is a reflexive or reciprocal pronoun coreferent with the subject:

(52) a. Gianni e Mario insegnarono la procedura a Carlo/l'uno all'altro
G. and M. taught C./each other the procedure
b. Gianni e Mario gli/*?si insegnarono la procedura

(53) a. Gianni e Mario regalarono un disco a Carlo/l'uno all'altro
G. and M. gave a disk to C./to each other
b. Gianni e Mario si regalarono un disco

If so, the conclusion that there are object control "restructuring" verbs finds no justification.

4.3. The unavailability of external arguments

The idea that "restructuring" verbs in "restructuring" contexts do not assign thematic roles has the even stronger consequence that they cannot have an external argument either. To put it differently, there cannot be subject control but only raising "restructuring" verbs, as auxiliaries (in this respect).[37]

This appears at first glance to be an unwelcome result. Even though most of the "restructuring" verbs, like ordinary (non-"restructuring") raising verbs (as *rivelarsi* 'to manifest oneself'), fail to impose selectional requirements on the subject of their clause [cf. (54)], some do, for example, *volere* 'want,' *osare* 'dare,' *sapere* 'know how,' and *provare* 'try' [cf. (55)]:

(54) a. La casa gli doveva piacere 'The house had to appeal to him.'
b. La casa non gli poteva piacere 'The house could not appeal to him.'
c. La casa gli tendeva ad apparire piccola 'The house tended to appear little to him.'
d. La casa gli smise di piacere, da allora 'The house stopped appealing to him, since then.'
e. La casa non gli riusciva ad apparire bella 'The house did not manage to appear nice to him.'
f. La casa gli stava per piacere 'The house was about to appeal to him.'
g. La casa gli stava dando molti dispiaceri 'The house was giving him a lot of troubles.'
h. La casa gli seguitò ad apparire piccola 'The house continued to appear small to him.'
i. La casa gli cominciò a piacere 'The house started to appeal to him.'
j. La casa gli finì per piacere 'The house ended up being appealing to him.'
k. La casa gli finì di apparire piccola 'The house finished to appear small to him.'

(55) a. *La casa gli voleva appartenere 'The house wanted to belong to him.'
b. *La casa non gli osava piacere 'The house did not dare to appeal to him.'
c. *La casa non gli sapeva piacere 'The house didn't know how to appeal to him.'
d. *La casa gli provò a piacere 'The house tried to appeal to him.'

If we abstract momentarily from the problem raised by (55), to which we will return, the bulk of the evidence indeed appears to support the conclusion that restructuring verbs take no external arguments.

The first piece of evidence comes from an observation of Burzio (1986: 390), who notes that extraction of *ne* 'of-them/it' from the inverted subject of an apparently transitive/unergative "restructuring" verb is possible just in case the embedded infinitival verb is unaccusative. See (56), containing the "restructuring" verb *volere* 'want,' and (57), showing the same with the "restructuring" verbs *osare* 'dare,' *sapere* 'know how,' and *provare* 'try':

(56) Ne vorrebbero intervenire molti (Burzio 1986: 390)
Of them would like to intervene many
'Many would like to intervene.'

(57) a. Ne osarono rimanere solo due
Of them dared to stay only two
'Only two dared to stay.'

b. Ne seppero risalire ben pochi
Of them knew how to climb up really few
'Really few knew how to climb up.'

c. Ne provarono a intervenire solo un paio
Of them tried to intervene only a couple
'Only a couple tried to intervene.'

Similar facts are noted for Catalan in Picallo (1985: 210). See also Rosen (1990b, 483):

(58) N'hi volien entrar alguns
Of them there wanted to enter some
'Some wanted to enter there.'

The fact that *ne*-extraction in Italian (and Catalan) is only possible from an object position, or the 'inverted' subject position of an unaccusative, passive, or *si*-passive verb (namely, from a structural object position—Burzio 1986: 20–42), suggests that *molti, solo due, ben pochi, alguns,* and so on, are indeed in the structural object position of the embedded unaccusatives *intervenire* 'intervene,' *rimanere* 'remain,' *risalire* 'climb up,' and *entrar* 'enter' in (56), (57), and (58).

This is confirmed by the fact that *ne* can also appear on the infinitive [cf. (59)] and by the fact that replacing the embedded unaccusative with an unergative verb leads to ungrammaticality [cf. (60)]:

(59) a. Vorrebbero intervenirne molti
Would like to intervene of them many
'Many would like to intervene.'

b. Osarono rimanerne solo due
Dared to stay of them only two
'Only two dared to stay.'

c. Seppero risalirne ben pochi
Knew how to climb up of them really few
'Really few knew how to climb up.'

d. ?Provarono a intervenirne solo un paio
Tried to intervene of them only a couple
'Only a couple tried to intervene.'

(60) a. *Ce ne vorranno mangiare ben pochi
There of them will want to eat really few

b. *Non ne osò piangere nessuno
Not of them dared to cry no-one

c. *Non ne seppe rifiutare nessuno
Not of them knew how to refuse no-one

d. *Gliene provarono a parlare due
To him of them tried to talk two

This means that what looks like the (inverted) subject of the matrix "restructuring" verb is actually generated (and remains) in the object (inverted subject) position of the embedded infinitival verb (with nothing, as a consequence, being generated in the external argument position of the "restructuring" verb).[38]

Another piece of evidence that transitive/unergative "restructuring" verbs take no external argument (when used as functional verbs) comes from a property of the impersonal(-passive) *si* construction of Italian.

In nonfinite contexts under a raising verb, *si* is found with verbs that assign an external theta role (transitive and unergative) but not with those that fail to assign one (unaccusative, passive, psych-, copular, and raising verbs). See (61) and (62) and the discussion in Cinque (1988):

(61) a. Sembra esser**si** finalmente trovato il colpevole
seems to be *si* finally found the culprit 'The culprit seems to have been found.'
b. Non sembra esser**si** lavorato a sufficienza
Not seems to be *si* worked sufficiently 'One does not seem to have worked sufficiently.'

(62) a. *Sembra esser**si** arrivati troppo tardi
Seems to be *si* arrived too late
'One seems to have arrived too late.'
b. *Sembra non esser**si** stati apprezzati
Seems not to have been appreciated
'One seems not to have been appreciated.'
c. *Sembra esser**si** preoccupato solo un genitore (irrelevantly good in the intransitive use of *preoccuparsi*)
Seems to be *si* worried only one parent
'One seems to have worried only one parent.'
d. *Sembra non esser**si** benvenuti qui
Seems not to be *si* welcome here
'One seems not to be welcome here.'
e. *Sembra risultar**si** ignorare il problema
Seems to appear *si* to ignore the problem
'One seems to appear to ignore the problem.'

Whatever the account is for this contrast (cf. Cinque 1988 and Dobrovie-Sorin 1998), it constitutes a diagnostic for external-theta-role-assigning verbs.

Now, if there were subject control (hence transitive or unergative) "restructuring" verbs, one would expect them to allow *si* in nonfinite contexts [like those of (61)]. Yet, whether they allow it or not depends entirely on the nature of the verb in their infinitival complement. They do if the latter is transitive or unergative; otherwise they don't. In other words, they appear to inherit their status from that of the embedded verb, which again suggests that they do not have an external argument of their own but are transparent to the arguments of the embedded verb, much like auxiliaries. See (63) and (64), with the "restructuring" verb *volere* 'want':[39]

(63) a. (?)Non sembra esserglisi voluto dare sufficiente credito
Not seems to be to-him *si* wanted to give sufficient credit

b. (?)Non sembra essersene voluto parlare molto, di questi problemi
Not seems to be of-it *si* wanted to talk much, of these problems

(64) a.*Non sembra esserglisi voluto/i venire in aiuto[40]
Not seems to be him *si* wanted to come in support
b.*Non sembra esserglisi voluto/i essere presentati
Not seems to be to-him *si* wanted to be introduced
c.*Non sembra esserglisi voluto/i essere fedeli
Not seems to be to-him *si* wanted to be faithful
d.*Non sembra esserglisi voluto/i risultare simpatici
Not seems to be to-him *si* wanted to appear nice

From the evidence just reviewed, the conclusion that (when transparency effects obtain) "restructuring" verbs do not take external arguments seems inescapable, though it is in conflict with the evidence based on (55) above, where some such verbs appear to impose selectional restrictions on the subject (giving the appearance that they take a subject of their own). A possible solution to the paradox (in the spirit of Zubizarreta's 1982: chap. 3 proposal that such predicates assign not primary but adjunct theta roles) would consist in taking their selectional requirements to be a consequence of their semantics. If verbs like 'want,' just like volitional adverbs such as *willingly, voluntarily*, and so on. (cf. *The house willingly belonged to Bill*), or, for that matter, manner adverbs (cf. **The house hid the horizon carefully*), must be predicated on a sentient being, the ungrammaticality of (55) versus (54) follows without having to assume that they take an external argument of their own.

5. The optional character of transparency effects in (standard) Italian

5.1. The optionality of Clitic Climbing

It is widely assumed that Clitic Climbing obtains *obligatorily* in the "restructuring" configuration (cf. Rizzi 1976a, 1978, but see his notes 18 and 26, respectively for a different view; Burzio 1986: 393 n. 44; Rochette 1988: 96; Rosen 1990a: 144; among others). Evidence for that assumption primarily comes from the interaction of Long Object Preposing and Clitic Climbing. When Long Object Preposing obtains (indicating the presence of the "restructuring" configuration), Clitic Climbing must apparently also obtain. See the ungrammaticality of (65b), adapted from Rizzi (1978: 132), where the clitic has failed to climb, versus the grammaticality of (65c), where it has climbed:

(65) a. Si vorrebbe vender**gli** queste case a caro prezzo
Si (one) would like to sell him these houses at a high price
b.*Queste case si vorrebbero vender**gli** a caro prezzo
These houses si would like to sell him at a high price
c. Queste case **gli** si vorrebbero vendere a caro prezzo

The evidence, however, is less solid than it appears. First, as already noted in Rizzi (1976a: n. 18; 1978: n. 26; see also Longobardi 1978: n. 5), clitics may fail to climb in the presence of Auxiliary Change. See (66a), from Rizzi (1978), and (66b), from Boysen (1977: 289):

(66) a. Maria è dovuta veni**rci** molte volte
M. is had to come-there many times
'M. must have come there many times.'
b. Un'ora più tardi sarebbe dovuto esse**rvi** arrivato, ma nessuno lo vide (Silone)
One hour later he should be had to be there arrived, but nobody saw him
'One hour later he should have had to be there, but nobody saw him.'

This would seem to indicate that Clitic Climbing is optional, in contrast with what (65b) appeared to show. The paradox, however, is only apparent, as (65b) turns out to be ill formed for a different reason.

In Italian, when an unergative or transitive verb (which takes auxiliary *avere* 'have' in the perfect) is in the impersonal(-passive) *si* form, the perfect auxiliary shifts to *essere* 'be' (Rizzi 1978: n. 22). See (67) and (68):[41]

(67) a. Gianni **ha/*è** lavorato molto 'G. has/is worked a lot'
b. Si **è/*ha** lavorato molto 'One is/has worked a lot.'

(68) a. Gianni **ha/*è** perso molti soldi 'G. has/is lost a lot of money'
b. Si **son/*hanno** persi molti soldi 'A lot of money was/has been lost.'

This also holds in infinitival contexts (cf. Cinque 1988: 524ff.):

(69) I colpevoli non risultano **essersi/*aversi** ancora trovati 'The culprits do not seem yet to *si* be found'

When the higher verb is a "restructuring" verb, Object Preposing, as noted, can apparently span over two clauses:

(70) I colpevoli si vorrebbero trovare subito 'the culprits *si* would want to find immediately'

In such cases, a surprising instance of auxiliary shift is found on the embedded infinitival verb when this is in the perfect. In spite of the fact that the impersonal(-passive) *si* is on the "restructuring" verb, the perfect auxiliary of the embedded infinitival must be *essere* 'be.' Consider (71):

(71) a. Questi libri gli si vorrebbero **esser** già dati
These books to-him si (one) would like to be already given
b. *Questi libri gli si vorrebbero **aver** già dato
These books to-him si (one) would like to have already given

As there is no other reason why the auxiliary should be *essere* in (71a) except for *si*, we can infer that *si* must have originated with the embedded verb. In turn this means that its appearing in front of the "restructuring" verb in (71a) must be due to Clitic Climbing.[42]

If so, the reason for the ungrammaticality of (65b), which is an instance of impersonal(-passive) *si* (see the agreement with the object), is different. It is the same reason that rules out (72) and (73), where only one of the two clitics has climbed [vs. (74) and (75), in which the clitics have not split]:[43]

(72) a.*__Mi__ sta dicendo__lo__
(He) to-me is saying it
b.*__Lo__ sta dicendo__mi__
(He) it is saying to-me
'He is saying it to me.'

(73) a.*__Mi__ sta per dir__lo__
(He) to-me is about to say it
b.*__Lo__ sta per dir__mi__
(He) it is about to say to-me
'He is about to say it to me.'

(74) a. Sta dicendo__melo__
(He) is saying to-me it
b. __Me lo__ sta dicendo
(He) to-me it is saying
'He is saying it to me.'

(75) a. Sta per dir__melo__
(He) is about to say to-me it
b. __Me lo__ sta per dire
(He) to-me it is about to say
'He is about to say it to me.'

If the ill-formedness of (65b) indeed reduces to that of (72) and (73) (*si* has climbed, while *gli* has not), it becomes possible to maintain Clitic Climbing in restructuring contexts as optional (with the two options possibly depending on factors distinct from the restructuring configuration). The optionality of Clitic Climbing is already indicated by (66), as noted, and by such cases as (74) and (75), for which no (literally) biclausal source appears plausible. It is also indicated by the fact that clitics may fail to climb in the presence of the climbing of the weak pronominal *loro* 'to-them' (for which see Rizzi 1978: 138ff.; Cardinaletti 1991):[44]

(76) Ho __loro__ cominciato ad insegnar__lo__ più di un anno fa
'I began to teach it to them more than a year ago.'

All of this suggests that clitics may appear in the same clause either on the finite verb or on the nonfinite one (infinitive or gerund). From this point of view, it is past participles (the other nonfinite form of Italian) that are surprising in not allowing clitics to attach to them in the presence of a finite verb. See the impossible **Ho mangiatolo* 'I have eaten it' (vs. *L'ho mangiato*).[45] In contrast to Italian, which in "restructuring" configurations allows clitics to appear in either position, one finds Romance varieties where the clitic can only appear in the *higher* one, that is, varieties in which Clitic Climbing (hence "restructuring") looks obligatory, like most Central and Southern Italian dialects (Benincà 1986: 131f.; Monachesi 1995: 200ff.; Ledgeway 1998, 2000) and Sardinian (Jones 1993), as well as varieties where the clitic can appear only in the *lower* position. This is the case of (modern) French, which displays no regular Clitic Climbing nor Long Object Preposing nor Auxiliary Change but has other restructuring effects—the marginal climbing of *y* 'there' and *en* 'of it/them' in more careful styles[46] (cf. Kayne 1977: chap. 2, n. 7; Pollock 1978: n. 18; Taraldsen 1983: 308; Cinque 2002b), Long *Tough* movement, and Long Passive (see Kayne 1989b: 250ff.; Rochette 1988: 245, n. 23, Cinque 2002b; and the examples given in note 47). Still other varieties display a clitic in both positions, that is, a copy in the lower one (Benincà 1986: 130; Kayne 1989b: n. 37). See, for example, Chilean Spanish ***Los** vamos a ver**los*** 'Them (we) are going to see them' (from Uriagereka 1995: 86, n. 21), and Neapolitan ***L'**amu pruvatu a **ru** vida* 'Him (we) tried to him see' (from Ledgeway 1996: chap. 3, n. 6).[47]

5.2 The optionality of Long Object Preposing and *Loro* Climbing

The optionality of Clitic Climbing in "restructuring" contexts in Italian is not unique. Long Object Preposing (as noted in Rizzi 1978: 132) and *Loro* Climbing are likewise optional. See (77), where the presence of Clitic Climbing does not force Long Object Preposing, and (78)–(80), where the presence of Clitic Climbing, Auxiliary Change, and Long Object Preposing, respectively, does not force *Loro* Climbing:

(77) Gli si vuole vendere queste case a caro prezzo
To-him *si* wants to sell these houses at a high price
'One wants to sell him these houses at a high price.'
(Cf. Queste case gli si vogliono vendere a caro prezzo)

(78) a. Le ho dovute consegnar loro in ritardo
Them (I) have had to give to-them late
'I had to give them to them late.'
b. Le ho loro dovute consegnare in ritardo

(79) a. Mi chiedo come sia potuta andar loro incontro
I wonder how she could go to-them toward
'I wonder how she could go toward them.'
b. Mi chiedo come sia loro potuta andare incontro

(80) a. Si sarebbero dovute consegnar loro subito
They *si* would have to give to-them immediately
'One would have had to give them back to them immediately.'
b. Si sarebbero loro dovute consegnare subito

5.3 Auxiliary Change

The case of Auxiliary Change[48] appears to be more complex. On one side, the ungrammaticality of (81a) versus (81b), (from Rizzi 1978: 136) would seem to suggest that it is obligatory:

(81) a. *?Maria **ci ha** dovuto venire molte volte
'M. has had to come there many times.'
b. Maria **c' è** dovuta venire molte volte

On the other side, the acceptability of (82a) alongside (82b) would seem to point to its optionality (in that Auxiliary Change fails to apply even in the presence of *Loro* Climbing):[49]

(82) a. Avremmo loro potuto rimanere più vicini 'We could have to-them remained closer'
b. Saremmo loro potuti rimanere più vicini 'We could have to-them remained closer'

I tentatively interpret this paradox as showing that in Standard Italian, Auxiliary Change is per se optional (like all the other transparency effects) but is favored by Clitic Climbing in more careful styles of Italian. This could be made sense of if in these styles clitics climb via adjunction to the head, which, raising, effects the change *avere* → *essere* on the "restructuring" verb (whence the implication Clitic Climbing → Auxiliary Change in a language that has both, though not vice versa [cf. (66)].[50]

6. The functional status of "restructuring" verbs in the absence of transparency effects

So far, following the traditional opinion, I have been assuming that the presence of one or more transparency effects is an unequivocal indication of the presence of a monoclausal configuration, while the variant without transparency effects indicates a biclausal one. Given their optionality, however, the variant without transparency effects tells us nothing about sentence structure. A restructuring verb could well be functional (directly inserted under a functional head in a monoclausal configuration) even when the clitic is on the embedded verb, *loro* has not climbed, or Long Object Preposing has not applied.

This opens up the theoretical possibility that restructuring verbs are always functional, even in the absence of transparency effects.

The existence of varieties where transparency effects are obligatory (such as most Southern Italian dialects) would already seem to suggest that restructuring verbs indeed are only functional. In this section, I consider some evidence supporting this first indication. We shall see that except for *sembrare* 'seem' and motion verbs (which also have genuine lexical usages), restructuring verbs are always functional, and hence necessarily enter a monoclausal configuration. This has the conceptual advantage that such verbs do not need to be marked in the lexicon as either lexical or functional, with the ensuing problem of having to account for the complete synonymy of the two uses and for what looks like a single subcategorization option (the uniform selection of either *di* 'of,' *a* 'to,' or *0* (cf. Rizzi 1978: 150). They need only be marked as functional.

In addition to this conceptual argument, there is some empirical evidence for their exclusively functional nature (see sections 6.1–3).

6.1. More on the relative order of restructuring verbs

In section 3.2 above, we observed that restructuring verbs come in a rigid order when transparency effects obtain. The same rigidity is, however, found even in the absence of transparency effects. See (83) and (84) (and Hernanz and Rigau 1984: n. 6 for the similar rigid ordering of restructuring verbs in the absence of transparency effects in Catalan):

(83) a. **Suole provare a farle/provarle a fare** da solo 'He uses to try to do them by himself'
b. ***Prova a soler farle/ solerle fare** da solo 'He tries to use to do them by himself'

(84) a. **Soleva smettere di vederla/ ?smetterla di vedere** ogni sei mesi 'He used to stop seeing her every six months.'
b. ***Smetteva di soler vederla/solerla vedere** ogni sei mesi 'He stopped using to see her every six months'

This suggests that such verbs are only functional. If they were (also) lexical, taking a full-fledged CP complement, it would not be clear how they could determine the choice of the verb of their sentential complement. Note that the reason for the ill-formedness of (84b) can hardly be semantic. It would make perfect sense to "stop having the habit of doing something." Yet, the sentence is unacceptable.

6.2. "Imperfect" (partial) versus "strict" (exhaustive) Control

Further evidence for the exclusively functional character of restructuring verbs appears to come from a property of (obligatory) Control recently discussed by Wurmbrand (1998: chap. 4) and Landau (1999, 2000: chap. 2). Wurmbrand (1998:163ff.) observes that the class of Control infinitives splits into two distinct subclasses: one in which the infinitive subject is referentially strictly identical to the controller, and one in which it only needs to include the reference of the controller (what she terms "imperfect" Control). This can be seen in the contrast between (85) and (86):

(85) a. *(They said that) John tried to meet in front of the Post Office.
b. *(They said that) John managed to gather at 6.

(86) a. (They said that) John had planned to meet in the castle.
b. (They said that) John had regretted meeting in the castle.

The latter, but not the former, are grammatical because only the latter allow the infinitive subject (which is plural, given the semantics of the verb) to partially overlap with (include) the controller (which is singular). The former, instead, require strict referential identity between controller and controllee, a condition violated in (85).[51]

Wurmbrand (1998) further argues that the class requiring strict identity coincides with the class of restructuring infinitives, whereas the class allowing imperfect Control coincides with that of nonrestructuring infinitives, and she suggests that the difference follows from a difference between restructured and nonrestructured configurations. The latter have a subject PRO (which can be imperfectly controlled). The former have no syntactic subject, their understood subject being semantically controlled. I think Wurmbrand's generalization is correct, but I would like to suggest that the strict referential identity between controller and controllee in the restructuring case requires no additional semantic mechanism. It is simply a consequence of the fact, already discussed, that restructuring configurations involve *raising* even in the few apparent Control cases of 'want,' 'try,' 'dare,' 'know (how).' In this view, the traditional notion of (obligatory) Control comes to coincide with imperfect Control, and what looks like strict Control is nothing but raising.[52]

Now, if the strict referential identity of the two subjects in restructuring contexts necessarily follows from their raising character, the fact that the two subjects are also strictly identical in the variant without transparency effects is a direct argument for the raising (and monoclausal) character of the configuration that lacks transparency effects, and hence for the exclusively functional character of the restructuring verbs involved. If the variant without transparency effects involved a biclausal structure with PRO, imperfect Control would be expected to be possible, contrary to fact (**Ho provato a incontrarsi alle 5* 'I tried to meet at 5').

6.3. Apparent lexical usages of **volere** and aspectual verbs

The idea that restructuring verbs are always functional would seem to be contradicted by certain prima facie lexical usages of *volere* 'want' and of some of the aspectual verbs. See (87) and (88):

(87) Gianni vuole una bicicletta 'G. wants a bicycle.'

(88) a. Maria ha cominciato il romanzo 'M. began the novel.'
b. Mario ha finito il vino 'M. finished the wine.'
c. Il concerto sta cominciando/sta finendo/continua
'The concerts is beginning/finishing/continuing'

In all such cases, the verb, unlike what happens with functional verbs, does not take a nonfinite verbal complement but rather a DP, object or subject, thus apparently qualifying as a simple transitive, or unaccusative, lexical verb. The appearances, however, are misleading, as there is evidence that (87) and (88) are structurally more complex than it looks. Den Dikken et al. (1996), following earlier proposals by McCawley and Ross, provide syntactic arguments that in (87) 'want' does not directly take the DP as its object but takes an abstract verbal complement, whose head, roughly paraphrasable with HAVE, takes the DP as its object:[53]

(89) Gianni vuole [$_{XP}$ HAVE [$_{DP}$ una bicicletta]]

If this is so, *vuole* in (87) continues to be the functional verb seen so far, with *Gianni la vuole* 'G. wants it' a case of Clitic Climbing.[54]

Similarly, Pustejovsky (1995) and Jackendoff (1997: 60ff.) (cf. also Rochette 1999: 159ff.), in order to account for the variable, and highly restrictive, interpretations that aspectual predicates show, depending on the nature of the object,[55] have argued that they actually select an abstract verbal complement of activity, whose head is interpreted on the basis of the *qualia structure* of the object (differently from them, I assume here that they syntactically take an abstract verbal complement).[56]

Although such special usages of 'want' and of phasal aspectuals deserve more careful investigation, it seems that they can be rendered compatible with the idea that such verbs are exclusively functional, part of the extended projection of another, overt or abstract, lexical verb.

6.4. Restructuring and lexical usages of motion verbs and **sembrare**

The case of motion verbs and *sembrare* 'seem,' which appear to have genuine usages as lexical verbs in addition to their functional usage, is different. We have seen that when these verbs take an internal argument (either a directional PP or a subject, for the former, and a dative PP for the latter) they cease to behave as restructuring verbs (e.g., they do not allow Clitic Climbing). See, in particular, (43), notes 10 and 30, and (41) and (42), respectively.

These data are still compatible with the idea that restructuring verbs are *always* functional if, when they take a complement, motion verbs and *sembrare* are actually different verbs, in fact, genuine *lexical* verbs. This appears to be confirmed by the fact that the case with and the case without a complement display a subtle difference in meaning.

Motion verbs, when they take a complement of their own and an optional adjunct clause (cf. note 10), are interpreted literally as verbs of locomotion, part of whose meaning is the means of transportation [cf. (90a) below]. When they are used as restructuring verbs, instead, they are not verbs of locomotion for which one can ask the means of transportation—whence the ungrammaticality of the answer to (90b), where *come* 'how' can only ask 'the way he will (come to) paint the door.' They merely indicate that some distance is traversed before the action depicted by the lexical verb is carried out (much as with the so-called distantive suffix of Fula/Fulfulde, seen in note 4 above):[57]

(90) a. A: Come verrà da te a dipingere la porta? 'How will he come by you to paint the door'
B: In bicicletta 'With his bicycle'
b. A: Come ti verrà a dipingere la porta? 'How will he come to paint your door?'
B:*In bicicletta 'With his bicycle.'

Similar considerations hold for *sembrare* when it takes a dative argument versus restructuring *sembrare* without one. The former literally means that a certain state of affairs seems true to someone [hence the perfectly noncontradictory status of (91a)]. The latter is instead an evidential functional verb, which (mildly) commits the speaker to the truth of a certain state of affairs [whence the contradictory status of (91b)]:[58]

(91) a. Gianni sembra a tutti apprezzarlo molto, ma io non credo che lo apprezzi
'G. seems to everybody to appreciate it much, but I don't believe he appreciates it.'
b. #Gianni lo sembra apprezzare molto, ma io non credo che lo apprezzi
'G. seems to appreciate it much, but I don't believe he appreciates it.'

This, of course, does not exclude the possibility that the functional (restructuring) usage of motion verbs, and *sembrare*, have their ultimate basis in the lexical usages of these verbs (because of their semantics). But it shows that their functional and lexical usages should be kept distinct.

7. Presence versus absence of transparency effects: Syntactic contrasts

I have argued so far that restructuring verbs are always functional, appearing in a monoclausal configuration with their infinitival complement whether or not they show transparency effects. This requires reassessing the syntactic contrasts noted in the literature between the variant with and the variant without transparency effects; and in particular, it requires explaining them in ways that have nothing to do with constituency differences (such as the monoclausal vs. biclausal distinction).

Before attempting that (sections 7.2 and 7.3), we should put to the side the few genuine (and irrelevant) cases of actual alternation between a monoclausal and a biclausal configuration, when a restructuring verb also has lexical usages.

7.1. The special status of **volere, sembrare,** and motion verbs

As seen above (note 54), such cases as *Gianni vuole restare* 'G. wants to stay' are structurally ambiguous even if *volere* is exclusively functional. That depends, as seen, on the additional possibility for *volere* to be followed by an abstract verb (OBTAIN), which itself takes the infinitival phrase as a complement:

(92) a. Gianni$_i$ vuole . . . [$_{VP}$ t$_i$ restare]
b. Gianni$_i$ vuole . . . [$_{VP}$ t$_i$ OBTAIN [$_{CP}$ PRO$_i$ restare]]

This, we take it, is at the basis of the contrasts in (23)–(26) above. These are found with *volere* but in fact with no other modal or aspectual verb.[59]

The case of *sembrare* and motion verbs is different because they actually enter either a monoclausal or a biclausal structure, depending on whether they are used as functional or lexical verbs (section 6.4). We have already seen (section 2.3 and note 10) that such Heavy NP Shift contrasts as (18b) and (19b), repeated below as (93a and b), are not imputable to a constituency difference but derive, for (93b), either from an illicit application of scrambling of the PP *a Firenze* or from an illicit extraction of the clitic out of the adjunct *ad esporre la mia idea*:

(93) a. . . . verrò a Firenze ad espor**ti** la mia idea ' . . . I'll come to F. to explain-to-you my Idea'
b.*. . . **ti** verrò a Firenze ad esporre la mia idea ' . . . to-you I'll come to F. to explain my idea'

7.2. Right Node Raising contrasts and ellipsis with restructuring

We have also already seen that under a deletion analysis of Right Node Raising (Kayne 1994), such contrasts as (13a and b), repeated here as (94a and b), and in particular the ungrammaticality of (94b), reduce to the independent ungrammaticality of such cases as (17), repeated here as (95):

(94) a. Piero voleva—ma francamente adesso non so se vorrà ancora—parlar**ne** con Gianni
'P. wanted to—but frankly now I don't know if he still will—speak about it with G.'
b.*Piero **ne** voleva—ma francamente adesso non so se **ne** vorrà ancora—parlare con Gianni
'P. about it wanted to—but frankly now I don't know if he still will—speak about it with G.'

(95) a.*Gianni voleva parlare di questo, ma Piero non **ne** voleva______
G. wanted to talk about this, but P. not (about-it) wanted
b.*Certe cose si possono fare, ma queste non si possono______
Certain things one can do, but these not one can
c.*Gianni poteva andare a casa, ma non *è voluto______
G. could go home, but not has/is wanted

It is worthwhile examining more closely the ungrammaticality of (95) as it appears to play a role in such Cleft Sentence contrasts as (7a and b) above. Depiante (1998), following Zubizarreta (1982), suggests that it is due to the kind of null anaphora licensed by restructuring verbs, which is a form of "deep anaphora," in Hankamer and Sag's sense: namely, an empty category with no internal syntactic structure. Deep anaphors [pronominals, the pro-form *do it*, and null complement anaphora (NCA)], as opposed to surface anaphors (like VP deletion, Gapping, Sluicing, etc.), (i) do not need an identical syntactic antecedent, (ii) can be pragmatically controlled, (iii) cannot host missing antecedents, and (iv) eliminate scope ambiguities (see Hankamer & Sag 1976; Depiante 1998). Bošković (1994: 266f.) and Depiante show that the null complement that follows restructuring verbs indeed behaves like a deep anaphor with respect to these properties. If so, the contrasts in (96) follow from the fact that the clitic cannot be paired with a trace within the (unstructured) elliptical constituent:[60]

(96) a. A: La può tenere per sé? B: No. Non può/*Non la può
A: Can he keep it for himself? B: No. He can't.
b. A: Lo riuscirai a tradurre? B: No. Non riuscirò/*Non lo riuscirò
A: Will you manage to translate it? B: No. I will not manage.
c. A: Gianni la vede? B: Sì. Ha ricominciato/*L'ha ricominciata
A: Does G. see her? B: Yes. He started again.
d. A: Gianni la vede ancora? B: Sì. Continua/*La continua
A: Is G. still seeing her? Yes. He continues.
e. A: L'hai provato a riparare? B: Sì. Ho provato/*L'ho provato
A: Have you tried to repair it? B: Yes. I have tried.

Bošković (1994: 266f.) takes the deep anaphor status of the null complement of restructuring verbs to show that they must be able to assign an external theta role (because their subject cannot enter any antecedent-trace relation with a category inside the null complement).[61] But this is not necessarily so. It depends on the precise analysis of the deep anaphor involved in NCA, which since Hankamer and Sag (1976) has been left rather vague. Deep anaphors are (beside pronominals) the *do it* pro-form, as well as our NCA. I take this to be no accident, and I suggest that the NCA following restructuring verbs is literally the null counterpart of *do it* (with agentive predicates, and perhaps *be it* with stative predicates). Thus . . . *ma io non posso 0* ' . . . but I can't 0' will have the structure . . . ma [io$_k$ non posso . . . [$_{VP}$ t$_k$ [[$_V$~~far~~] [$_{DP}$~~lo~~]]] ' . . . but I can't do it,' with the subject *io* outside of the pro-form *farlo* 'do it,' an analysis also compatible with my previous conclusion that restructuring verbs all involve raising.[62]

7.3. Cleft Sentence contrasts

Recall the different behavior of the variant with transparency effects and the variant without under Cleft Sentence Formation [(7), repeated here as (97)]:

(97) a. E' proprio a parlar**ti** di questi problemi che verrà.
It's just to talk to-you about these problems that he'll come.'
b.*É proprio a parlare di questi problemi che **ti** verrà

On the basis of the well-formedness of the Focus Movement and Topicalization cases corresponding to (97b) [cf. (8) above], we concluded that the contrast in (97) cannot be due to constituency reasons but probably to the selective character of Cleft Sentence Formation (which is less free than Focus Movement and Topicalization). We explore here what property of the construction may be responsible for such contrasts.

If restructuring verbs are always functional (whether transparency effects are present or not), the acceptability (or near acceptability) of the sentences on the lefthand side of (98a–e) suggests that the unacceptability of the sentences on the righthand side of (98a–e) and (97b), cannot be attributed to the fact that some illicit constituent (say, a functional XP, rather than DP, PP, or CP) has been clefted:

(98) a. E' tenerla per sé che **non può**/*E' tenere per sé che **non la può**
It's to keep it for himself that he cannot

b. ?E' a tradurlo che **non riuscirò**/*E' a tradurre che **non lo riuscirò**
It's to translate it that I will not manage
c. ?E' a vederla che **ha ricominciato**/*E' a vedere che **l'ha ricominciata**
It's to see her that he started again
d. ?E' a vederla che **continuerò**/*E' a vedere che **la continuerò**
It's to see her that I will continue
e. E' a ripararla che **ho provato**/*E' a riparare che **l'ho provata**
It's to repair it that I have tried

The generalization underlying all such contrasts appears to be that Cleft Sentence Formation is possible just in case the stranded predicate supports NCA. Compare (97b) and (98a–e) with (99) and (100a–e), respectively:

(99) A: Non credo che mi verrà a parlare di questo. B: Vedrai che verrà/*Vedrai che **ti** verrà
A: 'I don't think he will come to talk to me about this. B: You'll see that he will come.'

(100) a. A: La può tenere per sé? B: **No. Non può/*Non la può**
A: Can he keep it for himself? B: No. He can't
b. A: Lo riuscirai a tradurre? B: **No. Non riuscirò/*Non lo riuscirò**
A: Will you manage to translate it? B: No. I will not manage.
c. A: Gianni la vede? B: **Sì. Ha ricominciato/*L'ha ricominciata**
A: Does G. see her? B: Yes. He started again.
d. A: Gianni la vede ancora? B: **Sì. Continua/*La continua**
A: Is G. still seeing her? Yes. He continues.
e. A: L'hai provato a riparare? B: **Sì. Ho provato/*L'ho provato**
A: Have you tried to repair it? B: Yes. I have tried.

The generalization appears to be supported by the existence of a number of predicates that can neither be stranded under Cleft Sentence Formation [cf. (101)] nor support NCA [cf. (102)]:

(101) a. *E' essere ubriaco che sembrava (*sembrare*)
'It is to be drunk that he seemed'
b. *E' essergli caro che deve (epistemic *dovere*)
It's be dear to-her that he must
c. *E comprandolo che stava (progressive *stare*)
It's buying it that he was
d. *E' per comprarla che sta (prospective *stare per*)
It's to buy it that he is about
e. *E per aiutarlo che finirà ('delayed aspect' *finire per*)
It's helping him that he will end up

(102) a. A: Era ubriaco? B: ***?Sembrava**.
A: Was he drunk? B: He seemed

b. A: Pensi che gli sia caro? B: ***Sì, deve**
A: Do you think he is dear to him? B: Yes, he must

c. A: Sta comprandolo? ***Sì, sta**
A: Is he buying it? B: Yes, he is.

d. A: Sta forse per comprarlo? B: ***Sì, sta**
A: Is he about to buy it? B: Yes, he is.

e. A: Finirà per accettarlo? B: ***Non finirà**
A: Will he end up accepting it? B: He won't end up

Note that the contrast between (98) and (100), on the one side, and (101) and (102), on the other, is not one between Control and Raising predicates. This is shown by the fact that certain unmistakably raising predicates can be stranded under Cleft Sentence Formation [cf. (103)] and can be followed by NCA]cf. (104)]:

(103) a. (Forse è un imbroglio) E' trattarsi di un errore che **non può**
(Maybe it's a fraud.) It's be a mistake that it cannot

b. E' piovere in abbondanza che **deve** (se si vuole che le piante sopravvivano)
It's rain abundantly that it must (if one wants the plants to survive)

(104) a. A: Forse si tratta di un errore. B: No. **Non può**
A: Maybe it's a mistake. B: No, it cannot

b. A: Pioverà? B: **Deve**!, se si vuole che le piante sopravvivano
A: Will it rain? B: It must, if one wants the plants to survive.

Furthermore, even *sembrare*, when negated, appears to become strandable under Cleft Sentence Formation and capable of supporting NCA (thus strengthening the generalization about Clefts and NCA). Compare (101a) and (102a) with (105):

(105) a. (Sembrava assonnato) ?E' essere ubriaco che **non sembrava**
(He seemed sleepy.) It's to be drunk that he didn't seem

b. A: Era ubriaco? B: **Non sembrava**
A: Was he drunk? B: He didn't seem

If the generalization connecting the strandability of certain predicates under Cleft Sentence Formation and their ability to support NCA is correct, it becomes tempting to say that it derives from the fact that the empty category following the stranded predicate in Clefts is nothing other than an instance of NCA, whether the empty counterpart of *do it* or of an empty DP or PP (cf. note 62). More accurately, the empty counterpart of *(do) it*, as well as the empty DP or PP, is perhaps what allows the correct operator-variable structure accompanying the base-generated phrase in focus (in Chomsky's 1977: 44ff. analysis of Cleft Sentence Formation). Such cases as (106a–c) under this analysis would receive the derivation indicated in (107a–c):

(106) a. E' tenerla per sé che non può
It's to keep it for himself that he can't

b. E' di ripararla che non ha ancora finito
It's to mend it that he has not yet finished

c. E' a ripararla che ho provato/non sono riuscito
It's to mend it that I tried/did not manage

(107) a. DP è [$_{CP}$ PRO tenerla per sé] 0_i che non può FARE ('DO') t_i
(cf. E' tenerla per sé ciò che non può fare 'It's to keep it for himself what he can't do')

b. DP è [$_{CP}$ PRO di ripararla] 0_i che non ha ancora finito t_i
(cf. E' di ripararla ciò che non ha ancora finito 'It's to mend it what he has not yet finished')

c. DP è [$_{CP}$ PRO a ripararla] 0_i che ho provato/non sono riuscito [$_{PP}$ P t_i]
(cf. A ripararla, non ci ho provato/non ci sono riuscito 'to mend it, there I did not try/I did not manage to')

If something along these lines is correct, then, the contrast between (97a and b) and the like follows from the impossibility of construing the clitic with an appropriate trace in (97b). See (108b):

(108) a. E' [$_{CP}$ proprio a parlar**ti** di questi problemi] 0_i che verrà [$_{PP}$ P t_i]
(cf. A parlarti, non **ci** verrà 'To talk to you, he won't come to it/there')

b. E' [$_{CP}$ proprio a parlare di questi problemi] 0_i che **ti**$_k$ verrà [$_{PP}$ P t_i]

8. Some residual questions

8.1. Restructuring and null subjects

Kayne's (1989b) analysis, in making both restructuring and null subjects depend on the strength of INFL, formally related Clitic Climbing to the null subject character of the language (a relation originally conjectured in Kayne 1980).[63] The present analysis of restructuring instead establishes no necessary link between the two. It is thus important that subsequent work has shown the relation between Clitic Climbing and null subjects not to hold systematically. Haverkort (1993: 76f.) and Martins (1995: 229) both point out that in seventeenth-century French, Clitic Climbing was still a robust phenomenon, whereas null subjects had already been lost one century before. Haverkort (1993: 77) also discusses the case of Kru languages, which have Clitic Climbing but no null subjects, referring to Koopman (1984: 56) (See also Sportiche 1983 & Tellier 1987).

8.2. Restructuring and negation

It is generally assumed (cf. the references cited in Kayne 1989b: n.14) that negation blocks Clitic Climbing (and other transparency effects). This in turn is often taken to depend on the minimality violation caused by the crossing of the head of NegP by another head—arguably the clitic itself, in the case of Clitic Climbing, and a covert INFL or T, in the case of Long Object Preposing (an instance of XP-movement). See, for example, Bok-Bennema and Kampers-Manhe (1994: 209).[64] Although in principle compatible with the present approach (modulo the occurrence of head-movement within a single extended projection) such conclusion appears in need of further scrutiny. Alongside often-cited examples like (109), there are others in which Clitic Climbing appears to cross over negation. See (110) and Napoli (1981: 853):[65]

(109) a. *Gianni lo smise di non mangiare (più)
'G. it stopped not eating it (any longer)'
b. ??Lo sta per non amare (più)
'(She) was about not to love him (any longer)'
c. *?Lo tornò a non apprezzare (affatto)
'(He) once again did not see him (at all)'
d. *Gianni li vuole non vedere (Kayne 1989b: 243) (for me "?" if *vorrebbe* replaces *vuole*)
'G. them wants not to see'

(110) a. Lo sembra non apprezzare affatto
'(He) it seems not to appreciate at all'
b. Per stare meglio, la dovresti non rivedere più
To feel better, her (you) should not see any longer
c. La potrebbe anche non rivedere mai più
(He) her could even not see ever again
d. Non ci si può non pensare[66]
One cannot not think about it

The contrast between (110) and the much more marginal (109) could have to do (in a monoclausal analysis of restructuring, where restructuring verbs are always functional) with the (canonical, or unmarked) locus of sentential negation, which in Italian is lower than the head hosting *sembrare* 'seem,' plausibly $\text{Mood}_{\text{evidential}}$ [hence (110a)], but higher than most aspectual heads [hence (109)], with scope elements like modals activating different positions of negation [hence (110b–d)]. See Cinque (1999: sect. 5.4) for evidence that sentential negation can occupy more than one position in the presence of scope-bearing elements.

8.3. Variation in the membership of restructuring verbs

The often-made observation that the membership in the class of restructuring verbs varies across languages—and, within one language, even among speakers—would seem to go against the UG approach taken here and argue for an essentially lexical approach. This impression, however, is quite misleading. Consider, first, variation across languages. The idea that restructuring verbs correspond to distinct functional heads of a universal functional hierarchy does not per se entail that all languages should have a verb (a free morpheme) corresponding to *each* such head. It could well be that a language expresses a certain functional head via a bound morpheme (say, a suffix) or via no head category at all (but rather via an AdvP, arguably in the specifier of that head). Italian, for example, appears to instantiate the latter case when compared to Spanish (or French). Spanish has a restructuring usage of *acabar de* '(lit.) finish,' which seems to correspond to the so-called Retrospective Aspect (cf. Cinque 1999: 96–98, and references cited there):

(111) Lo acabo de ver
(Lit.) Him (I) finish to see 'I have just seen him.'

The same aspect is rendered in French by the verb *venir de* [(Lit.) 'come from' (*Je viens de le voir* 'I have just seen him')]. In Italian, however (and English, for that matter), the only way to render such an aspect is by using the AdvP *appena* 'just' (in one of its uses) combined with the verb in the perfect form: *L'ho appena visto* 'I have just seen him.' Such lexical variation among Spanish *acabar de*, French *venir de*, and Italian 0 (or rather *appena*) is of little significance from a UG point of view. It only obscures the fact that the three languages express one and the same functional head through different morphological means. Another case in point is the restructuring verb *faillir* in French ('to almost'), which renders the grammatical notion of "action narrowly averted," variously expressed in the languages of the world (see Kuteva 1998), and to which in Italian and English no restructuring verb corresponds but, instead, an AdvP (*quasi/almost*).

One could easily multiply such examples. The fact that Spanish *seguir* '(lit.) follow' (Zagona 1986: 236) or Catalan *procurar* '(lit.) procure' (Hernanz & Rigau 1984: 45), behave as restructuring verbs, whereas the corresponding verbs of Italian do not, is only of historical interest—of how a certain functional notion ($\text{Aspect}_{\text{continuative}}$, $\text{Aspect}_{\text{conative}}$) has come to be "grammaticalized." The same is true of the restructuring verb *cuider* '(lit.) believe' in Middle French, also used with the (prospective) aspectual meaning of 'be about to' (Martineau 1991: 242f.), or of *prendere* '(lit.) catch' in colloquial Italian, which is also a restructuring verb with the meaning of 'start (suddenly)': *lo prese ad insultare* 'him (he) started (lit. 'caught') to insult.' Again, such cases obscure the fact that the same set of functional notions across languages comes to be expressed via different lexical means.

Apparently more serious for a UG approach is the fact that the same verb, with essentially the same meaning, is a restructuring verb in one language but not in another or, within one and the same language, for some speakers but not others.

One example is 'seem,' which is taken not to be a restructuring verb in Spanish (Zagona 1986: 232) or in Portuguese (Quicoli 1976: 215; Pizzini 1981: 427, n. 24) but is a restructuring verb, at least for many speakers, in Italian (cf. note 27 above). Even if true, this fact is not necessarily troublesome. It could mean that in Spanish and Portuguese *parecer* has only the lexical usage seen in section 6.4 above (alternatively, it could be that the speakers Zagona and Pizzini based their conclusion on, as opposed to other speakers, are as the Italian speakers that do not have *sembrare* as a restructuring verb).

Much of the cross-linguistic and interspeaker variation involves verbs that belong to certain classes (typical is the class of 'desideratives'), which are related to particular functional heads without being the prototypical, or basic, exponent of the class (*volere* 'want'). Thus, many accept *desiderare* 'desire,' *amare* 'love,' *intendere* 'intend,' and *preferire* 'prefer' as restructuring verbs, whereas others find them marginal or outright impossible.[67] These verbs appear to add specific nuances of meaning to the basic sense of 'volition,' and hence complying to a lesser degree with the semantics of the corresponding functional head ($ModP_{volition}$): a probable cause of their oscillating status. If so, such variation is not incompatible with the general UG approach taken here.

8.4. The prepositional complementizers

The prepositions [*di* 'of' and *a* 'to'; less commonly *per* 'for' and *da* 'from': *lo sto per fare* 'it (I) am about to do'; *lo finì per accettare* 'it (he) ended up accepting'; *lo avrà da riconsegnare entro domani* 'it (he) will have to give back by tomorrow'] that introduce the nonfinite complement of many restructuring verbs are generally taken to be complementizers (one of the lowest, in the split CP field of Rizzi 1997). In the present analysis, in which restructuring verbs are always functional, they must be reinterpreted as introducers of smaller portions of the extended projection of the lexical VP, namely, as introducers of the complement of one of the functional heads that make up that extended projection: . . . F . . . [$_{PP}$ P [$_{INFP}$ Inf [$_{FP}$ F . . . [$_{VP}$]]]]. Much as Kayne's (1993) participial projection (a nominal type of projection) is not directly the complement of (auxiliary) BE but is contained in a PP/DP-projection, so the infinitival complement of many restructuring verbs (also a nominal type of projection) is contained in a PP lexicalized by *a* or *di* (or *per* and *da*).[68]

Notes

I thank Paola Benincà, Marcel den Dikken, Richard Kayne, Idan Landau, and Elisabeth Pearce for their comments on an earlier draft of this chapter.

1. Besides structure simplification approaches like Rizzi's (1976a, 1976b, 1978) and, in a different framework, Aissen and Perlmutter's (1976, 1983) (cf. also Rivas 1977 and Luján 1978), one may mention two other major families of analyses: the "double (Sentence/VP) subcategorization" analyses of Strozer (1976, 1981), Fresina (1981, 1982, 1997), Picallo (1985, 1990), Rochette (1988, 1990), Moore (1989, 1990, 1996), Pearce (1990), Rosen (1990a, 1990b), Bošković (1994), Wurmbrand (1998, 2001), and so on, as well as the (embedded-I-to-(matrix-)I biclausal analysis of Kayne (1989b), adopted in different forms by Martineau (1991), Rivero (1991), Terzi (1992, 1994, 1996), Roberts (1993, 1997), Bok-Bennema and Kampers-Manhe (1994), Bonneau and Zushi (1994), and Rooryck (1994). Other analyses that have been proposed for the restructuring phenomenon are the biclausal analyses of Burzio (1981, 1986), Baker (1988), Haverkort (1990, 1993), and Sabel (1995a, 1995b, 1996, 1999) in terms of VP raising to the left of the embedded subject; and the parallel structure analyses of Zubizarreta (1982), Manzini (1983), Haegeman and Riemsdijk (1984), Goodall (1987), and Di Sciullo and Williams (1987: 97ff.). Restructuring has also received treatments in more recent minimalist terms (Watanabe 1993; Martins 1995), as well as in LFG (Andersen 1987), in Tree-adjoining Grammar (Bleam 1994; Kulick 1997), in HPSG (Miller 1992; Monachesi 1993, 1995, 1998), and in Categorial Grammar (Nishida 1991).

2. Besides Romance, transparency effects have been reported to exist (with roughly the same verbs) in Germanic (see Evers 1975; Haider 1986, 1987, 1992; Grewendorf 1987; Fanselow 1989; Bayer & Kornfilt 1990, Koopman & Szabolcsi 2000, etc.); in Slavic (George & Toman 1976: 241ff.; Dyła 1983; Spencer 1991: 357f.; Progovac 1993; Sabel 1995a, 1995b, 1996, 1999; Veselovská 1995: 377; Przepiórkowski & Kupš 1997; Stjepanović 1998, 2001;

Medová 2000; etc.); in the African languages Abe (Tellier 1987), Bete (Sportiche 1983; Haverkort 1990, 1993), and Édó (Stewart 1999); in Eskimo (Baker 1988: 204ff); in Basque (Ortiz de Urbina 1989: 26ff.); in Turkish (Kornfilt 1996); in Japanese (Miyagawa 1986; Nishigauchi 1993; Zushi 1995; Wurmbrand 1998); in Malayalam (Baker 1988: 204ff.); in Chamorro (Chung 1988); in Tagalog (Kroeger 1993: 167–207); in Hungarian (Choe 1998, 1989; Farkas & Sadock 1989, Koopman & Szabolcsi 2000); in Choktaw (Broadwell & Martin 1993: 5ff); in Ancash Quechua (Cole 1984); in Chukchee (Spencer 1991: 361; Baker 1999: 369); in Hindi (Mahajan 1989: 233ff.; Zushi 1995); in Kashmiri (Wali & Koul 1994: 988), among many other languages. The long-distance agreement of Godeberi (Caucasian: Haspelmath 1999) has all the characteristics of restructuring, too. For the claim that French also displays restructuring effects, see Taraldsen (1983: 299f.), Kayne (1989b), Bok-Bennema and Kampers-Manhe (1994), and Cinque (2002b). Haïk (1985: 76, n. 49), Goodall (1991), Hornstein (1995: 77f., 85f.), Roberts (1997), and Kayne (1998: n. 36) claim that restructuring effects are even detectable in English.

3. 'XP>YP' should be interpreted as 'YP is the complement of the head of XP.'

4. In many languages, 'andative' ('itive/ventive') or 'distantive' morphemes are attested which can be glossed in English as 'go/come and.' For example, the derivational suffix, *-oy-*, of Fula/Fulfulde (West Africa) has exactly this function (cf. Fagerli 1994: 53):

(i) Min mabb-it-ir-an-ilaw-oy-i mo ngal sembe
we close-REVERS-INSTR-BENEF-CELER-DISTANTIVE-PAST him it strength
'We went and opened it for him with strength quickly.'

Mishmi (Tibeto-Burman) verbs can likewise be "inflected for movement" (Devi Prasada Sastry 1984: 156). Analogous "coming and going aspectual affixes" are attested to in a number of Australian languages (cf. Evans 1995: 311 and references cited there). Myhill (1988: 357) reports Georgian, Maricopa, Tarascan, Kiowa, and Nahuatl as having grammatical morphemes expressing the meaning of 'go' and 'come.' On the special syntactic properties of 'come' and 'go' verbs in English and in Sicilian, see Jaeggli and Hyams (1993) and Cardinaletti and Giusti (2000). In Cinque (1999: sect. 4.28), the existence of other aspectual heads is mentioned for which no order is provided (see, now, Cinque 2001). Among these, particularly relevant here are *conative* aspect ('try'), *frustrative* or *'success'* aspect ['(not) manage'], *inceptive* aspect ('begin'), and *predispositional* aspect ('tend').

5. The approach taken here differs from most analyses of restructuring, which assume the phenomenon to be lexically governed and optional; but also from such analyses as Wurmbrand's (1998), which share with ours the idea that it is universally based but take it to depend on a cluster of different semantic and syntactic properties of the restructuring verbs (for her, the semantic properties [-tense] and [-subject] and the syntactic property [-structural case] of their complement).

6. Small capital letters indicate focused constituents. Incidentally, the grammaticality of (8) shows that the ungrammatiality of (7b) cannot be due to the fact that the clitic fails to c-command its trace (contra Zubizarreta 1980: 148ff). For the same conclusion, see Burzio (1981: chap. 6, n. 2) and Fresina (1981: chap. 2, n. 2).

7. Similar cases are noted in Napoli (1981: 864), who concludes from that [incorrectly, given (12)] that the past participle forms a constituent with the auxiliary rather than with its complement. That the ungrammaticality of (7b) should be seen as related to that of sentences like (10) is also suggested in Fresina (1981: 119, n. 62; 1982: 289), and Moore (1996: 48f).

8. Rizzi (1976a: n. 8, 1978, 1982a: n. 14) notes that, under special conditions, a bare infinitive can sometimes be clefted in the presence of Clitic Climbing. Such conditions appear to crucially involve a contrastive phrase [*E' ringraziare che lo dovremmo, *(non*

rimproverare) 'It's thank that we him should, not scold'], a context that also improves the clefting of an infinitive plus its complement [?*E' ringraziare per ciò che ha fatto che lo dovremmo,* *(*non per ciò che non ha fatto*) 'It's thank for what he did that we him should, not for what he didn't do']. The cases mentioned in Napoli (1981: n. 7) also involve either an explicit or an implicit, contrastive phrase. These exceptions remain to be understood. The constrast in (i), noted in Rizzi (1982b) and attributed by him to the Empty Category Principle (ECP), may also have to do with the selective character of Cleft Sentence Formation:

(i) a. E' avere più fortuna che vorrei 'It is to have more luck that I would like'
b.*E' avere più fortuna che sembra 'It is to have more luck that he seems'

The fact that no such contrast is found under Focus Movement or Topicalization would be hard to understand in terms of ECP:

(ii) a. AVERE PIÙ FORTUNA, sembra! 'To have more luck (focus), he seems'
b. Avere più fortuna di noi, non sembra 'To have more luck than us, he doesn't seem'

I thank Richard Kayne for pointing out this implication.

9. On the basis of examples such as (i), it has sometimes been claimed that nonconstituents can also be Right Node Raised, and hence that the phenomenon is not a reliable diagnostic for constituency (Abbot 1976):

(i) Mary baked and George frosted twenty cakes in less than one hour.

Note, however, that in Larson's (1988) and Kayne's (1994) analyses, even such Right Node Raised sequences qualify as constituents.

10. The ungrammaticality of (20) is noted by Rizzi himself (1978: 126, n. 16), who analyses it as derived by leftward movement of the adverbial PP into the auxiliary structure.

Another potential derivation of (19b) does not derive it from (18a) via Heavy NP Shift (or its leftward analogue). In (18a) the PP *a Firenze* either modifies just the embedded infinitive (and is interpreted as a locative) or both *venire* and the embedded infinitive (in which case it is interpreted as directional). In (18b), instead, the PP *a Firenze* can only be interpreted as a directional complement of *venire*, used as a lexical verb (cf. section 6.4), with *ad esporti la mia idea* an adjunct purpose clause rather than a CP complement. The adjunct status of *ad esporti la mia idea* in (18b) is shown by the fact that no complement or adjunct can be extracted from it (which would be unexpected if it were a complement CP). Compare (i) with (ii), which nothing prevents from containing restructuring *venire* (and a complement CP following it):

(i) a.*A chi è venuto a Firenze ad esporre la sua idea? 'Whom did he come to F. to clarify his idea?'
b.*Come$_k$ è venuto a Firenze ad esporti la sua idea t_k? (Molto chiaramente) 'How has he come to Florence to illustrate his idea to you? (Very clearly)

(ii) a. A chi è venuto ad esporre la sua idea? 'Whom did he come to clarify his idea?'
b. Come ti è venuto ad esporre la sua idea? (Molto chiaramente) How has he come to illustrate his idea to you? (Very clearly)

If so, Clitic Climbing out of the adjunct is (a fortiori) impossible. Contrasts such as those between (iiia and b), noted in Fresina (1981: 285) also cast doubt on the presence of a systematic relation between (18a and b):

(iii) a. Vengo da te a riportarti i libri 'I come by you to bring back to you the books'
b. ?*Vengo a riportarti i libri da te 'I come to bring back the books to you by you'

Benucci (1990: 19) notes the grammaticality in older stages of French of the equivalent of (19b): *Un de ces jours, on me viendra chez moi couper la gorge* (Molière, L'avare 151). 'One of these days, they will come to my place to cut my throat.' We conjecture that scrambling between auxiliary and past participle was also possible in the French of that period.

11. Rizzi (1976a, 1978) also claims that the infinitive and its complement do not pied-pipe under wh-movement when transparency effects obtain, giving contrasts such as (i):

(i) a. Questi argomenti, a parlarti dei quali verrò al più presto . . .
'These topics, to talk to-you about which I will come soon . . .'
b. *?Questi argomenti, a parlare dei quali ti verrò al più presto . . .
'These topics, to talk about which I will to-you come soon . . .'

First, although there is some contrast between (ia and b), there are cases just like (ib) that sound quite acceptable. See (iii):

(iii) Maria, presentare alla quale non lo vorrei . . . .
'M., to introduce to whom I him wouldn't like . . . '

Second, there are auxiliary + past participle cases where a clitic cannot be easily left behind under pied piping:

(iv) *?Il conto, trasferita nel quale la somma non ti verrà . . .
'The account, transferred to which the sum to-you will not be . . . '
(vs. Il conto, trasferita nel quale la somma non verrà . . .)

So, it seems that the phenomenon needs to be better understood before any conclusions can be drawn from it.

12. Many adverbs can occur more than once in the same simple clause (e.g., *Gianni spesso vede le stesse persone spesso* 'G. often sees the same persons often'; *Gianni rapidamente alzò il braccio rapidamente* 'G. quickly lifted his arm quickly'; etc.—cf. Cinque 1999: chap. 1). These, of course, would not discriminate between the two variants, with and without transparency effects.

13. See section 6.3 below for lexical usages of *volere*. Another potential argument for monoclausality involving adverbial modification is suggested in Napoli (1981: 873ff.). In the absence of transparency effects, certain adverbs appear capable of modifying either the matrix or the embedded verb. *Voglio di nuovo imprigionarli* 'I want again to imprison them' is compatible with a context where I never imprisoned them before though I had the intention (here, *di nuovo* 'again' modifies just *voglio* 'I want'); but it is also compatible with a context where I imprisoned them before (though I may not have wanted to), and now I want to send them back to prison (*di nuovo* in this case modifies the embedded verb). Napoli claims that when Clitic Climbing obtains (Li *voglio di nuovo imprigionare* 'them I want again to imprison') *di nuovo* 'again' can only modify the two verbs together (as in a simple sentence with an auxiliary and a nonfinite form). Although I tend to share this intuition, the judgment is not very sharp, and speakers disagree. For critical discussion of this argument, see Wurmbrand (1998: 214ff.).

14. This restructuring verb appears to correspond to the so-called Predispositional Aspect (head) found in American Sign Language (Klima & Bellugi 1979: 253ff) and to the 'tendency' aspect suffix found in Southeastern Tepehuan (Willet 1991).

15. For the apparent case of speakers also accepting (27b), see the discussion in Cinque (2001: n. 4).

16. The adverbs that correspond to $\mathbf{Asp}_{\mathbf{terminative}}$ and $\mathbf{Asp}_{\mathbf{continuative}}$ are *non più* 'no longer' and *ancora* 'still.' As expected, their relative order is also fixed and matches that found with the corresponding functional verbs (cf. Cinque 1999: 95):

(i) a. ?Spero che tu non sia **più ancora** arrabbiato con me!
'I hope that you are no longer still angry at me.'
b. *Spero che tu non sia **ancora più** arrabbiato con me!
'I hope that you are still no longer angry at me.'

[(ib) is grammatical in the irrelevant reading in which *ancora* directly modifies *più* "even more angry at me"].

17. The order in (31) implies by transitivity a number of other relative orders among restructuring verbs; for example, *solere* should precede *volere, smettere,* and *continuare*; *tendere* should precede *smettere* and *continuare*; and so on. These expectations appear to be confirmed quite generally. Here, I give only two relevant examples:

(i) a. Certe cose si sogliono voler fare subito 'Certain things *si* use to want to do immediately'
b. *Certe cose si vogliono soler fare subito 'Certain things *si* want to use to do immediately'

(ii) a. La tenderebbe a continuare a vedere tutti i giorni '(He) her would tend to continue to see every day'
b. *La continuerebbe a tendere a vedere tutti i giorni '(He) her would continue to tend to see every day'

18. Another potential argument for monoclausality would seem to come from Rizzi's (1976a: 39, 1978: 155f.) observation that transparency phenomena are blocked by an Aux $V_{participle}$ Aux $V_{participle}$ sequence. See, for example,

(i) a. Avrei voluto aver*vi* conosciute prima
'I would have liked to have met you earlier.'
b. **Vi* avrei volute aver conosciute prima
'They you would have liked to have met earlier'

The marginality of (ib) would seem to follow (in constrast to *Gli avrei voluto esser presentato prima* 'To-him I would have liked to be introduced earlier,' where the two Aux Vparticiple sequences express different heads) from the fact that in a single clause only one Perfect Aspect head is available. Things, however, are more complex. Fresina (1981: 309, 315; 1997: 111, 115) notes that some cases similar to (ib) are in fact possible:

(ii) a. Maria l'avrebbe dovuta aver letta
'M. it would have had to have read'
b. La somma prestata da Mario gli sarebbe potuta esser già stata resa se la contabilità fosse stata buona.
'The sum loaned by M. to-him could have already been given back if the accounting had been fine.'

Boysen (1977: 289) reports another such case with Auxiliary Change rather than Clitic Climbing: *Un'ora più tardi sarebbe dovuto esservi arrivato, ma nessuno lo vide* (Silone) 'One hour later, he should have had to be there, but nobody saw him.' This may suggest that (active)

Aux $V_{participle}$ can actually correspond to two distinct functional heads ($Asp_{perfect}$ and $T_{anterior}$). See Cinque (1999) for some discussion, but more work is needed on this question.

19. This may suggest a reason for the often-made observation that the presence of negation is crucial for the well-formedness of (33). On the special status of the locution "know how," see also Chomsky (1973: n. 26). The same limitations appear to hold for the analogous cases of Clitic Climbing out of wh-phrases in Serbo-Croatian [cf. (ia and b), Nedzhad Leko and Ljljiana Progovac, personal communication):

(i) a. ?Ja **mu** to ne bih znao kako da objasnim
I him it not would know how to explain 'I wouldn't know how to explain it to him.'
b. *Ja sam ih pitala (Milana) kako da predstavim
I have them asked (M.) how to introduce 'I asked (M.) how to introduce them.'

20. A similar assumption (a single CP layer over the functional XP complement of the deontic modal) might be appropriate for Spanish *Los tiene que ver* '(He) them has to see' if *que* is a complementizer. Its alternation with *de* in Portuguese (*Tenho que vê-lo, Tenho de vê-lo* 'I have to see him'—Martins 1995: 226) would make it appear closer to prepositional 'complementizers,' which may not be instances of clausal CP (see section 8.4 below).

21. *Ku* can (but need not) be missing when the matrix and embedded subjects are coreferential (Terzi 1992, 1994, 1996). When *ku* is present, no Clitic Climbing is possible (in contrast to what happens in Serbo-Croatian; see below):

(i) a. Voggyu ku **lu** kkattu
want-1sg particle it buy-1sg
b. ***Lu** voggyu ku kkattu
It want-1sg particle buy-1sg
'I want to buy it.'

22. Cf. Terzi (1996: n. 15): "The verb of the embedded clause can only occur in the present Tense." Furthermore, as Terzi (1994: 116f.) herself notes, "Salentino subjunctive subordinates appear to demonstrate fewer Tense dependences than their standard Romance counterparts—i.e. they are not subject to the usual Tense dependencies of Romance subjunctives."

23. Another transparency phenomenon, which at first sight appears to be able (for many, though not all, speakers) to cross the **finite** (subjunctive) CP complement of restructuring verbs, is L-*tous* in French. See (i), from Kayne (1977: para. 1.11), and (ii):

(i) a. Il faut toutes qu'elles s'en aillent 'it is necessary that they all go'
b. Il faut tous qu'on se tire 'it is necessary that we all shoot'

(ii) a. Il faut tout qu'on lui dise 'it is necessary that we tell him everything'
b. Il veut tout qu'on lui fasse 'he wants that we make him everything'

Such cases have quite peculiar restrictions (Kayne 1977: 69f.), which led Déprez (1997: n. 18) to conclude that "they do not seriously threaten the generalization that *tous à gauche* is essentially clause-bounded." Cinque (2002b), in fact, argues that in French Quantifier and Adverb, Climbing (as opposed to *En* and *y* Climbing and Long Movement in *easy-to-please* constructions) are not dependent on Restructuring.

24. This recalls Fresina's (1981, 1982, 1997), Napoli's (1981), and Rochette's (1988) idea that in their restructuring use these verbs act much like auxiliaries (cf. also Ledgeway 2000: chap. 5). It is also reminiscent of Rosen's (1990a, 1990b) notion of "light verb" (without the need for an unspecified argument structure and a process of argument structure "merger"

with the arguments and event specification of the embedded verb). See also Emonds's (1999) idea that verbs in restructuring contexts lack semantic features.

25. See section 4.2 for a discussion of the few apparent cases of object control restructuring verbs, which Kayne conjectures (correctly, I will argue) to be hidden causatives.

26. This would either lead to contraindexing or, with identical indexes, to a violation of principle B or C, depending on whether the object controller is a pronominal or an R-expression, respectively:

(i) a.*Gianni$_{i/k}$ lo INFL$_k$ ha costretto lui$_k$ a PRO$_k$ t$_k$ fare
G. it has forced him to do
b.*Gianni$_i$ lo ha costretto il poveretto$_i$ a fare
G. it has forced the poor guy to do

The only permissible case would be one with an anaphor as object controller. But in a structure like (ii), no Clitic Climbing is possible either [cf. (iii)]:

(ii) Gianni ha costretto se stesso a farlo

(iii) *Gianni lo ha costretto se stesso a fare
G. has forced himself to do it.

It could be claimed that the latter is too restricted a case to warrant a restructuring use of *costringere* 'force,' but this is not obvious given the restricted restructuring use of *sembrare* 'seem' documented below in the text.

27. *Sembrare* allows Clitic Climbing for Radford's (1976), Napoli's (1981: 883), and Ledgeway's (2000: 299, n. 15) informants, as well as for Burzio (1986: 354) but not for Rizzi (1976b: 173 and n. 12) or Fresina (1981: 49). My own judgment is that it allows it selectively, that is, with third-person Clitics, as in (41a) or in *Non **gli**$_i$ sembra essere fedele* t$_i$ 'not to him (she) seems to be faithful,' but not with first- and second-person Clitics: **Non **mi**$_i$/**ti**$_i$ sembra essere fedele* t$_i$ 'not to me/you (she) seems to be faithful' or *si* (impersonal or other): **Quelle case **si** sembrano poter costruire con poche spese* 'those houses *si* seem to be able to build inexpensively' (Rizzi 1976b: 173). *Sembrare* followed by a small clause appears to pattern in the same way, suggesting that it, too, is a case of restructuring (cf. Stowell 1991): *Non gli$_i$ sembra fedele* t$_i$ 'he to-him does not seem faithful' versus **Non mi$_i$/ti$_i$ sembra fedele* t$_i$ 'he to me/you does not seem faithful.' The contrast between *Ne sembravate contenti* '(you) of-it seemed glad' and **Giorgio gliene sembrava contento* 'G. to-him-of-it seemed glad,' as well as **Giorgio ne sembrava a tutti contento* 'G. of-it seemed to everybody glad,' with an overt dative complement of *sembrare* (noted in Cinque 1981/1982: 257), in fact exactly parallels that between (41a and b). Other restructuring verbs that apparently allow third-person, but not first- and second-person Clitics and *si*, are (for me) the following: *preferire* [?***Lo** preferì fare Gianni* 'G. preferred doing it' vs. ****Se ne** preferì andare* '(He) preferred to go away'], *scordare* 'forget' [***Lo** scordò di fare* '(He) forgot to do it' vs. ****Mi** scordai di presentare all'esame* 'I forgot to appear at the exam'], *stentare* 'to be hardly able' [***Lo** stento a credere* 'I am hardly able to believe it(?him)' vs. *Lui ***ci** stenta a credere* 'He is hardly able to believe us'], *sperare* 'hope' [?*Lo spera di poter fare anche lui* '(He) hopes to be able to do it himself' vs. **Ce la spera di fare anche lui* 'He hopes to make it himself'], and so on. The phenomenology in question could have to do with the kind of empty category that third-person, on the one hand, and first- and second-person Clitics and *si*, on the other hand, co-occur with (pro or trace, respectively, as proposed in Kayne 1999b).

28. The contrast in (41) is noted in Radford (1976). See also Napoli (1981: 875).

29. Raising *menacer* 'threaten' and *promettre* 'promise' [roughly '(unpleasantly) appear to' and '(pleasantly) appear to'] behave analogously, as noted in Pollock (1978: 84f.):

(i) a. Pierre avait **tous** menacé (*Marie) de les importer
P. had threatened (M.) to take them all away.
b. Pierre avait **tout** promis (*à Marie) de lire
P. had promised (M.) to read everything.

Likewise, Wurmbrand (1998: 306) notes that Scrambling is only possible with *versprechen* 'promise' when it has no dative argument. Sabel's (1999) observation that Scrambling out of the infinitival complement of *versprechen* is possible even in the presence of a dative can perhaps be reconciled with Wurmbrand's if Sabel's is a control usage of *versprechen* that falls in the same category as that of the hidden causatives discussed in section 4.2.

30. Fresina (1981: 164ff.) also notes that *andare* 'go' and *venire* 'come' cease to allow Clitic Climbing when they take an internal directional complement:

(i) a. Li andiamo (*alla stazione) a ricevere '(We) them go (to the station) to receive'
b. Lo venne (*a casa) a prendere '(He) it came (home) to fetch'

Again, this is expected if functional verbs cannot take arguments. For evidence that the infinitival constituent following *andare* and *venire* is an adjunct clause when these take a directional complement, see note 10 above. A potential problem is constituted by the possibility of Clitic Climbing out of the infinitival complement of certain impersonal verbs that take a dative argument in certain varieties of Catalan, noted in Rigau (2000: sect. 6):

(i) No vos hi cal anar 'Not to-you (pl.) there is necessary to go'

Such cases would cease to be problematic if, as Richard Kayne pointed out to me, the dative DP were in fact the subject of the lexical V, raising with *cal* and similar verbs to a dative (rather than nominative) subject position.

31. For this reason I do not share Burzio's (1981: sect. 6.2.1, 1986: 333f.; cf. also Schroten 1986) conclusion that "matrix ergative verbs do not 'lose' their direct object when restructuring applies" (Burzio 1981: 555). His argument, based on small clause relatives (in which only structural direct objects can be relativized), actually gives contradictory results. Whereas first- and second-person clitics and *si* are (marginally) possible [cf. (i), (accusative)] third-person clitics are to my ear ungrammatical [cf. (iia) and (iiia), which contrast with the potentially nonrestructuring (iib) and (iiib), possible because the relative head can originate in the structural object position of the motion verb):

(i) a. ?Le uniche persone venute**vi** a salutare . . . 'the only persons come to greet you. . . . '
b. ?[G.C.)]Un vicino venuto**mi** a chiedere un favore . . . (Burzio 1986: 334) 'A neighbor come to ask me a favor. . . . '
c. ?L'unico ragazzo venuto**si** a presentare . . . 'the only boy *si* come to introduce himself . . . '

(ii) a.*L'unico ragazzo andato**lo** a prendere . . . 'the only boy gone to fetch it . . . '
b. ??L'unico ragazzo andato a prender**lo** . . . 'the only boy gone to fetch it . . . '

(iii) a.*Le sole persone venute**lo** a raccogliere . . . 'the only persons come to gather it . . . '
b. Le sole persone venute a raccoglier**lo** . . . 'the only persons come to gather-it . . . '

This divide in clitic types is reminiscent of that found with present participles in Italian, which allow for first- and second-person clitics and *si* but disallow (accusative) third-person clitics (cf. Benincà and Cinque 1991: 609; see also note 27 above). As for Burzio's argument based on auxiliary selection, which is *essere* 'be' even in the presence of Clitic Climbing [*Lo è venuto a prendere* '(He) is come to fetch it'], we do not have a clear answer. It may prove to depend on the proper analysis of Auxiliary Change (cf. the discussion in Kayne 1993: n. 50); or it may depend on the semifunctional character of motion verbs, which, like causatives (cf. Cinque 2002a: n. 19), contribute an argument even if entering a specific slot of the functional hierarchy. The different interpretation of the PP *da Torino* 'from Turin' in (iva) and (ivb), below indeed shows that it must be *venire* 'come' that contributes a source argument to *venire a operare* 'come to operate':

(iv) a. Lo verranno a operare da Torino '(They) will come to operate him from Turin'
b. %Lo opereranno da Torino '(They) will operate him from Turin'

On the notion of semifunctional predicates, see also Cardinaletti and Shlonsky (2000) (some of whose judgments and conclusions, however, we do not share), Cardinaletti and Giusti (2000), and Wurmbrand (2001).

32. The account sketched in Kayne (1989b: n. 52) of the similar contrast between **Lo è andato Gianni a prendere* 'It has gone G. to fetch' and *Lo è andato a prendere Gianni* 'It has gone to fetch G.' (cf. Burzio 1986: 333 and 386, n. 11) is incompatible with the antisymmetric framework because it crucially rests on rightward extraposition of *a prendere* around *Gianni*.

33. As a matter of fact, there is evidence that when *venire* 'come' has an inverted subject (as in (43a), the infinitival clause is an adjunct; an even stronger reason for why Clitic Climbing fails (cf. note 10 above). This is shown by the impossibility of extracting an argument PP from it: **A chi ne sono venuti molti a portare un regalo?* 'To whom have many of them come to bring a present?' Acceptable sentences are *Molti ti sono venuti a portare un regalo*; (?)*Ti sono venuti a portare un regalo molti* 'Many have come to bring you a present,' for which the absence of *ne* 'of-them' makes it possible for *molti* to originate not as the internal subject of unaccusative *venire* 'come,' but as the external subject of the unergative *portare* 'bring,' with *venire* functional. *Ne* is licit when the embedded verb is unaccusative, which is again compatible with *venire* being a complementless functional verb. Compare *Te ne sono venuti a morire vicino molti* 'Many of them have come to die near you.' The same reason may account for the nonrestructuring nature of *mettersi a* 'start' (vs. *cominciare a*); see (i), and other verbs with ('inherent') *si*, if this *si* betrays a necessarily unaccusative origin of the subject (namely, its generation in an internal argument position):

(i) a. Maria si mise a legger**lo**
b. *Maria **lo** si mise a leggere
'Maria started reading it.'

Ledgeway (1998: 531), however, lists *metterse a* among the restructuring verbs of Neapolitan.

34. The restructuring nature of verbs of this kind is also assumed in the literature on Germanic. See, for example, Wurmbrand (1998: 39) and Sabel (1999).

35. This is a case of indirect object control, as are the Spanish cases discussed in the text. As far as I can tell, Italian (the same is true for other languages: Bordelois 1988: 73; Sabel 1999) does not allow Clitic Climbing with any *direct* object control verb (see, e.g., **Me lo invitarono/aiutarono a leggere* 'They invited/helped me to read it'; **Me lo costrinsero/ obbligarono/forzarono a leggere* 'They forced me to read it'; **Me lo convinsero/*

persuasero a leggere 'They convinced me to read it'). An exception appears to be *mandare* 'send,' as in *Me lo mandarono a prendere* 'They sent to get it for me.' This, however, is not related to *Mi mandarono a prenderlo* 'They sent me (ACC) to get it' (via Climbing of *lo*), for *mi* must be dative (cf. *Glielo mandarono a prendere* 'They sent to get it for him'). Rather, it seems related to *Mandarono a prendermelo* 'They sent (scilicet: someone) to get it for me,' though climbing is impossible if the implicit object of *mandare* ('someone') is present: **Me lo mandarono qualcuno a prendere* 'They sent someone to get it for me.' *Mandare* 'send' appears to be the causative of 'go' but can also render 'cause to go (by saying)': *Mi ha mandato al diavolo* '(He) sent me to hell (lit. to the devil)' can be used to report someone saying to the speaker *vai al diavolo!* 'go to hell.'

36. In a decomposition analysis à la Hale and Keyser (1993), *allow, order*, and *teach*, for example, would closely correspond to something like 'cause to be able to,' 'cause to do (by saying)' (cf. the previous note), and 'cause to learn' (or 'cause to come to know'), respectively.

37. This is, of course, orthogonal to the question of whether (obligatory) control reduces, or not, to movement (local raising from and into a theta position), as in O'Neil (1995, 1997), Hornstein (1999), Manzini and Roussou (2000) (cf. also Bošković 1994). For critical discussion of this possibility, however, see Landau (1999, 2000). The evidence below concerning control restructuring verbs argues for movement into a nontheta position, as in classical raising configurations.

38. The possibility found in (56) to (59), though, is apparently restricted to unaccusative verbs whose subject can receive a volitional interpretation. See the contrast between the latter sentences and (ia–c):

(i) a. *Ne sarebbero voluti morire molti 'Many would have liked to die.'
b. *Ne vorrebbero essere ricevuti pochi 'Few would like to be welcomed.'
c. *Ne vorrebbero esser noti molti 'Many would like to be well known.'

The contrast is plausibly an effect of the selectional requirement of *volere* 'want' and the ability or inability of the 'inverted' subject to be interpreted volitionally. The same requirement can perhaps account for why purely presentational contexts like *ce ne sono molti* 'there are many of-them' are unacceptable in this construction (vs. the one with raising *dovere* 'must,' which does not impose any volitionality requirement). See (iia and b), from Burzio (1986: 362), which in this view no longer instantiate a control versus raising contrast:

(ii) a. *Ci vorrebbe essere molta gente alla festa 'there would like to be many people at the party'
b. Ci dovrebbe essere molta gente alla festa 'there should be many people at the party.'

The contrast between (iiia) and (iiib) (also from Burzio 1986: 389) can analogously be attributed not to control versus raising but to a failure in complying with the volitionality requirement on the subject (theme of the embedded passive verb):

(iii) a. *Un interprete ciascuno$_i$ vorrebbe essere assegnato a quei visitatori$_i$
'One interpreter each would want to be introduced to those visitors.'
b. Un interprete ciascuno$_i$ potrebbe essere assegnato a quei visitatori$_i$
'One interpreter each could be introduced to those visitors.'

When such a subject is more easily interpretable as volitional, the contrast, indeed, tends to disappear:

(iv) ?A quei visitatori$_i$ vorrà forse andare incontro un interprete ciascuno$_i$
'To those visitors will want to go up one interpreter each'

Rizzi (1976b: 172ff.) mentions the existence of another Control versus Raising contrast in the restructuring construction. Raising, but not Control, verbs would seem to allow for the impersonal *si* on the embedded infinitival. See (v), given with Rizzi's judgment:

(v) a. Queste case devono/possono costruir**si** alla svelta
'These houses must/can *si* build quickly
b. *Queste case vogliono costruir**si** alla svelta
These houses want to *si* build quickly

I (and other speakers), however, find such cases as (vb) not to be impossible, and actually quite natural, with other moods and lexical choices: *Certe esperienze vorrebbero poter*si *fare subito* 'Certain experiences would want to be able to do *si* immediately.' The (near-) impossibility of the other case given by Rizzi (the one with *andare*: **Queste medicine vanno a comprar*si *in farmacia* 'These medicines go to *si* buy at the chemist's') can perhaps be due to the fact that impersonal *si* is located higher than the functional head hosting motion verbs (indeed a very low one: cf. Cinque 2002a). Similar considerations may apply to the (near-) impossibility of ??*Certe esperienze vorrebbero/dovrebbero poter far***si** *subito* 'Certain experiences would want to/should be able to *si* do immediately,' where the clitic is found on the lexical verb.

39. Analogous cases of transparency of 'want' in various languages are noted in the relational grammar literature. Frantz (1976: 182f), for example, notes that in MicMac (Algonkian) the complex verb formed by 'want' and the embedded verb retains the valency properties of the embedded verb (it shows transitive or intransitive inflection, depending on the transitive or intransitive nature of the embedded verb). Similarly, Gerdts (1988: 845f.) notes that in Eskimo and Halkomelem Salish the subject of 'want' receives absolutive Case if the embedded verb is intransitive and ergative Case if it is transitive (thus apparently inheriting the status of the latter). Gonzales (1986, 1990) reports that with *querer* 'want' (and more marginally *tratar* 'try') in certain varieties of Spanish, the "inversion property of an embedded predicate like *gustar* can in effect "transfer" to the matrix" (1990: 87). In *A Juan le quieren gustar las matematicas* 'J. wants to like mathematics,' it is Juan who "wants" even if *querer* does not normally take a dative subject. This suggests that the selectional requirement of *querer* can be satisfied under restructuring by the dative argument of the embedded psych-verb *gustar*. For more general discussion of the optional inheritance property of desideratives across languages, see Gerdts (1988).

40. The presence of Clitic Climbing is meant to exclude the lexical use of *volere* (for which see section 6.3 below). Plural number agreement on *volere* also appears to exclude it (**Sembra essersi voluti andare volentieri* 'Seems to be *si* wanted to go willingly') because 'lexical' *volere* is followed by an abstract predicate taking an object clause (cf. section 6.3), whence third-person singular agreement on the participle. The third-person singular agreement, indeed, is acceptable in the same context: *Sembra non essersi voluto andare incontro a nessuno* 'Seems to be *si* wanted to go toward nobody.'

41. In addition to impersonal(-passive) *si*, which absorbs the external theta role and Accusative Case (thus forcing a direct object, when present, to become the subject), another *si* exists (cf. Cinque's 1988 [—arg *si*]), which absorbs no external theta role or Accusative, only Nominative, and which can thus render impersonal those predicates that have no external theta role or Accusative Case (unaccusative, passive, psych-, copular, and raising verbs). When this *si* applies to transitives, there is no object promotion to the subject (Cinque 1988: Dobrovie-Sorin 1998):

(i) a. Si è perso molti soldi 'One has lost (sing.) a lot of money (pl.).'
b. Li si è persi 'them one has lost'

This construction (which is somewhat marked with transitive verbs, giving rise to a special interpretation in specific time reference contexts) is the only possible one when there is no agreement [as in (ia)], the object is cliticized [as in (ib)], it contains the *ci si* form (replacing an impossible *si si* sequence), or it has floating *tutti* 'all' (cf. Cinque 1988; see also the next note).

42. The contrast in (71), in fact, provides additional evidence for the already discussed non-argument-taking nature of *volere* 'want' in restructuring contexts. If it could assign an external theta role and thus license impersonal(-passive) *si*, it is not clear why it should require the embedded transitive verb to select *essere* when Long Object Preposing occurs. In the absence of such preposing, no *avere* → *essere* change on the embedded verb can in fact take place [cf. (i); Fresina 1981: 335), even in the presence of other transparency effects [like *Loro*-climbing; cf. (ib)]:

(i) a. Si vorrebbe averle (*esserle) vendute a un prezzo più alto 'One would have liked to have sold them at a higher price.'
b. Si vorrebbe loro averle (*esserle) già vendute 'One would like to have already sold them to them.'

These examples would seem to show that *si*, after all, can originate directly with *volere*; hence that the modal assigns an external theta role. But (ib) and the Clitic Climbing variant of (ia)—***Le*** *si vorrebbe aver vendute a un prezzo più alto*—show that the *si* of (i) is not the impersonal(-passive) one (i.e., the [+arg] one of Cinque 1988, which absorbs the external theta role and Accusative Case) but the pure impersonal one mentioned in the previous note (the [-arg] one of Cinque 1988, which absorbs only Nominative Case and which renders impersonal unaccusative, passive, psych-, copular, and raising verbs. Also (ib) also suggests that, in one and the same clause, [–arg] *si* is higher than complement clitics. Now, the following facts indeed suggest that such *si* is higher in the functional structure of the clause than impersonal(-passive) *si* (and the other types of *si*). See, for example, the contrast between (iib), with the [-arg] impersonal *si* of note 41, and (iiib) and (ivb), with impersonal(-passive) *si*:

(ii) a. **Si** stava convincendo**lo** tutti a restare 'We were all convincing him to stay.'
b.**Stava convincendo**losi** tutti a restare

(iii) a. Questi articoli **si** stanno vendendo a prezzi stracciati 'These items are being sold very cheap.'
b. ?Questi articoli stanno vendendo**si** a prezzi stracciati

(iv) a. Loro **si** stanno scrivendo dei biglietti 'They are writing cards to each other.'
b. Loro stanno scrivendo**si** dei biglietti

Examples (72) and(74) in the text below show that the progressive periphrasis in Italian, like other contexts, does not allow split clitics. In this respect, (ii) is not exceptional in our analysis as *si* actually originates higher than all other complement clitics. As Richard Kayne pointed out to me, (ii) recalls such Friulian examples as *Si vjodilu* 'One sees it/him' (cf. Benincà 1989: 572), which would make such cases as *Si lu vjodi* (and *Lo si stava convincendo*) cases of Clitic Climbing.

43. The requirement of "uniform cliticization" found in Italian in restructuring contexts (Rizzi 1976b: n. 18), in the progressive and prospective periphrasis of (74) and (75), and in negative imperatives (Kayne 1992: n. 5—cf. **Non gli datelo* vs. *Non dateglielo* or *Non **glielo** date* 'Don't give it to-them') remains to be understood, especially given the fact that it is not found in other Romance languages or dialects (Kayne 1989: 248, 256, n. 34) or in Serbo-

Croatian (Stjepanović 1998). The presence/absence of the requirement could turn out to depend on whether clitics form a cluster (i.e., each one is adjoined to the next) or not. That the ill-formedness of (65b) may have to do with one but not the other clitic climbing up is also found in Longobardi (1979: n. 7) and Burzio (1981: chap. 6, n. 4).

44. Taraldsen (1982: 273) gives *Maria deve loro averlo già dato* 'M. must to-them have it already given' as ungrammatical, but this and similar sentences seem to me quite acceptable. The optionality of Clitic Climbing in 'long' *tough*-movement contexts, also a diagnostic for the restructuring configuration (Rizzi 1978: 140ff.), is not easy to check. Although examples such as *Questa tavola è difficile da poter venderti* 'this table is difficult to be able to sell to you' are, according to Zubizarreta (1980: 154, 175) accepted by some native speakers on a par with *Questa tavola è difficile da poterti vendere* 'this table is difficult to be able to you to sell,' for others, myself included, clitics (in either position) are quite marginal. In this connection, see also Radford (1977: 109), Napoli (1981: 850f.) and Rizzi (2000: 101). Additional evidence for the optionality of Clitic Climbing is provided by the paradigms in (i) (prompted by an observation of Anna Cardinaletti), and (ii), adapted from Longobardi (1980: n. 5):

(i) a. Gianni **lo** tornò a salutare 'G. greeted him again.'
b. Gianni tornò a salutar**lo** 'G. greeted him again' or 'G. came back to greet him.'

(ii) a. ??Dovrebbe detestare studiare questa materia 'He should detest studying this subject.'
b. ??Vorrebbe potere fare questo anche lui 'Even he would like to be able to do this.'
c. **Lo** vorrebbe poter(??e) fare anche lui 'Even he it would like to be able to do'
d. Vorrebbe poter(??e) far**lo** anche lui

In (ia), with Clitic Climbing (which forces the restructuring configuration), *tornare* '(lit.) go/come back' is unambiguously interpreted as a marker or 'iterative aspect' (= 'do again'). In (ib), where the clitic is on the embedded infinitival, *tornare* is ambiguous between the literal meaning 'go/come back' and 'do again.' This suggests that the restructuring option is available even when the clitic does not climb. (iia and b) exemplify a constraint against the sequence of two infinitives, one of which is the complement of the other (Longobardi 1980); (iic) shows that with restructuring verbs that display Clitic Climbing the constraint becomes inoperative, provided that the final vowel of the first infinitive is deleted. But the same is true of (iid), even though the clitic has not climbed. This suggests that (iid) is a case of restructuring despite the lack of Clitic Climbing [note that deletion of the 'e' of *detestare* in (iia) does not improve its status; retention of the –e in (ii) is better than the retention of the –e with enclitics: ***Farelo sarebbe difficile* 'To do it would be difficult']. See also Monachesi (1999) for experimental evidence that restructuring verbs and their infinitival complement form a prosodic unit whether or not Clitic Climbing has applied.

45. *Ho mangiatolo* is possible in other Romance dialects (cf. the references cited in Rizzi 2000: 100). When no finite verb is present, a clitic can attach to the past participle even in Standard Italian: (*Una volta*) *mangiatolo, si alzò e se ne andò* '(Once) eaten it, (he) stood up and left.' On such 'absolute' usages of the past participle, see Belletti (1981, 1990), Kayne (1989a), and Cinque (1990: sect. 4.1).

46. Though, apparently, only with a subset of the verbs that allow Clitic Climbing in Spanish and Italian.

47. One context where Clitic Climbing appears *obligatory* is Long Passive, a construction only possible with restructuring verbs (Rizzi 1976a: n. 21; Aissen and Perlmutter 1983:

postscript; Burzio 1986: 373ff; Cinque 2002a). Here, a clitic cannot remain on the infinitive. See (ib) (a similar observation is made in Rizzi 2000: 101):

(i) a. I pezzi **gli** furono finiti di consegnare l'anno dopo
'The parts were finished delivering to him a year later'
b. *I pezzi furono finiti di consegnar**gli** l'anno dopo

But even this obligatoriness may prove illusory. As noted in the above references, Long Passive in Romance is restricted to restructuring verbs of 'finishing,' 'beginning,' and (more marginally) 'motion' and 'continuation'—in fact, a subset of these (cf. Cinque 2002a, In that article, I argue that such limitations can be understood if restructuring verbs are taken to be functional verbs inserted directly under the corresponding functional heads. In such cases it is to be expected that only those restructuring verbs that correspond to aspectual heads lower than Voice (completive, inceptive, continuative, and motion) will be able to be passivized (in addition to the lexical verb). All other aspectual, modal, and mood heads higher than Voice cannot be passivized, as lowering is barred. If that is correct, the ungrammaticality of (ib) could be due, then, not to the obligatory character of Clitic Climbing but to the fact that no clitic position is available (in Italian) under Voice. Although the same generalization concerning Long Passive in restructuring Romance languages appears to hold in French (The only cases cited in Grevisse 1993: 1124f. are with 'finish'-type verbs: *Le chateau n'était pas achevé de meubler* 'the castle was not finished furnishing'; *une boite qui n'était pas tout à fait finie d'installer* 'a box which was not at all finished installing') and Japanese (Nishigauchi 1993), Wurmbrand (1998: 34f., 119ff.) notes that in German Long Passive is not as restricted as in Romance. For example, it is also found with such restructuring verbs as 'try,' 'manage,' 'dare,' and so on. Rather than taking the contrast to depend on the different location of these aspectual heads, I conjecture it may depend on the higher location of passive morphology in German, which corresponds more to an impersonal than to a personal Voice (it can, e.g., affect unergative verbs, like Italian *si*, which, interestingly, also "passivizes" 'try,' 'manage,' 'dare,' etc.). For further discussion on this topic, see Taraldsen (2002).

48. Auxiliary Change is possible only from *avere* 'have' to *essere* 'be' (not vice versa) and with a subset of the restructuring verbs (*volere* 'want,' *potere* 'can,' *dovere* 'must,' *cominciare, iniziare* 'begin,' and *continuare* 'continue') for reasons that remain to be understood. Cf. Kayne (1989b, 253) and references cited there.

49. Burzio (1986: 365) also attributes equal status to the variant with Auxiliary Change and to that without in (ia and b), and (iia and b), in the presence of Clitic Climbing. (I, in fact, find the variant without Auxiliary Change slightly better):

(i) a. Giovanni le ?sarebbe dovuto essere fedele 'G.would have had to be faithful to her.'
b. Giovanni le ?avrebbe dovuto essere fedele 'G.would have had to be faithful to her.'

(ii) a. Giovanni ne ?sarebbe dovuto essere il presidente 'G. would have had to be the president of it.'
b. Giovanni ne ?avrebbe dovuto essere il presidente 'G. would have had to be the president of it.'

In more colloquial styles of Italian, Auxiliary Change may in fact fail to apply even in the presence of Clitic Climbing. See (iii) and the case in (iv), given by Rizzi (1978: 136). The same is true in Occitan [see (v), from Hernanz & Rigau 1984: 47]:

(iii) a. Maria c'ha (*ci ha) dovuto venire molte volte 'M. there had to come many times'

b. Gli hai per caso potuto andare incontro? 'him could you by chance go toward?'
c. Non ne ha mai voluto venir fuori 'he from-it has never wanted to get out'

(iv) ??Laura ci ha cominciato ad andare un mese fa 'L. has begun to go there a month ago'

(v) a. Me **son** volgut venjar 'I wanted to take revenge'
b. M'**ai** volgut venjar

Concerning the contrast **ci ha* vs. *c'ha* [tʃa] in (iii), note that (81b) and the like also degrade considerably with *ci è* in place of *c'è*.

50. In this connection, Pearce (1990: 21) reports that Auxiliary Change was lost in the history of French more or less at the same time (early seventeenth century) that Clitic Climbing began to be lost (which is also the time when Aux-to-COMP apparently was lost: Roberts 1993a: 203).

51. Landau (1999, 2000) draws a comparable distinction between what he calls "exhaustive" Control (with implicative, aspectual, and modal predicates) and "partial" Control (with factive, propositional, desiderative, and interrogative predicates). I'll come back to his analysis, as he explicitly claims that exhaustive Control does not coincide with restructuring (contrary to what I am proposing below).

52. Landau (2000: chap. 2, sect. 6) explicitly claims that 'strict,' or in his terms, 'exhaustive,' Control does not reduce to raising (because of the Control character of some of the modal and aspectual verbs), nor does it coincide with restructuring (given that exhaustive control is a property of modal, aspectual, and implicative verbs, regardless of whether they are in a restructuring context or not, and given that some of the implicative verbs that show exhaustive control are not, according to him, restructuring). In the context of my analysis, none of these arguments is compelling. For one thing, we saw above evidence for the raising character of even apparent Control restructuring verbs like 'want.' As to the second claim, I am suggesting that restructuring verbs enter a restructuring (monoclausal) configuration even in the absence of transparency effects; that is, they enter only restructuring contexts—whence their exclusively raising character (which derives their exhaustive Control property in all situations). Finally, the claim that there are nonrestructuring implicative verbs, which still display exhaustive Control, does not seem to be substatiated by the facts. Among implicative verbs, we find that only the restructuring ones (*riuscire* 'manage,' *dimenticare* 'forget,' *mancare* 'fail,' and *osare* 'dare') display exhaustive control [cf. (i)]. Nonrestructuring ones (all the others) appear to us to allow (in Italian) partial Control [cf. (ii)]:

(i) *Loro dissero che Gianni non riuscì a (/dimenticò di/mancò di/osò) incontrarsi alle 5
'They said that G. did not manage (/forgot/failed/dared) to meet at 5.'

(ii) Gianni fece in modo di/ritenne opportuno/accondiscese a/evitò di incontrarsi alle 5
'G. made sure/saw fit/condescended/avoided to meet at 5.'

"Weak implicatives" (Pesetsky 1991)—which are plausibly hidden causatives (cf. Kayne 1989b: 248 and sect. 4.2 above—also seem to me to allow partial Control [cf. (iii)]. At any rate, (ii) and (iii) sharply contrast with (i), which indeed makes it plausible that exhaustive Control and restructuring coincide:

(iii) Gianni costrinse/forzò Maria a incontrarsi alle 5 'G. compelled/forced M. to meet at 5.'

53. Here, I in fact assume, immaterially for the argument, that the abstract understood verb is something like OBTAIN (= [COME [TO HAVE]]). '*Vorrei* DP,' as opposed to '*Vorrei avere* DP' cannot be interpreted as "I would like to be in the state of having DP.' Cf. *Vorrei *(avere) vent'anni* 'I would want (to have) 20 years.'

54. As pointed out to me by Dominique Sportiche, this also means that the *che*-clause following *volere* in *Gianni vuole che Maria resti* 'G. wants that M. stays' is not directly a complement of *volere* but of HAVE (or OBTAIN):

(i) Gianni vuole [$_{VP}$ OBTAIN [$_{CP}$ che Maria resti]]

This introduces a systematic ambiguity in infinitival cases such as (iia), which can thus instantiate either the structure in (iib), or that in (iic):

(ii) a. Gianni vuole restare 'G. wants to stay.'
b. Gianni$_i$ vuole . . . [$_{VP}$ t$_i$ OBTAIN [$_{CP}$ PRO$_i$ restare]]
c. Gianni$_i$ vuole . . . [$_{VP}$ t$_i$ restare]

Evidence supporting such structural ambiguity is discussed in section 7.1 below.

55. That is, *Mary began the novel* can be interpreted as '. . . began to read/write' but not as '. . . *to hate/*to appreciate/etc.'); similarly, *John finished the beer* can be interpreted as '. . . finished drinking' but not as '. . . *pouring/*selling/etc.'

56. In the case of (88c), the abstract verbal complement must be one of existence, presumably.

57. As is perhaps to be expected, motion verbs without an overt directional PP are still ambiguous between the lexical and the restructuring use. This can be seen from the double possibility they allow under *fare* (cf. Rizzi 1978: 153; Burzio 1986: 388, n. 26):

(i) a. Gianni lo farà andare a prenderlo 'G. him will make go to fetch it'
b. Gianni glielo farà andare a prendere 'G. to him it will make go to fetch'

In the first, causativization treats *andare* as intransitive, assigning Accusative to its subject (cf. also the split clitics); in the sencond, it takes the restructured *andare a prendere* as a transitive configuration, assigning Dative to its subject.

58. That the commitment on the part of the speaker in the evidential, restructuring usage of *sembrare* is not due to the presence of an optionally deleted dative *a me/mi* 'to me' is shown by the fact that the restructuring use is no longer possible when *a me/mi* is actually present:

(i) a. *Non me lo sembra apprezzare molto 'He doesn't seem to me to appreciate it much.'
b. *Non lo sembra a me apprezzare molto 'He doesn't seem to me to appreciate it much.'
c. *A me, non lo sembra apprezzare molto 'To me, he doesn't seem to appreciate it much.'

59. The peculiar pause required in the (a) cases of (23)–(26), noted in section 3.1, is perhaps a reflex of the more complex, biclausal structure. Replacement of *volere* with other modals or aspectuals (which have no access to the biclausal option) leads to ungrammaticality. See, for example,

(i) a. *Maria deve già averlo già lasciato 'M. already must have already left him.'
b. *Maria comincia già ad esserci già antipatica 'M. already begins to already be unpleasant.'

60. *Non (*la) può [0]* 'He (it) cannot' of (96a) thus contrasts with *Mangiare fredda, non la può* 'eat cold, he it cannot,' which has a structured empty category ([$_{XP}$Mangiare ~~la~~ fredda] non la può [~~mangiare la fredda~~]) under the copy theory of movement (Chomsky 1995: 3.5).

61. This conclusion, coupled with the evidence for the raising nature of restructuring verbs ('want' included), leads him to suggest that movement can be from a theta position to another theta position. If my analysis of NCA below is correct, no such conclusion is warranted.

62. The *partial* visibility of the internal structure of the null complement in NCA (the subject, but not the verb and its complements, "covered" by *do it*) is also shown by the possible appearance of benefactive PPs (and other adjuncts) modifying the understood predicate (problematic in an opaque '[$_{CP/IP}$ 0]' pro-form) versus subcategorised PPs. See (Porterai da mangiare?) *Potrò, solo per qualcuno* '(Will you bring something to eat?) I will be able [to do it] only for someone' versus **Potrò, solo a qualcuno* 'I will be able [to do it] only to someone.' The NCA appears not to be reducible to an abstract *do it* in all cases. In addition to restructuring verbs, many other predicates allow null complements. See (i), adapted from Grimshaw (1979: 288ff.):

(i) A: John is telling lies.
B: I know/ I have already found out/ I am not surprised/ It's too bad . . .

For these, the analysis must be different. The understood complement is not *do it* but a pronominal DP or PP, as also suggested by the obligatory presence in Italian of a clitic for direct object DPs, though not for PPs, which recalls the English and Italian contrast between empty operators and resumptive clitics in Topicalization and CLLD:

(ii) A: Dice bugie (He tells lies.)
B: *(Lo) so/ *(L')ho già scoperto/Non (ne) sono sorpreso
'I know/ I already found out/I'm not surpised.'

What all the different types of NCA appear to have in common is some kind of pronominal element ('it,' pro-PPs, 'do it,' etc.): the exponents of 'deep anaphora.' The possibility of *Je sais* 'I know' in French is perhaps related to that of *Ça, je sais* 'That, I know.'

63. As the strength of INFL is a necessary but not a sufficient condition for Clitic Climbing (Kayne 1989b: 251), only the presence of Clitic Climbing implies, for Kayne, the presence of null subjects, not vice versa.

64. Kayne (1989b: 243) attributes the blocking effect of negation to the inability of the NegP head to L-mark VP.

65. Note that the sentences in (110) do not require the special intonation discussed in Rizzi (1976a: n. 9), which rescues even the negation between an auxiliary and a participle. It remains to be determined whether Long Object Preposing and Auxiliary Change are less sensitive to the intervention of negation than Clitic Climbing (as claimed in Watanabe 1993: 366 and Kayne 1989b: 253, respectively). I do not find any appreciable difference between Watanabe's example (30)—(?)*Quei libri si potrebbero non leggere subito* 'these books SI would-be-able not read immediately' and *Li potresti non leggere subito* 'Them you could not read immediately'—or between Kayne's example (45)—??*Sarebbe voluto non andare al mare* '(He) would-be wanted NEG to go to the seaside' and ?*Ci sarebbe voluto non andare subito* 'There (he) would-be wanted NEG to go immediately.'

66. This sentence was pointed out to me by Richard Kayne.

67. For example, Fresina (1981: 49) does not accept Clitic Climbing with *desiderare*, while Monachesi (1998: 362 n. 9) does. For Spanish, Roldán (1975: 344) does not allow Clitic Climbing with *preferir*, whereas Luján (1978: 105) does. Some Italians have *pensare* 'think' as a restructuring verb, not in its propositional meaning [cf. (ia)] but in its volitional

one, of intending/planning to [cf. (ib)]. For an analogous contrast in Spanish, see Suñer (1980: 314):

(i) a.*Lo penso di aver trattato male 'It (I) think to have treated badly'
b. Lo penso di vedere domani 'Him (I) think to see tomorrow'

Similarly, *dimenticare* 'forget' is restructuring, for some speakers, in the implicative sense of *mancare di* 'fail to,' but not in its propositional sense (for the analogous behavior of German *vergessen*, see Wurmbrand 1998: 222ff.):

(ii) a. Lo dimenticò di spegnere 'It (he) forgot to switch off.'
b.*Lo dimenticò di aver spento 'It (he) forgot he had switched off.'

68. We abtract here from the possibility, argued for in Kayne (1999a), that such prepositions are in fact higher than the selecting verb and act as attractors of the infinitival phrase to their Spec, then raising to the next higher head, and attracting the remnant to the higher Spec (cf. also the rollup derivation proposed in Koopman & Szabolci 2000 for restructuring verbs in Hungarian and Dutch). We also abstract from additional projections that may make up such "small clauses," which include the agreement heads discussed in Kayne (1993) and possibly Topicalization and Focalization projections, if such restructuring cases with "middle field" Focalization and Topicalization are possible: *?Avrebbero loro voluto I SOLDI riconsegnare al più presto (non i vestiti)* '(they) would have to-them wished the money (focus) hand back immediately (not the suits)'; *Avrebbero loro voluto, i soldi, poterli riconsegnare più avanti* '(they) would have to-them wished the money to be able to hand back later.'

References

Abbot, Barbara. (1976). "Right Node Raising as a Test for Constituenthood." *Linguistic Inquiry* 7, 639–642

Aissen, Judith, & David Perlmutter. (1976). "Clause Reduction in Spanish." In *Proceedings of the Second Annual Meeting of the Berkeley Linguistics Society*. Berkeley, Cal.: Berkeley Linguistics Society, pp. 1–30.

Aissen, Judith, & David Perlmutter. (1983). Postscript to Republication of "Clause Reduction in Spanish." In D. Perlmutter, ed., *Studies in Relational Grammar*, vol. 1. Chicago: University of Chicago Press, pp. 383–396.

Andersen, Peggy M. (1987). "Restructuring in Italian: An LFG Analysis." In *Proceedings of the Third Eastern States Conference on Linguistics*. Pittsburgh: University of Pittsburgh, pp. 13–24.

Baker, Mark. (1988). *Incorporation. A Theory of Grammatical Function Changing*. Chicago: University of Chicago Press.

Baker, Mark. (1999). "Clitic Climbing and the Boundedness of Head Movement." In H. van Riemsdijk, ed., *Clitics in the Languages of Europe*. Berlin: Mouton de Gruyter, pp. 369–373.

Bayer, Joseph, & Jaklin Kornfilt. (1990). "Restructuring Effects in German." In E. Engdahl, R. Cooper, M. Mellor, & M. Reape, eds., *Parametric Variation in Germanic and Romance. Proceedings from the DYANA Workshop, September 1989*. Edinburgh: Center for Cognitive Science, University of Edinburgh, pp. 21–42.

Belletti, Adriana. (1981). "Frasi ridotte assolute." *Rivista di grammatica generativa* 6, 3–32.

Belletti, Adriana. (1990). *Generalized Verb Movement*. Turin: Rosenberg e Sellier.

Benincà, Paola. (1986). "Punti di sintassi comparata dei dialetti italiani settentrionali." In G. Holtus & K. Ringger, eds., *Raetia antiqua et moderna. W.Th.Elwert zum 80. Geburtstag*. Tübingen: Niemeyer, pp. 457–479. (Cited from republication in Benincà 1994.)

Benincà, Paola. (1989). "Friaulisch." In G. Holtus, M. Metzeltin, and C. Schmitt, eds., *Lexicon der romanistischen Linguistik. 1.Grammatik.*Tübingen: Niemeyer, pp. 563–585.

Benincà, Paola. (1994). *La variazione sintattica. Studi di dialettologia romanza.* Bologna: Il Mulino.

Benincà, Paola, & Guglielmo Cinque. (1991). "Il participio presente." In L. Renzi & G. Salvi, eds., *Grande grammatica italiana di consultazione*, vol. 2. Bologna: Il Mulino, pp. 604–609.

Benucci, Franco. (1990). *Destrutturazione. Classi verbali e costruzioni perifrastiche nelle lingue romanze antiche e moderne.* Padova: Unipress.

Bleam, Tonia. (1994). "Clitic Climbing and the Power of Tree Adjoining Grammar." In A. Abeillé & O. Rambow, eds., *Tree Adjoining Gramars: Formalism, Interpretation and Linguistic Analysis.* Stanford, Cal.: CSLI.

Bok-Bennema, Reineke. (1981). "Clitics and Binding in Spanish." In R. May & J. Koster, eds., *Levels of Syntactic Representation.* Dordrecht: Foris, pp. 9–32.

Bok-Bennema, Reineke, & Brigitte Kampers-Manhe. (1994). "Transparency Effects in the Romance Languages." In M. L. Mazzola, ed., *Issues and Theory in Romance Linguistics.* Washington, D.C.: Georgetown University Press, pp. 199–217.

Bonneau, José, & Mihoko Zushi. (1994). "Quantifier Climbing, Clitic Climbing and Restructuring in Romance." *McGill Working Papers in Linguistics* 8, 1–37.

Bordelois, Ivonne. (1974). The Grammar of Spanish Causative Constructions, Ph.D. diss., Massachusetts Institute of Technology, Cambridge.

Bordelois, Ivonne. (1988). "Causatives: From Lexicon to Syntax." *Natural Language and Linguistic Theory* 6, 57–93.

Bošković, Željko. (1994). "D-Structure, Theta-Criterion, and Movement into Theta-Positions." *Linguistic Analysis* 24, 247–286.

Boysen, Gerhard. (1977). "L'emploi des verbes auxiliaires **essere** et **avere** avec les verbes modaux en italien." *Studia Neophilologica* 49, 287–309.

Broadwell, George Aaron, & Jack Martin. (1993). "The Clitic/Agreement Split: Asymmetries in Choctaw Person Marking." In *Proceedings of the 19th Annual Meeting of the Berkeley Linguistics Society (Special Session on Syntactic Issues in Native American Languages).* Berkeley, Cal.: Berkeley Linguistics Society, pp. 1–10.

Burzio, Luigi. (1981). Intransitive Verbs and Italian Auxiliaries. Ph.D. diss., Massachusetts Institute of Technology, Cambridge.

Burzio, Luigi. (1986). *Italian Syntax.* Dordrecht: Reidel.

Calabrese, Andrea. (1993). "The Sentential Complementation of Salentino: A Study of a Language Without Infinitival Clauses." In A. Belletti, ed., *Syntactic Theory and the Dialects of Italy.* Turin: Rosenberg e Sellier, pp. 28–98.

Cardinaletti, Anna. (1991). "On Pronoun Movement: The Italian Dative *Loro.*" *Probus* 3, 127–153.

Cardinaletti, Anna, & Giuliana Giusti. (2000). "'Semi-lexical' Motion Verbs in Romance and Germanic." In N. Corver & H. van Riemsdijk, eds., *Semi-lexical Categories. On the Function of Content Words and Content of Function.* Berlin: Mouton de Gruyter.

Cardinaletti, Anna, & Ur Shlonsky. (2000). "Restructuring in Italian, Clitic Positions and Clausal Strata." University of Bologna and Venice and University of Geneva.

Choe, Hyon-Sook. (1988). Restructuring Parameters and Complex Predicates. A Transformational Approach. Ph.D. diss., Massachusetts Institute of Technology, Cambridge.

Choe, Hyon-Sook. (1989). "Restructuring in Korean and Hungarian." In L. Maràcz & P. Muysken, eds., *Configurationality.* Dordrecht: Foris, pp. 267–292.

Chomsky, Noam. (1977). "On Wh-movement." In P. Culicover, T. Wasow, & A. Akmajian, eds., *Formal Syntax.* New York: Academic Press, pp. 71–132.

Chomsky, Noam. (1995). *The Minimalist Program.* Cambridge, Mass.: MIT Press.

Chung, Sandra. (1988). "Restructuring, Passive and Agreement in Chamorro." Talk given at Stanford University, Stanford, Cal., July.

Cinque, Guglielmo. (1981/1982). "On the Theory of Relative Clauses and Markedness." *Linguistic Review* 1, 247–294.

Cinque, Guglielmo. (1988). "On *si* Constructions and the Theory of Arb." *Linguistic Inquiry* 19, 521–581.

Cinque, Guglielmo. (1990). "Ergative Adjectives and the Lexicalist Hypothesis." *Natural Language and Linguistic Theory* 8, 1–39.

Cinque, Guglielmo. (1998). "On Clitic Climbing and Other Transparency Effects." Talk given at New York University, New York City, and Massachusetts Institute of Technology, Cambridge, February and March.

Cinque, Guglielmo. (1999). *Adverbs and Functional Heads. A Cross-linguistic Perspective.* New York, Oxford University Press.

Cinque, Guglielmo. (2001). "Restructuring and the Order of Aspectual and Root Modal Heads." In G. Cinque & G. Salvi, eds., *Current Studies in Italian Syntax. Essays Offered to Lorenzo Renzi.* Amsterdam: Elsevier, pp.137–155.

Cinque, Guglielmo. [1997] (2002a). "The Interaction of Passive, Causative, and "Restructuring" in Romance." In C. Tortora, ed., *The Syntax of Italian Dialects.* New York: Oxford University Press, pp. 50–66.

Cinque, Guglielmo. (2002b). "A Note on 'Restructuring' and Quantifier Climbing in French." *Linguistic Inquiry* 33(4).

Cole, Peter. (1984). "Clause Reduction in Ancash Quechua." In E.-D. Cook & D. B. Gerdts, eds., *Syntax and Semantics 16: The Syntax of Native American Languages.* New York: Academic Press, pp. 105–121.

Contreras, Heles. (1979). "Clause Reduction, the Saturation Constraint, and Clitic Promotion." *Linguistic Analysis* 5, 161–182.

Depiante, Marcela. (1998). "On the Interaction Between 'Ellipsis' and Restructuring in Spanish and Italian." Ms., University of Connecticut, Storrs.

Déprez, Viviane. (1997). "Two Types of Negative Concord." *Probus* 9, 103–143.

Devi Prasada Sastry, G. (1984). *Mishmi Grammar.* Manasagangotri, Mysore: Central Institute of Indian Languages.

Dikken, Marcel den, Richard Larson, & Peter Ludlow. (1996). "Intensional 'Transitive' Verbs and Concealed Complement Clauses." *Rivista di Linguistica* 8, 331–348.

Di Sciullo, Anna-Maria, & Edwin Williams. (1987). *On the Definition of Word.* Cambridge, Mass.: MIT Press.

Dobrovie-Sorin, Carmen. (1998). "Impersonal *se* Constructions in Romance and the Passivization of Unergatives." *Linguistic Inquiry* 29, 399–437.

Dyła, Stefan. (1983). "Evidence for S'-Deletion in Polish." *Folia Linguistica* 17, 327–337.

Emonds, Joseph. (1999). "How Clitics License Null Phrases: A Theory of the Lexical Interface." In H. van Riemsdijk, ed., *Clitics in the Languages of Europe.* Berlin: Mouton de Gruyter, pp. 291–367.

Evans, Nicholas D. (1995). *A Gramar of Kayardild.* Berlin: Mouton de Gruyter.

Evers, Arnold. (1975). The Transformational Cycle of Dutch and German. Ph.D. diss., Utrecht University, Utrecht.

Fagerli, O. T. (1996). "Verbal Derivations in Fufulde," University of Trondheim Working Papers in Linguistics, 21, 1–129.

Fanselow, Gisbert. (1989). "Coherent Infinitives in German: Restructuring vs. IP-Complementation." In C. Bhatt, E. Löbel, & C. Schmidt, eds., *Syntactic Phrase Structure Phenomena in Noun Phrases and Sentences.* Amsterdam: Benjamins, pp. 1–16.

Farkas, Donka, and Jerrold M. Sadock. (1989). "Preverb Climbing in Hungarian." *Language* 65, 318–338.

Frantz, Donald G. (1976). "Equi-Subject Clause Union." In *Proceedings of the Second Annual Meeting of the Berkeley Linguistics Society*. Berkeley, Cal.: Berkeley Linguistics Society, pp. 179–187.

Fresina, Claudio. (1981). *Aspects de la grammaire transformationnelle de l'italien*, Thèse de troisième cycle. Paris: Université de Paris VIII.

Fresina, Claudio. (1982). "Les verbes de mouvement et les aspectuels en italien." *Linguisticae Investigationes* 6, 283–331.

Fresina, Claudio. (1997). "L'auxiliation en italien." *Linguisticae Investigationes* 21, 97–138.

George, Leland, & Jindrich Toman. (1976). "Czech Clitics in Universal Grammar." *Papers from the 12th Regional Meeting of the Chicago Linguistic Society*. Chicago: Chicago Linguistic Society, pp. 235–249.

Gerdts, Donna B. (1988). "Semantic Linking and the Relational Structure of Desideratives." *Linguistics* 26, 843–872.

Gonzalez, Nora. (1986). "Interaction of Inversion and Clause Reduction in Spanish." *Proceedings of the Second Eastern States Conference of Linguistics*. Columbus: Dept. of Linguistics, Ohio State University, pp. 80–91.

Gonzalez, Nora. (1988). *Object and Raising in Spanish*. New York: Garland.

Gonzalez, Nora. (1990). "Unusual Inversion in Chilean Spanish." In P. M. Postal & B. D. Joseph, eds., *Studies in Relational Grammar*, vol. 3. Chicago: University of Chicago Press, pp. 87–103.

Goodall, Grant. (1987). *Parallel Structures in Syntax. Coordination, Causatives, and Restructuring*. Cambridge: Cambridge University Press.

Goodall, Grant. (1991). "*Wanna*-contraction as Restructuring." In C. Georgopoulos & R. Ishihara, eds., *Interdisciplinary Approaches to Language. Essays in Honor of S.-Y. Kuroda*. Dordrecht: Kluwer, pp. 239–254.

Grevisse, Maurice. (1993). *Le bon usage. Grammaire française refondue par André Goosse*, 3rd ed. Paris: Duculot.

Grewendorf, Günther. (1987). "Kohärenz und Restrukturierung." In B. Asbach-Schnitker & J. Roggenhofer (hrsg.). *Neuere Foschungen zur Wortbildung und Historiographie der Linguistik*. Tübingen: Narr, pp. 123–144.

Grimshaw, Jane. (1979). "Complement Selection and the Lexicon." *Linguistic Inquiry* 10, 279–326.

Haïk, Isabelle. (1985). The Syntax of Operators. Ph.D. diss., Massachusetts Institute of Technology, Cambridge.

Haegeman, Liliane, & Henk van Riemsdijk. (1986). "Verb Projection Raising, Scope, and the Typology of Rules Affecting Verbs." *Linguistic Inquiry* 17, 417–466.

Haider, Hubert. (1986). "Fehlende Argumente: Vom Passiv zu kohärenten Infinitiven." *Linguistische Berichte*. 101, 3–33.

Haider, Hubert. (1987). "Nicht-sententiale Infinitive." *Groninger Arbeiten zur Germanistischen Linguistik* 28, 73–114.

Haider, Hubert. (1992). "Fakultativ kohärente Infinitivkonstruktionen im Deutschen." *Arbeitpapiere des Sonderforschungsbereichs 340, Nr. 17*, Universität Stuttgart.

Hale, Ken, & S. Jay Keyser. (1993). "On the Argument Structure and the Lexical Expression of Syntactic Relations." In K. Hale & S. J. Keyser, eds., *The View from Building 20*. Cambridge, Mass.: MIT Press, pp. 53–109.

Hankamer, Jorge, & Ivan Sag. (1976). "Deep and Surface Anaphora." *Linguistic Inquiry* 7, 391–426.

Haspelmath, Martin. (1999). "Long Distance Agreement in Godoberi (Daghestanian) Complement Clauses." *Folia Linguistica*, 33(1–2), 131–151.

Haverkort, Marco. (1990). "Clitic Climbing and Barrierhood of VP." In J. Hutchinson & V. Manfredi, eds., *Current Approaches to African Linguistics*, vol. 7. Dordrecht: Foris.

Haverkort, Marco. (1993). *Clitics and Parametrization*. Eurotyp Working Papers, vol. 8. Tilburg, Neth.: University of Tilburg.

Hernanz, Maria L., & Gemma Rigau. (1984). "Auxiliaritat i reestructuració." *Els Marges* 31, 29–50.

Hinterhölzl, Roland. (1999). Restructuring Infinitives and the Theory of Complementation, Ph.D. diss., University of Southern California, Los Angeles.

Hornstein, Norbert. (1995). *Logical Form. From GB to Minimalism*. Oxford: Blackwell.

Hornstein, Norbert. (1999). "Movement and Control." *Linguistic Inquiry* 30, 69–96.

Jackendoff, Ray. (1997). *The Architecture of the Language Faculty*. Cambridge, Mass.: MIT Press.

Jaeggli, Osvaldo, & Nina Hyams. (1993). "On the Independence and Interdependence of Syntactic and Morphological Properties: English Aspectual *Come* and *Go*." *Natural Language and Linguistic Theory* 11, 313–346.

Jones, Michael. (1993). *Sardinian*. Routledge: London.

Kayne, Richard. (1977). *Syntaxe du français*. Paris: Editions du Seuil.

Kayne, Richard. (1980). "Vers une solution d'un problème grammatical: **Je l'ai voulu lire, j'ai tout voulu lire*." *Langue française* 46, 32–40.

Kayne, Richard. (1989a). "Facets of Past Participle Agreement." In P. Benincà, ed., *Dialect Variation and the Theory of Grammar*. Dordrecht: Foris, pp. 85–103.

Kayne, Richard. (1989b). "Null Subjects and Clitic Climbing." In O. Jaeggli & K. Safir, eds., *The Null Subject Parameter*. Dordrecht: Kluwer, pp. 239–261.

Kayne, Richard. (1991). "Romance Clitics, Verb Movement, and PRO." *Linguistic Inquiry* 22, 647–686.

Kayne, Richard. (1992). "Italian Negative Infinitival Imperatives and Clitic Climbing." In L. Tasmowski & A. Zribi-Hertz, eds., *Hommages à Nicolas Ruwet*. Ghent: Communications et Cognition, pp. 300–312.

Kayne, Richard. (1993). "Toward a Modular Theory of Auxiliary Selection." *Studia Linguistica* 47, 3–31.

Kayne, Richard. (1994). *The Antisymmetry of Syntax*. Cambridge, Mass., MIT Press.

Kayne, Richard. (1998). "Overt Versus Covert Movement." *Syntax* 1, 128–191.

Kayne, Richard. (1999a). Clitic Doubling and pro. Class lecture, University of Venice, May.

Kayne, Richard. (1999b). "Prepositional Complementizers as Attractors." *Probus* 11, 39–73.

Klima, Edward, & Ursula Bellugi. (1979). *The Signs of Language*. Cambridge, Mass.: Harvard University Press.

Koizumi, Masatoshi. (1995). Phrase Structure in Minimalist Syntax. Ph.D. diss., Masschusetts Institute of Technology, Cambridge.

Koopman, Hilda. (1984). *The Syntax of Verbs*. Dordrecht: Foris.

Koopman, Hilda, & Anna Szabolcsi. (2000). *Verbal Complexes*. Cambridge, Mass.: MIT Press.

Kornfilt, Jaklin. (1996). "NP-Movement and 'Restructuring.'" In R. Freidin, ed., *Current Issues in Comparative Grammar*. Dordrecht: Kluwer, pp. 120–147.

Kroeger, Paul. (1993). *Phrase Structure and Grammatical Relations in Tagalog*. Stanford, Cal.: CSLI.

Kulick, Seth. (1997). "Generalized Transformations and Restructuring in Romance." In J. Austin & A. Lawson, eds., *Proceedings of the 14th Eastern States Conference on Linguistics*, pp. 103–114.

Kuteva, Tania. (1998). "On Identifying an Evasive Gram: Action Narrowly Averted." *Studies in Language* 22, 113–160.

Landau, Idan. (1999). Elements of Control. Ph.D. diss., Massachusetts Institute of Technology, Cambridge.

Landau, Idan. (2000). *Elements of Control. Structure and Meaning in Infinitival Constructions.* Dordrecht: Kluwer.

LaPolla, M. (1988). "Clitic Movement in Spanish and the Projection Principle." In D. Birdsong and J.-P. Montreuil, eds., *Advances in Romance Linguistics.* Dordrecht: Foris, pp. 217–231.

Larson, Richard. (1988). "On the Double Object Construction." *Linguistic Inquiry* 19, 335–391.

Ledgeway, Adam. (1996). The Grammar of Complementation in Neapolitan. Ph.D. diss., University of Manchester, Manchester, Eng.

Ledgeway, Adam. (1998). "La ristrutturazione in napoletano." In Giovanni Ruffino, ed., *Atti del XXI Congresso Internazionale di Linguistica e Filologia Romanza.* Centro di Studi filologici e linguistici siciliani. Università di Palermo 18-24 settembre 1995. Sezione 2 Morfologia e sintassi delle lingue romanze. Tübingen: Niemeyer, pp. 529–541.

Ledgeway, Adam. (2000). *A Comparative Syntax of the Dialects of Southern Italy: A Minimalist Approach.* Oxford: Blackwell.

Lefebvre, Claire, & Pieter Muysken. (1982) *Mixed Categories. Nominalizations in Quechua.* Dordrecht: Kluwer.

Longobardi, Giuseppe. (1978). "Doubl-inf." *Rivista di grammatica generativa* 3, 173–206.

Longobardi, Giuseppe. (1979). "Postille alla regola di ristrutturazione." *Rivista di grammatica generativa* 4, 213–228.

Longobardi, Giuseppe. (1980). "Remarks on Infinitives: A Case for a Filter." *Journal of Italian Linguistics* 5, 101–155.

Luján, Marta. (1978). "Clitic Promotion and Mood in Spanish Verbal Complements." *Montreal Working Papers in Linguistics* 10, 103–190; also *Linguistics* 18 (1980), 381–484.

Mahajan, Anoop. (1989). "Agreement and Agreement Phrases." In I. Laka & A. Mahajan, eds., *Functional Heads and Clause Structure.* vol. 10. Massachusetts Institute of Technology Working Papers in Linguistics, pp. 217–252.

Manzini, M. Rita. (1983). Restructuring and Reanalysis, Ph.D. diss., Massachusetts Institute of Technology, Cambridge.

Manzini, M. Rita, & Anna Roussou. (2000). "A Minimalist Theory of A-movement and Control." *Lingua* 110, 409–447.

Martineau, France. (1991). "Clitic Climbing in Infinitival Constructions of Middle French." In D. Wanner & D. A. Kibbee, eds., *New Analyses in Romance Linguistics.* Amsterdam: Benjamins, pp. 235–251.

Martins, Ana Maria. (1995). "A Minimalist Approach to Clitic Climbing." *Proceedings of the 31st Regional Meeting of the Chicago Linguistic Society. Vol. 2: The Parasession on Clitics.* Chicago: Chicago Linguistic Society, pp. 215–233.

Medová, Lucie. (2000). *Transparency Phenomena in Czech Syntax.* Hovedfagsoppgave: University of Tromsø.

Miller, Philip H. (1992). *Clitics and Constituents in Phrase Structure Grammar.* New York: Garland.

Miyagawa, Shigeru. (1986). "Restructuring in Japanese." In T. Imai & M. Saito, eds., *Issues in Japanese Linguistics.* Dordrecht: Foris, pp. 273–300.

Monachesi, Paola. (1993). "Restructuring Verbs in Italian HPSG Grammar." In *Proceedings of the 29th Regional Meeting of the Chicago Linguistic Society.* Chicago: Chicago Linguistic Society, pp. 281–295.

Monachesi, Paola. (1995) A Grammar of Italian Clitics. Ph.D. diss., Tilburg University, Tilburg, Neth.

Monachesi, Paola. (1998). "Italian Restructuring Verbs: A Lexical Analysis," In E. Hinrichs, A. Kathol, & T. Nakazawa, eds., *Complex Predicates in Nonderivational Syntax*. New York: Academic Press, pp. 313–368.

Monachesi, Paola. (1999). "Phonological Phrases in Italian." In *Recherches de linguistique française et romane d'Utrecht* 18, 79–89.

Moore, John. (1989). "Spanish Restructuring and Psych Verbs: A Case for VP-Complementation." In E. J. Fee & K. Hunt, eds., *Proceedings of the 8th West Coast Conference on Formal Linguistics*, pp. 262–275.

Moore, John. (1990). "Spanish Clause Reduction with Downstairs Cliticization." In K. Dziwirek, P. Farrell, & E. Mejías-Bikandi, eds., *Grammatical Relations. A Cross-Theoretical Perspective*. Stanford, Cal.: CSLI, pp. 319–333.

Moore, John. (1994). "Romance Cliticization and Relativized Minimality." *Linguistic Inquiry* 25, 335–344.

Moore, John. (1996). *Reduced Constructions in Spanish*. New York: Garland.

Munro, Pamela, & Dieynaba Gaye. (1997). "Introduction." *Ay Baati Wolof. A Wolof Dictionary*. UCLA Occasional Papers in Linguistics 19, iii–xiii.

Myhill, John. (1988). "The Grammaticalization of Auxiliaries: Spanish Clitic Climbing." *Proceedings of the Fourteenth Annual Meeting of the Berkeley Linguistics Society*. Berkeley: Berkeley Linguistics Society, pp. 352–363.

Myhill, John. (1989). "Variation in Spanish Clitic Climbing." In T. J. Walsh, ed., *Synchronic and Diachronic Approaches to Linguistic Variation and Change (Georgetown University Roundtable 1988)*. Washington, D.C.: Georgetown University Press, pp. 227–250.

Napoli, Donna J. (1981). "Semantic Interpretation vs. Lexical Governance: Clitic Climbing in Italian." *Language* 57, 841–887.

Nishida, Chiyo. (1991). "A Non-transformational Analysis of Clitic Climbing in Spanish." In A. Halpern, ed., *Proceedings of the Ninth West Coast Conference on Formal Linguistics*, Stanford, Cal., pp. 395–409.

Nishigauchi, Taisuke. (1993). "Long Distance Passive." In N. Hasegawa, ed., *Japanese Syntax in Comparative Grammar*. Tokyo: Kuroshio Shuppan, pp. 79–114.

O'Neil, John. (1995). "Out of Control." *Proceedings of the 25th Annual Meeting of the North Eastern Linguistic Society*, University of Massachusetts, Amherst, pp. 361–371.

O'Neil, John. (1997). Means of Control: Deriving the Properties of PRO in the Minimalist Program. Ph.D. diss., Massachusetts Institute of Technology, Cambridge.

Ortiz de Urbina, Jon. (1989). *Parameters in the Grammar of Basque*. Dordrecht: Foris.

Pearce, Elisabeth. (1990). *Parameters in Old French Syntax. Infinitival Complements*. Dordrecht: Kluwer.

Pesetsky, David. (1991). Zero Syntax II: An Essay on Infinitives. Ms., Massachusetts Institute of Technology, Cambridge.

Picallo, Carme. (1985). Opaque Domains. Ph.D. diss., City University of New York.

Picallo, Carme. (1990). "Modal Verbs in Catalan." *Natural Language and Linguistic Theory* 8, 285–312.

Pizzini, Quentin A. (1981). "The Placement of Clitic Pronouns in Portuguese." *Linguistic Analysis* 8, 403–430.

Pizzini, Quentin A. (1982). "The Positioning of Clitic Pronouns in Spanish." *Lingua* 57, 47–69.

Pollock, Jean-Yves. (1978). "Trace Theory and French Syntax." In Samuel Jay Keyser, ed., *Recent Transformational Studies in European Languages*. Cambridge, Mass.: MIT Press, pp. 65–112.

Pollock, Jean-Yves. (1989). "Verb Movement, Universal Grammar, and the Structure of IP." *Linguistic Inquiry* 10, 365–424

Postal, Paul. (1974). *On Raising*. Cambridge, Mass.: MIT Press.

Progovac, Lilijana. (1991). "Polarity in Serbo-Croatian: Anaphoric NPIs and Pronominal PPIs." *Linguistic Inquiry* 22, 567–572.

Progovac, Lilijana. (1993). "Locality and Subjunctive-like Complements in Serbo-Croatian." *Journal of Slavic Linguistics* 1, 116–144.

Przepiórkowski, Adam, & Anna Kupš. (1997). "Verbal Negation and Complex Predicate Formation in Polish." *Texas Linguistic Forum* 38, 247–261.

Pustejovsky, James. (1995). *The Generative Lexicon*. Cambridge, Mass.: MIT Press.

Quicoli, Carlos. (1976). "Conditions on Clitic-Movement in Portuguese." *Linguistic Analysis* 2, 199–223.

Radford, Andrew. (1976). Constraints on Clitic Promotion in Italian. Ms., Oxford University, Oxford.

Radford, Andrew. (1977a). *Italian Syntax: Transformational and Relational Grammar*. Cambridge: Cambridge University Press.

Radford, Andrew. (1977b). "La teoria della traccia, la condizione del soggetto specificato e la salita dei pronomi nelle lingue romanze." *Rivista di grammatica generativa* 2(2), 241–315.

Rigau, Gemma. (2000). Number Agreement Variation in Catalan Dialects. Ms., UAB, Barcelona.

Rivas, Alberto. (1974). Impersonal Sentences and Their Interaction with Clitic Movement in Spanish. Ms., Massachusetts Institute of Technology, Cambridge.

Rivas, Alberto. (1977). Clitics in Spanish. Ph.D. diss., Massachusetts Institute of Technology, Cambridge.

Rivero, Maria Luisa. (1991). "Clitic and NP Climbing in Old Spanish," In H. Campos & F. Martínez-Gil, eds., *Current Studies in Spanish Linguistics*. Washington, D.C.: Georgetown University Press, pp. 241–282.

Rizzi, Luigi. (1976a). "Ristrutturazione." *Rivista di grammatica generativa* 1, 1–54.

Rizzi, Luigi. (1976b). "La MONTEE DU SUJET, le *si* impersonnel et une règle de restructuration dans la syntaxe italienne." *Recherches Linguistiques* 4, 158–184.

Rizzi, Luigi. (1978). "A Restructuring Rule in Italian Syntax." In S. J. Keyser, ed., *Recent Transformational Studies in European Languages*. Cambridge, Mass.: MIT Press, pp. 113–158 (also in Rizzi 1982a).

Rizzi, Luigi. (1981). "Nominative Marking in Italian Infinitives and the Nominative Island Constraint." In F. Heny, ed., *Binding and Filtering*. London, Croom Helm, pp. 129–157.

Rizzi, Luigi. (1982a). *Issues in Italian Syntax*. Dordrecht: Foris.

Rizzi, Luigi. (1982b). "Comments on Chomsky's Chapter 'On the Representation of Form and Function.'" In J. Mehler, E. C. T. Walker, & M. Garrett, eds., *Perspectives on Mental Representation*. Hillsdale, N.J.: Lawrence Erlbaum, pp. 441–451.

Rizzi, Luigi. (1997). "The Fine Structure of the Left Periphery." In L. Haegeman, ed., *Elements of Grammar*. Dordrecht: Kluwer, pp. 281–337.

Rizzi, Luigi. (2000). "Some Notes on Romance Cliticization." In L. Rizzi *Comparative Syntax and Language Acquisition*. London: Routledge, pp. 96–121.

Roberts, Ian. (1993a). Restructuring, Pronoun Movement and Head-Movement in Old French. Ms., University of Wales, Bangor.

Roberts, Ian. (1993b). *Verbs and Diachronic Syntax*. Dordrecht: Foris.

Roberts, Ian. (1997). "Restructuring, Head Movement and Locality." *Linguistic Inquiry* 28, 423–460.

Rochette, Anne. (1988). Semantic and Syntactic Aspects of Romance Sentential Complementation. Ph.D. diss., Massachusetts Institute of Technology, Cambridge.

Rochette, Anne. (1990). "On the Restructuring Classes of Verbs in Romance." In A. Di Sciullo & A. Rochette, eds., *Binding in Romance. Essays in Honour of Judith McA'Nulty*. Special Publication. Ottawa: Canadian Linguistic Association, pp. 96–128.

Rochette, Anne. (1999). "The Selection Properties of Aspectual Verbs." In K. Johnson, & I. Roberts, eds., *Beyond Principles and Parameters. Essays in Memory of Osvaldo Jaeggli*. Dordrecht: Kluwer, pp. 145–165.

Roldán, Mercedes. (1975). "Clitic Climbing and Unrelated Matters." *Linguistic Inquiry* 6, 342–346.

Rooryck, Johan. (1994). "Against Optional Movement for Clitic Climbing." In M. L. Mazzola, ed., *Issues and Theory in Romance Linguistics*. Washington, D.C.: Georgetown University Press, pp. 417–443.

Rosen, Sara T. (1990a). *Argument Structure and Complex Predicates*. New York: Garland.

Rosen, Sara T. (1990b). "Restructuring Verbs Are Light Verbs." *Proceedings of the Ninth West Coast Conference on Formal Linguistics*, Stanford, Cal., pp. 477–492.

Sabel, Joachim. (1995a). "On Parallels and Differences Between Clitic Climbing and Long Scrambling and the Economy of Derivations." *Proceedings of the 25th Annual Meeting of the North Eastern Linguistic Society*, University of Massachusetts, Amherst, pp. 405–423.

Sabel, Joachim. (1995b). "A Unitary Account of Long Scrambling and Clitic Climbing in Restructuring Contexts: Parallels Between German, Polish and Spanish." In *ConSOLE II*, 210–226.

Sabel, Joachim. (1996). *Restrukturierung und Lokalität*. Berlin, Akademie Verlag (Studia Grammatica 42).

Sabel, Joachim. (1999). "Coherent Infinitives in German, Polish, and Spanish." *Folia Linguistica*, 33(3–4), 419–440.

Schroten, Jan. (1986). "Ergativity, Raising and Restructuring in the Syntax of Spanish Aspectual Verbs." *Linguisticae Investigationes* 10, 399–465.

Spencer, Andrew. (1991). *Morphological Theory*. Oxford: Blackwell.

Sportiche, Dominique. (1983). "Bete Reciprocals and Clitic Binding." In J. Kaye, H. Koopman, D. Sportiche, & A. Dugas, eds. *Current Approaches to African Linguistics*, vol. 2. Dordrecht: Foris, pp. 297–316.

Sportiche, Dominique. (1996). "Clitic Constructions." In J. Rooryck & L. Zaring, eds., *Phrase Structure and the Lexicon*. Dordrecht: Kluwer, pp. 213–276.

Stewart, Ó. Thompson. (1999). "Infinitive Clauses, Restructuring, and the Modal-Aspectual Verb Construction." *Linguistic Analysis* 29, 87–136.

Stjepanović, Sandra. (1998). "On the Placement of Serbo-Croatian Clitics: Evidence from Clitic Climbing and VP Ellipsis." In Ž. Bošković, S. Franks, & W. Snyder, eds., *Annual Workshop on Formal Approaches to Slavic Linguistics. The Connecticut Meeting 1997*. Ann Arbor, Mich.: Slavic Publications, pp. 267–286.

Stjepanović, Sandra. (2001). "Clitic Climbing without Climbing out of Seemingly Finite Clauses and Implications for Restructuring," abstract of a paper presented at the Workshop on Slavic Pronominal Clitics, ZAS, Berlin, February 8–9.

Stowell, Tim. (1991). "Small Clause Restructuring." In R. Freidin, ed., *Principles and Parameters in Comparative Grammar*. Cambridge, Mass.: MIT Press, pp. 182–218.

Strozer, Judith. (1976). Clitics in Spanish. Ph.D. diss., UCLA.

Strozer, Judith. (1981). "An Alternative to Restructuring in Romance Syntax." In H. Contreras & J. Klausenburger, eds., *Proceedings of the Tenth Anniversary Symposium on Romance Linguistics, Papers in Romance*, Supplement II, vol. 3. Seattle: University of Washington, pp. 177–184.

Suñer, Margarita. (1980). "Clitic Promotion in Spanish Revisited." In F. Neussel, ed., *Con-*

temporary Studies in Romance Languages. Bloomington: Indiana University Linguistics Club, pp. 300–330.

Taraldsen, Tarald. (1982). "Remarks on Government, Thematic Structure and the Distribution of Empty Categories." In R. May & J. Koster, eds., *Levels of Syntactic Representation*. Dordrecht: Foris, pp. 253–291.

Taraldsen, Tarald. (1983). Parametric Variation in Phrase Structure: A Case Study. Ph.D. diss., University of Tromsø, Norway.

Taraldsen, Tarald. (2002). "Complex Passives in Germanic and Romance," talk given at the 25th GLOW Colloquium, Amsterdam.

Tellier, Christine. (1987). "Restructuring and Complement Order in Abe infinitives." In D. Odden, ed., *Current Approaches to African Linguistics*, vol. 4. Dordrecht: Foris, 369–381.

Terzi, Arhonto. (1992). PRO in Finite Clauses. A Study of the Inflectional Heads of the Balkan Languages. Ph.D. diss., City University of New York.

Terzi, Arhonto. (1994). "Clitic Climbing from Finite Clauses and Long Head Movement." *Catalan Working Papers in Linguistics* 3(2), 97–122.

Terzi, Arhonto. (1996). "Clitic Climbing from Finite Clauses and Tense Raising." *Probus* 8, 273–295.

Tsujimura, Natsuko. (1993). "Adjuncts and Event Argument in Restructuring." In S. Choi, ed., *Japanese/Korean Linguistics, vol. 3*. Stanford, Cal.: CSLI, pp. 121–136.

Uriagereka, Juan. (1995). "Aspects of the Syntax of Clitic Placement in Western Romance." *Linguistic Inquiry* 26, 79–123.

Van Tiel-Di Maio, M. Francesca. (1975). "Una proposta per la sintassi dell'italiano: V-Raising." In *La grammatica. Aspetti teorici e didattici*. Roma: Bulzoni, pp. 445–477.

Van Tiel-Di Maio, M. Francesca. (1978). "Sur le phénomène dit du déplacement 'long' des clitiques et, en particulier, sur le constructions causatives." *Journal of Italian Linguistics* 3(2), 73–136.

Veselovská, Ludmila. (1995). Phrasal Movement and X° Morphology. Ph.D. diss., Palacky University, Olomouc.

Wali, Kashi, & Ashok Kumar Koul. (1994). "Kashmiri Clitics: The Role of Case and CASE." *Linguistics* 32, 969–994.

Watanabe, Akira. (1993). "The Role of Equidistance in Restructuring Verbs: Italian vs. French." *Proceedings of the 10th Eastern State Conference on Linguistics*, pp. 360–371.

Wexler, Ken, & Peter Culicover. (1980). *Formal Principles of Language Acquisition*. Cambridge, Mass.: MIT Press.

Willet, T. L. (1991). *A Reference Grammar of Southeastern Tepehuan*. Arlington: Summer Institute of Linguistics and University of Texas.

Wurmbrand, Susanne. (1998). Infinitives. Ph.D. diss., Massachusetts Institute of Technology, Cambridge.

Wurmbrand, Susanne. (2001). *Infinitives. Restructuring and Clause Structure*. Berlin: Mouton de Gruyter.

Zagona, Karen. (1986). "Las Períphrasis de gerundio y la restructuración." *Revista Argentina de Lingüística* (Mendoza, Arg.), 2, 232–244.

Zubizarreta, Maria-Luisa. (1980). "Pour une restructuration thématique." *Recherches Linguistiques* 9, 141–187.

Zubizarreta, Maria-Luisa. 1982. On the Relationship of the Lexicon to Syntax. Ph.D. diss., Massachusetts Institute of Technology, Cambridge.

Zushi, Mihoko. (1995). Long-distance Dependencies. Ph.D. diss., McGill University, Montreal.

5

RICHARD S. KAYNE

Prepositions as Probes

1. Introduction

In this chapter, I will argue that some prepositions (and, by extension, some postpositions) are probes, in the sense of Chomsky's (1998, 1999, 2001) recent work. The particular case I will take up here is that of dative prepositions preceding subjects in French (and Italian) causatives. If the conclusion is correct for these, it will carry over to dative prepositions preceding subjects in causatives in other languages, as well as to parallel cases with postpositions.

The conclusion reached here will reinforce that reached in recent work of mine concerning prepositional complementizers.[1] On the other hand, it is likely that some prepositions and postpositions are not probes (or at least not in any simple way). Thus it would be plausible to take the arguments given below for French dative *à* to generalize beyond causatives to other instances of *à* and to prepositions (and postpositions) like *of, at, to, by, with, from, for*, and their counterparts in other languages, without necessarily generalizing (directly) to locatives like *above, below, behind, inside,* and *outside* (and perhaps not either to *in, on, off,* and *out*).

Chomsky (2001) distinguishes external ("pure") Merge and internal Merge ("movement") and suggests a correlation between these two subtypes of Merge and two subtypes of semantic conditions. More specifically, he suggests that external Merge is associated with argument structure, that is, external Merge is into theta positions, whereas internal Merge covers everything else.

Put another way, internal Merge covers all cases of merger into nontheta positions. This includes scope and discourse-related positions, as well as what would earlier have been called movement into nonthematic A-positions (with T or *v* as probe).

I will now argue that from this general perspective the by far most natural conclusion is that French dative *à* preceding the embedded subject in causative constructions does not "get togther with" that subject via external Merge but rather via internal Merge (movement). The position of this subject following *à* is not a theta position; the construction is rather more like a case of ECM with raising. Therefore we would expect *à* to act as a probe much in the way that T and *v* do.[2]

2. Causatives in French

2.1. "Dativization" of the subject of a transitive infinitive

As discussed in Kayne (1975) and Rouveret and Vergnaud (1980) (cf. Burzio 1986 on Italian), the basic facts are as follows: the subject of the embedded infinitive in a French causative with *faire* ('make'/'do') cannot precede the infinitive, contrary to the usual position of subjects:[3]

(1) *Jean a fait Paul manger (la tarte). ['J has made/had P eat (the pie)']

The infinitival subject must follow the infinitive (abstracting away from wh-movement, cliticization, etc.):

(2) Jean a fait manger Paul. ('J has made/had eat P')

But when the infinitive has a direct object, the infinitival subject must be preceded by the preposition *à*:

(3) *Jean a fait manger Paul la tarte.

(4) *Jean a fait manger la tarte Paul.

As seen in these two examples, lack of *à* leads to ungrammaticality. Rather, one has

(5) Jean a fait manger la tarte à Paul.

2.2. This *à* looks like a preposition

In the causative (5), '*à* Paul' acts in general just like other 'P DP.' First, with respect to extraction from within adjuncts (cf. Chomsky 1982: 72, citing Adriana Belletti):

(6) ??le professeur que je me suis endormi après avoir écouté ('the professor that I fell asleep after having listened-to')

(7) *le professeur à qui je me suis endormi après avoir parlé ('the professor to whom I fell asleep after having spoken')

Extraction of a DP from within an adjunct, as in (6), though marginal, is appreciably better than extraction of a PP, as in (7). Example (9) shows that extraction from an adjunct of the subject-related '*à* DP' in causatives is every bit as bad as in (7):

(8) ??l'enfant que je me suis endormi après avoir fait manger ('the child that I fell asleep after having made eat')

(9) *l'enfant à qui je me suis endormi après avoir fait manger une tarte ('the child to whom I fell asleep after having made eat a pie')

Second, the subject-related '*à* DP' of causatives is similar to ordinary 'P DP' with respect to its position relative to a direct object:

(10) J'ai montré la tarte à Jean. ('I have shown the pie to J')

(11) (?)J'ai montré à Jean la tarte.

(12) J'ai fait manger la tarte à Jean. ('I have made/had eat the pie to J')

(13) (?)J'ai fait manger à Jean la tarte.

Third, the subject-related '*à* DP' of causatives acts like any PP with respect to subextraction of *en* or *combien*, which is possible out of direct objects and (many) postverbal nonprepositional subjects, but not out of PPs:[4]

(14) Le capitaine en a fait ramper trois dans la boue. ('the captain of-them has made crawl three in the mud')

(15) *Le capitaine en a fait manger de la boue à trois. ['the captain of-them has made eat of-the-mud to three.]

(16) Combien a-t-elle fait manger d'enfants. ('how-many has she made eat of children')

(17) *Combien a-t-elle fait manger cette tarte à d'enfants. ('how-many has she made eat this pie to of children')

In both (15) and (17), subextraction is blocked by *à* just as it would be by any other preposition.

Fourth, the '*à* DP' in question acts sharply differently from direct objects with respect to the "obligatoriness" of clitic placement:[5]

(18) Elle *(les) a fait manger tous les deux. ('she them has made eat all the two')

(19) Elle (leur) a fait manger une tarte à tous les deux. ('she them has made eat a pie to all the two')

A direct object quantifier phrase like *tous* (*les deux*) is not possible without an accompanying clitic. The '*à* DP' of (19) is possible with just QP being overt, as would be the case with other prepositions, for example:

(20) Elle a parlé de tous les deux. ('she has spoken of all the two')

Fifth, the French counterpart of English topicalization (Cinque's 1990 CLLD) requires a clitic when the topicalized phrase is a (derived) direct object:

(21) *Paul elle a déjà fait manger. ('P she has already made eat')

(22) Paul, elle l'a déjà fait manger. ('P she him has already made eat')

But the subject-related '*à* DP' of causatives does not need a clitic:

(23) A Paul elle a déjà fait manger une tarte. ('to P she has already made eat a pie')

Again, this is simply behavior that it shares with ordinary prepositions:

(24) De Paul elle ne parle jamais. ('of P she neg speaks never')

Sixth, floating/stranded quantifiers in French relatives can, for many speakers, be linked to a relativized direct object but never to a relativized prepositional object:

(25) ces garçons, que j'inviterai tous ('those boys, who I will-invite all')

(26) *ces garçons, à qui je téléphonerai tous ('those boys, to whom I will-telephone all')

For such speakers, the *à* under consideration shows the same restriction:[6]

(27) *ces garçons, à qui ton ami faisait tous boire du vin ('these boys, to whom your friend made all drink of-the wine')

The general conclusion of this section is that the *à* that appears before subjects in certain French causatives is a preposition with the usual properties of prepositions.

2.3. This causative construction is not an instance of control

There are many reasons to think that the sentences we have been concerned with, such as (28), are not instances of control, that is, that the '*à* DP' is not at all like a matrix controller:

(28) Jean a fait manger une tarte à Paul. ('J has made/had eat a pie to P')

First, a control construction would not care about the transitivity of the embedded infinitive:

(29) *Jean a fait manger à Paul. ('J has made eat to P')

In the absence of a direct object of the infinitive, the embedded subject in the causative generally cannot be preceded by *à*. Ordinary cases of control act quite differently:

(30) Jean a dit à Paul de manger (une tarte). ['J has said to P to eat (a pie)']

In the true control structure (30), the presence of an embedded object is irrelevant.

Second, French control constructions never allow clitic climbing, whereas causative constructions do:

(31) Jean les a fait manger à Paul. ('J them has made eat to P')

(32) *Jean les veut manger. ('J them wants to-eat')

(33) *Jean les a dit à Paul de manger. ('J them has said to P to eat')

The clitic *les* has moved up into the matrix in (31) (a causative with the *à* under study) in a way that is not allowed in the control examples (32) and especially (33).

Third, control constructions always allow a clitic to remain on the infinitive, whereas in causatives this is marginal at best (apart from reflexives) and often impossible:

(34) *Jean a fait les manger à Paul.

(35) Jean veut les manger.

(36) Jean a dit à Paul de les manger.

Fourth, control constructions generally have the controller preceding the infinitive, whereas in causatives the order is the reverse. In causatives, the order is as in (28) and (31), not as in (37) or (38):

(37) *Jean a fait à Paul manger une tarte.

(38) *Jean les a fait à Paul manger.

This contrasts sharply with control examples:

(39) Jean a avoué à Paul avoir mangé une tarte. ('J has confessed to P to-have eaten a pie')

(40) Jean a dit à Paul de manger une tarte. ('J has said to P to eat a pie')

Finally, were (28) and (31) to be analyzed as control examples, they would violate an otherwise exceptionless generalization about French infinitival complementizers:

(41) Infinitives with true object control[7] must have an overt (prepositional) complementizer.

Example (40) is a typical case of object control and contains the complementizer *de*; (39) has no overt complementizer but in fact can only be interpreted as subject control. The fact that there is no complementizer in (28) and (31) indicates clearly that those causatives do not involve control at all.

In conclusion, then, the DP following *à* in (28) and (31) is not a matrix controller.

2.4. An ECM/raising analysis

If the DP under consideration is not a matrix controller, then what is its origin? Subjects of French transitives are not normally preceded by *à*:

(42) Jean a mangé la tarte. ('J has eaten the pie'.)

(43) *A Jean a mangé la tarte.

This is also true of postverbal subjects in finite sentences. French allows postverbal subjects with transitives to a limited extent in the so-called 'stylistic inversion' construction:[8]

(44) ?le jour où les a mangées Jean-Jacques ('the day when them has eaten J-J')

Again, *à* is sharply impossible:

(45) *le jour où les a mangées à Jean-Jacques

The contrast between (45) and (31) suggests that this *à* is closely linked to the causative matrix verb *faire* in (31). *Faire* is not unique in French; there is one other verb that productively (probably less so than with *faire*) allows this *à*, namely, *laisser*:

(46) Jean a laissé manger la tarte à Paul. ('J has let eat the pie to P')

In addition, to a minor extent, the perception verbs *entendre* and *voir* allow it:

(47) J'ai entendu dire cela à un de tes amis. ('I have heard say that to one of your friends' = 'I have heard one of your friends say that.')

(48) J'ai vu faire des bêtises à Jean. ('I have seen do some stupid-things to J' = 'I have seen J do some stupid things.')

As far as I know, no other class of matrix verbs allows the *à* of (28), (31), and (46)–(48).

At the same time as this *à* seems clearly to be part of the matrix, the DP following it seems clearly to be part of the embedding. In part, we have already seen this in (28)–(41), which shows that the DP following *à* is not a matrix controller. In part, there is the simple fact that this DP is, semantically speaking, an argument of the infinitive.

The range of theta and interpretive roles (relative to the infinitive) that can be filled by the subject DP following *à* is fairly wide, as these further examples (from Kayne 1975) illustrate:

(49) Son dernier bouquin a fait gagner beaucoup d'argent à Jean-Jacques ('his last book has made earn a-lot of money to J-J')

(50) Tu vas faire perdre son poste à ton copain. ('you are-going to-make lose his job to your friend')

(51) Elle fera entendre raison à Jean. ('she will-make listen-to reason to J')

(52) Cela fera changer d'avis à Jean. ('that will-make change of opinion to J' = 'That will make J change his mind.')

(53) Ce qui est arrivé a fait perdre de l'importance au fait que Jean aime Marie. ('that which has happened has made lose (of the) importance to-the fact that J loves M')

(54) On ne peut pas faire jouer un rôle important à tout. ('one neg can not make play a role important to everything' = 'One cannot have everything play an important role.')

(55) Elle fera effleurer le filet à la balle. ('she will-make touch the net to the ball' = 'She will make the ball touch the net.')

(56) Le coup de vent a fait traverser l'étang au petit voilier. ('The blast of wind has made cross the pond to-the little sailboat' = 'The blast of wind has made the little sailboat cross the pond.')

(57) Cela fait préférer à Jean la syntaxe à la phonologie. ('that makes prefer to J the syntax to the phonology' = 'That makes J prefer syntax to phonology.')

Whereas *Paul* in (46) is an agent, the embedded subjects following *à* in (49)–(57) are not, in various ways. If Spec,*v*P is limited to agents, then the embedded subjects of (49)–(57) will originate lower down in the VP structure. This seems to be perfectly compatible with their ending up preceded by *à* in these causative sentences.[9]

We have arrived at the following intermediate and apparently paradoxical conclusion: the lexical DP preceded by *à* in (49)–(57) and similar causative examples is the subject of the embedded infinitival clause; yet the *à* itself, to judge by the discussion following (45), properly belongs to the matrix.

This leads naturally to

(58) Causatives with *à* preceding the embedded subject are instances of raising/ECM.

Put another way, the lexical DP preceded by *à* IS the subject of the infinitive at some point in the derivation; *à* itself IS in the matrix. The embedded subject comes to look like the object of *à* as the result of raising.[10] The intent of (58) is to establish a clear partial link between these French causative constructions and the more familiar English ECM of (59):[11]

(59) John considers Bill to have made a mistake.

The two differ dramatically in that (59) contains no preposition comparable to *à*, an important but, I think, limited difference. They also differ in the type of matrix verb. A still closer parallel between French and English from this ECM perspective is

(60) Jean a fait manger une tarte à Paul. ('J has made eat a pie to P')

(61) John made Paul eat a pie.

2.5. French and English

One question that arises is why English (perhaps all of Germanic) lacks sentences comparable to the French ones with an overt preposition preceding the embedded subject:

(62) *John made/had eat the cereal to his children.

A partial answer might well be that English (61), (and similarly in other Germanic languages) actually does contain a dative preposition comparable to French *à*, except that in English this preposition must be unpronounced.

This would establish a very plausible link between these causatives and double object constructions, which differ in a parallel way, that is, the following match, with respect to presence versus absence of an overt preposition, the pair in (60) and (61):

(63) Jean a donné un livre à Paul. ('J has given a book to P.')

(64) John gave Paul a book.

Of course, English also allows

(65) John gave a book to Paul.

Thus, the ungrammaticality of (62) must reflect some more specific property of French *à* versus English *to*, probably related to the following differences:[12]

(66) i. English distinguishes *to* and *at*, while French doesn't.
ii. *to* can introduce purpose clauses, whereas French must use *pour* rather than *à*.
iii. French *à* can correspond to English *from* (with verbs like *take* and *steal*).
iv. French *à* can be benefactive, whereas English *to* is never benefactive.

This may indicate that *to* is associated with a more specific interpretation than *à* and that that extra specificity precludes it from appearing in (62) [cf. especially (66iii and iv].

A second important question is why French does not allow an exact counterpart of (61) or (64):

(67) a. *Jean a fait manger Paul une tarte.
b. *Jean a fait Paul manger une tarte.

(68) *Jean a donné Paul un livre.

The (government-based) proposals I made in earlier work[13] clearly need to be updated, something that I will not attempt here. What will suffice for present purposes is simply the idea that French (60) and (63) are very close counterparts of English (61) and (64).

2.6. English double object sentences

Collins and Thráinsson (1993, 140) develop an analysis of double object constructions in which there are two Agr-O positions above VP (separated by AspP), one for each of the two objects. For my purposes, it is not so much the label Agr-O that is important.[14] What is essential, rather, is that there be two licensing positions, one for each of the objects. Important also is their taking the higher of the two Agr-Os to be associated with (and higher than) an abstract causative V. Of further importance to what follows is their claim that in Icelandic object shift of both objects the indirect object moves to the higher Agr-O and the direct object moves to the lower.

Setting aside the question of whether the objects move overtly or covertly in Icelandic sentences where the verb has (apparently) not raised in the familiar fashion, and continuing to use the (perhaps appropriate) label Agr-O, I would like to take over from their discussion the following:

(69) Double object constructions are akin to causatives.

(70) The indirect object is licensed in an Agr-O position above the causative V.

(71) That licensing is at least sometimes effected by overt movement.

Let us now reconsider the idea that French (60) and (63) are very close counterparts of English (61) and (64). For the French example (63), this suggests an analysis parallel to theirs, with *à* playing a role akin to their higher Agr-O. For the French construction with an overt causative verb, as in (60), this kind of analysis is especially natural. We saw earlier in the discussion of (45)–(51) that there was every reason to think that the *à* that precedes the embedded subject is really part of the matrix. That is extremely close to Collins and Thráinsson's (1993) proposal that the Agr-O that licenses the indirect object is above the abstract causative V. I conclude that the *à* of French causative (60) is either identical to or closely related to their higher Agr-O, and that it is above the causative verb *faire*.

Similarly, although I won't pursue this, it is now natural to take the embedded subject *Paul* in (72) to be licensed by an indirect-object-licensing type of Agr-O above *make*:

(72) John made Paul eat the pie.

2.7. *à* as probe

To grant that *à* in causatives like (60) (repeated here) is a high functional head strongly similar to Collins and Thráinsson's (1993) above-causative-V Agr-O is to grant, within the framework of Chomsky (1998; 1999; 2001), that *à* is a probe:

(73) Jean a fait manger une tarte à Paul. ('J has made eat a pie to P')

The same is certainly then true of (63), also repeated:

(74) Jean a donné un livre à Paul. ('J has given a book to P.')

This expresses the idea put forth earlier, namely, that *à* in (73) belongs to the matrix, even though the DP following it originates as the embedded subject. [In (74), similarly, *à* is above the higher causative V, whereas *Paul* originates within the lower VP.]

In Agr-less terms, this amounts to taking *à* in these examples to act as a probe parallel to *v* (and to T).[15] In other words, *à* (along with similar adpositions in other languages) is part of the Case-agreement system, in Chomsky's (2001) sense. The fact that in French it does not actually show overt agreement with any DP is simply parallel to the fact that *v* usually doesn't (even if it is involved in past participle agreement), nor does T in many languages (including English, where T shows overt agreement in a very limited class of cases). On the other hand, like *v* and T, P (adposition) does show overt agreement in some/many languages.[16]

2.8. Word order

The parallelism between the *à* of (73)/(74) and Collins and Thráinsson's higher Agr-O is imperfect as far as word order is concerned. In their Icelandic examples with overt indirect object shift, the indirect object moves leftward, as does the finite verb. The desired word order is achieved immediately. The indirect object remains to the left of the direct object.

In French, the DP whose movement is induced by *à* functioning as probe [i.e., the DP *Paul* in both (73) and (74)] ends up to the right of the direct object *une tarte/ un livre* and also to the right of the causative V (*faire*) in (73). The question is how to derive the French-English word order difference without losing the strong parallelisms that we have seen to hold in other respects.

The challenge does not only concern the position of *Paul* in these examples but also the position of *à* itself. If it is a functional head above the causative, parallel to Collins and Thráinsson's (1993) higher Agr-O, then we would expect it to precede the causative, which is not the case. One possibility would be to take *à* to be unusual for French heads and to have it follow its complement, that is, to have it follow the causative VP.

This is, of course, incompatible with my universal Spec-Head-Complement proposal 1994. On the other hand, Chomsky (2001: 7) considers an intermediate position, whereby one would have the Spec-Head part be universally valid, but not the Head-Complement part; Specs would always precede their head, but Complements could either precede or follow. From that perspective, taking *à* to be higher than and yet to follow the causative VP would not be impossible.

The problem is, that wouldn't suffice. Taking *à* to follow the causative VP in (73) and (74) might be a way of having *à* appear after the direct object, but if the Spec of *à* necessarily precedes it, then movement of *Paul* in (73) and (74) will not succeed in getting *Paul* to its desired position following *à*. In a Spec-Complement-Head configuration, movement of a phrase to Spec from within the Complement will place that phrase to the left of the complement, giving in the cases at hand the radically ill-formed

(75) *Jean a Paul fait manger une tarte à.

(76) *Jean a Paul donné un livre à.

I conclude that if one grants the universality of Spec-Head order, then, even if one does not grant the universality of Head-Complement order, derivation of the correct word order in (73) and (74) requires more movement than is sometimes assumed.

A proposal akin to one I have made for prepositional complementizers in recent work[17] is as follows. First, *à* (located above the causative VP) induces movement of *Paul*, yielding (abstracting away from the subject of the causative V and from the auxiliary)

(77) . . . Paul_i à fait t_i manger une tarte

(78) . . . Paul_i à donné t_i un livre

Since *à* is a preposition (rather than a postposition), it then raises to an immediately higher head (labeled W in that earlier work but perhaps assimilable to one of Cinque's 1999 functional heads):

(79) . . . à_j+W Paul_i t_j fait t_i manger une tarte

(80) . . . à_j+W Paul_i t_j donné t_i un livre

Subsequently, the causative VP raises:

(81) . . . [fait t_i manger une tarte$]_k$ à_j+W Paul_i t_j t_k

(82) . . . [donné t_i un livre]$_k$ à$_j$+W Paul$_i$ t_j t_k

An alternative derivation of a type suggested to me in the context of prepositional complementizers by Ur Shlonsky would differ from the preceding in taking *à* to be 'twinned' with another functional head, call it Agr-IO.[18] This Agr-IO could be taken to match the higher of Collins and Thráinsson's (1993) two exactly, with French then having an "extra" *à* that is lacking in English. The derivations would look like this, starting from

(83) . . . fait Paul manger une tarte

(84) . . . donné Paul un livre

This Agr-IO acts as a probe for *Paul*:

(85) . . . Paul$_i$ Agr-IO fait t_i manger une tarte

(86) . . . Paul$_i$ Agr-IO donné t_i un livre

Then *à* enters the derivation as the next head, acting as a probe for the causative VP and inducing movement:[19]

(87) . . . [fait t_i manger une tarte]$_j$ à Paul$_i$ Agr-IO t_j

(88) . . . [donné t_i un livre]$_j$ à Paul$_i$ Agr-IO t_j

The derivations sketched in (83)–(88), (as well as the earlier ones in (77)–(82)), derive the desired word order, and they do so while maintaining the status of *à* as a functional head above the causative and, simultaneously, the idea that *Paul* originates as the subject of the infinitive.

2.9. Complementizers

Movement of *Paul* in (85) and (86) to Spec,Agr-IO will be similar to the derivation of sentences with prepositional complementizers, adopting Shlonsky's suggested modification and taking Agr-Infin to occur in place of Agr-IO. For example, the derivation of *Jean commence à comprendre* ('J begins to understand') will look like this (abstracting away from subjects):

(89) . . . commence comprendre

Agr-Infin enters the derivation and induces movement of the infinitival (nominal[20]) IP:

(90) . . . comprendre$_i$ Agr-Infin commence t_i

Then *à* enters the derivation, inducing movement of the VP headed by *commence*:

(91) [commence t_i]$_j$ à comprendre$_i$ Agr-Infin t_j

With a matrix verb like *essayer* ('try') instead of *commencer*, the prepositional complementizer would be *de* ('of') rather than *à*:

(92) Jean essaie de comprendre. ('J tries to understand.')

I assume that there is a head-to-head relation between Agr-Infin and V and a distinction between Agr-Infin(*à*) and Agr-Infin(*de*) such that the appropriate Agr-Infin is introduced above (not below, as in more familiar approaches) a given V. Another head-to-head relation between *à/de* and Agr-Infin will ensure the desired matching.

This way of thinking about prepositional complementizers has the property that movement of IP into the Spec of the prepositional complementizer (or its Agr-twin) is not limited to head-final languages. It is rather the (unique) way in which UG allows these complementizers to "get together with" their associated IP. Furthermore (contrary to Kayne 1994: 53), the movement in question is not movement of the complement of some head into the Spec of the same head.

One intuition behind this proposal is that the relation between a prepositional complementizer and its associated IP is not akin to the relation between a verb and a thematic argument but rather to the relation between a head like T or *v* (or Agr) and a DP that moves into its Spec (or into the Spec of its twin). If the relation between prepositional complementizer and associated IP is not akin to a theta relation, then Chomsky's (2001: 8) division of labor between external and internal Merge would independently have led us to question the familiar and traditional, but I think incorrect, idea that complementizer and IP "get together" as the result of one merging directly with the other.

The same intuition holds for the dative *à* that I have primarily been concerned with in this chapter. The relation between it and its associated DP is not a theta relation but rather much more like the relation between *v* (or Agr-O) and the accusative DP that moves into its Spec. If so, then *à* and DP should not be put together by external Merge but only by internal Merge (movement).

As we have seen, this leads to the conclusion that (leftward) VP-movement must play a role in derivations involving either complementizer *à* or dative *à*. We might think of this kind of VP-movement as being to English VP-preposing [illustrated in (93)] what scrambling is to topicalization:[21]

(93) He said he would do it and do it he will.

2.10. Finite complementizers

The derivational similarities between prepositional complementizers and prepositions are strong if the preceding is on the right track. (I take all prepositions of the *of, at, to, by, with, from,* and *for* type to be good candidates for derivations of the sort under discussion.) Complementizers like English *that* can be analyzed in parallel fashion (i.e., as entering the derivation above VP and acting as a probe for a finite IP merged within VP), as I suggested briefly in earlier work for the case of relative clauses.[22]

Finite sentential complements might be directly parallel to infinitival sentential complements. On the other hand, there might be a requirement to the effect that arguments must invariably be nominal.[23] Now I mentioned in the discussion of (89)–(91) that French infinitival clauses are in fact nominal, in which case they can be an argument of V (later to be moved up to *à* or *de*, setting aside cases where there is no overt complementizer).

Finite clauses in French (and English) are, however, almost certainly not nominal in and of themselves. If so, it may be that they are not permitted to be arguments of V. Although I will not pursue this question here, I think this suggests that finite complement clauses must be associated with something like *it*, in the spirit of Rosenbaum (1967), whereas gerunds usually must not be, and what we call infinitives may or may not be. The complementizer *that*, or in French, *que*, may still enter the derivation outside of VP and induce movement of (finite) IP, in a way similar to what happens in the case of relative clauses.

2.11. Case

From the perspective of Chomsky (2001), we would expect the lexical DP that ends up preceded by *à* to have structural Case. This is, of course, compatible with the fact that French lexical DPs never have any Case morphology (nor do non-clitic pronouns). There are some morphological distinctions in third-person clitics, which may or may not be assimilable to Case morphology.[24] Let me set them aside and briefly turn to a question concerning French causatives, namely, Why is dativization apparently sensitive to transitivity? That is, why do we have the following?

(94) Jean a fait manger une tarte *(à) Paul. ('J has made eat a pie to P')

(95) Jean a fait manger (*à) Paul.

There are at least two distinct questions here. One is why *à* is required in (94). I take Rouveret and Vergnaud (1980) to be correct in seeing this in terms of Case licensing.[25] In present terms, without the *à*/Agr-IO pair, there would in French not be enough functional heads of the required kind. A second question is why *à* is not possible in (95). This question is complicated by the fact that although (95) is perfectly representative of sentences in which the infinitive has no complement whatsoever, it is not completely true that *à* requires the presence of a direct object. For example, Rouveret and Vergnaud (1980: 133) give[26]

(96) Cela a fait changer d'avis/*de chemise à tout le monde. ('that has made change of mind/of shirt to all the world' = 'That made everyone change their mind/shirt.')

It may be that Agr-IO (for the most part) requires the presence of Agr-DO.

A third question is why the embedded subject *Paul* in (95) follows the infinitive. It does in (94), according to the analyis developed above, as the result of its moving up to *à*, plus the subsequent preposing of the causative VP (which no longer contains it). This does not carry over to (95). It may be that the verb-subject order in (95) is to be related to that in "stylistic inversion" sentences such as (97):[27]

(97) Qu'a mangé Paul? ('What has eaten P.')

3. Conclusion

Prepositions are not merged with what we think of as their objects. Rather, prepositions enter the derivation outside VP and subsequent to merger of a phonetically unrealized Case-licensing functional head (perhaps dispensed with by postpositions). That functional head acts as a probe attracting to its Spec what we think of as the object of the preposition. The preposition itself is a probe for VP, which moves to Spec of the preposition, producing the desired word order. The argument has been pursued here almost entirely with respect to (certain instances of) French *à*, but if correct, must generalize well beyond.

Appendix. Constituent structure

The derivations sketched in (83)–(88) produced the derived structures repeated here:

(98) . . . [fait t_i manger une tarte]$_j$ à Paul$_i$ Agr-IO t_j

(99) . . . [donné t_i un livre]$_j$ à Paul$_i$ Agr-IO t_j

These have the property that *à Paul* is, strictly speaking, not a constituent (*Paul* is in Spec,Agr-IO and *à* is the next head above that). This bears on the question of Pied-piping, in sentences like the following:

(100) A Paul, Jean a fait manger une tarte. ('to P, J has made eat a pie')

(101) A Paul, Jean a donné un livre. ('to P, J has given a book')

and similarly for their wh-counterparts:

(102) le garçon à qui Jean a fait manger une tarte ('the boy to whom J has . . . ')

(103) le garçon à qui Jean a donné un livre

If *à Paul* and *à qui* are not constituents, how can they be moved?

One possible answer would be based on the observation that in (98) and (99) *à Paul Agr-IO t* is a constituent, so that (100) and (101) could be thought of as involving moving of that (remnant) constituent, and similarly for (102) and (103). A consideration that goes against this approach would be the following: Webelhuth (1992:

129) has noted that the Germanic languages other than English have the counterpart of (104) but not the counterpart of (105):

(104) the boy whose sister John invited to the party

(105) the boy the sister of whom John invited to the party

Webelhuth's (1992: 121) generalization is that Pied-piping is Spec-based; *who* in (104) is in the Spec of the larger phrase *whose sister* and can therefore Pied-pipe it. In (105), *whom* is not in the Spec of *the sister of whom* and therefore cannot (in non-English Germanic) Pied-pipe it. English (1992: 131) will have some means of evading this restriction.

Now Webelhuth further notes that non-English Germanic does allow the counterpart of

(106) the boy to whom John spoke

This leads him (p.142) to treat preposition-based Pied-piping as special. If (106) is truly an exceptional kind of Pied-piping, then taking (100)–(103) to be instances of movement of *à Jean/qui Agr-IO t* is plausible.

The alternative is to take (106) not to be an exceptional case of Pied-piping, by taking it not to be a case of Pied-piping at all, and similarly for

(107) To whom did John speak?

This alternative is more natural from the present perspective on prepositions than it would be from the more usual perspective in which prepositions are merged directly with their objects (and form a constituent with them right away).

What I have in mind more specifically is the following: take (107) to involve object scrambling across the subject, in a way intended to recall Japanese or German. This will require a stage in the derivation (abstracting away from the auxiliary) such as

(108) whom Agr_{to} John . . .

Whether Agr_{to} is merged directly in this high position or moved there from a lower position is left an open question. But granted (108), it is natural to have the next step in the derivation be the introduction of *to* itself:

(109) to whom Agr_{to} John . . .

to enters the derivation just above Agr_{to} much as *à* enters just above Agr-IO in (98) and (99).[28]

In this way, the derivation of (107) need involve no Pied-piping, that is, no movement of a constituent containing both *to* and *whom*.

This would give us a partially new way of thinking of (6)–(9), repeated here with essentially equivalent English examples:

(110) ?Who did John fall asleep while talking to?

(111) *To whom did John fall asleep while talking?

Instead of (111) reflecting a restriction on PP-movement, it could now reflect a restriction on Agr_{to}, which cannot appear above the matrix subject and yet be related to an argument originating within an adjunct IP.

Relevant here are sentences such as

(112) ?To whom was John speaking to?

These are sometimes found/heard. They could be thought of as having two instances of Agr_{to}, one below the (derived position of) the subject and one above. At issue is the status of

(113) ?To whom did you think he was speaking to?

(114) ??To whom were you wondering what to say to?

(115) *To whom did he fall asleep while talking/speaking to?

Sentence (113) does not seem appreciably different from (112). Sentence (114) is a bit worse by virtue of being a case of extraction from a wh-island. But (115) seems much worse, essentially like (111).

If these judgments are accurate, the strong deviance of (111) must be due, not to the absence of *to* inside the adjunct, but rather to its presence in the matrix. The formulation given above holds: Agr_{to} cannot appear within the matrix and simultaneously be related to a position within the adjunct. (It may be that the adjunct-introducing element, here *while*, blocks movement of Agr_{to}.)

In conclusion, the analysis of (110) and (111) and their French counterparts (6)–(9) does not depend on P-DP being a constituent in the strict sense; nor does prepositional Pied-piping in general, whether thought of as movement of 'P DP Agr-P t' or in terms of scrambling, as in the discussion beginning at (107). Similarly, an account of the facts of (10)–(27) above, which falls outside the scope of this chapter, does not depend on P-DP being a PP-constituent.

Notes

I am grateful to Jean-Yves Pollock for helpful comments on an earlier version of this chapter.

1. Cf. Kayne (2000: chaps. 14, 15).

2. I will set aside the question of why dative (as opposed to accusative) is generally preserved in passives, with notable exceptions, at least with single object verbs (see Kayne 1975: sect. 3.6 and Barnes 1994: 213).

3. If the subject of the infinitive is an accusative clitic, there are exceptions; see Kayne (1975, chap. 3, n. 31; chap. 4, n. 23) and Rouveret and Vergnaud (1980: 129). These should perhaps be related to the 'loista' phenomenon of certain varieties of Spanish, whereby clitics of accusative form appear where a dative would be expected (see Kany 1976: 135).

4. Cf. Kayne (1975: sect. 4.9).
5. Cf. Kayne (1975: sect. 2.17, 2000: chap. 9).
6. For further details, see Kayne (1975: sect. 4.9).
7. There is no overt complementizer in

(i) Il me semble avoir compris. ['it(explet.] me seems to-have understood' = 'I seem to have understood.']

(ii) Il me faut partir. ['it(explet.) me is-necessary to-leave' = 'I have to leave.']

Although the controller in (i) and (ii) seems to be an object (dative), these are almost certainly to be analyzed as dative subjects of the sort seen prominently in Icelandic (see Fernández-Soriano 1999 and references cited there).

8. Cf. Kayne and Pollock (1978, 2001).

9. There is a restriction against embedding certain kinds of psych verbs under *faire* that does not seem to be specific to sentences with *à*-v. (Kayne 1975: chap. 3, n. 63).

A partially distinct point is made by

(i) Elle fera lever la main à Jean. ('she will-make raise the hand to J' = 'She will make/have J raise his hand.')

insofar as in this example, *Jean* may originate within the DP *la main* (cf. in part Landau 1999).

The variety of interpretation in (49)–(57) goes beyond the benefactive case focused on by Guasti (1996).

10. Some speakers of English accept the following, with ECM and a preposition:

(i) ?We're counting on there to be a solution.

See also McCloskey (1984). The raising analysis being suggested for *à* leads to the expectation that an idiom of the form 'DP V DP,' with the subject DP part of the idiom, could be embedded under *faire* and have the subject DP preceded by *à*. This needs to be looked into. A similar expectation arises for expletive subjects. But French has no expletive *there* that's a subject, so no test is readily available. It does have expletive *il*, but this expletive is incompatible with accusative Case and so would probably not be expected to ever surface with dative Case.

11. To some extent, French has counterparts of (59)-v (Pollock 1985). On English ECM, see Postal (1974).

12. See also Déchaine et al. (1995) and Klipple (1997).

13. See Kayne (1981, 1983).

14. See Chomsky (1999: n. 14) and references cited there.

15. Then *à* must have an EPP feature and phi-features.

16. Although apparently never in SVO languages, for reasons that must be more intricate than those suggested in Kayne (1994: 49), given the analysis to follow.

17. See Kayne (2000: chap. 14).

18. See Chomsky (1999: n. 14).

19. The derivation given in (87) does not immediately account for the possibility of having a stranded quantifier in

(i) Ils ont fait manger tous une tarte à leurs enfants. ('they have made eat all a pie to their children' = 'They all made their children eat a pie.')

As Guasti (1991: 214) notes, the presence of a *tous* related to *ils* yet following the infinitive appears to support the idea that the infinitive incorporates to the causative (which is not necessarily incompatible with the text proposal). Alternatively, stranded quantifiers, rather than being analyzed a la Sportiche (1988), should be related to sentences like the following (cf. Kayne 1975: sect. 1.9):

(ii) They went, the one to Paris, the other to London.

These in turn look like intricate cases of gapping. An approach to gapping a la Johnson (1994) might then carry back over to (i), without requiring incorporation.

20. The infinitive morpheme *-r(e)* is nominal in Romance languages (see Kayne 2000: sect. 14.1).

21. For extensive argumentation in this direction, see Koopman and Szabolcsi (2000). Note that this VP preposing of (93) is sometimes obligatory:

(i) I said he would do it and do it he has.

(ii) . . . and he has done/*do it.

Example (i) recalls the Dutch and German IPP phenomenon (for a recent discussion, see Koopman and Szabolcsi 2000).

22. See Kayne (2000: chap. 15).

23. See Kayne (1982).

24. See Emonds (1976: 232).

25 See also Koopman (1992).

26. Cf. also Kayne (1975: chap. 3, n. 9) (and chap. 4, n. 4):

(i) Cela fera voir juste à ton ami. ('that will-make see right to your friend')

(ii) *?Elle fera téléphoner à Marie à Jean. ('she will-make telephone to M to J' = 'She will have J call M.')

If the infinitive has both a direct object and a PP complement, *à* is necessary, and the word order facts are complex (see chap. 3, n. 82). Additional examples of a dativized subject are available if one looks at causatives in which the embedded subject becomes a dative clitic, but I am setting those aside in this chapter.

27. On which, see Kayne and Pollock (1978, 2001). Some link with stylistic inversion is suggested by Rouveret and Vergnaud (1980: 133), at least for some cases in which the infinitive is unaccusative. That (95) does not involve head-raising of V is suggested for unergatives by the fact that the construction is "delicate" in the presence of a complement PP (see Kayne 1975: chap. 4, n. 24):

(i) ?Cela fera penser tout le monde à Jean. ('that will-make think all the world to J' = 'That will make everyone think of J.')

28. This bears on the question of whether all functional heads need to attract something to their Spec-v. (Kayne 2000: 322).

References

Barnes, M. P., with E. Weyhe. (1994). "Faroese." In E. König & J. van der Auwera, eds., *The Germanic Languages*. London: Routledge, 190–218.

Burzio, L. (1986). *Italian Syntax. A Government-Binding Approach*. Dordrecht: Reidel.

Chomsky, N. (1982). *Some Concepts and Consequences of the Theory of Government and Binding*. Cambridge, Mass.: MIT Press.

Chomsky, N. (1998). "Minimalist Inquiries: The Framework." *MIT Occasional Papers in Linguistics* 15, MITWPL, Cambridge, Mass.

Chomsky, N. (1999). Derivation by Phase. Ms., Massachusetts Institute of Technology, Cambridge.

Chomsky, N. (2001). Beyond Explanatory Adequacy. Ms., Massachusetts Institute of Technology, Cambridge.

Cinque, G. (1990). *Types of A'-Dependencies*, Cambridge, Mass.: MIT Press.

Cinque, G. (1999). *Adverbs and Functional Heads. A Cross-Linguistic Perspective*. New York: Oxford University Press.

Collins, C., & H. Thráinsson. (1993). "Object Shift in Double Object Constructions and the Theory of Case." In C. Phillips, ed., *Papers on Case & Agreement II. Vol. 19*. Cambridge, Mass.: *MIT Working Papers in Linguistics*, 131–174.

Déchaine, R.-M., T. Hoekstra, & J. Rooryck. (1995). "Augmented and Non-augmented HAVE." In L. Nash and G. Tsoulas, eds., *Actes du premier colloque Langues & Grammaire*, Paris: Université de Paris 8, 85–101.

Emonds, J. E. (1976). *A Transformational Approach to English Syntax. Root, Structure-Preserving and Local Transformations*. New York: Academic Press.

Fernández-Soriano, O. (1999). "Two Types of Impersonal Sentences in Spanish: Locative and Dative Subjects." *Syntax* 2, 101–140.

Guasti, M. T. (1991). "Incorporation, Excorporation, and Lexical Properties of Causative Heads." *Linguistic Review* 8, 209–232.

Guasti, M. T. (1996). "Semantic Restrictions in Romance Causatives and the Incorporation Approach," *Linguistic Inquiry* 27, 294–313.

Johnson, K. (1994). Bridging the Gap. Ms., University of Massachusetts, Amherst.

Kany, C. E. (1976). *Sintaxis Hispanoamericana*. Madrid: Editorial Gredos.

Kayne, R. S. (1975). *French Syntax. The Transformational Cycle*. Cambridge, Mass.: MIT Press.

Kayne, R. S. (1981). "On Certain Differences Between French and English." *Linguistic Inquiry* 12, 349–371 (reprinted in Kayne 1984).

Kayne, R. S. (1982). "Predicates and Arguments, Verbs and Nouns." Paper presented at the GLOW Conference, *GLOW Newsletter* 8, 24.

Kayne, R. S. (1983). "Le datif en français et en anglais." In M. Herslund, O. Mordrup, & F. Sorensen, eds., *Analyses grammaticales du français. Etudes publiées à l'occasion du 50e anniversaire de Carl Vikner, Revue Romane*, Numéro spécial 24, 86–98 (English version in Kayne 1984).

Kayne, R. S. (1984). *Connectedness and Binary Branching*. Dordrecht: Foris.

Kayne, R. S. (1994). *The Antisymmetry of Syntax*. Cambridge, Mass.: MIT Press.

Kayne, R. S. (2000). *Parameters and Universals*. New York: Oxford University Press.

Kayne, R. S., & J.-Y. Pollock. (1978). "Stylistic Inversion, Successive Cyclicity and Move NP in French." *Linguistic Inquiry* 9, 595–621.

Kayne, R. S., & J.-Y. Pollock. (2001). "New Thoughts on Stylistic Inversion." In A. Hulk and J.-Y. Pollock, eds., *Subject Inversion in Romance and the Theory of Universal Grammar*. New York: Oxford University Press.

Klipple, E. (1997). "Prepositions and Variation." In A.-M. di Sciullo, ed., *Projections and Interface Conditions. Essays on Modularity*. New York: Oxford University Press, 74–108.

Koopman, H. (1992). "On the Absence of Case Chains in Bambara." *Natural Language and Linguistic Theory* 10, 555–594.

Koopman, H., and A. Szabolcsi. (2000). *Verbal Complexes*. Cambridge, Mass.: MIT Press.

Landau, I. (1999). "Possessor Raising and the Structure of VP." *Lingua* 107, 1–37.

McCloskey, J. (1984). "Raising, Subcategorization and Selection in Modern Irish." *Natural Language and Linguistic Theory* 1, 441–485.

Pollock, J.-Y. (1985). "On Case and the Syntax of Infinitives in French." In J. Guéron, H.-G. Obenauer, & J.-Y. Pollock, eds., *Grammatical Representation*. Dordrecht: Foris, 293–326.

Postal, P. M. (1974). *On Raising. One Rule of English Grammar and Its Theoretical Implications.* Cambridge, Mass.: MIT Press.

Rosenbaum, P. S. (1967). *The Grammar of English Predicate Complement Constructions.* Cambridge, Mass.: MIT Press.

Rouveret, A., & J. R. Vergnaud. (1980). "Specifying Reference to the Subject: French Causatives and Conditions on Representations." *Linguistic Inquiry* 11, 97–202.

Sportiche, D. (1988). "A Theory of Floating Quantifiers and Its Corollaries for Constituent Structure." *Linguistic Inquiry* 19, 425–449.

Webelhuth, G. (1992). *Principles and Parameters of Syntactic Saturation*. New York: Oxford University Press.

6

JACQUES MEHLER AND MARINA NESPOR

Linguistic Rhythm and the Acquisition of Language

Introduction

In organisms endowed with a disposition to acquire grammar, the beginnings of language learning can be detected at the onset of life (Chomsky 1965, 1980). Under the assumption that some universal properties of grammar are part of the human genetic endowment, we still have to explain how particular languages are acquired. One strong hypothesis that is currently under evaluation is that an essential aspect of language acquisition consists in the setting of parameters to the value that corresponds to the first language of exposure, hereafter L1. Basically, the genetic endowment can be thought of as switches that are to be set to the values that characterize the grammatical properties of L1. Whether there is an initial value of these parameters and how often they can be switched to take another value (for instance, to account for the presence of another language in the learning situation) is currently being explored. The grammars of natural languages are limited by the values that the parameters can take. There may, of course, be a noise generator, as described for the expression of other biological properties (Changeux & Dehaene 1989), in which case a novel situation may arise.

We take it for granted that one version or another or the parameter-setting approach is correct. Thus, we need to ask how the parameter-setting account actually works. Most accounts assume that infants have somehow managed to learn the lexicon when they begin to acquire grammar. Mazuka (1996) underscored the problems that arise when one makes this assumption. In this chapter we assume, following Mazuka, that some physical properties of L1 determine the setting of some basic parameters, thus facilitating further language learning.

What are the specific environmental stimuli that contribute to setting parameters to their values? This essential question remains unanswered. As we shall see, rhythm is an important cue that helps acquire different aspects of grammar (Gleitman & Wanner 1982; Morgan 1986; Nespor et al. 1996). That is, determining the rhythmic properties of L1 affects the acquisition of its phonology, as well as of other aspects of grammar. Specifically, rhythm provides infants with information that is used to form a representation that influences continuous speech segmentation and ultimately the way in which lexical items are identified. In addition, rhythm makes it possible to determine some basic syntactic properties responsible for the variation in word order observed in natural language. That is, the rhythm of language is essential to the acquisition of both grammar and the lexicon. To understand how language learning is bootstrapped, it is essential to understand the way in which rhythm can help set parameters and to determine exactly which properties of a linguistic system may be derived from a specific rhythm.

1. Rhythm and language

Rhythm refers to the periodicity with which certain events recur. The alternation of day and night is rhythmic, and so are the horse's trot and the beat of the heart. The modality and the nature of the events that recur with a certain periodicity are irrelevant to the definition of rhythm. Rather, it is the periodicity of their recurrence that is central to the percept we call rhythm.

If we want to understand what linguistic rhythm is and how it contributes to the development of a linguistic system, it is necessary to identify the language-specific events responsible for periodicity in speech. In other words, it is necessary to determine the properties that make speech appear to have an intrinsic rhythm. Past attempts have failed to establish the validity of any single property to account for linguistic rhythm. As we shall see below, the most influential view was that different linguistic rhythms arise because the components that recur regularly differ for each rhythm.

It has long been acknowledged that natural languages may be classified according to their rhythm. Lloyd James (1940) first noticed that some languages, Spanish among them, have a rhythm that resembles that of a machine gun, whereas other languages, notably English, have a rhythm evocative of messages in Morse code. Pike (1948) labeled the two types of rhythm "syllable timed" and "stress timed," respectively. Abercrombie (1967) went a step further and claimed that isochrony either of syllables or of interstress intervals is at the basis of rhythm in the languages of the world. The first type of language would be characterized by the isochrony of syllables and the second by the isochrony of interstress intervals. A third rhythmic class was added later (Ladefoged 1975) to account for the fact that some languages, typically Japanese, appeared to be neither syllable- nor stress-timed but to be isochronous at a sub-syllabic level, that is, the *mora*. The mora is a constituent established in phonological theory to distinguish light from heavy syllables: light syllables consist of one mora, heavy syllables of two (Hayes 1995). Languages whose basic rhythmic unit is the mora are labeled "mora-timed."

Phonetic research aimed at discovering the physical properties that characterize rhythmic classes failed to find isochrony in either syllables or interstress intervals, the latter coinciding with the notion of metrical foot in phonological theory (Liberman & Prince 1977). Instead, the variation of their duration has been shown to be similar in syllable-timed and in stress-timed languages (Shen & Peterson, 1962; Manrique & Signorini 1983; see however, Port et al. 1987, who find isochrony at the level of the mora). This finding gave rise to two proposals: one, by Dasher and Bolinger (1982), suggesting that rhythmic classes do not result from a rhythmic distinction across languages but rather are the byproduct of either the coexistence or the absence of different phonological phenomena within a language. The second, by Lehiste (1973, 1977), is that the rhythmic classes are due to a perceptual illusion. The source of this illusion may or may not be due to the cues pinpointed by Dasher and Bolinger.

The first of these two proposals finds support in the existence of phonological properties characteristic of stress-timed languages. Indeed, these languages tend to have a large syllabic repertoire, vowel centralization in unstressed syllables, and quantitative sensitivity in stress location. Syllable-timed languages fail to have any of these three properties (Dauer 1983). The properties that characterize the stress-timed languages, which are all absent in syllable-timed ones are, prima facie, to be independent of each other. If so, it is natural to conjecture that some languages may have one or two of the above properties. One ought thus to find languages that are not classifiable as either syllable- or stress-timed because they would lie in between. In fact, this is what actually happens. Indeed, on the one hand, there are languages with a rich syllabic repertoire but with no vowel centralization, for example, Polish, and, on the other hand, languages with a relatively poor syllabic repertoire but with vowel centralization, for example, Catalan or European Portuguese (Nespor 1990). This line of thinking brought both Dauer and Nespor to reject the notion of rhythmic classes. They propose that languages be spread out along a continuum that would have at one extreme stress-timed languages and at the opposite extreme syllable-timed languages.[1]

The second line of research—according to which the division of languages into rhythmic classes might be due to a perceptual illusion—stems from and is congruent with the notion that neither syllables nor interstress intervals are isochronous. Rather, Lehiste conjectures that the speech signal gives rise to perceptual processes responsible for the illusionary perception of isochronicity. To ground their hypothesis, a number of investigators set out to establish whether languages are discriminated from one another only if they are not in the same rhythmic class. Language discrimination studies have been carried out with both infants and adults and, more recently with non-human animals (Ramus et al. 2000). To be certain that languages are distinguished on the basis of rhythmic properties rather than of phonetic or morphological cues, utterances are often delexicalized. The main outcome of these investigations is that both infants and adults can discriminate between a pair of languages if they belong to different rhythmic classes but not otherwise.

A large number of experiments have been carried out to ground the aforementioned claims. Both adults and newborns are able to discriminate between two languages belonging to different rhythmic classes but not between languages belonging to the same class (Mehler et al. 1988, 1996; Moon et al. 1993; Nazzi et al. 1998;

Bahrick and Pickens 1988).[2] Interestingly, the outcome of most of these experiments is that languages appear to cluster into classes that correspond to those proposed by linguists, namely, stress-timed, syllable-timed, and mora-timed.

To confirm that the rhythmic class hypothesis can explain perceptual behavior, Nazzi and his colleagues (1998) carried out an experiment with sentences drawn from two languages belonging either to the same or to different rhythmic classes. The results show that both newborns and adults discriminate between stimuli of mixed Spanish and Italian sentences and stimuli of mixed Dutch and English sentences, whereas they do not discriminate between a mixture of Spanish and English sentences and a mixture of Italian and Dutch sentences.

The conclusion that may be drawn from the aforementioned work is that languages may form perceptually grouped rhythmic classes rather than being spread out along a continuum. Of course, all these studies are based upon a handful of languages, and it is entirely possible that future studies will uncover more rhythmic "classes" and that, in the end, what now seems to be groups of languages will again appear as a continuum. Discrimination would then occur between any two languages that are sufficiently distant along the continuum but not otherwise. Alternatively, the classes identified so far are not exhaustive; possibly two or three additional classes will be discovered after more languages are studied. For example, on the basis of a typological study on a variety of unrelated languages, it has been proposed that languages belong to one of five classes defined on the basis of syllable complexity (Levelt & van de Vijver 2004). It is entirely possible that investigations of more languages along the line of Ramus et al. (1999), to be discussed below, will uncover the existence of exactly two more rhythmic classes. At the moment, we cannot help being agnostic about how many rhythmic classes there are, if there are classes at all. We will pursue the notion that there are rhythmic classes because their existence presents an advantage for the language learner, as will be illustrated below.

2. Physical correlates of rhythmic classes

As was stated above, languages are perceived as belonging to one rhythmic class or another. Yet isochrony of either syllables or feet has not been found in acoustic-phonetic measurements. Hence, it becomes necessary to explore other characteristics of speech that may account for perception. Mehler et al. (1996) conjectured that infants perceive speech as a sequence of vowels, interrupted by consonants (or consonant clusters). This proposal is entirely reasonable since infants may very well pay attention to the parts of speech that have higher energy and longer duration, namely, vowels. This could give rise to the percept of rhythm underlying the discrimination performance observed in infants, as well as in adults. Ramus et al. (1999) pursued this conjecture and set out to investigate whether the way in which different vocalic intervals alternate forms the basis to our impression of speech rhythm.

Specifically, Ramus et al. (1999) propose that the representation of rhythm is computed on the basis of two measures: the proportion of utterances occupied by vowels and the variability of the consonantal intervals that separate them (see figure 6.1).

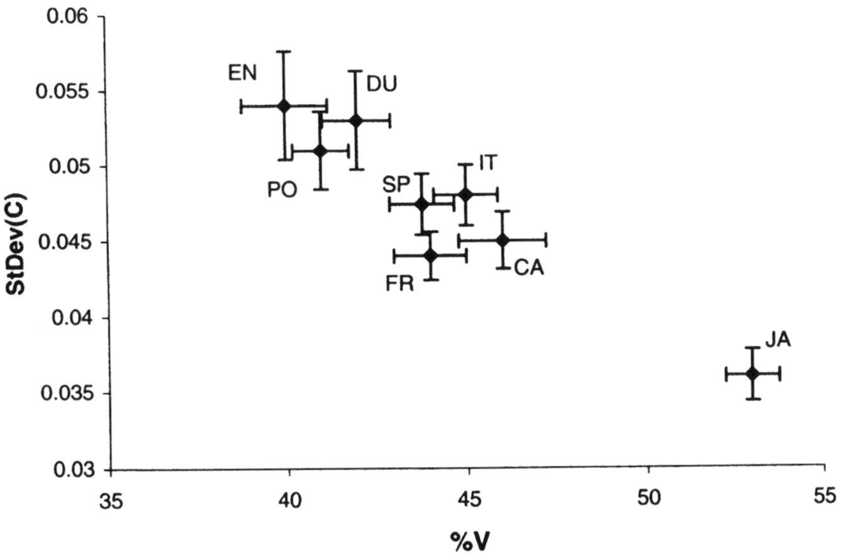

FIGURE 6.1. Results from the study by Ramus et al. (1999). Distribution of languages over the percentage of vowels per utterance versus the standard deviation of the consonants. Error bars represent ± one standard error.

The proportion of vocalic intervals, together with the regularity of their occurrence, can be used to sort the eight languages studied into three groups consistent with the classes proposed by linguists. This intriguing result strengthens our conviction that some rhythmic aspects of L1 may play an important role in early language acquisition.

3. From rhythmic classes to basic phonological representations

Linguists assume that phonological units (as morae, syllables, and feet) are part of the speaker's knowledge. Psycholinguists have evidence, however, that different languages highlight one or the other of these representations, to make it the basic phonological unit exploited in segmenting utterances.

Experimental studies have established that the mora is the representation that guides the behavior of Japanese speakers, the syllable of speakers of French, and the foot of speakers of English (Cutler et al. 1986; Otake et al. 1993; Mehler et al. 1996). To illustrate one of the standard procedures used in this area, we describe one of the tests designed to discover the relevance of the syllable for native speakers of French (Mehler et al. 1981). The participants in this study were asked to respond as soon as they recognized the sequence *pa* in either *palace* or *palmier*, and reaction times were measured. Participants responded faster to *pa* in *palace* than to *pa* in *palmier*. In the first case, but not in the second, *pa* coincides with the first syllable. The same subjects were then asked to recognize the sequence *pal* in the same two words, and turn out to be faster in recognizing it in *palmier*, where it is a syllable, than in *palace*, where it corresponds to one syllable plus the onset of the next. The same experiment was then conducted with native speakers of English and of Japanese (Otake et al.). Their reaction times turned out to be the same in all tasks. These results may be interpreted as showing that, whereas the syllable is used as a parsing unit by native speakers of French, it is not so used by native speakers of either Japanese or English.

Let us now assume that the mora, the syllable, and the foot are the representations used to parse the languages in the experiments just mentioned, as well as all other languages of the respective rhythmic class. Under this assumption, one of the problems that must be addressed is how one goes from a representation of rhythm, understood as the proportion of vowels and the regularity with which these are produced, to a representation in terms of moras, syllables, or stress periodicity.[3] This is a difficult question to answer and one that is not usually addressed in the psycholinguistic literature.

Is it possible to make some conjecture that would link the rhythmic classes, as illustrated in Ramus et al. (1999), with one of the three phonological units mentioned above? We will risk making one conjecture even though the exact details have not yet been worked out. Consider speakers of Hawaiian or Japanese. It is likely that infants will rapidly discover that their L1 is mainly composed by CVs. In some of these languages, codas may exist, for example, post-vocalic nasals or geminate consonants in Japanese. This, however, may not be too problematic for the infant. Indeed, given that the majority of the units they hear are actually CVs [the infant may be able to figure this out from the fact that the standard deviation of Cs (ΔC) is very low], the codas may be rated as having a special status. In due time, the infant might even notice that their average duration is not that different from CVs and assimilate codas to moraic units. Notice, moreover, that Japanese codas are quite different from codas in languages belonging to other rhythmic groups.

Consider the other extreme case, that in which the infant's L1 is a stressed-timed language. In this case, infants may discover that these are languages that have a very high ΔC. Given that L1 has a high ΔC, a salient regularity may become apparent, namely, that besides word primary stress, secondary stress is also clearly marked. This gives rise to the percept of an alternation of stressless and stressed vowels and thus of strong and weak syllables. What happens when the infant's L1 is a syllable-timed language? In all likelihood, this is a property that is correlated with an intermediary value of ΔC. In this case, the syllable will become the representational unit that will be most highlighted, a fact that becomes clear in adult psycholinguistic experiments with speakers of Romance languages, as shown above.

4. Syllabic repertoires and expectations for segmentation

The preceding sections can lead one to conclude that rhythm may help determine how many syllable types a language has, that is, the size of the syllabic repertoire of the language the infant is acquiring. This is a hypothesis that Ramus et al. (1999) mention explicitly. In fact, languages appear to have syllabic repertoires that jump quantically. Some languages, like Japanese or Hawaiian, have a small syllabic repertoire consisting of two or three syllable types. Other languages, like Greek, Spanish, and Italian, have six to eight syllable types, and English and Dutch have a syllabic repertoire of sixteen or even more syllable types (Dauer 1987; Nespor 1990). Sorting languages according to the size of their syllabic repertoire coincides with the previously mentioned rhythmic classes. Determining the rhythmic class to which a language belongs is, however, not sufficient to determine exactly which syllable types the language has.[4] It may, however, provide some information about the level of complexity of syllabic structure.

Is there some additional information besides the rough estimate of the syllabic repertoire in L1 that the prelinguistic infant can gain from paying attention to rhythm? This is a hard question to answer without further research. However, we are willing to venture the hypothesis that rhythm may bias the infant to segment signals into smaller or larger chunks. In other words, the rhythmic class to which a language belongs may provide some information about the mean size of the more frequent words in L1. Indeed, low-frequency words are very often long in most languages (Zipf 1936; Dehaene and Mehler 1992).

Indeed, it seems reasonable to conjecture that languages with a small repertoire of syllables, that is, mora-timed languages, will tend to have long frequent words, like Japanese or Hawaiian, whereas the languages with the richests syllablic repertoire, that is, stress-timed languages, will be rich in monosyllables, like Dutch or English. Syllable-timed languages will, of course, fall in between, as is the case for Spanish, Italian or Greek.

The above conjecture makes intuitive sense. Indeed, in a language with a very poor syllabic repertoire, the number of monosyllables is insufficient to express even the most frequent concepts. Conversely, in a language with a rich syllabic repertoire, there are enough monosyllables to cover the basic vocabulary, rendering the use of polysyllables unnecessarily costly. Of course, this assumes that languages have a similar tolerance for polysemy.

Given the connections between rhythmic class and syllable types and between syllable types and minimal word size, it is indeed plausible that through the identification of the rhythmic class of L1, infants will tend to postulate possible word units of different sizes.

In addition to the above conjucture about the possible function of rhythm in language acquisition, others have proposed that higher levels of the rhythmic organization can help the acquisition of syntax. The representation of rhythm, in fact, in language as in music, is hierarchical in nature. While at the basic level, the elements that recur in time to make speech rhythmic are vowels, at higher levels it is prominent vowels, that is, vowels characterized by different suprasegmental properties that, alternating with less prominent vowels, establish the rhythmic flow (Liberman & Prince 1977; Selkirk 1984).

The two levels of phonological—and rhythmic organization—relevant to syntax are the phonological and the intonational phrase. In both cases, the relative prominence of their elements has been proposed as a specific signal to some properties of syntax (Nespor & Vogel 1986; Hayes & Lahiri 1991 for the first and the second constituent, respectively). If this proposal is right, these cues may be essential to the prelexical setting of basic syntactic parameters governing word order (Nespor 1995; Nespor et al. 1996; Nespor & Guasti 2002).[5] Future research will uncover whether the different cues to phrasal prominence are actually used by infants. In a first experiment, the sensitivity of infants to the phonological phrase prominence makes plausible the idea that at least the Head-Complement parameter could be set through prosody (Christophe et al. 2002).

5. Conclusions

In this chapter, we have suggested that, on the basis of the specific rhythmic class of their L1, infants might be able to highlight the phonological representation that they will eventually come to use to segment speech. Moreover, infants may also obtain information about the size of the syllabic repertoire of the language they hear. Indeed, we have speculated that the size of the syllabic repertoire might give a bias as to mean word length. Finally, we mentioned that basic syntactic parameters might also be set through the signal conveyed by the prosody of utterances.

The idea that rhythm may provide an initial perspective into the structure of language is fascinating. However, how exactly an infant derives phonological knowledge from rhythmic information remains to be studied in greater detail.

Future research will clarify exactly the ways in which the rhythmic properties of the speech signal contribute to learning the language-specific aspects L1. The appeal we see in the hypothesis that rhythm is directly responsible for part of the knowledge necessary to learn grammar is that the child could start quite early to work on segmentation. According to our proposal, the infant starts to learn grammar with the onset of life. The signal could set parameters in an automatic fashion, without requiring the postulation that the infant adopts an intentional stance or engages in *heavy* computations. Those two assumptions seem to us incompatible with what is otherwise known about the infant's brain.

Finally, further research will also have to clarify where language-specific learning starts and general learning stops. We know that tamarins behave similarly to babies in some linguistic discrimination (Ramus et al. 2000). At least one part of the task involved in the identification of rhythm might thus not be language specific.

Notes

1. The third class, mora-timed languages, was not considered in these investigations.

2. Of course, the stimuli presented to adult subjects are either low-pass filtered or resynthesized. These manipulations destroy segmental content while preserving the different aspects of prosody.

3. Cutler and her colleagues have argued that strong syllables are the segmentation unit that is used by speakers of English and languages in that class (Cutler 1992). If so, speakers of Japanese would use moras, speakers of Romance languages syllables, and speakers of stress-timed languages strong syllables to segment the speech signal.

4. For example, one language with two syllable types, may have CV, V, like Cayuvava; another language with the same number of syllable types may have CV, CVC, like Thangari; and yet another might have CV, CCV, like Arabela (cf. Blevins 1995).

5. See also Donati and Nespor (2003).

References

Abercrombie, D. (1967). *Elements of general phonetics*. Chicago: Aldine.

Bahrick, L. E., & J. N. Pickens, (1988). "Classification of Bimodal English and Spanish Language Passages by Infants." *Infant Behavior and Development* 11, 277–296.

Blevins, J. (1995). "The syllable is phonological theory." In J. A. Goldsmith (ed.), *The Handbook of Phonological Theory*. Blackwell, Cambridge, 206–266.

Changeux, J. P., & S. Dehaene. (1989). "Neuronal Models of Cognitive Functions." *Cognition* 33, 63–109.

Chomsky, N. (1965). *Aspects of the Theory of Syntax*. Cambridge, Mass.: MIT Press.

Chomsky, N. (1980). *Rules and Representations*. Oxford: Blackwell.

Christophe, A., M. Nespor, M. T. Guasti, & B. van Ooyen. (2002) "Prosodic Structure and Syntactic Acquisition: The Case of the Head-Complement Parameter. *Developmental Science* 6.2, 213–222.

Cutler, A. (1992). "The Production and Perception of Word Boundaries." In Y. Tohkura, E. Vatikiotis-Bateson, & Y. Sagisaka, *Speech Perception Production and Linguistic Structure*. Tokyo and Amsterdam: Ohmsha and IOS Press.

Cutler, A., J. Mehler, D. Norris, & J. Segui. (1986). "The Syllable's Differing Role in the Segmentation of French and English." *Journal of Memory and Language* 25, 385–400.

Dasher, R., & D. Bolinger, (1982). "On Pre-accentual Lengthening." *Journal of the International Phonetic Association* 12, 58–69.

Dauer, R. M. (1983). "Stress-timing and Syllable-timing Reanalyzed." *Journal of Phonetics* 11, 51–62.

Dehaene, S., & J. Mehler. (1992). "Cross-linguistic Regularities in the Frequency of Number Words." *Cognition* 43, 1–29.

Donati, C., & M. Nespor. (2003). "From Focus to Syntax." *Lingua* 113, 11, 1119–1142.

Gleitman, L. R., & E. Wanner. (1982). "Language Acquisition: The State of the State of the Art." In G. E. Wanner & L. R. Gleitman (eds.) *Language Acquisition: State of the Art*. New York: Cambridge University Press, 3–48.

Hayes, B. (1995). *Metrical Stress Theory*. Chicago and London: University of Chicago Press.

Hayes, B., & A. Lahiri. (1991). Bengali intonational phonology. *Natural Language and Linguistic Theory* 9, 47–96.

Ladefoged, P. (1975). *A Course in Phonetics*. New York: Harcourt Brace Jovanovich.

Lehiste, I. (1973). "Rhythmic Units and Syntactic Units in Production and Perception." *Journal of the Acoustical Society of America* 54, 1228–1234.

Lehiste, I. (1977). "Isochrony Reconsidered." *Journal of Phonetics* 5, 253–263.

Levelt, C., & R. van de Vijver. (2004). "Syllable Types in Cross-linguistic and Developmental Grammars." In R. Kager, J. Pater, & W. Zonnereld (eds.) (2004) *Constraints in Phonological Acquisition*. Cambridge. OUP, 204–218.

Liberman, M., & A. Prince. (1977). "On Stress and Linguistic Rhythm." *Linguistic Inquiry* 8, 240–336.

Lloyd James, A. (1940). *Speech Signals in Telephony*. London.

Manrique, A. M. B. D., & A. Signorini. (1983). "Segmental Durations and Rhythm in Spanish." *Journal of Phonetics* 11, 117–128.

Mazuka, R. (1996). "How Can a Grammatical Parameter Be Set Before the First Word?" In J. L. Morgan & K. Demuth, *Signal to Syntax: Bootstrapping from Speech to Grammar in Early Acquisition*. Mahwah, N.J.: Erlbaum, 313–330.

Mehler, J., Y. Dommergues, U. Frauenfelder, & J. Segui. (1981). "The Syllable's Role in Speech Segmentation." *Journal of Verbal Learning and Verbal Behavior* 20, 298–305.

Mehler, J., E. Dupoux, T. Nazzi, & G. Dehaene-Lambertz. (1996). "Coping with Linguistic Diversity: The Infant's Viewpoint." In J. L. Morgan & K. Demuth, *Signal to Syntax: Bootstrapping from Speech to Grammar in Early Acquisition*. Mahwah, N.J.: Erlbaum, 101–116.

Mehler, J., P. W. Jusczyk, G. Lambertz, N. Halsted, J. Bertoncini, & C. Amiel-Tison. (1988). "A Precursor of Language Acquisition in Young Infants." *Cognition* 29, 143–178.

Moon, C., R. Cooper, & W. Fifer. (1993). "Two-day-olds Prefer Their Native Language." *Infant Behavior and Development* 16, 495–500.

Morgan, J. L. (1986). *From Simple Input to Complex Grammar*. Cambridge, Mass.: MIT Press.

Nazzi, T., J. Bertoncini, & J. Mehler. (1998). "Language Discrimination by Newborns: Towards an Understanding of the Role of Rhythm." *Journal of Experimental Psychology: Human Perception and Performance* 24(3), 756–766.

Nespor, M. (1990). "On the Rhythm Parameter in Phonology." In I. M. Roca, *Logical Issues in Language Acquisition*. Dordrecht: Foris, 157–175.

Nespor, M. (1995). "Setting Syntactic Parameters at a Prelexical Stage." *Proceedings of the XXV ABRALIN Conference*, Salvador de Bahia, Brazil, 97–100.

Nespor, M., & M. T. Guasti. (2002). "Stress-to-Focus alignment." *Lingue e Linguaggio* 1, 79–106

Nespor, M., M. T. Guasti, & A. Christophe. (1996). "Selecting Word Order: The Rhythmic Activation Principle." In U. Kleinhenz, *Interfaces in Phonology*. Berlin: Akademie Verlag, 1–26.

Nespor, M., & I. Vogel. (1986). *Prosodic Phonology*. Dordrecht: Foris.

Otake, T., G. Hatano, A. Cutler, & J. Mehler. (1993). "Mora or Syllable? Speech Segmentation in Japanese." *Journal of Memory and Language* 32, 258–278.

Pike, K. L. (1945). *The Intonation of American English*. Ann Arbor: University of Michigan Press.

Port, R. F., J. Dalby, & M. O'Dell. (1987). "Evidence for Mora-timing in Japanese." *Journal of the Acoustical Society of America* 81(5), 1574–1585.

Ramus, F., M. D. Hauser, C. Miller, D. Morris, & J. Mehler. (2000). "Language Discrimination by Human Newborns and by Cotton-Top Tamarin Monkeys." *Science* 288, 349–351.

Ramus, F., M. Nespor, & J. Mehler. (1999). "Correlates of the Linguistic Rhythm in the Speech Signal." *Cognition* 73(3), 265–292.

Selkirk, E. O. (1984). *Phonology and Syntax: The Relation Between Sound and Structure*. Cambridge, Mass.: MIT Press.

Shen, Y., & J. J. Peterson. (1962). "Isochronism in English." *University of Buffalo Studies in Linguistics. Occasional Papers* 9, 1–36.

Zipf, G. K. (1936). *The Psycho-biology of Language*. London: Routledge.

7

LUIGI RIZZI

Locality and Left Periphery

1. Relativized Minimality and the cartography of structural positions

The goal of this chapter is to provide a new, refined formal characterization of the locality principle known as Relativized Minimality. At the same time, we will try to show how the study of locality interacts with the "cartographic approach," the attempt to draw maps of syntactic configuratons as precise and detailed as possible. A fundamental discovery of modern formal linguistics is that, if the length and depth of syntactic representations is unbounded, core structural relations are local. According to the Relativized Minimality approach, a local relation is one that must be satisfied in the smallest environment in which it can be satisfied. One traditional implementation of this idea is that, in a configuration like (1), a local structural relation cannot hold between X and Y if Z is a potential bearer of the relevant relation and Z intervenes between X and Y.[1]

(1) . . . X . . . Z . . . Y . . .

Consider for instance the local relation linking a phrase to its trace. The relation holds in (2) but not in (3b): the wh-operator *who* in the embedded Spec of C intervenes between *how* and its trace in (3b), and *who* is a potential bearer of the antecedent relation in the relevant kind of chain; so the required antecedent-trace relation fails, and one cannot ask a wh-question about the manner adverbial in (3b):

(2) a. How did you solve the problem?
b. How did you solve the problem t?

(3) a. I wonder who could solve the problem in this way.
b.*How do you wonder *who* could solve this problem t?

RM can be intuitively construed as an economy principle in that it severely limits the portion of structure within which a given local relation is computed: elements trying to enter into a local relation are short-sighted, so to speak, in that they can only see as far as the first potential bearer of the relevant relation. The principle reduces ambiguity in a number of cases: whenever two elements compete for entering into a given local relation with a third element, the closest always wins. So, whatever its precise implementation, RM has desirable properties and appears to be a natural principle of mental computation. It is the kind of principle that we may expect to hold across cognitive domains: if locality is relevant at all for other kinds of mental computation, we may well expect it to hold in a similar form: you must go for the closest potential bearer of a given local relation.

For the principle to work, it is necessary to define a refined enough typology of positions to capture the selectivity of the effect; for instance, we must be able to express the fact that the subject position (a possible binder of certain types of traces in the VP) does not affect the chain link connecting *how* and its trace in (2a). Here the study of locality meets with the recent attempts to draw very detailed maps of structural representations, a research trend that is sometimes referred to as the cartographic approach (Rizzi 1997, 2004, and this volume; Cinque 1999, 2002). On the one hand, the results of the cartographic study provide a sound theoretical and empirical basis for drawing a typology of positions that the study of locality can build on. On the other hand, selective locality effects can provide evidence for differentiating structural positions, thus providing relevant evidence for the cartographic endeavor. One of the aims of the present chapter is to illustrate this interaction between the two research topics.

This chapter is organized as follows. We will define an approach to locality in chains that formally implements the RM-idea, and we will suggest that the postulated locality principle may extend to local processes distinct from chain formation: phonological processes, certain kinds of ellipsis, and head-XP-interactions. We will then look at locality in A'-chains and review certain argument/adjunct asymmetries that arise in the context of Weak Islands, and will take such asymmetries as a "signature" of RM-related phenomena. We will then focus on various empirical puzzles raised by selective locality effects on adverbial chains, and we will show that they are amenable to two theoretical ingredients: a detailed cartography of the left peripheral positions occupied by adverbs and a proper typology of structural positions that RM is sensitive to.

2. Minimal configurations and chains

The idea we now want to formally express is that local relations must be satisfied in a minimal configuration, the smallest configuration in which they can be satisfied. Consider the following definition:

(4) Y is in a Minimal Configuration (MC) with X iff there is no Z such that
i. Z is of the same structural type as X, and
ii. Z intervenes between X and Y.

Statement (4) gives a definition of the minimal configuration that must hold in local relations, eliminating reference to the spurious notion "Antecedent government" and generalizing the notion to all local relations: the assumption here is that (4) is the fundamental locality principle; hence different subtheories for which the concept of locality is relevant will refer to (4). I will continue to refer to (4) as Relativized Minimality (RM) in informal discussion. As for "sameness" of structural type, if we assume a theory not allowing phrasal adjunction, the relevant potential interveners will be heads or specifiers. So, heads are of the same structural type as other heads; as for specifiers, to capture the fact that, for example, the subject does not determine a minimality effect in (2b) we must introduce some distinction. Let us assume, for the moment at least, the distinction between A and A' specifiers, as in Rizzi (1990), a point that will be refined later on: so, an A specifier, the subject, does not affect an A'-chain in (2b), but an A'-specifier, the embedded wh-element, interferes in the A'-chain of *how* in (3). Thus,

(5) "Same structural type" = (i) head or Spec and, in the latter class, (ii) A or A'

As for the notion of intervention, for the cases that will concern us more directly, the relevant concept is hierarchical intervention, defined in terms of c-command:

(6) Z intervenes between X and Y iff Z c-commands Y and Z does not c-command X.

If locality also applies to some processes not involving c-command, as is suggested below, intervention will be calculated in linear terms in such cases (see the discussion in section 3 below).

We will continue to express RM as a representational principle, a principle that must hold of chains at LF. For the purposes of this chapter, this can simply be considered the choice of a particular style of presentation, admitting a straightforward translation into a derivational style if need be. The rationale behind the choice of the representational style is the following. If there is LF, a level of representation through which the language faculty "talks to" other cognitive systems, chains must be expressed on this level for a structure to be interpretable. Ideally, chains should be easily "legible" on inspection of the LF representation: we would not want the external systems to have access to the derivational history of the representation (this is basically the conceptual argument given in Rizzi 1986, where an attempt is made to provide empirical evidence for this approach). A simple way to achieve this result is to give a definition of chain that can directly read chains off LF. Consider the following:

(7) (A_1, . . . A_n) is a chain iff, for $1 \leq i < n$
i. $A_i = A_{i+1}$.
ii. A_i c-commands A_{i+1}.
iii. A_{i+1} is in a MC with A_i.

So, a chain is defined by the following elementary syntactic properties:

1. Identity: each position is identical to any other position in internal structure. This is the copy theory of traces of Chomsky (1995) and subsequent work. Only the highest position in a chain is pronounced in the normal case, but all the positions have the same internal structure. Familiar reconstruction effects follow at once from this way of looking at traces. Following the formalism of Starke (1997), I will express traces as substructures within angled brackets.
2. Prominence, defined by c-command. I will assume for concreteness the definition of c-command given in Chomsky (2000).[2]
3. Locality, defined by the notion Minimal Configuration, as in principle (4).

(7) can be seen as an algorithm, identifying chains at LF. Whenever a sequence of positions meets identity, prominence, and locality at LF, it constitutes a chain. If one of the ingredients is not satisfied, the definition of chain is not met and, if a chain connection is needed for well-formedness, the structure is ruled out. So, as locality (MC) is not met in (3b), no chain connects the operator *how* to a variable, and the structure is ruled out as a violation of Full Interpretation.

3. Combining elementary relations

If identity, prominence, and locality are basic ingredients of syntactic computations, we expect them to show some degree of modular independence. Linguistically significant relations should exist, involving some but not all of these elements. In fact, this expectation appears to be fulfilled. We will now do the following exercise: we will freely combine two of the three ingredients that have been assumed to constitute chains, and we will try to determine if the combination expresses a significant linguistic relation.

A structural relation involving c-command and (some kind of) identity, but no locality, is pronominal binding: a pronoun can be bound by a quantified DP when the pronoun matches at least in part its featural makeup (whence the impossibility of (8d) in the bound interpretation of the pronoun) and c-command holds (whence the ungrammaticality of (8e)), but no locality is involved: no matter how deeply embedded the pronoun may be into islands, binding is fine, as in (8a, b, and c):[3]

(8) a. *No candidate* can predict how many people will vote for *him*.
b. *Every politician* is worried when the press starts attacking *him*.
c. *Which politician* appointed the journalist who supported *him*?
d. *Which politician thinks that we'll vote for them?
e. *The fact that *no candidate* was elected shows that *he* was inadequate.

A similar case is provided by languages that use a fully grammaticalized resumptive pronoun strategy in relative clauses (e.g., modern Hebrew) and in other A'-constructions (e.g., Left Dislocation of the English kind or Hanging Topic in the sense of Cinque

1990): the head of the relative or the Topic must c-command the matching pronoun, but no island sensitivity is shown. (Constructions apparently involving pronominal resumption but sensitive to locality, such as Romance Clitic Left Dislocation, are better analyzed as involving full traces alongside the pronoun, as in many current analyses, which correctly predicts full reconstruction effects in such constructions.)

A linguistic process apparently involving identity and locality, but not c-command, is Gapping. Koster (1978) observed that in cases like the following, with several conjoined clauses, the gapped verb can only be interpreted as identical to the closest overt verb (here *read*, not *sell*):

(9) John sells books, Mary buys records, and Bill V newspapers.

Koster interpreted this as a manifestation of locality, and the similarity with the basic RM configuration is striking. Identity is obviously involved but c-command is not: under standard structural assumptions, the string controlling gapping does not c-command the elided string.[4]

Other plausible cases involving locality and (feature) identity but no c-command can be found in phonology (I thank Morris Halle for useful discussion of this point). Consider, for instance, a process of assimilation in Sanskrit, according to which "a Coronal nasal assimilates the Coronal features from a retroflex consonant that precedes it. . . . The nasal can be arbitrarily far away from the retroflex, provided that no Coronal consonant intervenes" (Halle 1995: 22, based on work by D. Steriade).

(10) a. kṣobh-aṇ 'quake' c. kṣved-ana 'lament'
b. b kṛp-aṇa 'hum' d. kṛt-ana 'cut'

In (10c and d) the intervening coronals d and t block assimilation, even if they do not undergo the assimilation process, which is restricted to the nasals. So here an active intervener does not have to have the exact same featural makeup as the target of the process: sharing same superfeature, presumably the articulator in the phonological example, is sufficient. As we will see later on, this is exactly the kind of situation that is found in syntax: not individual features, but feature classes, defined by some appropriate feature hierarchy, trigger minimality effects. Thus, the parallel syntax-phonology in this case seems not to be superficial, which again argues for the width of the locality principle involved.

Another phonological phenomenon illustrating the point, taken again from Halle (1995), is Vowel copy in Ainu (based on work by J. Ito):

(11) tas-a 'cross' ray-e 'kill'
per-e 'tear' hew-e 'slant'
nik-i 'fold' ciw-e 'sting'
tom-o 'concentrate' poy-e 'mix'
yup-u 'tighten' tuy-e 'cut'

Certain morphemes are spelled out in this language as vowel suffixes whose quality is identical to that of the stem vowel, as in the lefthand column. But if a glide intervenes (defined by the same articulator, dorsal, according to the analysis adopted), vowel copying is blocked and the default vowel *e* is used (righthand column).

Do we also find genuine linguistic relations that involve c-command and locality but drop identity? I would like to suggest that this corresponds to head-XP-relations. Heads and phrases can interact locally for such processes as the licensing of inflectional features of the Case-agreement system and for the licensing of special elements, null pronominals, and so on. These processes clearly involve distinct elements, heads and phrases, and are local. The claim here is that no special local environment, distinct from what is given by the fundamental locality principle, must be defined to deal with this case: the possible interactions are limited by the ingredients we already have, c-command and the notion of Minimal Configuration expressing RM. Head-XP-interactions seem to be possible in three basic cases: Specifier/head, head/complement, and head/specifier-of-the-complement. The first case is, for example, nominative Case licensing. The second is, for instance, the licensing of an inherent Case by the theta-marking head, for example, partitive assignment, with consequences for the definiteness effect (Belletti 1988). The third is, for example, the relation of a Case-assigning complementizer to the subject:

(12) [For [John to do that]] would be a mistake.

Such relations apparently cannot go further than that: a head cannot reach a position higher than its specifier or lower than its complement's head (it cannot reach the complement of the complement, for instance). On the other hand, cases of a head influencing the properties of the specifier of its complement (for Case licensing or the licensing of null pronominals, on which see Roberts (1993)) are numerous and well documented. That a direct relation is established in cases like (12) is suggested by adjacency effects like the following:

(13) a. . . . that, tomorrow, John will do that
b. *For, tomorrow, John to do that would be a mistake.

(14) *[For [tomorrow X [John to do that]] would be a mistake.

An adverb, which can normally intervene between a C and the subject, as in (13a), cannot do so in this case. This is explained by the fundamental locality principle if the structure of (13b) must be something like (14), with X the head that licenses the adverb position in the left periphery (Rizzi 1997). Then, *for* cannot reach the subject because of the intervention of X.[5]

So, rather than postulating a special government relation for this case or a special computational process (covert movement, feature movement, a follow-up checking operation, etc.), we can simply assume that the elementary relations of c-command and locality combine here, giving the desired effect. Suppose that Head-XP-interactions for feature licensing (feature checking and/or feature valuing in the system of Chomsky 2000, 2001) are expressed in the following format:

(15) Feature K is licensed (checked, valued . . .) on (H, XP) only if
 i. XP is in a MC with H, and
 ii. c-command holds.

The feature in question may be a Case feature or a feature involved in the formal licensing of a special category, *pro* and the like. As the XP must be in a MC with X, we find that any intervening head would cause the relation to fail, so a head can act upon the specifier of its complement, but not the complement of its complement (or in cases like (13)), because locality, as expressed by (4), would be violated.[6]

The following table summarizes the free combination of identity, c-command, and locality, as well as the kinds of linguistically significant relations that are generated:

(16)

Chains:	Identity,	C-command,	Locality
Pronominal Binding:	Identity,	C-command	
Ellipsis:	Identity,		Locality
Head/XP interactions:		C-command,	Locality

4. Asymmetries in the A'-system involving the moved element

Going back to chains, we see that the system of Relativized Minimality, in its simplest form, predicts that a chain relation will systematically fail if a position of the same kind as the target position (in terms of the typology in (5)) intervenes. The empirical evidence shows that some anomalies arise that require certain refinements. In this chapter we will focus on A'-chains. Two major kinds of anomalies have emerged:

1. Not all elements moved to an A'-specifier are subjected to RM-effects: for instance, wh-phrases with special formal and interpretive properties (D-linking, specificity, etc.) are not.
2. Not all intervening A'-specifiers trigger a minimality effect on A'-chains: some finer typology is then needed.

Here we will only hint at the first class of anomalies, which will be mainly used as a kind of "signature" of the class of phenomena we are interested in, and then we will address the second class in detail.

The initial empirical observation pointing to the first kind of anomaly is due to Jim Huang, who observed that there is a sharp distinction between arguments and adjuncts in cases of extraction from a wh-Island:

(17) a. ?Which problem do you wonder how to solve <which problem> (Huang 1982)
 b. *How do you wonder which problem to solve <how>?

Arguments may be marginally extractable from indirect questions, depending on language-specific properties and on certain characteristics of the construction, but adjunct extraction is strongly and uniformly banned in this environment. In one form or another, the argument-adjunct asymmetry became the distinctive characteristics of a certain kind of island environments, the Weak Islands (as opposed to Strong Islands, blocking argument and adjunct extraction on a par; see Szabolcsi 1999 for recent discussion).

But the distinction is not simply between argumental and adverbial material. In languages in which a DP-specifier alone can be wh-moved, as for *combien* movement in French (see (18a and b)), we observe a similar asymmetry between extraction of the whole argument and of its specifier, as in (19a and b), a paradigm based on observations in Obenauer (1994):

(18) a. Combien de problèmes sais-tu résoudre ______?
'How many of problems can you solve?'
b. Combien sais-tu résoudre [______ de problèmes]?
'How many can you solve of problems?'

(19) a. ?Combien de problèmes sais-tu comment résoudre ______?
'How many of problems do you know how to solve?'
b. *Combien sais-tu comment résoudre [______ de problèmes]?
'How many do you know how to solve of problems?'

Adverbs and DP-specifiers are not the only elements that resist extraction from Weak Islands: predicats are not extractable either, as Baltin (1992) observed: consider the contrast between the extraction of the subject and the predicate of a small clause from the Weak Island in (21), taking movement from the declarative in (20) as the baseline:

(20) a. How many people do you consider ______ intelligent?
b. How intelligent do you consider John ______?

(21) a. ??How many people do you wonder whether I consider ______ intelligent?
b. *How intelligent do you wonder whether I consider John ______?

Finally, Cinque (1990) observed that not all arguments are extractable from Weak Islands: to be successfully extracted, arguments must have special interpretive properties, they must be specific, presupposed, or D(iscourse)-linked, in the sense of Pesetsky (1987), with the range of the variable preestablished in previous discourse (see also Comorowski 1989). The relevant interpretive properties are particularly clear with certain wh-elements, for example, *how much/many*. Consider for instance the following examples in Italian (see Rizzi 2001a for more detailed discussion):

(22) a. ?Quanti problemi non sai come risolvere ______?
'How many problems don't you know how to solve?'
b. *Quanti soldi non sai come guadagnare ______?
'How much money don't you know how to make?'

(22a) may well be a request of information on the cardinality of a certain set of problems that is identified in previous discourse, for example, the problems listed on page 39 of my son's textbook. In that interpretation, extraction is at least marginally possible. But it's harder to imagine a context in which (22b) may be a question about specific sums of money: wh-phrases like *how much money* normally do not involve any contextually preestablished sets of sums. So, unless very special contextual conditions are set up to make a specific interpretation plausible (we've been talking, e.g., about particular sums of money that may be needed for different purposes) extraction is banned in (22b). But if a specific interpretation is enforced, say, by an explicit partitive form, extraction becomes marginally possible again:

(23) ?Quanti dei soldi che ti servono non sai come guadagnare ______?
'How much of the money that you need don't you know how to make?'

In conclusion, the only wh-elements successfully extractable from an indirect question are arguments with special interpretive properties (specific, presupposed, D-linked).

5. Asymmetries involving the intervener

Different theoretical accounts of the selective extractability of arguments have been proposed in the literature (see Cinque 1990; Rizzi 1990, 2000, 2001a; Frampton 1991; Szabolcsi & Zwarts 1999 and references there; Starke 2001). I will not address here the intricacies of the argument/adjunct asymmetries and will focus on the restrictive case, the ban on non-argument extraction, leaving open the proper treatment of the relaxation of RM-effects with (certain kinds of) arguments. Whatever the exact analysis of the asymmetries, we will take the observed selectivity as a marker of RM-effects in the A'-system.

So, the fact that we observe analogous kinds of selectivity with types of interveners different from wh-operators suggests that the RM-effects generalize to other types of configurations. For instance, Obenauer (1983, 1994) observed that the DP/DP-Specifier asymmetry is also found in French across negation (as in (24), a case of the Negative Island Constraint of Ross 1983; see also Kuno & Takami 1997 and references there for other interpretations), and across quantificational adverbs like *beaucoup*, *peu* (as in (25)):

(24) a. Combien de problèmes ne sais-tu pas résoudre ______?
'How many of problems can't you solve?'
b. *Combien ne sais-tu pas résoudre [______ de problèmes]?
'How many can't you solve of problems?'

(25) a. Combien de livres a-t-il beaucoup consultés ______?
'How many of books has he a lot consulted?'
b. *Combien a-t-il beaucoup consulté ______ de livres?
'How many has he a lot consulted of books?'

c. Combien de films a-t-elle peu aimés ______?
'How many films did she little like?'
d. *Combien a-t-elle peu aimé [______ de films]?
'How many did she little like of films?'

Under the natural assumption that the negative adverb and quantificational adverbs, on a par with wh-elements, fill specifier positions in the clausal system, Obenauer's observation provided the empirical basis for the proposal that the typology of phrasal positions is determined by the A/A'-distinction: in particular, A'-specifiers determine minimality effects on A'-chains (Rizzi 1990).

An immediate problem for this idea is raised by the fact that only certain adverbs determine minimality effects. An adverb like *attentivement* ('carefully') does not (Obenauer 1994; Laenzlinger 1998):[7]

(26) a. Combien de livres a-t-il attentivement consultés ______?
'How many of books did he carefully consult?'
b. Combien a-t-il attentivement consulté [______ de livres]?
'How many did he carefully consult of books?'

One could try to account for the selectivity of the effect by making the assumption that some adverbs fill A'-specifiers, whereas while others are adjoined to the phrase they modify, so that only the former count as interveners in the relevant sense. The distinction between A'-specifiers and phrasal adjunction is very dubious on general grounds, however (Kayne 1994). Moreover, Cinque's (1999) detailed theory of adverbial positions is based on the assumption that adverbs sit in Spec positions of dedicated functional heads (an assumption that is substantiated by the convergence of the ordering of adverbs and of verbal particles and inflections with the corresponding interpretive properties); so, no simple solution to the asymmetry in (25) and (26) seems to be available in terms of elementary tree geometry.

Analogous conclusions for the insufficiency of the A/A'-distinction in this context is provided by the fact that an intervening left-dislocated phrase determines only a mild degradation on both argument and adjunct movement in Italian:

(27) a. ?Non so come pensi che, a Gianni, gli dovremmo parlare t
'I don't know how you think that, to Gianni, we should talk to him.'
b. ?Non so a chi pensi che, queste cose, le dovremmo dire t
'I don't know to whom you think that, these things, we should say them.'

The absence of any argument-adjunct asymmetry suggests that we are not in the realm of RM-effects, and the parallel mild deviance of both examples is due to some independent principle (say, a subjacency-like constraint). Now, it is plausible that the left-dislocated phrase occupies an A'-specifier position (Rizzi 1997), a conclusion that is enforced if we assume that natural languages do not allow phrasal adjunction (clearly, the dislocated phrase could not fill an A-specifier, as the locality characteristics of the construction are totally different from those of A-chains). So, again, a typology of positions simply based on the A/A'-distinction for RM effects would incorrectly predict a strong and selective deviance in the case of (27a).

Clearly, a more refined typology of positions is called for than the simple A/A'-distinction. In fact, in recent years a much more selective theoretical account of RM-effects has been proposed. Consider Chomsky's (1995: 311) Minimal Link Condition:

(28) Minimal Link Condition: K attracts a only if there is no b, b closer to K than a, such that K attracts b.

This principle is an attempt to capture the same intuition as RM within a fundamentally derivational system. It differs in implementation from the original RM-approach in at least three respects:

(29) a. It is built into a particular syntactic operation, Attract (or Agree, in the system of Chomsky 2000).
b. It operates in the course of derivations.
c. It characterizes the intervener as identical in featural makeup to the target.

As for the first point, the similarity of the syntactic effect with the locality effects observed in phonology, in ellipsis processes, and so on seems substantive enough to support the view that these effects follow from a general locality principle, cutting across specific operations and components of grammar. So, we will continue to assume that there is a single locality principle that is appealed to by the different modules that involve locality. As for the second point, we will continue to disregard the derivational/representational issue in this chapter (but see Rizzi 2001a for discussion). The third point is the crucial one here. Principle (28) is highly selective in the identification of possible interveners: an intervener is an intervening position with the same featural constitution as the target, as in (30a). So, in this system, a wh-island violation is excluded in that the higher C in (30b) cannot attract the wh-element in the embedded question across a wh-position in the embedded C-system:

(30) a. X Z Y
[+f] [+f] [+f]

b. C you wonder [which problem C [to solve how]]

This is selective enough to not run into problems with (26) and (27). The trouble is that this approach is too selective. As negation and quantificational adverbs clearly do not have the same featural make up as wh-elements (wh-elements are not attracted to the positions of negation or quantificational adverbs, nor vice-versa), the explanation of (24) and (25), hence the generalization uniting these cases with (19), is lost. In sum, what seems to be needed is a system more selective than the one based on the simple A/A'-distinction but less selective than the one based on feature identity.

To arrive at such a system, we can now enrich the empirical basis of the discussion by studying other RM-effects in the system of adverb syntax.

6. RM with adverbs

Koster (1978) observed that adverbs can't cross other adverbs in certain constructions in Dutch. First, adverbs are strictly ordered in the middle field; for example, evaluative adverbs are higher than epistemic adverbs in IP-internal, postsubject position:

(31) a. Het is zo dat hij helaas waarschijnlijk ziek is
'It is so that he unfortunately probably sick is'
b.*Het is zo dat hij waarschijnlijk helaas ziek is
'It is so that he probably unfortunately sick is'

Both evaluative and epistemic adverbs can be moved to the left periphery to satisfy the V-2 constraint, as in (32a and c), but if both adverbs are present, the lower adverb cannot move to the C-system crossing the higher adverb:

(32) a. Helaas is hij ______ waarschijnlijk ziek
'Unfortunately is he probably sick'
b.*Waarschijnlijk is hij helaas ______ ziek
'Probably is he unfortunately sick'
c. Waarschijnlijk is hij ______ ziek
'Probably is he sick'

This is very reminiscent of the RM-effect and, as pointed out by Cinque (1999), Koster's (1978) original analysis was in terms of a very similar principle.

The ban against crossing is not limited to V-2 languages. Consider the following cases in Italian: the celerative adverb *rapidamente* can be moved to the front, as in (33b), but not across a higher epistemic adverb, as in (33c).

(33) a. I tecnici hanno (probabilmente) risolto rapidamente il problema
'The technicians have probably resolved rapidly the problem.'
b. Rapidamente, i tecnici hanno risolto ______ il problema
'Rapidly, the technicians have resolved the problem.'
c.*Rapidamente, i tecnici hanno probabilmente risolto ______ il problema
'Rapidly, the technicians have probably resolved the problem.'
d. Probabilmente, I tecnici hanno ______ risolto rapidamente il problema
'Probably, the technicians rapidly resolved the problem.'

The same conclusion holds for an adverb like *improvvisamente*, which can move to the front but not across the higher frequentative adverb *spesso*:

(34) a. Gianni ha (spesso) improvvisamente cambiato opinione.
'Gianni has (often) suddely changed opinion.'

b. Improvvisamente, Gianni ha ______ cambiato opinione.
'Suddenly, Gianni has ______ changed opinion.'
c. *Improvvisamente, Gianni ha spesso ______ cambiato opinione.
'Suddenly, Gianni has often changed opinion.'
d. Spesso, Gianni ha ______ improvvisamente cambiato opinione.
'Often, Gianni has quickly changed opinion.'

These judgments are relatively delicate, in that by manipulating somewhat intonational properties and discourse conditions the "crossing" cases can become acceptable. So such factors should be carefully controlled for.

The next observation is about one such factor. The ban against adverb crossing is selective. Schlyter (1974) observed that, if simple preposing of an adverb across another adverb in French is excluded, as in the previous examples in Dutch and Italian (see (35b)), preposing of the adverb to a focus position, such as the cleft construction in (35b), can successfully cross another adverb (examples due to Christopher Laenzlinger):

(35) a. Jean s'est probablement dirigé calmement vers la sortie.
'Jean has probably moved quietly toward the exit.'
b. *Calmement, Jean s'est probablement dirigé vers la sortie.
'Calmly, Jean has probably moved toward the exit.'
c. C'est calmement que Jean s'est probablement dirigé vers la sortie.
'It is calmly that Jean has probably moved toward the exit.'

Cinque (1999) points out that the amelioration due to focalization is observed in a V-2 language like German, with the lower frequentative adverb able to move across the higher epistemic adverb if focused:

(36) SEHR OFT hat Karl Marie wahrscheinlich gesehen
'VERY OFTEN has Karl Marie seen'

The same effect is observed in Italian: the equivalent of (33c) becomes acceptable if the adverb is focused:

(37) RAPIDAMENTE i tecnici hanno probabilmente risolto il problema (non lentamente).
'RAPIDLY the technicians have probably solved the problem (not slowly).'

One additional piece of the puzzle is that focalization, instrumental to allow movement of the lower adverb across the higher adverb, is of no help with negation: whether the adverb is focused or not, movement across negation is banned. This is illustrated in Italian and French in the following examples:

(38) a. Rapidamente, i tecnici (*non) hanno risolto il problema.
'Rapidly, the technicians have (not) solved the problem.'
b. RAPIDAMENTE i tecnici (*non) hanno risolto il problema.
'RAPIDLY the technicians have (not) solved the problem.'

(39) a. *Calmement, Jean ne s'est pas dirigé vers la sortie.
'Calmly, Jean didn't move toward the exit.'
b. *C'est calmement que Jean ne s'est pas dirigé vers la sortie.
'It is calmly that Jean didn't move toward the exit.'

Finally, in special discourse contexts, the "no crossing effect" observed in (33) disappears completely in Italian, even in the absence of focalization. This happens when the adverb has been mentioned in the immediately preceding discourse, a state of affairs that naturally arises, say, when a previous statement is corrected with a contrastive focus on some other constituent different from the adverb:

(40) A: Credo che i tecnici abbiano rapidamente risolto entrambi i problemi.
'I believe that the technicians have rapidly solved both problems.
B: Ti sbagli: Rapidamente, i tecnici hanno probabilmente risolto IL PRIMO PROBLEMA, ma non il secondo, che era più difficile.
'You are wrong: rapidly, the technicians have probably solved the first problem, but not the second, which was more difficult.'

In this kind of context, with a recent mention of the preposed adverb, even negation ceases to have an adverse effect on adverb movement:

(41) Speravo proprio che potessero sbarazzarsi rapidamente di questo problema, ma devo dire che, rapidamente, non lo hanno risolto.
'I really hoped that they could rapidly get rid of this problem, but I must say that, rapidly, they didn't solve it.'

Let us summarize the different pieces of the puzzle identified so far:

(42) i. Only certain types of adverbs, quantificational adverbs, affect wh-movement of an adjunct: (25) and (26).
ii. All intervening adverbs block simple (nonfocal) preposing of an adverb to the left periphery: (32)–(34).
iii. This does not happen if the adverb targets a focus position: (35)–(37).
iv. Negation blocks both simple adverb preposing and preposing to a focus position: (38) and (39).
v. But if the adverb has been mentioned in the immediately preceding discourse context, neither another adverb nor negation block preposing: (40) and (41).

To try to deal with these effects, we must now make some assumptions on the structural positions that adverbs can occupy in the left periphery of the clause. One step in the direction of understanding what is going on is the realization that preposed adverbs may target different positions in the C-space. Thus we need a structured theory of the C-space. Let me then introduce some elements of the cartography of the left periphery.

7. The structure of the left periphery

In Rizzi (1997), the left periphery of the clause is seen as a structural zone defined by a system of functional heads and their projections, along the following lines:

(43) Force Top* Foc Top* Fin IP

The system is delimited upward by Force, the head expressing the clausal typing, the kind of information that must be readily accessible to an external selector, and downward by Finiteness, the head differentiating finite and nonfinite constructions. Romance and Germanic typically overtly express the Force head in finite clauses, as *che* in the Italian example (44a) (with Topics and Focus following the Force indicator), but they may also express Fin, arguably the position of prepositional complementizers in Romance, as in (44b) (with the Topic preceding it in the linear order):

(44) a. Credo che ieri QUESTO a Gianni avreste dovuto dirgli.
Force Top Foc Top Fin IP
'I believe that yesterday THIS to Gianni you should have said.'
b. Penso a Gianni, di dovergli parlare
Force Top Fin
'I think, to Gianni, to have to talk to him'

Celtic languages like Irish appear to normally express Fin in finite clauses as well, so that the complementizer *go* normally is preceded by other left-peripheral material, such as the preposed adverbial in (45) (I am following here the reinterpretation of the distributional evidence put forth in McCloskey 1996 in terms of the "fine structure" approach to the left periphery suggested by Shlonsky (personal communication), and Roberts (2004)):

(45) Is doíche [faoi cheann cúpla lá [*go* bhféadfaí imeacht]]
'Is probable at-the-end-of couple day that could leave'

As Roberts (2004) points out, Welsh appears to express both Force and Fin, so that left-peripheral material is sandwiched between the complementizer particles *mai* and *a*:

(46) Dywedais i [*mai* 'r dynion fel arfer *a* [werthith y ci]]
'Said I C the men as usual C will-sell the dog'

As for topic, focus, and other discourse-related left-peripheral positions, the assumption is that they are created by the usual structure-building mechanism, in fact the only structure-building mechanism that is assumed: there are special functional heads of Topic and Focus that give rise to their own projections and whose Specs are positions dedicated to topical or focal interpretation.

In some languages the Top and Foc heads are overt: this is, for instance, a plausible analysis of the topic and focus particles *ya* and *we* in Gungbe, according to Aboh (1998):

(47) . . . do Kofi *ya* gankpa me *we* kponon le su I do
'. . . that Kofi Top PRISON IN Foc policemen Pl shut him there'

We may assume that other languages use analogous structures with null heads, thus differing from Gungbe and similar languages in the morphological manifestation of a fundamentally uniform syntactic system, a reasoning reminiscent of what is stardardly assumed in Case Theory ever since Vergnaud (1982).[8]

8. The positions of adverbs in the left periphery of the clause

What positions do left-peripheral adverbs occupy? In Rizzi (1997) it was assumed that they normally fill regular topic positions, which can proliferate quite freely in Romance (as many topics are possible as there are topicalizable elements). This hypothesis has some initial appeal in that the intonational contour of preposed adverbs is very similar to the topic intonation (the phrase is separated from the rest of the structure by "comma intonation"). Nevertheless, the assumption that preposed adverbials may be full-fledged topics is not very plausible on interpretive grounds. If the notional interpretation of a topic is "as for X (which is already present in the discourse context), I'm telling you that Y" ("As for your book, I'm telling you that I'll buy it tomorrow"), a sentence with a preposed adverb ("Quickly, John left the room") does not seem to be felicitously paraphrasable in such terms ("As for quick events . . . "). A straightforward way to highlight the difference between topics and preposed adverbs is the following: in Italian, a sentence with a topic (expressed here via the Clitic Left Dislocation construction) is not felicitous in out-of-the-blue (or "what happened?") contexts, whereas a preposed adverb is fine in such contexts:

(48) A: Che cosa è successo?
'What happened?'
B: La polizia stradale ha fermato l'autobus per Roma.
'The road police stopped the bus to Rome.'
B': L'autobus per Roma è stato fermato dalla polizia stradale.
'The bus to Rome was stopped by the road police.'
C: #L'autobus per Roma, la polizia stradale lo ha fermato.
'The bus to Rome, the road police stopped it.'
C': #L'autobus per Roma, lo ha fermato la polizia stradale.
'The bus to Rome, stopped it the road police.'
D: Improvvisamente, la polizia stradale ha fermato l'autobus per Roma.
'Suddenly, the road police stopped the bus to Rome.'
D': Improvvisamente, l'autobus per Roma è stato fermato dalla polizia stradale.
'Suddenly, the bus to Rome was stopped by the road police.'

Such contexts are compatible with both active and passive sentences (B) but not with topics expressed in the Clitic Left-Dislocation construction (C) (whether the subject is preverbal or postverbal), while a preposed adverbial is fine (D), both in active and passive. A preposed adverb seems to have something in common with a topic, the fact of being made prominent by movement to the left periphery, but it does not share with the topic the necessary connection to the background, whence its compatibility with "what happened" contexts.[9]

Distributional properties also suggest that preposed adverbs normally fill positions distinct from topic positions. On the one hand, preposed adverbs clearly can move to the left periphery, as they can precede bona fide left-peripheral material, such as a left-dislocated phrases (cf. also the fact that the preposed adverbial satisfies the V-2 constraint in Germanic examples such as (32), plausibly a property involving the C system):

(49) Rapidamente, i libri, li hanno rimessi a posto
'Quickly, the books, they put them to place'

But preposed adverbials, contrary to genuine topics (as in (50c), and (51c)), cannot naturally precede wh-elements in questions:

(50) a. Improvvisamente, Gianni è tornato a casa.
'Suddenly, Gianni went home.'
b. ?? Improvvisamente, chi è tornato a casa?
'Suddenly, who went home?'
c. Il mio libro, chi lo ha preso?
'My book, who took it?'

(51) a. Rapidamente, hanno fatto i compiti.
'Quickly, they did the homework.'
b. ??Rapidamente, che cosa hanno fatto?
'Quickly, what did they do?'
c. A Gianni, che cosa gli hanno fatto?
'To Gianni, what did they do to him?'

Evidently, there is a dedicated position for preposed adverbials, which contrary to (certain) Topic positions, is necessarily lower than the position filled by the wh-elements in (50) and (51). Preposed adverbials can't naturally occur in a position lower than the wh-element either, a property plausibly related to the obligatory adjacency between the wh-element and the inflected verb, whatever its ultimate theoretical status (see different chapters in Rizzi 2000 and much related work):

(52) *Che cosa, rapidamente, hanno fatto?
'What, rapidly, did they do?'

A particularly clear indication of the peculiar distributional properties of preposed adverbs emerges with wh-elements not requiring inversion, such as *perché* in Italian

(Rizzi 2001a): the preposed adverb can follow but cannot precede *perché*, whereas a topic can occur in both positions:

(53) a. Perché, improvvisamente, Gianni è tornato a casa?
'Why, suddenly, Gianni went home?
b.*Improvvisamente, perché Gianni è tornato a casa?
'Suddenly, why Gianni went home?

(54) a. Perché, il mio libro, Gianni lo ha portato via?
'Why, my book, Gianni took it away?'
b. Il mio libro, perché Gianni lo ha portato via?
'My book, why Gianni took it away?

Again, the judgment on the deviance of cases like (51b) is delicate. Such examples can improve to full acceptability in special contextual circumstances, that is, if the adverb has been mentioned in the immediately preceding discourse:

(55) Gianni mi ha detto che hanno fatto alcune cose lentamente e altre rapidamente. Ora, io vorrei sapere: rapidamente, che cosa hanno fatto?
'Gianni told me that they did some things slowly and others quickly. Now, I would like to know: quickly, what did they do?'

A natural interpretation of this state of affairs is the following. Only referential nominal expressions are natural topics; adverbs are not, so they cannot naturally occupy topic positions. In normal discourse conditions, they can acquire salience only by being preposed to special, dedicated adverbial positions in the left periphery, which have the distributional properties we have described. But even elements that are not natural topics can become topics in special contextual conditions, that is, when they have been mentioned in the immediately previous discourse. Under such conditions, a preposed adverbial can legitimately occupy a topic position, including the high (pre-operator) position of (51b). Notice that the special discourse conditions licensing a preposed adverb in topic position are the same under which the preposed adverbs seem to be insensitive to the stringent locality conditions constraining adverbial syntax (cf. (40) and (41)). Anticipating the discussion in the next sections, we can now see what the solution of this puzzle can be: under the special discourse conditions that license adverbs in topic positions, preposed adverbs will manifest the very loose locality conditions constraining topic movement rather than the rigid conditions proper of adverb movement.

Before reassessing the issue of locality on the basis of the new findings, let us conclude this section by observing two additional syntactic differences between topics and simple preposed adverbs. One is that topics often determine island effects on (at least certain types of) A'-movement, whereas preposed adverbs do not. The effect induced by an intervening left-dislocated phrase on the movement of a relative pronoun is very weak in Italian, but there is no detectable effect at all with an intervening preposed adverb:

(56) a. ? Questo è il libro che, a Gianni, gli hanno portato ieri.
'This is the book that, to Gianni, they brought to him yesterday.'
b. Questo è il libro che, ieri, hanno portato a Gianni.
'This is the book that, yesterday, they brought to Gianni.'
c. Questa è la proposta che, rapidamente, tutti i deputati hanno accettato.
'This is the proposal that, quickly, all the representatives have accepted.'

The difference may be sharper in other languages. A particularly sharp contrast between a topic and a preposed adverb is found in English in cases of subject extraction. If subject extraction takes place across a preposed adverb, a clear improvement of the that-t violation is detected, as in (57b), an "antiadjacency" effect (on which see Rizzi 1997 and references there). If a topic intervenes, no detectable improvement is observed, as in (57c):

(57) a. *This is the man who I think that t will buy your house next year
b. This is the man who I think that, next year, t will buy your house
c. *This is the man who I think that, your house, t will buy next year
d. This is the man who I think that, frequently, t takes his holidays abroad

In conclusion, preposed adverbs can occupy at least three distinct structural positions in the left periphery. Normally, they occupy a dedicated position that is intonationally similar to a topic position but differs from it in that the adverb position does not require a connection with the previous discourse context, it cannot naturally precede wh-operators, it does not give rise to any island effect, and it gives rise to antiadjacency effects.[10] In very special discourse contexts, that is, when they have been mentioned in the immediately preceding discourse, preposed adverbs can also be moved to a genuine topic position, with the familiar characteristics of ordinary topics (e.g., can precede wh-operators). And on top of these two options, adverbial elements can also be moved to the initial focus position [see (35), (36), (37), etc.]; in this case they behave as any other element moved to the left-peripheral focus (contrastive interpretation, uniqueness, etc.; see Rizzi 1997 for discussion).

9. Revised theory

We can now go back to the structure of the left periphery and integrate into our fine structural representation the position targeted by simple (nonfocal and nontopic) adverb preposing. Following the usual restrictive theory of syntactic positions, we assume that a phrasal slot can only arise as the Spec of a head that is licensing the position. As the left-peripheral position targeted by the adverb in simple preposing is neither topic nor focus, we need a third type of licensing head in the space sandwiched between Force and Fin (with the observed distributional properties). I will call this head "Mod(ifier)", assuming modification to be the substantive relation between an adverb and the structure it relates to. We assume Cinque's (1999) analysis of adverbial positions: each adverb is licensed in the Spec of a dedicated head, occurring in a given position of a universal hierarchy; so, a frequentative adverb occurs as modifier in the Spec of a dedicated frequentative head, for example. On top of the whole hierarchy, we assume that the left periphery can contain dedicated Mod heads that can host adverbs as their specifiers; the functional motivation for such heads is that they make the moved adverb prominent, a property that left-peripheral Mod has in common with Top; it differs from Top, though, in not requiring a connection to the discourse context, and from Foc in not requiring the contrastive focal interpretation proper of the left-peripheral Foc position in Romance (see Rizzi 1997; of course the adverb can also move to the Spec of Foc; in that case it will receive the interpretation and intonational contour of a contrastive focus, as in (37)).

So, a frequentative adverb can either remain in the Spec of its licensing IP-internal Mod head or move to the Spec of the left-peripheral Mod head, thus acquiring structural prominence. The alternation is somehow akin to the one available for a deep object in a passive structure in a Null Subject language: it may remain in its thematic position VP-internally (with the EPP presumably fulfilled by *pro*) or acquire structural prominence by moving to the IP-initial preverbal subject position. So, (58a) is to (58b) what (59a) is to (59b):

(58) a. E' stato dato un premio al presidente
'Was given a prize to the president'
b. Un premio è stato dato al presidente.
'A prize was given to the president.'

(59) a. Gianni è improvvisamente tornato a casa.
'Gianni has suddenly come back home.'
b. Improvvisamente, Gianni è tornato a casa.
'Suddenly, Gianni has come back home.'

In the terms of the system of Chomsky (2000), we may think that the relevant heads are endowed with an EPP-feature, triggering the creation of a specifier and the attraction of an element (with which the relevant head has established an "agree" relation). We may now think that the interpretive import of an EPP-feature is to make the element moved to the newly created specifier "prominent," "salient," "figure" (as opposed to "ground," or whatever the right concept distinguishing a and b will turn out to be).

Going back to the position of left-peripheral Mod, we have seen that it is lower than the operator zone that includes different types of wh-operators. If this zone is (or starts at) the Focus layer, we end up with the following fine structure of the C system (Int is the position in which higher wh-elements such as *perché* in Italian can occur; see Rizzi 2001a for motivation).

(60) Force Top* Int Top* Focus Mod* Top* Fin IP

At this point, we can go back to the classification of the structural positions, in view of improving on the definition of "same structural type" for locality. We focus on phrasal chains. Under binary branching, and the assumption that there is no phrasal adjunction, the only possible interveners in a phrasal chain are specifiers. Following standard practice, we continue to assume that specifiers are licensed by the substantive featural content of their heads (possibly through the mediation of the EPP-feature, a kind of meta-feature formally licensing specifiers, as in Chomsky 2000, 2001). So, the typology of specifiers is the typology of the licensing substantive features. Consider the following typology:

(61) i. Argumental: person, number, gender, case
ii. Quantificational: Wh, Neg, measure, focus . . .
iii. Modifier: evaluative, epistemic, Neg, frequentative, celerative, measure, manner, ...
iv. Topic

The argumental features of (61a) are the traditional Phi features: they define the positions relevant for the argumental system, A-positions in the standard terminology. It is entirely conceivable that this class will require finer distinctions, but for the purposes of this chapter we can stick to the traditional assumption that there is a unitary class of A-positions. On the other hand, we have seen that there are good reasons to split the class of A'-positions into subclasses. First, we want to isolate the features characterizing quantificational specifiers, as in (61ii): the features licensing interrogative and negative operators and, within the class of adverbials, the features licensing measure or amount adverbials such as French *beaucoup*. Second, following much work in syntax and semantics, we consider Focus a form of quantification (Rooth 1992; Rizzi 1997 and references there). Third, under the label "modifier" we include in (61iii) all the features licensing adverbs, that is, the whole of Cinque's (1999) hierarchy, and the dedicated Mod positions in the left periphery that make adverbs "prominent." Notice that there is a certain amount of cross-classification between the quantificational and the modifier class: quantificational adverbs and, I assume, negation belong to both classes. The assumption that negation is modificational is supported by the observation that in many languages negation is expressed by a special adverbial element (e.g., French *pas*). Topics seem to belong to none of the previous classes. They are not argumental (topic chains have none of the locality properties of argumental chains) or quantificational (topic and focus sharply differ with respect to the syntactic tests for quantificational elements; Rizzi 1997) or modificational. So, we assume a distinct class including topic constructions, such as Clitic Left-Dislocation in Romance. The typology in (61) then amounts to splitting the class of A'-positions into three classes: quantificational, modifier, and topic. We can now revise the definition of "same structural type" for phrasal chains in the obvious way:

(62) "Same structural type" = Spec licensed by features of same class in (61).

So, under (62), RM-effects are expected to arise within the same feature class but not across classes, much as in the phonological examples (10) and (11).

10. Consequences

We can now account for all the selective minimality effects observed in the previous sections. Let us consider the different generalizations summarized in (42), repeated here for convenience:

(42) i. Only certain types of adverbs, quantificational adverbs, affect wh-movement of an adjunct: (25) and (26).

Adverbs like *beaucoup* belong to both the modifier class and the quantificational class. As such, they trigger minimality effects in adjunct wh-chains, a kind of quantificational chain. Pure modificational adverbs like *attentivement* belong uniquely to the Mod class, so they do not have comparable effects on quantificational chains.

(42) ii. All intervening adverbs block simple nonfocal preposing of an adverb to the left periphery: (32)–(34).

Simple adverb preposing targets the dedicated Mod position in the left periphery. Any other Mod position, that is, any other adverbial position intervening in the path gives rise to a RM-effect.

(42) iii. This does not happen if the adverb targets a focus position: (35)–(37).

In cases of this sort, the adverb does not target Mod but rather the ordinary focus position. Therefore, the intervention of an adverbial position is not relevant to block the focus chain, a quantificational chain. Schlyter's (1974) observation is thus explained.

(42) iv. Negation blocks both simple adverb preposing and preposing to a focus position: (38) and (39).

Negation belongs to both the quantificational class and the Modifier class. So, it blocks both simple preposing (a Mod chain) and preposing to focus (a quantificational chain).

(42) v. But if the adverb has been mentioned in the immediately preceding discourse context, neither another adverb nor negation blocks preposing: (40) and (41).

In fact, in this special kind of context, the adverb can be extracted across negation, (63a); across a higher adverb, (63b); across a wh-island, (63c); across a contrastive focus, (63d):

(63) Tutti speravano che il primo problema si potesse risolvere rapidamente, ma . . .
'Everybody hoped that the first problem would be solved rapidly, but . . .

a. Rapidamente, non lo abbiamo risolto.
'Rapidly, we didn't solve it.'

b. Rapidamente, probabilmente non si può risolvere.
'Rapidly, probably one cannot solve it.'

c. Rapidamente, mi chiedo chi lo possa risolvere.
'Rapidly, I wonder who could solve it.'

d. Rapidamente, SOLO UN GENIO lo potrebbe risolvere.
'Rapidly, ONLY A GENIUS could solve it.'

Remember that we observed before that in this special context the preposed adverb shows a freer distribution than in simple preposing: it can, in fact, occupy ordinary topic positions (cf. (55)). My interpretation was that an adverbial is not a natural topic, so it cannot freely occupy topic positions, but it can function as a topic in case of mention in the immediately preceding discourse. This straightforwardly accounts for the lack of minimality effects in (63): as in this context the adverb can legitimately target a topic position, neither a quantificational nor a modificational element will give rise to a RM-effect.

11. Topics are special

If topics form a separate class from other A'-dependencies, we predict that we will not find locality interactions with other types of A'-dependencies. Example (63) shows that this is correct in one sense. We have already seen before that the lack of minimality interactions is also observed in the other sense: topics also do not act as interveners on other kinds of A'-dependencies. The relevant paradigm is reproduced here:

(64) a. ?Non so a chi pensi che, tuo fratello, lo potremmo affidare
'I don't know to whom you think that, your brother, we could entrust'

b. ?Non so come pensi che, tuo fratello, lo potremmo convincere
'I don't know how you think that, your brother, we could convince him'

Wh-extraction across a topic is slightly degraded in Italian (more severely in other languages) but with no manifestation of the argument/adjunct asymmetry that we have taken to be the earmark of RM-effects.

If topics form an autonomous class on a par with the other types of chain dependencies, as scheme (61) suggests, we would expect intervening topics to give rise to minimality effects on topic chains. The prediction is not borne out, though. The following examples show that adverbial topics of different kinds appear to be freely extractable across other topics in Italian:

(65) a. Rapidamente, penso che, questo problema, non lo possiate risolvere.
'Rapidly, I think that, this problem, you could not solve it.

b. In questo modo, credo che, il problema, lo risolverete senz'altro.
'In this way, I believe that the problem, you will solve it for sure.

c. In questo modo, credo che, senza troppe difficoltà, potreste risolvere il problema.
'In this way, I believe that, without too many difficulties, you could solve the problem.'

d. L'anno prossimo, penso che, le elezioni, le vincerà un altro candidato.
'Next year, I think that, the elections, another candidate will win them.'

Let us then briefly explore possible ways of addressing these special properties of topics. One possibility would be to relate the lack of minimality effects to the recursion of topics. Remember that in Italian (and, more generally, in Romance) it is possible to have any number of topics per clause:

(66) L'anno prossimo, in questo modo, le elezioni, senza troppe difficoltà, a Gianni, potreste fargliele vincere
'Next year, in this way, the elections, without trouble, (to) Gianni, you could make (to) him win them'

So, it is conceivable that, on its way to a higher topic position, a moving topic may find an intermediate landing site close enough to the intervening topic to circumvent the minimality effect via some notion of "equidistance," in the sense of Chomsky (1993, 1995).[11] This approach would predict that if a language lacks the possibility of allowing multiple topics per clause, then in this language intervening topics should give rise to minimality effects because no topic escape hatch could be provided through equidistance. For the moment, I am unable to find a fully convincing case to test this prediction.

There is a second, and more radical, way of interpreting the special character of topics. If we think of the members of the first three classes of (61) as positively specified with respect to at least one of the defining features (± Arg, ± Mod, ± Q), we may think of topics as defined in a purely negative way with respect to this system: topics are elements that are neither argumental, nor quantificational, nor modificational. This does not mean that topics have no properties at all; they certainly are defined by a number of interpretive properties, some of which (e.g., the connection to the discourse context) we have referred to in the previous discussion. But it could be that topics have none of the properties expressed by the feature system that identifies major position types, which RM is sensitive to: that is, they belong neither to the system of arguments, nor of quantification, nor of adverbial modification. In this case, if RM-effects are triggered by "sameness" of structural type, expressed by a positive feature specification, topics would be correctly excluded from the system of positions that exhibits RM-effects.

12. Conclusions

Core linguistic relations are local in the sense that they must be satisfied in the smallest structural environment in which they can be satisfied. So, local relations between two elements are blocked if a third element intervenes and this element has the potential of participating in the relevant relation. This is the core idea of Relativized Minimality. To implement it, we must identify the empirically correct notion of "sameness" of positions. Strict identity of featural specification seems to give rise to a system that is too liberal, one in which it is not possible to capture a variety of plausible minimality effects involving featurally distinct positions (negation and wh, for instance). On the opposite side of the spectrum, the classical typology in terms of the A/A'-distinction is too strict, as we have observed several cases in which an A'-chain can freely cross another

A'-specifier (wh can cross a nonquantificational adverb; various types of A'-chains can cross a topic). So, the theory of locality needs a precise typology of structural positions. In the A'-system, the cartographic approach is instrumental in building such a typology. It provides direct evidence for differentiating the left-peripheral positions of topics, focus (and other operators), and the dedicated positions of left-peripheral adverbials. This positional system is amenable to a typology of few featurally defined natural classes: argumental, quantificational, and modificational elements. Relativized minimality effects are found within the same featural class but not across classes (a quantificational specifier acts as an intervener on a quantificational chain, but a pure modificational specifier does not; etc.). This accounts for the very selective locality patterns that have been uncovered in the domain of adverbial syntax. Topics appear to fall outside the observed typology. Topic chains are not affected by other A'-specifiers, and topics do not act as interveners in other A'-chains. This may be a consequence of "equidistance" in systems that allow multiple topics or, perhaps, of a more radical difference between topics and the other types of A'-specifiers.

Notes

1. See Rizzi (1990) for the original representational formulation, and Chomsky (1995, 2000) for derivational formulations in terms of the Minimal Link Condition operating on Attract, or locality operating on Agree. On certain differences between these approaches, see below. The present chapter refines and extends the approach in Rizzi (2001c).

2. A c-commands B iff B is contained in the sister of A.

3. The identity requirement is restricted here to identity of Phi features. As there is no full identity, we do not have reconstruction effects in this case.

4. Notice that some configurational condition is at play; otherwise any linearly intervening verb would incorrectly block gapping:

(i) John wants to sell books, and Bill V to buy newspapers

Here *sell*, linearly intervening between *wants* and V, does not block gapping. Intuitively, this is so because *sell* is not itself in a position that could control gapping, presumably because the parallelism requirement is not met (see Fox 2000 for discussion of this requirement in other contexts). The formulation of intervention here cannot be expressed in terms of c-command, and it seems to require a sharper formulation of (4), according to which the intervener must structurally qualify as a potential participant in the process for which MC is calculated. We will omit this refinement here.

5. In the reference quoted, the English example is compared to an infinitival construction introduced by a prepositional complementizer in West Flemish (Haegeman 1986), but in which the subject of the infinitive is not Case-dependent on the complementizer as it presumably receives Case IP-internally. In this construction, adverb interpolation is possible, as predicted:

(i) Mee (?gisteren) zie nie te kommen . . .
'With yesterday she not to come . . .

A more minimal pair is provided by Brazilian Portuguese (Figueiredo 1996; Mioto 1999): the subject of the infinitive may receive IP-internal nominative Case or accusative assigned by the prepositional complementizer; only in the latter case is adverb interpolation forbidden:

(ii) a. Ela me deu o livro pra (amanha) eu ler
'She gave me the book for tomorrow I to read'

b. Ela me deu o livro pra (*amanha) mim ler
'She gave me the book for tomorrow me to read'

6. Here we leave the direction of c-command unspecified: if XP asymmetrically c-commands H, we have the Spec-head relation; if symmetric c-command holds, we have the head-complement relation; if the head asymmetrically c-commands the XP, we have the head/Specifier of the complement relation. A specific feature in a particular language may take a specific value of c-command: for instance, *pro* in Italian must asymmetrically c-command the licensing head, whereas *pro* in Old French must be asymmetrically c-commanded by the licensing head; hence a null subject is only possible in, for example, post-V-2 environments. This amounts, in essence, to the parametrization introduced in Koopman and Sportiche (1991) between agreement and government configuration for feature licensing, on which see also Roberts (1993). The parametrization is straightforwardly introduced in format (15) by imposing a particular direction in the C-command relation between H and XP for particular instances of K in particular languages. Notice that a head can enter into a direct relation with the specifier of its complement but not with the specifier of its specifier because of the violation of the c-command requirement (a head does not c-command the Spec of its Spec or vice versa). This appears to be correct: there is exceptional Case marking with object sentences but not with subject sentences; that is, a nominative assigning inflection cannot assign nominative Case to the subject of its sentential subject.

7. M. Starke (personal communication) also observes that examples like (26b) are degraded to some extent, which suggests that some kind of RM-effect may be operative in this case, too; in the remainder of this discussion I will continue to assume that the fundamental fact to explain is the relatively more severe degradation observed in cases like (25), along the lines of Obenauer (1994) and Laenzlinger (1998). See Starke (2001) for discussion of this issue.

8. The topic construction in Gungbe may be closer to Romance Hanging Topic than Clitic Left Dislocation (Cinque 1990), a point that does not affect the basic argument in the text.

9. Sentences like C become possible when the topic is given in context; the sentence sounds slightly redundant if the topic is the only element given in context (in this case, the most natural answer is to simply pronominalize the element):

(i) A: Che cosa è successo all'autobus per Roma?
'What happened to the bus to Rome?
B: L'autobus per Roma, lo ha fermato la polizia stradale
'The bus to Rome, stopped it the road police'

They become fully natural if the set of contextually given elements offers a choice, so that the mention of the topic is nonredundant:

(ii) A: Che cosa è successo all'autobus per Roma e a quello per Milano?
'What happened to the bus to Rome and to the one to Milan?'
B: Io so solo che, l'autobus per Roma, lo ha fermato la polizia stradale
'I only know that, the bus to Rome, stopped it the road police'

The felicitous character of sentences with preverbal subjects in "what happened" contexts, as in (B) and (D), as opposed to the Clitic Left-Dislocation construction (C), argues against a (complete) assimilation of preverbal subjects and topics, an assimilation often proposed for Null Subject Languages. So, if Clitic Left-dislocated phrases properly express Topics, the interpretive distinction between an active and a passive sentence (as in (B) and (B')) is not to be expressed in terms of the "topicality" of the logical object. Some finer distinction is needed.

10. Another important property distinguishing simple adverb preposing from movement to a topic position is that the former is clause bound:

(i) a. Rapidamente, (*Gianni dice che) hanno risolto il problema
'Rapidly, (Gianni says that) they solved the problem'
b. Il problema, (Gianni dice che) lo hanno risolto rapidamente
'The problem, (Gianni says that) they solved it rapidly'

Again, the long-distance construal of the adverb becomes possible if a context is set up so that "rapidly" has been mentioned in the immediately preceding discourse:

(ii) a. C'e qualche problema che hanno risolto rapidamente?
'Is there a problem that they solved rapidly?'
b. Rapidamente, Gianni dice che hanno risolto il primo problema, ma non gli altri
'Rapidly, Gianni says that they solved the first problem, but not the others.'

I will not address the issue of clause boundedness here. Let us simply note that perhaps any (overt or covert) element of the Cinque hierarchy occurring in the higher clause would determine a minimality effect on the chain of the extracted adverb.

11. This would be expressible in a particularly straightforward way if different topics could attach as specifiers to a single Top head: then, all the specifiers dependent of the same head could be assumed to count as "equidistant" with respect to a higher probe.

References

Aboh, E. (1998). From the Syntax of Gungbe to the Grammar of Gbe. Ph.D. diss., University of Geneva.

Baltin, M., & C. Collins, eds. (2001). *A Handbook of Syntactic Theory*. Oxford: Blackwell.

Baltin, M. (1992). "On the Characterisation and Effects of D-linking: Comments on Cinque." In R. Freidin, ed., *Current Issues in Comparative Grammar*. Dordrecht: Kluwer, 249–256.

Belletti, A. (1988). "The Case of Unaccusatives." *Linguistic Inquiry* 19, 1–34.

Chomsky, N. (1995). *The Minimalist Program*. Cambridge, Mass.: MIT Press.

Chomsky, N. (2000). "Minimalist Inquiries: The Framework". In R. Martin D. Michaels & J. Uriagereka, eds., *Step by Step—Essays in Minimalist Syntax in Honor of Howard Lasnik*, MIT Press, Cambridge, Mass., 89–155.

Chomsky, N. (2001). "Derivation by Phase". In M. Kenstowicz, ed., *Ken Hale: A Life in Language*, MIT Press, Cambridge, Mass., 1–52.

Cinque, G. (1990). *Types of A' Dependencies*. Cambridge, Mass.: MIT Press.

Cinque, G. (1999). *Adverbs and Functional Heads: A Cross-linguistic Perspective*. New York: Oxford University Press.

Cinque, G. ed. (2002). *The structure of IP and DP—The Cartography of Syntactic Structures*, Vol. 1, New York: Oxford University Press.

Comorowski, I. (1989). "Discourse-linking and the Wh Island Constraint." Proceedings of NELS 19, GLSA, University of Massachusetts, Amherst.

Figueiredo, C. (1996). *La position sujet en Portugais Brésilien*. Campinas, Brazil: Editora da Unicamp.

Fox, D. (2000). *Economy and Semantic Interpretation*. Cambridge, Mass.: MIT Press.

Frampton, J. (1991). "Relativized Minimality: A Review." *Linguistic Review* 8, 1–46.

Haegeman, L. (1986) 'INFL, COMP and Nominative Case Assignment in Flemish Infinitivals', in H. van Riemsdijk & P. Muysken (eds.) *Features and Projections*, Dordrecht: Foris, 23–137.

Haegeman, L. (1993). "Some Speculations on Argument Shift, Clitics and Crossing in West Flemish." In W. Abraham & J. Bayer, eds., *Dialektsyntax*. Opladen: Westdeutscher Verlag, 131–160.

Halle, M. (1995). "Feature Geometry and Feature Spreading." *Linguistic Inquiry* 26, 1–46.

Huang, J. (1982). Logical Relations in Chinese and the Theory of Grammar. Ph.D. diss., Massachusetts Institute of Technology, Cambridge.

Kayne, R. (1984). *Connectedness and Binary Branching*. Dordrecht: Foris.

Kayne, R. (1994). *The Antisymmetry of Syntax*. Cambridge, Mass.: MIT Press.

Koopman, H., & D. Sportiche. (1991). "The Position of Subjects." *Lingua* 85 (2/3).

Koster, J. (1978). *Locality Principles in Syntax*. Dordrecht: Foris.

Kuno, S., & K. Takami. (1997). "Remarks on Negative Islands." *Linguistic Inquiry* 28, 553–576.

Laenzlinger, C. (1998). *Comparative Studies in Word Order Variations: Adverbs, Pronouns and Clause Structure in Romance and Germanic*. Amsterdam and New York: John Benjamins.

McCloskey, J. (1996) "On the Scope of Verb Movement in Irish", *Natural Language and Linguistic Theory* 14: 47–104.

Mioto, C. (1999). "A periferia esquerda no português brasileiro." Ms., Universidade Federal de Santa Catarina, University of Siena.

Obenauer, H. (1983). "On the Identification of Empty Categories." *Linguistic Review* 4, 153–202.

Obenauer, H. (1994). Aspects de la syntaxe A-barre. Ph.D. diss., University of Paris VIII.

Pesetsky, D. (1987). "Wh in Situ: Movement and Unselective Binding." In E. Reuland, & A. Ter Meulen, eds., *The Representation of (In)definiteness*. Cambridge, Mass.: MIT Press.

Pollock, J.-Y. (1989). "Verb Movement, Universal Grammar and the Structure of IP." *Linguistic Inquiry* 20, 365–424.

Rizzi, L. (1986). "On Chain Formation." In H. Borer, ed., *The Grammar of Pronominal Clitics, Syntax and Semantics n. 19*, New York: Academic Press.

Rizzi, L. (1990). *Relativized Minimality*. Cambridge, Mass.: MIT Press.

Rizzi, L. (1997). "The Fine Structure of the Left Periphery." In L. Haegeman, ed., *Elements of Grammar*. Dordrecht: Kluwer.

Rizzi, L. (2000). *Comparative Syntax and Language Acquisition*. London: Routledge.

Rizzi, L. (2001a). Extraction from Weak Islands, Reconstruction, and Agreement. Ms., University of Siena.

Rizzi, L. (2001b). "On the Position Int(errogative) in the Left Periphery of the Clause." In G. Cinque & G. P. Salvi, eds., *Current Studies in Italian Syntax. Essays Offered to Lorenzo Renzi*. North Holland, Elsevier, Oxford.

Rizzi, L. (2001c) "Relativized Minimality Effects." In Baltin & Collins (2001).

Rizzi, L. ed. (2004). *The Structure of CP and IP—The Cartography of Syntactic Structures*, vol. 2, Oxford University Press, New York.

Roberts, I. (1993). *Verbs and Diachronic Syntax. A Comparative History of English and French*. Dordrecht: Kluwer.

Roberts, I. (2001a). "Head Movement." In Baltin & Collins (2001).

Roberts, I. (2004). "The C-System in Brythonic Celtic Languages, V2 and the EPP." In Rizzi (2004).

Rooth, M. (1992). "A Theory of Focus Interpretation." *Natural Language Semantics* 1, 75–116.

Ross, J. R. (1983). Inner Islands. Ms., Massachusetts Institute of Technology, Cambridge.

Schlyter, S. (1974). "Une hiérarchie d'adverbes et leur distribution—Par quelle transformation?" In C. Rohrer & N. Ruwet, eds., *Actes du Colloque Franco-Allemand de Grammaire Transformationnelle*, vol. 2, 76–84. Tübingen: Max Niemeyer.

Starke, M. (1997). LOC: A Sketch with Special Reference to Anaphora. Ms., University of Geneva.

Starke, M. (2001). Move Dissolves into Merge. Ph.D. diss., University of Geneva.

Szabolcsi, A. (1999). Weak Islands. SynCom, University of Tilburg, Neth.

Szabolcsi, A., & F. Zwarts. (1997). "Weak Islands and an Algebraic Semantics for Scope Taking." In A. Szabolcsi, ed., *Ways of Taking Scope*. Dordrecht: Kluwer, pp. 217–262.

Vergnaud, J.-R. (1982). *Dépendances et niveaux de représentation en syntaxe*. Ph.D. diss., University of Paris VII.

8

MICHAL STARKE

On the Inexistence of Specifiers and the Nature of Heads

This chapter argues that there is no such thing as a "specifier." What we mistook for specifiers are heads (in the sense that they provide the "label" for the merger they enter into). Put differently, there is no such thing as second merge in any theoretically relevant sense: every instance of merge has the properties of first merge.

Traditional representations postulate a "specifier" accompanied by an often invisible head terminal, both containing the same feature α, as in (1) with α = wh. Eliminating the invisible terminal causes the occurence of α inside the specifier to directly label the merger, with no duplication, as in (2):

(1) I wonder . . .

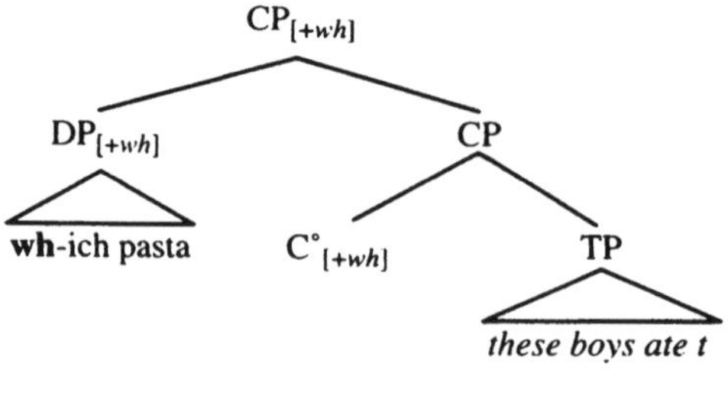

(2) I wonder . . .

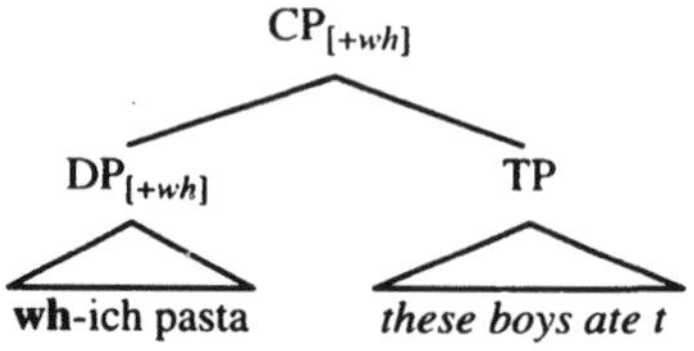

In (2), the DP 'which pasta' is the head of CP, in the same sense as the V° terminal 'ate' is the head of VP. No "C°" terminal is involved.

To put the proposal in perspective, consider this informal description: given a "small" representation, such as S'-S-VP or CP-TP-VP, specifiers are essentially a way of "adding space" around heads, so as to accomodate all the necessary material (subjects, wh-phrases, etc.). Once the representations become more refined (Pollock 1989; Rizzi 1997; Cinque 1999; etc.), however, space becomes abundant and the need to enlarge representations disappears. Space in fact becomes overabundant relative to the elements spelled out, and most "heads" become invisible. At the same time, given that specifiers agree with heads (whether directly, or indirectly with AGREE + EPP), specifiers contain the same feature as heads do. They are thus just as capable of "projecting" a label as the "head" is. Gone the need to add space, and with "specifiers" capable of doing the job alone, postulating an invisible head below each specifier becomes an anachronism, advantageously replaced by (2). The "specifier" has now taken over the role of the head, it has become a complex, non-terminal head. I will argue below that this simplification has many virtues beyond the significant cleanup of the theory that it provides.

Eliminating the notion "specifier" carries us one step further toward the reductionist program initiated by minimalism: minimalism eliminated the looser notion of government in favor of the more restricted notions of specifier-head relations. This chapter amounts to eliminating specifer-head relations also and restricting all syntactic relations to the most basic: head-complement relations.

1. Eliminating Specifier

1.1. The 'Doubly Filled Nothing' generalization

As a first step in motivating the elimination of "specifier," consider the following generalization: given finer-grained representations, there is almost no XP in which both the "specifier" and the "head" are filled.[1] Let us strenghten this to what we might call the "Doubly Filled Nothing" generalization, coming back to apparent exceptions below:

(3) Doubly Filled Nothing: no projection can have both its head-terminal and its specifier present at the same time.

If this is an accurate depiction, recent detailed empirical research is in effect telling us: the theory predicts two positions, but we only ever see one. Why?

Clearly, the optimal answer is that we see only one position because there *is* only one position. And this is what the spec-less (2) implements: if there are no "specifiers," the sole available position is the position of the "labeller," the "head" position. What we are seeing are the heads of the successive projections, with no additional material around them.

1.2. Why can't "specifiers" project?

The same conclusion comes from an inspection of current theories. As it turns out, the spec-less (2) is the result of pulling out undesirable tacit stipulations.

It is a common assumption that the "specifier-head" relation is an identity—'agreement,' 'matching,' 'checking'—relation with respect to some feature: both the specifier and the head contain the same feature f, and the specifier-head relation builds on this identity. That feature is furthermore the feature that labels the resulting constituent (it is immaterial whether this relation is a primitive or whether it is derived, as in *Agree* followed by EPP).

The fragment in (1) is thus properly represented as

(4) I wonder . . .

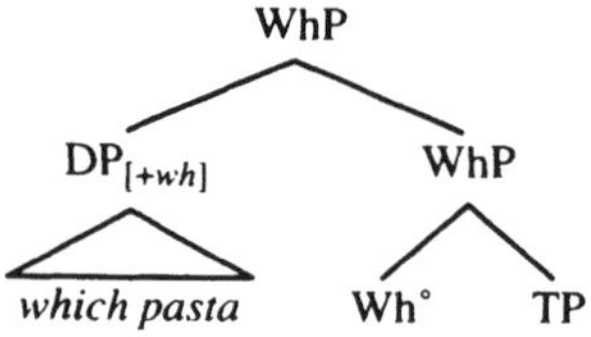

If the same feature f is contained in specifiers and in terminals acting as heads, the obvious question to ask is; Why does f in specifiers never project, whereas the same f in the corresponding terminal does project? What is it that prevents f inside the specifier from projecting?

The answer cannot be in terms of accessibility or usability of f inside the specifier; that is, it cannot be along the lines of 'f inside an XP is too deeply embedded to be visible outside of XP.' This is because the specifier-head relation requires f inside the XP-specifier to be visible outside that XP: f must be visible to the head with which it will enter into a checking relation. Given that f inside the specifier *is* visible to outside processes, why is it usable by the spec-head relation but not by labeling? That is, why do 'specifiers' never project? Equivalently, for our purposes, why must each insertion of an XP ("specifier") be preceded by an insertion of a corresponding terminal? Why can't a merged XP be "self-standing," as in (2)?

There are currently no answers to this question; current theories resort to tacit assumptions stipulating the need for a terminal along each specifier or the impossibility for f in a specifier to project, along the lines of either (5a) or (5b):

(5) a. Asymmetric Projection (AP): a feature f in an XP-node cannot legitimate its mother (it cannot 'project'), but the same f in an X° node can legitimize a maximal projection (it can 'project').
  b. Merging an XP requires prior merging of a corresponding terminal.

Of course, such assumptions are undesireable and are to be derived or eliminated once recognized. Simply eliminating (5) yields

(6) I wonder . . .

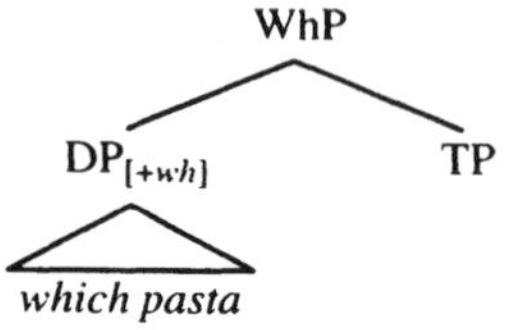

Below, I provide half a dozen other reasons to dispense with the notion of "specifier," before discussing what syntax would look like once specifiers are a thing of the past.

1.3. The Specifier-of relation is expletive

A third property making specifiers suspicious is a curious asymmetry between the specifier-of relation and the head-complement relation.

The head-complement relation is the basic syntactic relation, with the expected properties: it instantiates the core notion of concatenation (merge)—mapping onto (non-trivial) compositionality—and the set resulting from that composition is subject to the usual labeling algorithm, creating an asymmetry among the members of the set.

The specifier-of relation, on the other hand, has neither of these expected properties: it maps onto a semantically vacuous identity relationship, and it plays no role in labeling. This makes the specifier-of relation look like an "expletive relation," playing no meaningful role and on a par with expletive pronouns, uninterpretable features, or structural case.

If so, the hypothesis that there are specifiers needs serious justification; and again, the optimal state of affairs is that there is no such vacuous relation.

1.4. Specifiers complicate locality

Locality is standardly understood as a restriction on identity of two constituents with respect to some feature (quantificational features for A'-chains and agreement or case feature for A-chains). From the point of view of locality principles, then, the specifier-head relation is just another case of "identity with respect to some feature." In fact, the specifier-head relation is indistinguishable from an antecedent-trace relation, as far as locality is concerned.

To take an example, consider the classical analysis of a wh-moved element: XP_{wh} $X°_{wh}$ . . . t_{wh}. The relation between the anteposed XP_{wh} and its trace t_{wh} is restricted by locality because it is an identity wrt wh-features (or quantificational features). The specifier-head relation in CP—$R(XP_{wh}, X°_{wh})$—is, however, also an identity wrt. wh-features, and as far as the locality principle is concerned, it is indistinguishable from the antecedent-trace relation.

It then comes as a surprise that the locality of the specifier-head relation is completly different from the locality of wh-movement. Specifiers thus provoke a locality paradox, forcing some (unresolved) complication to current locality theories.[2]

Again, the whole issue disappears if syntax does not include second-mergers (and no 'checking' configurations need to be enforced).

1.5. Ordering stipulations

Fifth, another rarely noted fact is that assuming the existence of specifiers forces extrinsing rule ordering. Some mechanism must ensure that the merger of the wouldbe head is ordered before the merger of the wouldbe specifier. Nothing within current theories, however, forces that—although they all assume such an outcome. To achieve this, either the linearization algorithm must be made more complex or some independent stipulation must be added [as in (5)]. Again, this complication does not arise if syntactic structures are made only of heads and complements.

1.6. Redundancies

Duplication of every feature

A side effect of the idea that there are specifiers—and its accompanying tacit stipulation (5)—is the duplication of features: every feature present in an XP must be present twice, because a corresponding (local) head must bear it, too. Again, once the logic of functional projections is followed through, the scale of the issue becomes non-trivial. As before, no such consequence holds in a specifier-less syntactic structure.

Double-articulation of phrase structure

As a seventh point, consider that fact that specifiers require phrase structure to be split into two hierarchies: nodes are first assembled into "xBar units," and these ministructures are then assembled into a rigid sequence of projections. There is no clear relationship between these two layers, as contemporary investigations have been able to make very little sense of this, mostly leaving the issue aside for future scrutiny. Again, retiring specifiers relieves us of this unwanted side effect (by collapsing the two layers into one).

1.7. Triggering insertion: Specifiers versus fseq

Specifiers thus create a lot of trouble for the theory. It therefore comes as a surprise that they are also unnecessary in order to achieve the results they are used for.

In current theories, the only job of the apparatus surrounding specifiers, that is, (5) and the checking mechanism, is to trigger insertion (merge/move). This is based on the fact that if (5) holds, every insertion of an XP into phrase-structure creates an invariant local configuration between that XP and a corresponding head (the spec-head configuration). It is then trivial to equate the cause of the insertion with the need to create that configuration, which is what all current approaches do (cf. 'checking,' 'criteria,' etc.).

Should there be some other cause for insertion, however, the concept of "specifier" would ipso facto become jobless and merrily walk into retirement. And there is such a cause.

All modern theories of syntax assume that there is an ordering of projections: S is above VP and not vice versa; CP is above TP and not vice versa; TP is above VP (and not VP above TP); and so on. There are various ways to formulate this restriction, none particularly succesful qua explanation. Let us then adopt a simple description:

(7) There exists an 'fseq'—a sequence of functional projections—such that the output of merge must respect fseq.

In the simplified syntactic structures considered so far, fseq = <C, T, V>. Now consider the consequence of not moving the subject DP with a wh-question on the object such as (1–2). In a structure without specifiers, the result is that the T layer is never projected:

(8) I wonder . . .

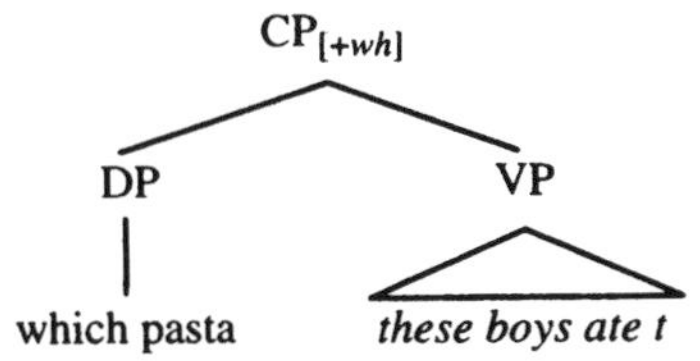

This produces fseq = <C, V>. But this is illegal, as fseq must be <C, T, V>.[3] In a spec-less theory, insertion is triggered directly by fseq: not moving or overmoving creates the wrong fseq.

Contrast this with a specifier-based structure. In the latter, the absence of the specifier has no bearing on the presence of the corresponding layer; the projection is already present via the prior insertion of a terminal head:

(9) I wonder . . .

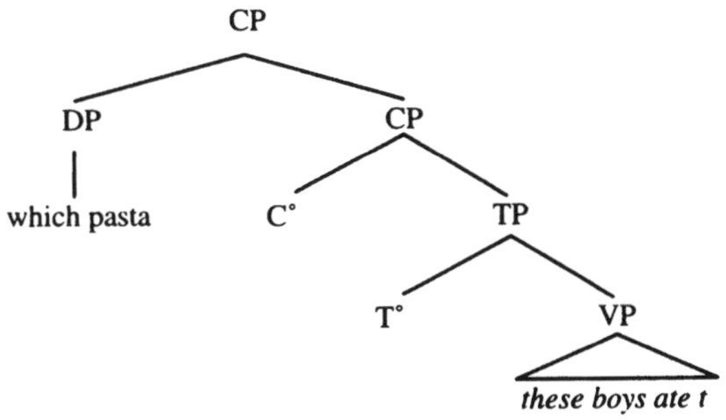

That is, in syntactic structures based on the head-complement relation, every insertion (or failure thereof) alters the fseq expressed by the structure, whereas this is not true in a specifier-based theory. This difference is a direct result of the fact that a head-complement-based theory does not duplicate features; each feature is represented only once.

Since (7) regulates possible fseqs, (7) dictates what can (and must) be inserted in a head-complement-based representation. The fseq requirement itself thus triggers merge/move. The beauty of this result is that fseq is independently needed in every theory. We thus get a trigger mechanism "for free."[4]

Thus, the eighth and final reason to dispense with specifiers is that they do not work for us. Worst, they obfuscate a way of making the independently needed fseq work for us. Taken together, these eight points show specifiers under a new light: as both useless and harmful.

2. Fseq as a replacement specifier

Let us thus proceed with the assumption that "specifiers" (non–first mergers) are an archaic concept, superceded by rich syntactic structures of the type initiated by Pollock

(1989) and followed up by such work as Beghelli and Stowell (1997), Rizzi (1997), Cinque (1999), among many others.

To get a handle on the structures without specifiers, here is the derivation of (1–2), adopting the common assumption the the object merges with V, whereas the subject merges with an agentivity head v, so that the simplified fseq is <C, T, v, V>.

Given the VP = {V, object} merger, of no interest here, the starting fseq = <V>. The only legal continuation of this is <v, V>, and the first step must therefore merge some v (agentivity) feature with VP. The DP 'these boys' provides such a property, resulting in

(10)

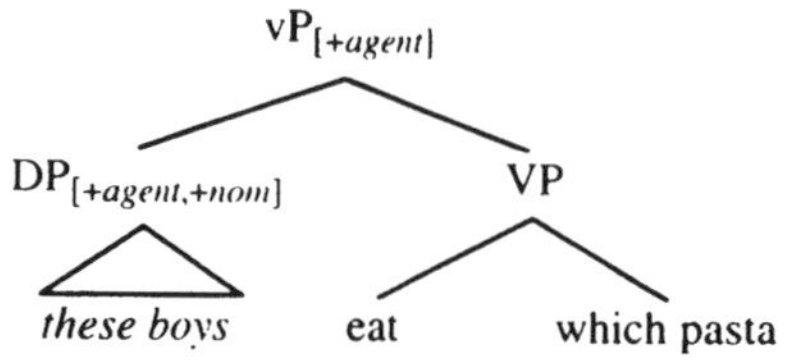

This step is parallel to a specifier-based structure in which the agentive property of the DP-subject enters into specifier-head agreement with an extra v° head:

(11)

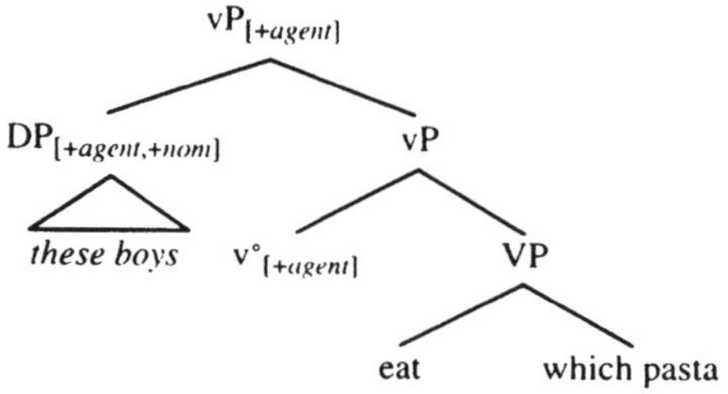

Given current fseq = <v, V> and the target fseq = <C, T, v, V>, the next step must involve projecting a T. There is currently no consensual approach to how the subject DP relates to T, but for convenience let us adopt a simplification of the idea that the nominative case properties of DP are the relevant nominal feature that are involved in TP 'checking' (adapting from Pesetsky & Torrego 2000). If so, movement of the DP allows the nominative feature to project T:

(12)

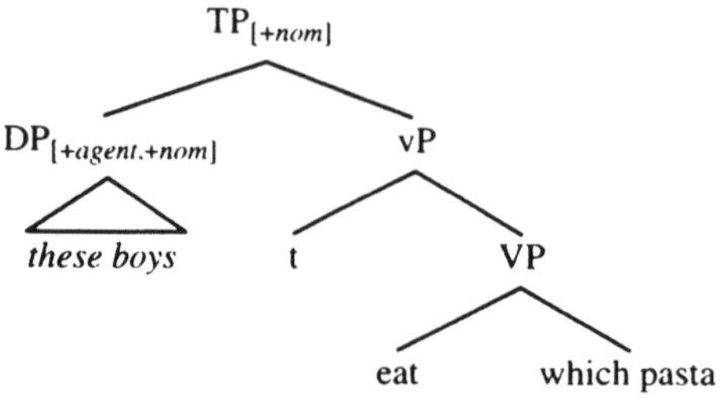

Again, this is stricIty parallel to moving the subject to specTP, but without the specifier and checking machinery. Finally, given this <T, v, V> structure and the

target fseq = <C, T, v, V>, the last step must project C, which is achieved by moving the object wh-phrase:

(13)

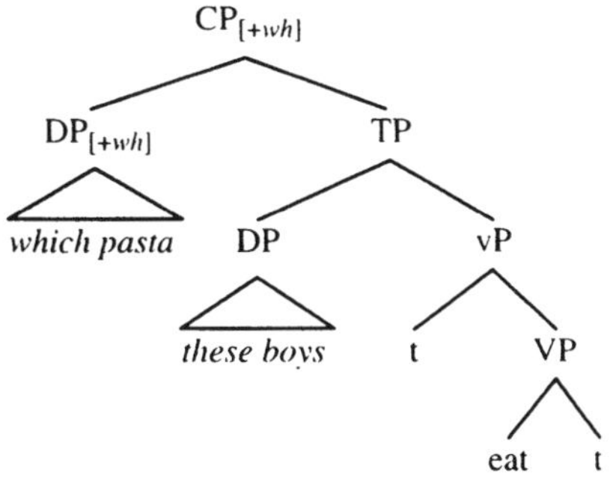

Generally, then, the logic is that given fseq = $<f_n \ldots f_1>$ and a phrasemarker whose top node is F_kP $(1 < k < n)$, insertion of f_{k+1} as the next step is forced by the need to build a legal fseq.

2.1. Fseq: laissez faire!

Now that fseq has come out of the closet and plays a central role in triggering insertion, let us give it some deserved attention. The identity of the features within fseq is not paramount to the current line of reasoning (although it is of central importance to any current P&P approach). What rather needs to be known is how much variation fseq allows, if any. Let us distinguish two questions:

- Is there more than one distinct fseq (where two fseqs are distinct if they are not in a subset relation)?
- Given a fseq, must all its features always be present, or are subsets legal instances of fseq?

Consensus seems to have developed around the most restrictive answer to the first question: there is one and only one legal fseq, universally (Starke 1995; Rizzi 1997; Cinque 1999; and numerous others). The second question is more controversial, with three types of answers repeatedly proposed: the 'rigid' approach—everything must always be present (e.g., Starke 1995; Cinque 1999); the 'peeling' approach—projections can be missing but only by peeling off from the top (e.g., Radford 1990; Rizzi 1994; Platzack 1996; Cardinaletti & Starke 1999); or, finally, the 'laissez-faire' approach—any projection can be missing (e.g., Wexler 1994). No argument has been put forward one way or another (pace Cinque 1999: 133).

Here are, however, two argument for the third, least normative line. Consider what happens to NegP in positive clauses. According to the first two approaches, there must be a null 'assertion' operator paralleling the negative operators (i.e. NegP is a PolarityP). The [-positive] operators, however, have some distinct properties, among which the quality of inducing weak islands ('negative islands'). All things being equal, we would expect the [+positive] assertion operators to have the same property. Any value of PolarityP would thus induce weak islands, and hence all clauses should always be weak islands, a reductio ad absurdum of the idea of 'positive operators' in a PolarityP of every clause. Is there any evidence that this abstract reasoning is correct? Factives provide a direct indication: it is a traditional observation that verbal predicates whose semantics involves asserting that their complement denotes a fact (*regret, know*) induce island effects (the 'factive' island), whereas their non-fact-asserting counterparts do not (*believe, think*)—an observation traditionally described with a factive (assertion) operator inducing weak islands. Since the assertion operator is a positive operator ('it is truly a fact that . . .'), factives indicate that positive operators induce weak island to the same extent as negative operators. The approaches to fseq that force the presence of an assertion operator thus seem stuck with the absurd conclusion that every clause is a weak island. (In fact, things get worse as the same logic applies to at least [±question] and [±focus]. Each clause is thus predicted to contain at least three weak islands.).

The same logic is massively required by Modifier-movement in Rizzi (2001). Rizzi postulates a third class of features relevant to *Relativised Minimality* to account for the fact that an adverb can be anteposed only if no other adverb intervenes on its path. If all positions were always present, a disaster would result: absence of an adverb would translate into a null adverbial/operator occupying the spec of the relevant projection, and that null adverbial/operator would block movement just as an overt adverbial does. The generalization that only actual occurring adverbs block anteposition would be lost. The account of adverbial Relativised Minimality thus presupposes that absent adverbs translate into a syntactic structure with interveners not represented.

2.2. Fseq as an external interface condition

We thus need a laissez-faire approach, allowing a projection to be absent if no element in the enumeration requires it, both to allow for the absence of NegP/PolP in positive clauses and to allow for the absence of unused adverbial positions. A radical implementation would replace (7) with

(14) There exists an 'fseq'—a unique sequence of functional projections—such that the output of merge must be a subset of fseq.

But this won't do: (14) is both too permissive, allowing many unattested combinations, and expresses the wrong generalization—the generalization that 'anything can drop'—Which is not what the facts are telling us. The facts are telling us that there is some regularity behind 'who can drop'; and it is this regularity that the fseq-requirement needs to express.

As an illustration, take negation, questions, and focus again: we never have any reason to think that [+neg], [+wh], or [+foc] are absent from the syntactic representation but interpreted semantically. Such cases—for example, *plum tastes good*, interpreted as *plum does not taste good*—indeed strike us as aberrant. (Cases in which elements are phonologically null but syntactically present, as in the classical analysis of English null complementizers, are of course irrelevant.) The only corresponding cases that ever do suggest radical absence from the syntactic representation (with concomitant semantic interpretation) are [-neg], [-wh], and [-foc].

Building on the traditional observation that speakers have systematic and strong intuitions about 'markedness' of values, whereby a declaration is 'unmarked' and an interrogation 'marked,' asserting is 'unmarked' and negating 'marked,' and a flat statement is 'unmarked' and focusing 'marked,' the correct generalization seems to be

(15) (Only) unmarked values can drop.

And therefore, descriptively,

(16) There exists an 'fseq'—a unique sequence of functional projections—such that the output of merge must respect fseq, modulo unmarked values.

Why should (16) hold? The fact that only unmarked values can 'drop' entails that dropped items are interpretatively recoverable (i.e., absent nodes are necessarily interpreted as receiving their unmarked value). Statement (15) thus amounts to a 'recoverability condition' in the vein of Vergnaud (1974): an element of fseq can be dropped only if it is recoverable at the LF interface. At the interpretative level, fseq is thus always complete (having recovered all pieces missing in the syntactic representation via the markedness route).

This transparently suggests that fseq is not a syntactic principle but rather an interface condition (*a bare output constraint*, in Chomsky's terminology). Thus (16) can be simplified to

(17) Semantic representations must respect fseq
(i.e., there exists an 'fseq'—a unique sequence of functional projections—such that LF must be readable as an instance of fseq).

This presupposes

(18) The interpretive component's reading of syntactic representations is based on recoverability: absence from syntactic structures corresponds to unmarked values.

It thus turns out that both the rigid and the laissez-faire approaches are right: the rigid approach is correct as far as the interpretative component goes (i.e. everything must always be present); the laissez-faire approach is correct for syntax but as an artifact of how interpretation of syntactic structures takes place.

As a second argument for the laissez-faire nature of the syntactic fseq requirement (and for the markedness-based formulation of that requirement), consider a massive and curious fact: only some values of a given feature trigger movement. In many languages a [+wh] feature triggers A'-movement to the CP-zone, but in no language does a [-wh] feature trigger a similar movement; in many languages a [+foc] feature triggers A'-movement to the CP-zone, but in no language does a [-foc] feature trigger a similar movement; or again, some constructions involve A'-movement of [+neg] phrases (such as negative inversion in English), but no constructions involve a similar movement triggered by a [-neg] feature. Why?

Again, the generalization seems to correspond to speakers' intuitions about markedness: only 'marked' values ever trigger movement. But why? Why should the same feature be subject to movement under one of its values but not under the other? and why should the moved value systematically be perceived as the 'marked' value by speakers? A rigid view of fseq makes this mystery thicker: it postulates a functional projection corresponding to [-neg], [-foc], and [-wh], ready to host movement and leading to the expectation that this projection will be used.

The laissez-faire approach, on the other hand, captures the contrast. Given our two assumptions that (1) features with marked values must be present in the syntactic structure, but features with unmarked values can be absent, and (2) the incentive for remerger (movement) is to extend fseq to comply with (17), it follows that unmarked features will never trigger movement. This is because fseq does *not* need to be extended in the case of unmarked features, and thus movement/remerger is superfluous. Marked features, on the other hand, correspond to projections that cannot be dropped, and thus fseq needs to be extended through movement or other means.

2.3. Dependent insertion

If everything is a head-complement relation, and no additional geometric relation is used by syntax, there should never be cases in which two different projections seem to interact. That is, there should never be anything looking like a specifer-head relation or a government relation.

Consider, then, cases like subject-aux inversion in English (19a) or focus-particle insertion under XP-focalization in Gun (19b) from Aboh (1997). Such cases are representative of many other constructions:

(19) a. . . . XP_{wh} aux [Subject t_{aux} . . . t_{wh}
b. . . . XP_{foc} wè [Subject . . . t_{foc}

In these cases, the anteposed XP and the Aux/PRT belong to two different projections and should, a priori, be entirely independent. It is thus unexpected that the insertion of the anteposed XP 'depends' upon the prior insertion Aux/PRT. This is a run-of-the-mill case if longer-distance 'specifier-head' relations exist, but it is out of grasp of the more local 'head-complement' relations.

Notice, however, that there is a clear pattern to the issue: the insertion of a higher node is dependent on the prior insertion of a node immediately below it. Let us call this 'dependent insertion.'

As it turns out, dependent insertion is already expressed in fseq: the fseq requirement dictates that insertion of a given feature depends on prior insertion of all features preceding it in fseq. Temporarily setting aside the optionality of unmarked features, the logic is as follows: given fseq = $< \ldots \alpha\ \beta\ \gamma \ldots >$, attempts to insert α directly on top of γ will create an illegal fseq and will thus fail. Given fseq = $<C, T, V>$ attempting to merge C directly with VP will fail since T is missing from the sequence. The same logic applies to subject-verb inversion: if α is the projection of the wh-phrase and γ the complement of the inverted verb, not inverting the verb creates $< \ldots \alpha\ \gamma \ldots >$, an illegal fseq. Dependent-insertion thus amounts to "fseq-filling."

The optionality of unmarked features provides an interesting refinement and a stronger prediction. The fseq $< \ldots \alpha\ \gamma \ldots >$ *is* a legal instance of $< \ldots \alpha\ \beta\ \gamma \ldots >$, provided that β has an unmarked value. The "fseq-filling" explanation thus predicts that dependent insertion will only occur when the sentence requires the marked value of the in-between features.

This in turn entails that the underlying cause of dependent insertion is dependence of the value of one feature on the value of another, a common phenomenon. As an example, suppose that in wh-subject-aux inversion the verb occurs in Q° (a plausible hypothesis since inversion is found with negation, focus, and wh):

(20)

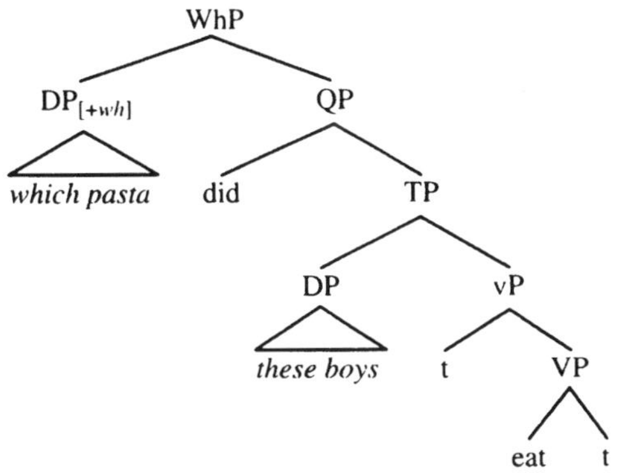

In this case, the generalization is that projecting whP requires prior projection of a QP-like projection. The filling-in phenomenon is now a consequence of the fact that +wh requires +Q rather than -Q (together with the fact that Q occurs lower than Wh in fseq).

This type of feature-value dependencies abound in a Cinquean refined fseq: if tense is split among several projections, for instance, a value + future in one projection is 'dependent' on a value + tensed in another. Again, that is an essentially interpretive phenomenon.

The "filling-in" approach to dependent-insertion makes different predictions with respect to the traditional spec-head approaches: the spec-head approach entails that the only case of dependent-insertion ever found is the case of a YP dependent upon the prior insertion of exactly one X°. The fseq approach, on the other hand, has no such entailment: insertion of a YP can require prior insertion of any number of elements, depending on how many fseq items are missing between the insertion site and the top node of the tree to be extended. The elements inserted to fill in fseq, furthermore, can be either terminals or phrases, whereas it can only be a terminal in a spec-head approach.

The fseq-based prediction seems correct. Cases with more than one element filling in are provided by the Scandinavian wh-constructions, where *two* particles ('complementisers') appear between the wh-phrase and the rest of the clause. A case in which a maximal projection is the filler is provided by Jamaican Creole focus structures, in which a particle *precedes* the focused phrase in the CP-area (Durrleman 2000); that is, a head triggers an XP-filler.[5]

3. Fseq and ϕ

According to the fseq logic, the only syntactically relevant geometrical relationship is complementation linked to sisterhood. This is because syntactic structures are nothing but raw layers of head-complement relationships, with each layer independent of the other.

However, two types of unexpected relations seem to occur. First, the agreement relation—though exceedingly rare—does occur with ϕ-features. A second type of case is illustrated by subject-verb inversion in root wh-questions: the insertion of one node (the inverted verb) depends on the insertion of another node (the wh-phrase). Both of these unexpected dependencies are straightforward in terms of spec-head agreement but seem unstatable with fseq, as they do not involve head-complement relations.

3.1. α-feature "agreement"

How do we express the fact that the morphology of the verb covaries with the morphology of the subject? Let us set our goals higher: since ϕ-feature agreement is the only credible instance of agreement, we not only want to explain how the agreement between the subject and the verb comes about, but we also want to explain why overt morphological agreement only ever happens with ϕ-features.

An obvious observation in this context is that there is one other phenomenon in grammar that again involves covariation in ϕ-features but in no other features: binding. Simple contrasts such as '*she* washes *herself*' versus '*he* washes *himself*' (cf. *'*she* washes *him*self') are formally identical to subject-verb agreement: the morphology of two nodes in the structure covaries with respect to ϕ-features (but no other features).

Why, then, do we have the same phenomenon twice? A natural answer is to reduce one to the other: verbal morphology enters into a binding relation with the argument of the verb. This captures the similarity between the two cases and solves the configurational aspect of the problem: no direct geometrical relationship of the "spec-head" type is involved, and thus no such geometrical relation is needed in grammar. The verbal infection and the covarying argument are in different projections, and the relationship is established via binding.

(This line of thought is reminiscent of approaches that hold that verbal agreement is 'pronominal,' e.g., Rizzi 1982. In that terminology, the present argument is that the 'pronominal nature of agr' allows it to enter binding relationships with verbal arguments and renders the idea of spec-head agreement redundant).[6]

3.2. EPP

Another type of problematic case is the EPP, which states that one particular projection in fseq is an exception in that it can never be dropped. Why?

Contrary to the cases above, this problem is not particular to the fseq approach. Traditional theories are confronted by the same issue and need to appeal to such stipulations as asserting that a particular feature has the property of being 'strong' or simply stating the facts through an 'EPP'-feature. The analysis of ϕ-agreement in terms of binding, however, opens up a path for explanation: if verbal agreement enters a binding relationship with the argument, the relationship is either pronominal or anaphoric. Suppose it is anaphoric. It then follows that a local antecedent must be present. Supposing that it is a general property of language to have anaphoric agreement on the verb (often null), the EPP follows.

(This opens up an additional intriguing possibility for the well-known correlation between null subjects and rich agreement. We know that anaphors are morphologically poorer than pronouns. Accordingly, only languages with poor verbal inflection have an anaphoric inflection, and thus only infl-poor languages show EPP-effects. Languages with rich inflection have a pronominal infl along traditional lines and thus escape the EPP-requirement.)

3.3. Verb Movement as an artefact of ϕ-placement

Consider the following potentially serious objection: according to Cinque (1999), verbs can occur anywhere in fseq. To provide these positions, it seems that we need to double fseq. Instead of <a b c d>, we need a fseq along the lines of <V1 a V2 b V3 c V4 d>, with each Vn a potential landing site for V°. But, of course, doing so basically recreates the null head positions that the specifier-head approach postulates.[7]

The problem disappears once we follow up on a further question: why is it that verbs have this special liberty of appearing anywhere? Why is it that within a given "construction" of a given language, verb movement has such widespread optionality as it has, according to Cinque's (1999) system, with no correlation with either semantics or morphology? Why are the boundaries of the 'optionality zone' of verb movement arbitrary (again, no semantic or morphological correlate)? It is only because verb movement turns out to have such bizarre properties that the above issue arises.

There are however two regularities that make the situation less desperate than seems at first sight.

First, not all 'verb movement' is bizarre: subject-aux inversion in questions, V2 antepositions, and so on do not display the above bizarre properties. Such antepositions do not result in optionality and are correlated to interpretation (±question, ±finite, etc.). It is only the "IP-internal" step of verb movement that behaves oddly, suggesting that some property of the IP-zone is responsible for this erratic behaviour.

Second, verbs are not the only category with these bizarre symptoms. Agreement and negation suffer from the same syndrome: "The evidence points to the possibility of generating a NegP on top of every adverb-related functional projection" (Cinque 1999:126), and a similar conclusion is reached by Cinque for "DP-related" projections, that is, AgrP or, more precisely, ϕP.

A slight restatement of Cinque's (1999) solution is that ϕ (and neg) can be inserted anywhere in fseq. This (surprising) fact provides the solution to the V-movement issue: since verbs move to ϕ and ϕ can be inserted anywhere in fseq, it follows that verbs will seem to be anywhere in fseq. But, of course, this is simply an artefact of the syntax of ϕ.

Given an fseq = <C Mod Adv1 ϕ Adv2 . . . >, the verb will appear between Adv1 and Adv2, but if fseq = <C Mod ϕ Adv1 Adv2 . . . >, the verb will appear between

Mod and Adv1. No enrichment of fseq is involved. What is rather at stake is the bizarre and ill-understood capacity of ϕ to occur anywhere.[8]

(Reducing the verb-movement issue to the behavior of ϕ also provides an explanation of the first generalization above: the difference between the 'IP-related' part of verb-placement and the higher parts derive from the fact that "liberal ϕ insertion" is a property of the IP zone of syntactic structures.)

4. Results

The core asset of the present proposal is to replace a more complex and more heterogeneous theory by a simpler and more homogeneous counterpart, thanks to the elimination of the notion of specifiers. The older—traditional—theory takes 'merge,' adds the distinction between first merge and non–first merge on top of it [ie., Asymmetric Projection, (5)], grafts an agreement/checking mechanism on top of this, and then proceeds to leave fseq lying around in a dusty corner. In doing so, it ends up with {merge; fseq; AsymmetricProjection; checking}, a curious bag of heterogeneous tools.

In contrast, eliminating specifiers results in everything being a head-complement relation. The corresponding tools are thus {merge; fseq}, which are part of every theory and form a homogeneous pair: one creates an object; the other decides the type of the object just created.

The newer theory is simpler in that it is a proper subset of the old theory, but maybe more importantly, it leaves us with a more homogeneous state of affairs. This gain is supplemented by a number of side gains: no duplication of features, no gratuitous null heads, no bizarre locality, no expletive relation, no two intermixed theories of phrase structure, no explanation of the "Doubly Filled Nothing" generalization, and so on.

Notes

1. Counting traces (but ignoring traces of verb movement until section 1.6). See Koopman and Szabolscsi (2000) for a recent example of this observation, albeit in a weakened form that is restricted to phonologically overt material.

2. Notice that this also holds if spec-head relations are recast as EPP-relations, as long as the latter are understood as feature-checking mechanisms.

3. See below for a discussion of the obligatory or optional nature of elements within fseq. I take them to be obligatory here only to simplify the illustration of the logic.

4. Conversely, another advantage of this result is to squeeze more juice out of preexisting assumptions: since every theory has the fseq condition—implicitly or explicitly—leaving it lying around in a dusty corner, barely used, is the worst-case scenario.

5. An attractive implementation of the fact that unmarked values are syntactically inert—or absent—would be to adopt the approach taken by Kaye et al. (1985) for broadly similar facts in phonology: the unmarked value simply does not exist, and features are unary (and presence corresponds to the marked value). Transposing: the reason the unmarked value never moves and can drop from *fseq* is that it doesn't exist. Unfortunately, this appealing approach does not seem to be workable in syntax since realized instances of unmarked values of syntactic

nodes seem to abound. Notice however that such an answer would amount to a laissez-faire approach to fseq: only marked (i.e., existing) features can project.

6. An interesting question is why some languages allow binding (agreement) only in some positions; for example, Arabic is noted for having the verb covary with the subject only if the subject precedes the verb, and similar facts hold for French participles wrt. an object. This is, however, orthogonal to the present issue and depends on two interesting areas: (a) that coreference is possible in some structural configurations but not others, a traditional issue of Binding Theory, and (b) the dependent-insertion phenomenon discussed below.

7. I owe this formulation of the objection to Luigi Rizzi. The metaphor of verb 'movement' is used here only for convenience. I am, in fact, assuming the more elegant technology proposed by Brody (2000) whereby no actual movement of the verb occurs. This, however, makes no difference for the argumentation.

8. A slightly radical solution along the same general lines is to allow insertion of the verb directly in the position of ϕ, discarding the traditional idea that verbs are generated in the lowest projection. I will not pursue this line here, but it is interesting to note that there is surprisingly little evidence for the common assumption that verbs must be generated very low.

References

Aboh, Enoch. 1997. From the Syntax of Gungbe to the Grammar of Gbe. Ph.D. diss., University of Geneva.

Beghelli, Filippo, & Tim Stowell. 1997. "Distributivity and Negation." In Anna Szabolcsi, ed., *Ways of Scope Taking*, chap. 3. Dordrecht: Kluwer, 71–107.

Brody, Michael. 2000. "Mirror Theory: Syntactic Representation in Perfect Syntax." *Linguistic Inquiry* 31, 29–56.

Cardinaletti, Anna, & Michal Starke. 1999. "The Typology of Structural Deficiency: On the Three Grammatical Classes." In Henk Van Riemsdijk, ed, *Clitics in the Languages of Europe*. Berlin: Mouton de Gruyter, 145–290.

Cinque, Guglielmo. 1999. *Adverbs and Functional Heads: A Cross-linguistic Perspective*. Oxford: Oxford University Press.

Durrleman, Stéphanie. 2000. The Left Periphery in Jamaican Creole. Ms., University of Geneva.

Kaye, Jonathan, Jean Lowenstamm, & Jean-Roger Vergnaud. 1985. "The Internal Structure of Phonological Representations: A Theory of Charm and Government. *Phonology Yearbook* 2, 305–328.

Koopman, Hilda, & Anna Szabolscsi. 2000. *Verbal Complexes*. Cambridge, Mass.: MIT Press.

Pesetsky, David, & Esther Torrego. 2000. "T-to-c Movement: Causes and Consequences." In Michael Kenstowicz, ed., *Ken Hale: A Life in Language*. Cambridge, Mass.: MIT Press.

Platzack, Christer. 1996. "The Initial Hypothesis of Syntax. A Minimalist Perspective on Language Acquisition and Attrition." In Harald Clahsen, ed., *Generative Perspectives on Language Acquisition*. Amsterdam: John Benjamins.

Pollock, Jean-Yves. 1989. "Verb Movement, Universal Grammar, and the Structure of IP." *Linguistic Inquiry* 20(3), 365–424.

Radford, Andrew. 1990. *Syntactic Theory and the Acquisition of English Syntax: The Nature of Early Child Grammars of English*. Oxford: Blackwell.

Rizzi, Luigi. 1982. *Issues in Italian Syntax*. Dordrecht: Foris.

Rizzi, Luigi. 1994. "Some Notes on Linguistic Theory and Language Development: The Case of Root Infinitives." *Language Acquisition* 3, 371–393.

Rizzi, Luigi. 1997. "The Fine Structure of the Left Periphery." In Liliane Haegeman, ed., *Elements of Grammar: A Handbook of Generative Syntax*. Dordrecht: Kluwer. 281–337.

Rizzi, Luigi. 2001. "Relativised Minimality Effects." In, Mark Baltin & Chris Collins, eds., *A Handbook of Syntactic Theory*. Oxford: Blackwell, 89–110.

Starke, Michal. 1995. "On the Format for Small Clauses." In, Anna Cardinaletti & Teresa Guasti, eds., *Small Clauses*, vol. 28, *Syntax and Semantics*. New York: Academic Press, 237–269.

Vergnaud, Jean-Roger. 1974. French Relative Clauses. Ph.D. Diss., Massachusetts Institute of Technology, Cambridge.

Wexler, Ken. 1994. "Optional Infinitives, Head Movement, and Economy of Derivation." In Norber Hornstein & David Lightfoot, ed., *Verb Movement*. Cambridge: Cambridge University Press, 305–350.

SUBJECT INDEX

NAME INDEX

LANGUAGE INDEX

Printed in the United States
135433LV00002B/42/A

1634677R0016

Printed in Great Britain
by Amazon.co.uk, Ltd.,
Marston Gate.